JIHAD
IN THE WEST

PAUL FREGOSI

JIHAD

IN THE WEST

MUSLIM CONQUESTS FROM THE 7TH TO THE 21ST CENTURIES

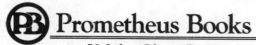 Prometheus Books

59 John Glenn Drive
Amherst, New York 14228-2197

Published 1998 by Prometheus Books

02 01   5 4 3

Library of Congress Cataloging-in-Publication Data

Fregosi, Paul.
    Jihad in the West : Muslim conquests from the 7th to the 21st centuries /
Paul Fregosi.
        p.   cm.
    Includes bibliographical references (p.   ) and index.
    ISBN 1–57392–247–1 (hardcover : alk. paper)
    1. Jihad—History. 2. Islamic countries—Relations—Europe.
3. Europe—Relations—Islamic countries. 4. Islam—Doctrines. 5. Islamic
fundamentalism. 6. Islam and world politics. I. Title.
BP182.F74   1998
297.7′2′09—DC21   98–34324
                                                          CIP
                                                          Rev.

Printed in the United States of America on acid-free paper

I DEDICATE THIS BOOK TO the memory of Bosko Brcik, 25, Christian Serb, and of his bride-to-be Admira Ismic, 25, Bosnian Muslim, who were shot and killed by an unknown sniper as they tried to escape from the beleaguered city of Sarajevo on May 20, 1993, and who died in each other's arms on the banks of the Miljacka River. God be with them.

CONTENTS

PART VII. ONSLAUGHT FROM THE EAST

PART VIII. BY LAND AND SEA

PART IX. THE WANING OF HOLY WAR

PART X. WARRIORS OF A WILLING DOOM

PART XI. THE JIHAD RETURNS

GLOSSARY OF USEFUL ARABIC
AND TURKISH TERMS

AL-ANDALUS. The part of Spain under Muslim rule. Its frontier fluctuated with the fortunes of war.

ALMOHAD. Berber dynasty (1130-1269) which followed a policy of religious purity and was defeated in Spain in 1212.

ALMORAVIDS. Berber dynasty from the Sahara which ruled over much of Morocco and Spain in the eleventh and twelfth centuries.

ANSAR. Inhabitants of Medina who helped Muhammad and the early Muslims after they moved from Mecca to Medina in the year 622.

BURAQ. The animal with the body of a mule and the head of a woman that carried Muhammad from Mecca to Paradise through Jerusalem on the Night Journey in the year 619.

CALIPH. Successor to Muhammad as head of the Muslim (Sunni) community. The caliphate (which was based in Istanbul) was abolished by Kemal Ataturk in 1924.

DAR-AL-HARB. The Land or Domain of War, where Islamic rule does not reign and which has historically been considered a legitimate target for the Jihad.

DAR-AL-ISLAM. The Land or Domain of Islam, where Islamic law and rule prevail.

11

DHIMMI. A nonbeliever (notably Jews, Christians, and Zoroastrians) who lives on Muslim territory, under Islamic law and protection. In lands under the rule of the Ottoman Turks dhimmis were known as *rayahs*.

FATWA. A religious or judicial edict that can be passed by the caliph, a mufti, or a judge (qadi).

GHAZI (Turkish term). A fighter for the faith engaged in a Jihad against the infidels.

HADITHS. The most holy of Muslim books after the Koran, usually translated as "The Traditions." The practices, utterances, and events of Muhammad's life. They number many thousands, were assembled by a number of official collectors several decades (usually one to two hundred years) after the Prophet's death, and many are considered historically suspect.

HEJIRA (or HIJRA). The emigration in 622 of Muhammad and his first disciples to Medina from Mecca, where they were unwanted and subjected to abuse. This event marks the beginning of the Muslim calendar.

IMAM. The leader of a Muslim religious community. Also among the Shiites, Ali and his descendants, who are considered the legitimate Leaders of Islam.

KAFIR. Infidel who has deliberately rejected the message of Islam.

KORAN (often spelled QURAN). The Muslim holy book revealed to Muhammad by God through the Angel Gabriel during a number of appearances in Mecca and Medina.

KOREISH (also spelled QURAISH). Influential Mecca tribe to whose minor branch Muhammad belonged and who at first opposed the founding of Islam and fought the new faith.

MAHDI. For the Sunnis, the awaited Messiah. The Shiites await, however, the Twelfth Iman.

MALIKI. A disciple of Malik, an eighth-century scholar who propounded the Maliki austere school of Islam, particularly strong in North Africa and among the Almoravids.

MAWALI. Non-Arab convert to Islam.

MILLET. A non-Muslim religious community living in Islam.

MORISCOS. Muslims in Christian Spain, mainly Castile, who had on the surface accepted Christianity but continued to practice secretly their Muslim faith.

MOSLEMAH. The Muslim nation in its entirety.

MOZARABS. Spanish Christians living in Muslim al-Andalus. They retained their Catholic faith but their everyday language and culture were Arabic.

MUDEJARES. Muslims who lived and worked in Christian Spain.

MUEZZIN. The person who calls the faithful to prayer in a mosque.

MUHAJIRUN. The Meccan followers of Muhammad who moved to Medina with the Prophet at the time of the hejira. The word means "emigrant."

MUFTI. Religious expert on the sharia, the Muslim law.

MUJAHID. Warrior of Islam engaged in a Jihad.

MUWALLADS. Native Spanish Muslims in al-Andalus, as opposed to those of Arab or Moorish stock.

QADI. A judge who administers Muslim law.

QURAN. See KORAN.

RAYAH. See DHIMMI.

SHARIA. The laws of Islam which originate in the Koran and the Hadiths.

SURA. A chapter in the Koran. There are 114 in all, each of which contains a number of verses.

TAIFA. One of the numerous minor Muslim kingdoms, usually centered in a town, which made up the Muslim Spanish state of al-Andalus during much of its 800-year history. The main taifas were Cordova, Seville, Toledo, and Granada.

ULAMA. A learned Muslim religious functionary.

UMMA. The Muslim community.

VIZIER. The Ottoman Sultan's chief minister and war leader.

PREFACE

T HE JIHAD HAS HAD A long presence on our planet, going back to
the early 600s, when Muhammad preached the Koran, ruled
over Medina, and sent his followers to fight against the pagan Arab
tribes of the peninsula, demanding they acknowledge his suzerainty and
convert to Islam. The terrorism called Jihad we know today is linked,
even if only by name, with these Muslim holy wars which began more
than 1,300 years ago in Arabia and spread during the next 13 centuries
to the Middle East, Europe, Africa, and Asia, and which are now also
part of the North and South American scene. The military conflicts of
former centuries, which all Muslims called the Jihad, and the terrorist
campaigns of recent decades, which some extremists consider a Jihad
also, not only share the same name. They are also an expression of the
distaste and basic antagonism which Islam has always manifested
toward the non-Muslim world, be it atheist, pagan, Hindu, Sikh,
Zoroastrian, Jewish, Buddhist, or Christian, and has often shown it by
fighting it—through the Jihad. We had forgotten this fact of international life, for most Muslim countries during the past century and a half
were politically impotent, ruled mainly as colonies or protectorates of
Britain, France, Italy, Spain, and Holland. They all regained their sovereignty late in the twentieth century. Recent events have reminded us
of their existence and of their independence. Islam is back.

The Jihad, the *force de frappe* of Islam, is a word which until a couple of decades ago had practically disappeared from the vocabulary of the Western world. It had become an esoteric term covering an epoch of forgotten confrontation between the Muslim East and the Christian West. In the elation of United Nations euphoria and international goodwill, of multiculturalism and multiracialism, of hands extended to one another in friendship and brotherhood, we had forgotten that "the battle between free expression and Islam still rages" as the *London Times* expressed it bluntly in an editorial of June 18, 1994. Unlike other, more timorous publishers, this newspaper recalled "the ferocity of fundamental Islam in the face of perceived insults." The perceived insult, in this case, was a reported criticism of the Koran by the courageous Bangladeshi woman writer, Taslima Nasrin, which sent 10,000 enraged Islamic fundamentalists into the streets of Dacca, clamoring for her death. A few years previously, similarly enraged Muslims had stormed through the streets of European and Asian cities demanding the death of Salman Rushdie for his novel *The Satanic Verses,* which they claimed had denigrated the Prophet and his wives.

Faced with this spectacle of fanaticism and fury, the *Times* mildly observed that the conflict between the two clashing cultures of Islam and Christendom could not be easily resolved and warned the West not to underestimate the bitterness of the battles that may lie ahead. One must hope that the *Times*'s pessimism will prove unjustified.

But if, alas, the past is any guide to the present, overoptimism cannot be the order of the day. The Jihad, as the *Encyclopedia of Islam* commented in 1913, will continue until "Islam makes itself over." There is no sign of that yet. In fact, if events in Algeria, Egypt, the Sudan, Indonesia, Pakistan, and other Muslim countries are any guide, Islam is growing in violence. In the West, the so-called Jihad even spread beyond Europe and reached the Americas in 1993. Bombing attacks were carried out against Jewish interests in Buenos Aires, and more massively, on February 26 of that year, a group of Islamic extremists tried to blow up the twin 110-story World Trade Center towers in Manhattan. If the two buildings had collapsed, as planned, the casualties would have run into the tens of thousands—close to 100,000 visitors or employees are there every day. Fortunately, the effects of the blast did not extend beyond the underground parking location where the explosives had been placed near the foundations that support the structures. Six people were killed and over a thousand were injured, however.

Confrontation between the West and militant Islam assumed a new and unexpected virulence in August 1998, when Saudi millionaire and terrorist Osama bin Laden allegedly ordered his group to firebomb the American embassies in Nairobi, Kenya, and Dar-es-Salaam, in Tanzania. Some 260 people, twelve of them Americans, were killed and nearly five thousand were injured in the blasts.

Bin Laden, whose headquarters are located in Afghanistan, is the founder and funder of the extremist Islamic International Front for Fighting Jews and Crusaders, who, in February 1998, issued the order: "Kill Americans." The United States retaliated promptly by sending seventy-five Tomahawk cruise missiles to bomb the movement's training base in Afghanistan and also what President Clinton claimed was a chemical weapons facility near Khartoum in Sudan. So the United States has found itself propelled to the front rank of the Jihad targets. The hunting season against America is now open. A new Jihad may be in the offing, a prospect which is causing considerable international concern, very understandable in light of the 1,300 years of Jihad activity which the West has already experienced and which is described in this book. Americans will note that bin Laden has chosen the most disparaging term in the devout Muslim's vocabulary to describe his American and other foes, and has gone back hundreds of years to find it. That term is: *Crusader.*

Devout followers of Muhammad believe the Crusades responsible for the confrontation between Christendom and Islam. They believe it was the Crusaders who forced Islam to create the Jihad's self-defense. In fact, they have their facts the wrong way round. When, in 1096, the Crusades were launched, the Jihad had already been in action against Christendom for nearly five hundred years. It was the Jihad's recent successes in Spain that inspired, so to speak, the pope to create the Crusades and to order the Crusaders to march to the Holy Land.

For the world at large these latest bombings in Africa were simply modern-day terrorism in action; but some non-Muslims saw in these bomb plots a possible connection with the old, historic Jihad that goes right back to the 600s, to the Arabian peninsula and to the founder of Islam who, at the same time, created the Jihad in defense of his creed. Many modern-day Muslims condemn this new fanatical Jihad even more strongly than do Westerners. The Jihad of today for them is a political Jihad with no connection with the religious Jihads of the past. They do not recognize themselves in this new Jihad, nor their religion, nor the preachings of their Prophet. Non-Muslims, however, have other thoughts. They wonder, question, and fear. The problem is that the practitioners of this new, fanatical, and murderous Jihad see themselves as the heirs of the warriors of old. One Muslim extremist of the Islamic Liberation party reminded his interlocutors just before the scheduled opening of the party's international rally in London in August, 1994, that "there are 123 verses in the Koran about killing and fighting." And he added, quite unnecessarily, "Ours is not a passive religion."

INTRODUCTION

THE HOLY WAR THAT ISN'T

T HE JIHAD, THE ISLAMIC SO-CALLED Holy War, has been a fact of life
in Europe, Asia, Africa, and the Near and Middle East for more
than 1,300 years, but this is the first history of the Muslim wars in
Europe ever to be published. Hundreds of books, however, have appeared on its Christian counterpart, the Crusades, to which the Jihad is
often compared, although they lasted less than two hundred years and
unlike the Jihad, which is universal, were largely but not completely
confined to the Holy Land. Moreover, the Crusades have been over for
more than 700 years, while a Jihad is still going on in the world.

The Jihad has been the most unrecorded and disregarded major
event of history. It has, in fact, been largely ignored. For instance, the
Encyclopaedia Britannica gives the Crusades eighty times more space
than the Jihad. In the New South Wales State Library, where I did part
of my research while in Australia, there were 108 entries listed in their
catalogue cards for the Crusades, but only two for the Jihad! The Jihad
has been largely bypassed by Western historians, and this book is an
attempt to right the situation, for the Jihad has affected the lives—and
continues to do so—of far, far more people and regions in the world
than the long-extinct Crusades ever did.

Forgetting that the Jihad was nearly five hundred years old when
the Crusaders set out on their first campaign to recover the Holy Land,
Muslims see the Crusades as the starting point of the long military

19

confrontation between Islam and the Western World. I quote the Ayatollah Khomeini, modern hero and saint to hundreds of millions of
Muslims. The Jihad, he said, "means the conquest of non-Muslim territory. The domination of Koranic Law from one end of the earth to the
other is . . . the final goal . . . of this war of conquest." So it was for
hundreds of years before the Crusades, so it has been since.

Should we take the ayatollah's words as the vaporing of an angry old
man or as a recall of the past, a reminder of the present, and a warning of
things to come? The choice is ours. But the past calls for our special attention, as well as the present. The Jihad "war of conquest" is a historical
reality that has lasted so far more than 1,300 years. The terrorist Jihad that
exists today is a topical, political reality. The advent of the ayatollah
Khomeini on the international scene has strikingly heralded the return to
the world of an aggressive Islam after more than a century of quiet:
Western imperialism and colonial domination shackled Islam to the West
for a century and stifled the Jihad until the mid-twentieth century.

To understand the Jihad we must be clear in our minds about what
it is and, first of all, what it is not. To start, it is *not* what most people
think it is. Its purpose is not to convert unbelievers to Islam by force.
This may have been so in its first century of life, when the choice given
to the defeated was conversion to Islam or death, but this was soon
changed to conversion to Islam, death or tribute in the form of a special tax. It was a case of "your money or your life"! The purpose of the
Jihad became, and basically still is, to expand and extend Islam until
the whole world is under Muslim rule. The Jihad is essentially a permanent state of hostility that Islam maintains against the rest of the
world, with or without fighting, for more sovereignty over more territory. We should at this point recall the words of Jacques Ellal who, in
his foreword to Bat Yeors's *The Decline of Eastern Christianity* (p.
19), reminds us of an almost forgotten basic fact concerning the Jihad:
"*Jihad* is a religious obligation. It forms part of the duties that the
believer must fulfill; it is Islam's *normal* path to expansion." The Jihad
is an institution in Islam which in Christian language we could call a
sacrament. It is part of the normal functioning of the Muslim world, a
religious duty which the devout Muslim has to perform if called upon.

For well over a thousand years the Jihad has been first and foremost a fighting war, an imperialist form of war, like the wars of colonial or continental expansion of Rome or, more recently, of Britain,
France, Spain, Germany, Russia, and the United States. The Muslims
make no distinction between religion and the state, hence the "holy"

tinge that their imperialist wars have acquired. Let us not be deceived by the religious coloring Muslims gave to their territorial conquests. The Jihad wars were sheer imperialism, just as ours were.

There are still many Muslims who believe that it is Islam's manifest destiny to conquer the whole world. Obliged to face the realities of the modern world, many more may not be too sure about this article of their faith. But, just the same, many still ardently cling to it, even among the millions of immigrants who have made their home in France and Britain. The fundamentalists and those who have faith in the message of Ayatollah Khomeini do. So do those we can call Muslim revivalists, devout and sincere followers of the Prophet but unwilling to take part in the militant postures and actions of the fundamentalists. Profoundly disturbed by the moral degradation of Western society today, they are convinced the future belongs to Islam.

In the past, individual Muslims fought in wars against the Infidels in a supposed gesture of piety and loyalty. Yet the wars themselves were—and still are—usually essentially territorial and political. No change is visible in the offing. The *Encyclopedia of Islam,* published in Leyden in 1913, is quite explicit: "Islam must be completely made over before the Jihad is eliminated." But the elimination of the Jihad seems nowhere in sight. On the contrary, it is probably more deeply imbedded in the Muslim mind than at any time in the past two centuries, and its elimination seems very far off indeed.

The Jihad appears more and more as an interminable fact of life, almost a freak of nature. Like the earth going around the sun, the Jihad seems to have a power, if not of perpetual motion, at least of perpetual continuity. In this domain of the stars and planets, a friend of mine once compared it to Halley's Comet. "It streaks across the sky, then vanishes. But it's always there. It reappears, streaks across the sky and then vanishes again." The comparison is not quite true. Haley's Comet appears very rarely and does no damage. The Jihad appears frequently and does a lot of damage. So does its modern terrorist version.

Although there have been Jihads in the three old continents, I have limited this history to Europe. The world is too vast a stage. Asia, particularly the formerly Christian Near East and Central Asia, and the subcontinent of India undoubtedly deserve the history of their own Jihads also. So does Africa, with the Muslim conquest of old Christian Egypt and North Africa, as well as large parts of West and East Africa with their animist and black tribal religions. But for this first general history of the Jihad, Europe provides a sufficiently extensive setting.

This book will also give us a glimpse of some of the great military and heroic figures of Islam—and of its foes—during these centuries of fighting. In the course of over a millennium of warfare, there have been many, for Islam has always preached war. Its founder and its heroes were warriors. "The sword is the key to heaven and hell," Muhammad told his followers. Six hundred years earlier, Christ had said, "He who lives by the sword shall perish by the sword." Muslims who kill are following the commands of Muhammad, but Christians who kill—and there are many—are ignoring the words of Christ. Therein perhaps lies one of the basic philosophical differences, as well as one of the basic ethical differences, between Islam and Christianity.

The Jihad originates in the Koranic teaching and was practiced by Muhammad in his lifetime against Jewish and pagan tribes in the Arabian peninsula, and soon after his death against the Persians and against the Christian peoples of the Byzantine empire, Syria, and Palestine. Hundreds of years later it terrified Europe. "From the fury of the Mahommedan, spare us, O Lord" was a prayer heard for centuries in all the churches of central and southern Europe. Fear of the Jihad has not entirely vanished even now, particularly among peoples who have known Muslim domination. The French expert on Islam, Maxime Rodinson, reminded us of it a few years ago in the June 17, 1994, issue of the Paris newspaper *Le Monde*: "There are some words that scare people. Jihad is one of them. When Serbian leaders want to satanize the Bosnian army they declare that Alija Izet Begovic (the Bosnian Muslim leader) has proclaimed Holy War, the Jihad, the feared weapon of Islam."

With the decline of Islam from the eighteenth century, much of the fear it had once inspired vanished. Later, many Muslim countries became for over a century colonies and protectorates of Britain, France, Spain, Italy, Holland, and Russia. Muslim soldiers no longer served under the banner of Islam, but in the armies of their foreign masters. For over a century the Jihad vanished. It became, to Westerners, an almost forgotten word. Now, since decolonization in the 1950s and 1960s, it is back again, and has been so for the last few decades, strong, more assured, perhaps more structured, richer with vast oil money financing it, and as ruthless as ever, perhaps more so. To most people, the Jihad now is simply one of the components of the international terrorism of our day. For some Muslims, Europe and the non-Muslim world are still today what they have always been, Dar-al-Harb, the Land of War. Muslim countries are what they have always been, Dar-al-Islam, the Land of Islam, the land of God and peace.

The purpose of this book is not primarily to look into the Jihad of today, although today's Jihad is important as an extension of the thirteen previous centuries of militant Islam. Soon after Muhammad's death in 632, the Jihad manifested itself on the European mainland, outside the walls of Constantinople, in the year 668, when the Muslims first laid siege, unsuccessfully, to the capital of the Byzantine empire. The Jihad has been part of European history ever since. Its first big triumph in Europe was the invasion and occupation of Spain in 711. Nearly eight hundred years of fighting and occupation followed. The conquest, and subsequent reconquest by the Portuguese and Spaniards, lasted until 1492, but most Europeans still know virtually nothing about it. Yet it is part of our history, part of our European lore, as much as the Norman conquest of England, the Roman conquest of Gaul, the defeat of the Huns, the Hundred Years' War, Waterloo, the Somme, and Dunkirk. The Jihad is one of the facts of life that have made Europe what it is today.

The Jihad of today, the Pan American plane blown up over Lockerbie, the Air France airliner destroyed in midair flying over Chad, the Western hostages kidnapped and held in underground cells for years by the Hezbollah in Beirut, the hundreds of French soldiers and American Marines killed when their barracks were blown up in Lebanon, the American diplomats abducted and secreted in Teheran, the bombs planted in department stores across Paris: they are all part of the long tradition of the Jihad.

The Jihad has affected and engulfed far more countries than the Palestine-bound Crusades. The Crusades, eight in number, were concentrated on the Holy Land and all took place between the years 1096 and 1270, not quite two hundred years in all. The Crusaders wanted to establish themselves in the Holy Land, formerly Christian. Islam's motives, through the Jihad, were far grander. The Muslims wanted to take and occupy Europe and, hopefully, to Islamize it. A large part of Europe was taken, occupied for centuries, sometimes devastated, and some of it was Islamized. Spain, Portugal, France, Italy, Sicily, Austria, Bosnia, Serbia, Croatia, Hungary, Rumania, Wallachia, Albania, Moldavia, Bulgaria, Greece, Armenia, Georgia, Poland, Ukraine, and eastern and southern Russia were all Jihad battlefields where Islam conquered or was conquered. Many of those lands were occupied by the Muslims, in some cases by Arabs and Moors, in others by the Ottoman Turks, usually for hundreds of years: Spain 800 years, Portugal 600 years, Greece 500 years, Sicily 300 years, Serbia 400 years,

Bulgaria 500 years, Rumania 400 years, and Hungary 150 years. Hungary, particularly, was ruined, plundered and ravaged and took 200 years to recover from Muslim occupation. By comparison, the European occupation of the Muslim countries of the Near and Middle East and of North Africa lasted less than a century and a half. In some countries of Europe, Spain, Sicily, Bosnia, Albania, Macedonia, the Crimea, and Crete, many, sometimes most of the people gave up Christianity for Islam; but in Algeria, Morocco, Tunisia, Libya, Lebanon, Iran, and Iraq, few indeed were the adherents of the Muslim faith who gave up Islam for Christianity.

Muslims invaded and occupied a huge part of Europe, but sometimes Muslim raiders only came and went. The Turks besieged Vienna twice, in 1529 and 1683. Their cavalry raided central Europe, riding into Bavaria almost as far as Nuremberg. They fought in Poland and the Ukraine, crushed Hungary, occupied Belgrade and Budapest for hundreds of years. The Moors and the Arabs took Spain and Portugal, invaded France through the Pyrenees, turned Sicily into an Islamic island, raided Rome, sacked St. Peter's, and obliged the pope to pay them tribute. From their base near St. Tropez on the French Riviera, they raided Switzerland as far as Lake Constance on the German border. The pirates of the Barbary Coast raided England, Denmark, Ireland, and Iceland, and brought back thousands of slaves to be sold in the markets of Constantinople (after they conquered it and turned it into Istanbul) and North Africa. The Mongols threatened Moscow, occupied the Crimea and became Tatars. The Persians marched into Georgia; so did the Turks, who also occupied Armenia.

History has largely bypassed the Muslim attacks on and invasions of Europe that lasted from the seventh to the twentieth centuries, but has remained transfixed on the Christian Crusades to the Holy Land that lasted only from the eleventh to the thirteenth century. We could say that the historical perspective here is gravely out of focus. The spotlights have been on the less important places and the less significant events; this book is a modest endeavor to adjust the vision. This is not just an academic matter. For their perception of the Crusades—and later of colonialism—has greatly affected the attitudes and the modern political thinking of Muslims, particularly of those from the Middle East, toward the Christian West. When accusing the West of imperialism, Muslims are obsessed with the Christian Crusades but have forgotten their own, much grander Jihad.

In fact, they often denounce the Crusades as the cause and starting point of the antagonism between Christianity and Islam. They are putting the cart before the horse. The Jihad is more than four hundred years older than the Crusades. Amin Malouf in *The Crusades through Arab Eyes* sees the sack of Jerusalem by the Crusaders in 1099 as "the starting point of a millennial hostility between Islam and the West." There is only passing mention of the Muslim capture of Jerusalem from the Christians in 638, of the invasion of Spain some seventy years later by the Arabs and Moors, or of their subsequent 800-year occupation in whole or in part of the Iberian peninsula.

The fault, in Arab eyes, usually starts with the West and the Crusades, continues with the West and colonialism, and ends with the West and neocolonialism. Forgotten is the fact that it was the success of the Jihad that caused Pope Urban II in 1095 to call for a Crusade to redeem the Holy Land from Islam. The pope had been very impressed by the recent victories of the Moroccan Almoravids in Spain, where they had smashed the army of Alfonso VI of Castile at Zalaca. Holy War obviously worked fine for Islam. It should also work for Christianity, he reasoned. It must have seemed a good idea at the time. So the Catholic pope followed in the martial footsteps of the Tuareg warrior Yusuf, who led the Almoravids to victory against Christendom in Spain.

Colonialism, the other major cause of censure against the West (and rightfully so), was nevertheless a two-edged process in the Islamic-Christian connection. Simply put, the Muslim East conquered much of Europe from the seventh to the nineteenth centuries, the Christian West and the Muslim East conquered and colonized each other during a large part of the nineteenth century, and from the mid-nineteenth to the mid-twentieth century colonizing and conquest became a Western monopoly. Western colonization of nearby Muslim lands lasted 130 years, from the 1830s to the 1960s. Muslim colonization of nearby European lands lasted 1,300 years, from the 600s to the mid-1960s. Yet, strangely, it is the Muslims, the Arabs and the Moors to be precise, who are the most bitter about colonialism and the humiliations to which they have been subjected; and it is the Europeans who harbor the shame and the guilt. It should be the other way around.

The Muslim occupations of Europe have left a far deeper and more lasting trace of their former influence than any of the European occupations of Islamic North Africa and the Near and Middle East. There are still large Muslim populations in the Balkans; sometimes the majority, as in Albania and Bosnia. The European powers that a few decades ago ruled over their Muslim fiefs in Asia and Africa did not in any way counter their heavily Islamic culture. Muslims are still Muslim, devoutly so sometimes.

In western Europe, Muslims today can worship in their own mosques; but in some Muslim countries, Christians are not allowed to practice their own faith or to build churches for their own worship. Judaism in some of them is even more strictly forbidden. Some of the countries which forbid or hamper Christian worship have embarked on a quiet but widespread program of mosque building and religious pros-elytizing in Europe, backed by immense oil revenues. There is another aim, unspoken but certainly present: the conversion of the infidel to Islam. But let the neophyte beware: Muslims only change their religion at the risk of their lives. Once a Muslim, always a Muslim; that is the rule. Apostasy can be punishable by death. You abandon or criticize or attack Islam or the Prophet at your own risk. In Pakistan, under section 295C of the penal code, death is the penalty for anyone who "by words, either spoken or written, or by visible representation, or by any imputation, innuendo, or insinuation, directly or indirectly defiles the sacred name of the Holy Prophet." Christians are often jailed. Some have been sentenced to death. Islam is not a religion for the tender or the squeamish.

I am well aware of the often uncritical devotion with which most Muslims regard their Prophet Muhammad. He was a man of his times, with its faults and qualities. He was a brave warrior but also a devoted husband (to his eleven wives), a loving father, and a charismatic polit-ical leader of the Arab people. Muhammad was a great Arab patriot, highly intelligent, undoubtedly cruel and brutal, too. In our day and age, like other great men whatever their religion or nationality, he might have been regarded as a criminal, perhaps a war criminal or a mass murderer.

Muslims are very aware of his good qualities and seem unaware of his faults. The Islamic scholar Malise Ruthven has written that the Muhammad "lodged in the Muslim psyche" has no relationship to the Muhammad of history. This is often the case with great historical fig-ures, but there is an extra problem with the personality of Muhammad. He is also an ideological leader, a conqueror, and the founder of one of the world's great accredited religions. It makes any objective exami-nation of the person a difficult task, because any adverse criticism of him still evokes, 1,363 years after his death, a great deal of emotion and passion. And fury.

I feel that one cannot stress enough the importance of the ideological side of Islam, with which this religion is permeated as is none of the other great religions. It infiltrates, and even sometimes governs, often down to the tiniest detail of everyday life, the way of life of its millions of adherents in the world of today. Let me quote the Ayatollah Khomeini. "Eleven things are unclean: urine, excrement, sperm, blood, a dog, a pig, bones, a non-Muslim man and woman, wine, beer, perspiration of the camel that eats filth." This view of "non-Muslim man and woman" is expressed by a man of great influence who did not live in the Dark Ages, but who died only recently, and who believed that the Jihad "war of conquest," as he called it, will make our planet convert to Allah and to Muhammad, his Prophet.

War, finally, is what this book is all about, war holy or unholy, war the most unclean thing of all, which the ayatollah failed to mention in his list. This book covers nearly one and a half thousand years of European and Islamic military and political confrontation in the West. Chapters 1 to 60 concern antagonism and war. The epilogue features the great quality of man that this book, by its very nature, overlooks. Call it the brotherhood of man. It is, at any rate, a moment of the past that, unlike the ayatollah's sayings and writings, can show us all, Muslims and Christians alike, the way to the future and toward each other. The Jihad had no place in the friendship of Topal Osman and Vincent Arnaud.

PART ONE

THE DAYS OF THE PROPHET

1

THE BEGINNINGS:
MECCA 570–622

W ITH THE EXCEPTION OF JESUS Christ, perhaps the Lord
Buddha, maybe Napoleon, and much more doubtfully Karl
Marx and John Maynard Keynes, no one has had more influence by his
actions and ideas on the flow of so many people's lives than Muhammad the Prophet. The creator of Islam not only founded one of the
world's great religions; he also created the Jihad, the Muslim holy war,
and shaped the lives of what may be as many as 700 million to one bil-
lion Muslims living today and all those who lived before, gave them
hope and sustenance, and is still doing so.

Born in Mecca in 570, after a childhood stint as a shepherd,
Muhammad's first known job was a camel driver. He started to drive
camels professionally at the age of twenty-five—that means around the
year 595—when in the service of the widow Khadijah. Orphaned early
in life, Muhammad was brought up by a succession of relatives, and
although a member of the respected Koreish clan, very upper class in
Meccan terms, he was one of the poorer relations of his family. Families were large in pre-Islamic Arabia, and already polygamous. During
the years that followed Muhammad's birth, Arabia began to crack at
the seams. The population had increased to over two million people in
the Hejaz, the Arabian west where Mecca is located, too many for this
dry, desert, stony region with only a few oases to feed and keep the
population in minimum comfort, even by the stern standards of sixth-

31

century Arabia. The entire peninsula had a population of between five and six million people, which meant many mouths to feed with very little fertile, watered land available for the growing of crops. One of the favorite professions was the hijacking of caravans, at which Muhammad, after he and his followers moved to Medina in 632, became an expert. Many of the tribes engaged in this popular activity were in continual warfare against each other. It was to end this image abroad of an irresponsible Arabia that Muhammad paradoxically founded Islam and used it as an instrument to unite all the tribes under it. We can describe this early Islam as being essentially a patriotic movement aimed at asserting Arabian independence and prestige. The expansion of Islam and the Jihad which it spawned were therefore no mere accidents of history. Muhammad planned it that way.

It was his wife, the widow Khadijah, probably a Christian, who was its first follower and financier. When Khadijah, a forty-year-old Mecca businesswoman who owned four camels, met Muhammad, fifteen years younger than she was, she gave the poor but presentable and intelligent young man a job and sent him to Syria with her four camels loaded with trade goods. There was then a considerable flow of trade between the ports of Yemen in the south and Damascus and the cities of Syria to the north, and most of it passed through Mecca, the main commercial center in Arabia. These caravans, usually made up of several thousand camels and their attendants, who banded together for protection against robbers, were a twice-yearly feature of commercial life in the Hejaz. Trade goods carried north included spices, chinaware, and silk brought by dhow across the Indian Ocean from India, Java, and China; and ivory, gold powder, and slaves from Africa.

In Yemen the merchandise was all transferred to camels, as the winds and currents in the Red Sea were often too contrary and unreliable for sailing ships. As the camels ambled slowly north in the Hejaz desert, they were indeed "ships of the desert." Yemen itself, famous in biblical times for the Queen of Sheba and perfumes, provided incense and musk, often used in the preparation of dead bodies for burial, for the markets of the north. The returning caravans were loaded with cereals and olive oil. It was a two-way traffic, centered on Mecca, and it made many Meccans rich, including several of Muhammad's Koreish relatives and the widow Khadijah.

The marriage lasted 25 years, until Khadijah's death, and was unexciting but happy in spite of their age difference, or perhaps because of it. It was shortly after her death that Muhammad and his followers moved to Medina from the city of Mecca, which had become hostile to them, the event from which Muslims date the Hegira, the start of their calendar year. Muhammad had taken no other wife during Khadijah's lifetime, perhaps as she was the moneyed partner and had made it clear to Muhammad that she would tolerate no other wives. He married again soon after Khadijah's death and during the next few years took over Medina, where he acquired a harem of a dozen wives and concubines. Very poor at the time of his marriage to Khadijah, Muhammad became a politician and businessman in his middle years and later became a warrior and ruler, the commander-in-chief of the Arab armies and the virtual king of the desert. But it is as the proclaimed Prophet of God and founder of Islam that he became, and has remained, famous.

Khadijah is said to have given Muhammad several children, including at least one son who died in infancy, his daughter Fatima who survived him, and three other daughters, a biologically improbable circumstance given Khadijah's age when she and Muhammad married. Then many things that were impossible, biologically and otherwise, happened to Muhammad during these years, first in Mecca, and then in Medina, including his frequent meetings and conversation with the Angel Gabriel, who dictated the Koran to him on behalf of Allah and told him he was the Prophet of God.

2

GABRIEL COMETH:
MEDINA 622–632

I T WAS IN THE YEAR 611, when he was forty-one, that Muhammad's life began to change drastically. Muhammad, a patriotic Arab, had been for some time musing over the low esteem in which the neighboring People of the Book, as the Christians and Jews were called, held the Arabs. Many Jews, as well as Christians, then lived in Arabia. These foreigners despised Arabs because they were uncouth pagans who did not adore just one God, but worshiped a collection of gods and goddesses. Mecca alone had 360. But, thought Muhammad, "All idols and formulas are nothing but miserable bits of wood. There is only one God." Who in Mecca would believe him?

Many of these deities were worshiped at the holy Meccan site of the Kaaba, which included a huge black stone, probably a meteorite, that Islam has since decreed was a gift from the Angel Gabriel to Abraham, common ancestor of Jews and Arabs, to mark the spot where Adam, when he left the Garden of Eden, built his first house. Every year people from all over Arabia came to worship at the Kaaba and walk around it seven times. Their visits were a rich source of revenue to the local businessmen, chief among whom were the people of Muhammad's own Koreish clan.

One night in 611, the Angel Gabriel appeared before Muhammad to give him a message from God, or Allah as He is known among the Arabs. There are several versions of the meeting. The usually accepted one says that Muhammad was resting in a cave at the foot of the bleak and bare Mount Hira, a couple of miles north of Mecca, when a vision of light suddenly appeared before him and he heard the words coming from sky: "Oh Muhammad, thou art the Prophet of the Lord in truth and I am Gabriel." Terrified, Muhammad rushed home to tell his wife, who sat him on her lap and tried to soothe her distraught husband. The apparition followed him into the house, although Khadijah could not see it. Muhammad feared it might be a demon ready to possess him. To test the visitor Khadijah took off all her clothes. Other, more prudish versions say she just removed her veil from her face. The vision thereupon immediately disappeared. Comforted by its discretion, Khadijah told Muhammad not to be afraid. "It is an angel, not a devil," she assured him. The vision reappeared several more times in the ensuing months. "Arise and preach and magnify Allah," it said. Muhammad, who could neither read nor write (this is a disputed matter among historians and Muslim theologians), dictated the messages which are now the Koran, and thus Muhammad founded Islam.

His first disciples were the loyal Khadijah and his two adopted sons, Ali (Muhammad's first cousin) and Zeid, who was black. Muhammad's teaching did not impress the citizenry of Mecca. Most people laughed at him. His first outside convert was his kindly neighbor Abu Bakr, a merchant some three years older than Muhammad, who was one day to father a girl called Aisha, who became Muhammad's favorite wife, and himself to become Islam's first caliph (successor to Muhammad) when the Prophet died. Gradually and slowly the circle of converts expanded, but not among Muhammad's relatives. One exception was his uncle Hamza, a tough Bedouin chief not very religious but who became a Muslim by tribal loyalty to his nephew whom he felt was threatened. Other early converts included a number of the younger set, members of the better-off families of Mecca such as Othman, a tall, rather dandified young man who was also to become Muhammad's son-in-law.

Othman, who belonged to the socially and financially eminent Umayyad clan was more interested in Muhammad's daughter Ruqyah than in Muhammad's teaching, people said, and in due course she became one of his several wives. He was many years later to become Islam's third caliph and to be murdered by rebellious disciples. That the Koran exists now is due largely to him, for he had all the mutton and camel bones, the stones and palm leaves on which the passages of the holy book, the "suras," were written, gathered together, and tran-

scribed into one volume. His filing system, however, caused considerable theological and historical problems. Instead of listing the 114
suras chronologically, he set down the longest suras first (except for
the first sura) and the shortest ones last. Scholars took several hundred
years to sort out the puzzle. Othman saved one of the several versions
of the Koran that began circulating but, perhaps to minimize theological clashes, destroyed three others then in existence that may have
been in competition with his.

Another early convert was Bilal, the Negro slave with the stento-
rian voice, who summoned the faithful to prayer in the same tones as
those heard today in mosques all over the world, and who became
Islam's first muezzin, or crier. When Bilal refused to renounce his
Islamic faith, his first owner, a Meccan, had left him to die of thirst in
the desert with an enormous rock on his chest so that he could not
move. Abu Bakr, Muhammad's neighbor and an early disciple, had
immediately bought Bilal to save his life, gone to fetch him in the
desert, and given him his freedom.

The early group of believers grew to thirty-five and met in a house
near the Kaaba belonging to one of his first converts, al-Arkham. It is
into this house that the future conqueror of Jerusalem, Omar, choleric,
tall, and twenty-six years old, erupted one night and penitently asked
Muhammad if he could join the group. Omar was destined to become
the second caliph and the first of them to be assassinated. The owner
of the house lived to become a very old man—not too old, however, to
take part in the first Jihad campaigns after the death of Muhammad.

Bilal's death sentence by his furious master typified the spirit of
seventh-century Meccan capitalism at bay as Muhammad's teachings
spread and cut the incomes of businessmen. Islam, businessmen said,
was bad for business. Mecca, with its Kaaba and its myriads of deities
including idols, stones, spirits in the mountains, and stars in the sky
attracted pilgrims from all over the peninsula, who spent considerable
numbers of dinars in the shops, inns, and eating houses during their
stay in the city. The celebration of their rites must have turned Mecca
into a huge Luna Park, with much music and dancing and singing,
eating of shish kebabs, much drinking of date alcohol, much smoking
of *quot* and praying to the many-faceted deities of the city. Muhammad's Muslims, who preached that all who did not submit to the will
of Allah—that meant all the pilgrims—would burn in hell for all eternity, definitely lowered the jollity of the occasion. Muhammad and his
disciples had to be stopped.

Foremost among his opponents was Abu Sufyan, the ruthless and rapacious head of the Koreish clan, owner of one thousand camels, a descendant of the first Umayyad, who was related to Othman, Muhammad's son-in-law. Abu Sufyan made it clear he would oppose by any means available—and murder was a perfectly legitimate method of redress in pagan Mecca—Muhammad's unwelcome missionary zeal.

Muhammad versus Abu Sufyan. The revolutionary Muhammad versus the ultra-conservative Abu Sufyan, creator of the distinguished rival Umayyad dynasty which ruled over Islam in Spain for hundreds of years. This was the first big internecine clash of Islam. It wasn't the Jihad yet—Muhammad was still too weak—but nearly. Abu Sufyan's faction was Islam's first implacable enemy. Abu Sufyan was perhaps the wealthiest man in Mecca, certainly among the wealthiest, and he and his family were, in the end, to mark the future course of Islam more than any other living person, not even excepting the Prophet himself. Like many of the actors of this ancient stage, Abu Sufyan remains a shadowy figure, certainly an opportunist, perhaps even a slightly evil one. He is a hard person to gauge and judge. One of his wives, Hind, was an atrocious creature. We shall read about her later. The Abu Sufyans are one of the greatest families of Islam. They simply pushed Muhammad's family aside and took over. The Abu Sufyans had several children, three of whom subsequently acquired great fame in early Islam. Their son Muawiya, not well known in the western world, is in fact one of the great figures in world history, not out of place in the company of William Pitt, Washington, Cardinal Richelieu, and Bismarck. Even Charlemagne would have found him amenable company. He is the true founder of the Islamic world empire, although his motivations may be uncertain. Love of his native Arabia and love of power? Probably yes. Love of Islam? Probably no. In Islamic religious terms, he may well have been agnostic.

Another son of Abu Sufyan, Yazid, became a general and could have become a great one had he not not died early in his career of the plague. A daughter, Habiba, made a political marriage with Muhammad and became one of the Prophet's eleven wives. The Umayyads were to become caliphs in Damascus and Cordova and to reign for three hundred years in Muslim Spain.

The Abu Sufyans, in the early days of Islam, led the opposition to the Prophet. The opposition to the Muslims was murderous and unrelenting. As Muhammad's group grew, it became more and more ferocious. One young woman, who had confessed to the belief that Allah was great and that Muhammad was his prophet, was impaled by the chief of one of the Mecca tribes, Abu Jahl, who remained until his death at the battle of Badr the most relentless enemy of Islam. His name meant "Father of Folly" and he took his Mecca deities so seriously that he ordered three of his tribesmen tortured to death for converting to Islam. He and Muhammad were personal enemies. The two men had disliked each other since childhood, and they had once had a fight which left Muhammad's foe with a permanent scar on his leg. Muhammad had once punched Abu Jahl so hard in his private parts that that Abu Jahl did not only see stars as a result of the blow, but "a camel with teeth that did not look like camel's teeth and that tried to eat me." There was rarely anything gentle about the historic Muhammad, whatever may be the lofty opinions of his followers. "The Muhammad who is lodged in the Muslim psyche is not the same as the Muhammad of history," Malise Ruthven has pointed out in his account of the Prophet. Muhammad was tough and he never avoided a fight.

In those emotion-charged early days of Islam it was, however, the Muslims who were at risk, particularly after the death of Muhammad's protector, another uncle, Abu Talib, one of the most influential men of the Koreish tribe, who, although he disagreed with his nephew, defended him. After Abu Jahl's death, being a Muslim became a particularly high-risk situation in Mecca. Some of them took temporary refuge in the Christian kingdom of Abyssinia, on the other side of the Red Sea. In 620 Muhammad lost Khadijah. She was 65 when she died and he was 50. Two months later he married Sauda, the widow of one of the men who had gone to Abyssinia and become a Christian. At about this time a group of pilgrims, worshippers of the Kaaba, arrived in Mecca from the town of Yathrib, now known as Medina, a couple of hundred miles north of Mecca. Yathrib was located in a green and fertile oasis which grew more than a hundred different varieties of dates and harbored five tribes, three of them Jewish and two Arab. The clans in Yathrib were mixed, with Arabs and Jews in each. Twelve Arab representatives from Medina, as we shall from now on call Yathrib, suggested that Muhammad go there and become their leader, as they could not agree among themselves. They were impressed by Muhammad's religious teaching. They promised to obey his injunctions. "We will not worship any but the one God. We will not steal, neither will we commit adultery, nor kill our children (infanticide, particularly of baby girls, which Muhammad was anxious to stop, was widespread in Arabia at the time). We will not slander in anywise. Nor will we disobey the Prophet in anything that is right," they pledged, and they promised Muhammad and his followers their protection. The Jews, who were not officially consulted, perhaps hoped that Allah might turn out to be their Jehovah and that Muhammad might be their long-awaited Messiah.

Thus Muhammad and his followers moved to Medina. The Hegira, or Flight as it is known to the outside world, the greatest moment of Islamic history, was spread over two months. The journey across the desert by camel took ten days. Between one hundred and two hundred followers of the Prophet left Mecca for their new home, and none of their non-Muslim neighbors tried in any way to stop them. Muhammad was among the last to leave. His friend Abu Bakr bought two camels and on June 22, 622, the most important day in the Muslim calendar, the two men left Mecca in the middle of the night and headed north to Medina. "Flight" is too strong a word to describe their departure, as it implies an escape and a pursuit. The Arab word for it is closer to "emigration."

One is free to wonder whether the escapees did not sometimes exaggerate the perils of their journey. The Muslims who remained behind in Mecca after Muhammad's departure were left undisturbed, and his son-in-law Ali, Fatima's husband, went about untroubled until he too left three days later. The families of Muhammad and Abu Bakr were not inconvenienced either.

Abu Bakr's six-year-old daughter, Aisha, remained with relatives in Mecca until she joined her father in Medina, where soon afterward she married the Prophet, nearly fifty years her senior. All in all, the Flight, although considered the most momentous event in Muslim history, seems to have been a very unperilous enterprise. The traditions claim that the Koreish met to decide on his pursuit and murder, and sent off a posse, headed by Abu Jahl, to find them. Satan himself, shrouded in a mantle, was present at the meeting. Muhammad and Abu Bakr were nearly found hiding in a cave where they had taken shelter for the night, but were saved by a spider that had woven its web across the entrance. So Muhammad was saved for Medina and, later, for little Aisha and the world.

3

THE FIRST BATTLES

MEDINA WELCOMED THE PROPHET ENTHUSIASTICALLY, although there were some inhabitants who wondered whether the welcome was not overdone. The poetess Asma bint Marwan, who objected to the predominant presence of Muhammad in Medina, hoped that someone would cut off "the gull's hopes." Her wishes infuriated the Prophet.

The disciples who had accompanied Muhammad from Mecca set about building a first mosque and living quarters for their leader and his wives, present and future, on the site where Muhammad's camel had first rested, of her own volition, on their arrival in the city. The British explorer Richard Burton was the first person to describe the Medina mosque to his countrymen after a secret pilgrimage he made to the site. Muhammad, Burton said, spent the first year in Medina building the original mosque with the help of local youths and his followers from Mecca. It was built of rough stone, sunbaked bricks, and date palm trunks. Short of funds, Muhammad tried to turn a local house into part of the mosque in exchange for a house in Paradise, but the owner told him he was too poor to let him have the building. The mosque was hemmed in on three sides, with a view of the Kaaba. The Prophet spent the greater part of the day in the mosque with his companions, and received visitors and messages from the Archangel Gabriel. The Medina mosque, Masjidu 'N Nabi, as it is called, is the second most important mosque in Islam, ranking alongside the Sacred Mosque in Mecca, which contains the Kaaba. See Richard Burton, *Personal Narrative of a Pilgrimage to Medinah and Meccah* (London, 1853), p. 345.

Muhammad found temporary accommodation in the nearby home of Abu Ayub who let his guest and his wife (only Sauda was with him at this time) occupy the lower part of the house while he moved with his wife (or wives) upstairs. Muhammad and Sauda stayed there seven months, and it is also in the Abu Ayub house that the six-year-old Aisha may have arrived with her toys to become Muhammad's second wife, although the marriage was not consummated until three years later.

Abu Ayub figured prominently in the early life of Islam. He was not only Muhammad's first landlord in Medina, but also Muhammad's first cook—or maybe it was one of his wives. Muhammad had to train the Abu Ayubs not to put onions in his food. His hosts discovered the Prophet, who had a very delicate palate, particularly disliked onions when he sent them back his plate with the meal untouched. "No onions," Muhammad said. "No garlic either," he added, just to prevent another culinary disaster. Abu Ayub was still alive some fifty years later and still fighting fit. In fact, he took part in the first continental invasion of Europe by the Arabs when, in 668, nearly forty years after the death of the Prophet, they landed in Gallipoli and laid siege to Constantinople.

The presence of the Mecca refugees in Medina brought tension into the city. The new arrivals, by their unity, were stronger than the divided people of Medina whose life they had come to share. Dissension soon broke out between the Medinese, who were called the "Ansars," the Helpers; and the Meccans, who were called the "Muharirun," the Emigrants. The three Jewish tribes of Medina, the Qoreiga, the Nadir, and the Qaynuga, provided another discordant note. Muhammad cultivated their support at first by honoring Jerusalem, their sacred city, and ordered his followers to kneel and face Jerusalem when saying their prayers. When he discovered that the Jews were not impressed by either him or his movement and had decided that Allah was not their Jehovah or Muhammad their Messiah, he replaced Jerusalem with Mecca, thus making the Jews honor his own birthplace. The Muslims have been bowing to Mecca ever since.

In addition to Asma, several poets were outraged by the presence of Muhammad in their city and wrote verses mercilessly mocking their visitor. Muhammad regarded critics as the minions of Satan and in Medina he developed a new personality. He was much more aggressive, much surer of himself. He was no longer a small-time little preacher in Mecca, struggling to have his ideas accepted. In Arabian society, where state or government, as we know the terms, were unknown, he became a chief, a dictator, a prince, the uncrowned sovereign of a legally nonexistent but in fact very alive small kingdom. Or perhaps it will suffice to call it a principality, a city-state such as those that came to fruition in Italy. Medina was to be turned into the first focal point of a burgeoning Arab state and a later Arab empire. From this little domain Muhammad conquered the rest of the Arab world and united it by Islamizing it. Islam was to be the cement of Arab nationhood as democracy was to be for the United States. Under his successors, Islam was to be the cement for a new imperialism.

Muhammad fought the opposition in Medina as any political leader might have done. He maneuvered, he intrigued, and sometimes he killed and had opponents assassinated. He organized his supporters for war. Brigandage would become the nearest modern-day equivalent to warfare, although in that remote place and period and in the harsh environment of the Hejaz, it was viewed as a normal form of business activity. Medina stood near the trade route between Mecca and Syria. Mecca and the Koreish were now his enemy, and Muhammad sent out bands of armed followers to attack their caravans. Their first success was at Nakhla, where a handful of Muslim brigands intercepted a small caravan, captured two of the four men escorting it, and killed a third. Muhammad received a fifth of the proceeds, establishing a historical precedent that has continued down the centuries under the caliphs and the sultans, who always received a fifth of all the booty captured by their pirates and their warriors in treasure, money, women, and slaves.

The next attack on a caravan was much more devastating to the Meccans and culminated in a pitched battle at nearby Badr involving hundreds of warriors shouting, "Allah is great," armed with swords, spears, and bows and arrows. Unseen by anyone except Muhammad himself, an allied legion of eight thousand armed angels (according to the chronicler al-Baidawi; five thousand in a variant account*) plunged into the battle on the side of the Muslims. The angels were all wearing white turbans except for Gabriel, whose turban was yellow to be easily recognizable by the angels under his command. Muhammad, at the head of a little army of three hundred humans, ambushed a caravan of

---

*Comments Edward Gibbon in *The Decline and Fall of the Roman Empire,* vol. 6: "The loose expression of the Koran allows the commentators to fluctuate between the numbers of 1,000, 3,000, and 9,000 angels."

seven hundred camels returning from the north defended by Muhammad's old enemy Abu Jahl. The Meccans were trounced. Badr, mentioned in the Koran (iii. 123), was the first crucial battle of Islam, although in terms of the numbers involved (not counting the angels) it was not a major clash. Muslim casualties were fourteen men killed. Seventy-four of the Meccans were killed and forty captured.

The Badr victory gave Muhammad great standing among the Medinese. The victors captured 150 camels, ten horses, a considerable amount of merchandise, and 70 Meccans, most of whom were ransomed for 1,000 to 4,000 dirams apiece. Muhammad also had the great satisfaction of capturing Abu Jahl, now more cringing than truculent at being a prisoner in the hands of his foe. The Prophet not being a forgiving man, Abu Jahl's red-haired head was severed from his body and thrown at Muhammad's feet. Another prisoner not ransomed but cut to pieces instead was Bilal's former owner, who had once taken the slave into the desert and pinned him to the ground with a large stone. Abu Sufyan, who owned many of the camels and much of the merchandise in the caravan, lost a son in the battle but managed to make his own escape back to Mecca, vowing vengeance. Muhammad was now more than an enemy to Abu Sufyan. To kill him became his obsession. The Koreish leader swore at the shrine of one of the 360 Kaaba idols that he would not make love to any of his wives until he had defeated the Prophet.

Back in Medina, thanks to his victory, Muhammad's position was now unchallengeable, and he decided the time had now arrived to settle a few old scores with those who had opposed his arrival. High on the list was the poetess Asma bint Marwan. Muhammad could not tolerate criticism, particularly from writers. Poetry was the most widespread and respected form of artistic expression among the Arabs, and Asma was to become his first local victim. She had spoken and written most disparagingly of the Prophet, whom she regarded with deep suspicion and, in memorable verse, had called upon her fellow citizens to throw him out:

> Gutless men of Malik and of Nabit,
> And of Nawf,
> Gutless men of Khazraj
> You obey a stranger who has no place among you,
> Who is not of Murad, nor of Madhhij,
> Do you when your own chiefs have been murdered

Put your hope in him
Like men greedy for meal soup when it is cooking?
Is there no man of honor among you
Who will take advantage of an unguarded moment
And cut off the gull's hopes?
(From Maxine Radinson, *Mohammed* [London, 1973], p. 157)

Asma's words carried. They were repeated all round the suks and alleys of Medina in whispers and made the Prophet very angry. He had no intention of being the gull with its hopes cut off. For Asma bint Marwan, her poem was her death sentence. A killer stabbed her so hard while she slept that, with his dagger, he nailed her to the couch. She was not his only literary victim. Another poet, the centenarian Abu Afak, was similarly dispatched in his sleep. Thus did Muhammad set about securing Medina for Islam.

Terror is a weapon that has its origins in these first struggling years of Islam. The day Asma was assassinated "was the day when Islam first showed its power over the Banu Khatma [the local tribe to which Asma belonged]. . . . On the day bint Marwan ["Marwan's daughter"] was killed the men of the Banu Khatma were converted because of what they saw of the power of Islam," wrote the ancient chronicler Ibn Hisham. Assassination has remained a powerful weapon that the extremists of the GIA (Armed Islamic Group) still use. We can, alas, point to the villages of Algeria, where several hundred people have been murdered in recent years in the name of Allah. A group of seven Trappist monks were also kidnapped and murdered in May 1996 simply for being in Algeria.

Soon after the Muslim victory at Badr, a clash with the Jews was begun by the unexpected exposure of an Arab girl's derrière by a young Jewish lout who raised her skirt in the souk where she had gone to sell vegetables. Outraged, the Arab shoppers killed the Jewish youth on the spot. Furious at this crime of *lèse-majesté* against his budding establishment, Muhammad laid siege to the Qaynuga quarter in Medina to avenge this outrage to decency. The Jews capitulated and, in return for their lives, Muhammad allowed them to migrate elsewhere, leaving all their possessions to the Muslims. A fifth of the booty went to Muhammad in line with the new rules of plunder-sharing recently promulgated by the Prophet. The whole operation was therefore a great financial success for Muhammad and his followers.

The latent hostility between the old Jewish tribes of Medina and the Muslim refugees from Mecca was already apparent. After the departure of the Qaynugas from Medina, two Jewish tribes, the Nadirs and the Qoreigas, were still left there, and they all felt very uneasy over Muhammad's growing influence in their city. Since the murder of Asma, the messenger of Allah was definitely not a popular figure in local literary circles either, and Kab, another poet, traveled to Mecca to propose to Abu Sufyan that they should unite to take action against Muhammad before it was too late. Abu Sufyan hemmed and hawed, nothing was done, and Kab returned to Medina where, soon after his arrival, Muhammad gave the order that his throat should be cut. The power of the sword, or at least of the knife, was seemingly stronger than the power of the word.

4

A MAN OF MANY PARTS

MUHAMMAD WAS PITILESS WITH THOSE who fought him, stole from him, who acted against his interests, or whose wealth he hankered to acquire. Kinana, the chief of a Jewish settlement at Kheibar, automatically became Muhammad's foe when the Prophet learned that Kinana had a fortune in gold vessels hidden away somewhere, and Muhammad ordered him to be tortured until he revealed its hiding place. His executioners tied him down to the ground and lit a fire on his chest "till his breath had almost departed." When Kinana finally died under torture, Muhammad ordered his head to be cut off, and that night went to bed with the victim's widow, Safiya, aged 17, who later became one of his eleven wives.

The *Dictionary of Islam* exposes various instances of the Prophet's harsher side. A striking instance of the cruelty of Muhammad's character occurs in the *Sahibu al-Bukhari** (p. 1019 in the French translation, *Les traditions islamiques*), when he killed several tribesmen to whom he had given hospitality, who robbed him of several camels, killed one of his men, and then fled. "The Prophet sent some people after them and they were seized and brought back to Medina. Then the

---

*Bukhari is regarded by Sunni Muslims as the greatest of the Traditionalists. His compilation of sayings and acts of Muhammad is second only to the Koran as the source of Muslim doctrine and law.

Prophet ordered their hands and feet to be cut off as a punishment for theft, and their eyes to be pulled out. But the Prophet did not stop the bleeding and they died." Another entry reads: "The Prophet ordered hot irons to be drawn across their eyes, and then [for them] to be cast on the plain of Medina [where they were impaled] and when they asked for water it was not given to them and they died." With masterly British understatement, his biographer William Muir noted that "magnanimity and moderation were not among the Prophet's great qualities."

Muhammad's son-in-law Ali, who married Fatima and became the fourth caliph a few years after Muhammad's death, was sometimes requested to dispose of the unfortunate creatures who had earned the Prophet's ire. Muhammad's wives, by common consent, all hated the Coptic concubine Mary, who had been given to Muhammad by the governor of Upper Egypt, with whom they felt their husband spent too much time. They told Muhammad she was having an affair with her servant Nabur. Incensed at this treachery, Muhammad ordered Ali to kill the servant. Terrified at the finality of his impending fate, Nabur not only frantically denied the charge but claimed it was impossible for him to commit the act he was accused of committing with Mary. "I'm a eunuch," he pleaded, and to prove his good faith he whipped out his mutilated genitals and pointed to where their missing essentials should be. "Look," he said. Ali looked, agreed, sheathed his sword, and Nabur lived on to safely serve his mistress.

The Prophet also had a number of volunteer executioners, unpaid, competent, and pious, ready to rid him of antagonists or critics who stood in his way. Several foes were thus disposed of, both men and women. One, as we have seen, was the Medina poetess Asma who, shortly after Muhammad's flight from Mecca to Medina, wrote verses disparaging the new arrival. Omeir, a loyal follower of Muhammad, crept into her house and stabbed her to death while she lay sleeping with her infant in her arms. "Is there cause for apprehension?" the murderer anxiously asked Muhammad the next day. "None," replied the Prophet. "A couple of goats will hardly knock their heads together."

On another occasion he sent his disciple Abdallah ibn Oneis into the camp of the rival tribal chief, Sufyan ibn Khalid, to assassinate him and bring back his head; which Abdallah duly did, throwing the bloody trophy at the feet of Muhammad on his return to camp. The grateful Prophet, to reward his henchman, gave him his walking stick as a present. "It shall be a token betwixt thee and me on the day of Resurrection," he piously informed his devout disciple. When the head of a personal enemy, the Meccan Abu Jahl, was thrown at his feet after the battle of Badr, near Medina, Muhammad joyously exclaimed that the dead man's head was more acceptable to him than the best camel in Arabia.

Of course, these scabrous incidents have to be judged in the context of the 620s or thereabouts. Seventh-century Arabia was not a hotbed of culture, and the delicate and finer things of life were largely unrepresented among the warriors of the desert. The same could be said for the Europe of those times. After settling in Medina, when he was fifty-two, Muhammad financed his major entry into public life by hijacking a caravan in the desert. He was probably a typical male specimen of the time and place in which he lived, that is to say a robber and a fighter, but obviously smarter than most. Had he not been a man of God, preaching about love and compassion, and the founder of a merciful religion, there would probably be nothing in his behavior to shock in spite of the propensity he often showed for revenge killing and violence. The historic Muhammad, I repeat, had no relationship with the Islamic Muhammad. Muslims can always say, as did Henry Ford, "History is bunk." But often it isn't.

The explanation of Malise Ruthven that "the Muhammad who is lodged in the Muslim psyche is not the same as the Muhammad of history" is very relevant. Many Muslims must refuse to believe that such an immense gulf can exist between their mystic vision of Muhammad and the Muhammad of historic reality. Perhaps some see in this assertion only a Western fabrication, but al-Bukhari must have known what he was writing about. He was an honest and devout man, and he was so anxious to record only truthful traditions (he accepted only about seven thousand of the 600,000 stories he was told about the Prophet) that he went down on his knees and bowed in prayer asking for divine guidance before he wrote down each of the Traditions he accepted.

Muslims venerate their Muhammad, and regard him as a kindly man who helped the poor, saved baby girls from traditional Arab infanticide, lived the simple life of a good husband surrounded by his eleven wives (he had received, as leader of the Muslims, special dispensation from Allah through the Angel Gabriel to have many more wives than the permitted four) and assorted concubines. He was no macho man; he even mended his own clothes and sewed his own buttons, although one wonders why when he had so many women around him. They loved him. Muhammad had the sexual power of thirty men, his followers reverently attested.

One of his eleven wives, Zeinab, was the divorced wife of his adopted son Zeid. He decided to marry her after accidentally seeing her one day, scantily dressed. "Gracious Lord! Good heavens! How dost thou turn the hearts of men!" he had exclaimed, so Sir William Muir tells us in his very Victorian prose. Zeinab, an intuitive woman, immediately understood his message and told her husband, the ugly and pug-nosed Zeid. Zeid and Zeinab were officially divorced. It took only a few seconds for Zeid to say three times to Zeinab "I divorce thee" and to drop three stones on the ground, and Zeinab and Muhammad were then free to marry. The Angel Gabriel (whom Muhammad mistook for a time for the Holy Ghost), on a special visit to Muhammad, made it clear to the Prophet—the 33rd sura of the Koran carries his message—that it was God's will he should marry his daughter-in-law.

The text of the Angel Gabriel's message was widely spread around Medina, for Muhammad habitually used the Koran suras, as they were dictated to him by Gabriel, as announcements which were widely distributed among the local population. Count Caetani, in his voluminous *Annali dell'Islam,* referred to the Koran as being the seventh-century equivalent of a newspaper. In modern days the distribution of the Koran suras in dribs and drabs, as they came out, might be described as a public relations operation, to keep the public informed on the latest wishes of Allah, or to give the population instructions on various points of hygiene, diet, law, or anything else Muhammad (or Allah) felt they should know.

Through the Koran he could also take his revenge against people who had crossed him or whom he disliked, and whom he could thereby expose to public ridicule. After a bitter quarrel with his uncle Abu Lahab, a greedy businessman whose wife Muhammad found unbearable, the Koran castigated his uncle and aunt, both in the name of Allah, and consigned them both to the fires of eternal damnation. "Perish the hands of Abu Lahab, and perish he," thundered the 111th sura. "His wealth avails him not, neither what he has earned; he shall roast in a flaming fire and his wife, the carrier of the firewood, upon her neck a rope of palm-fiber!" Among his many talents, Muhammad possessed a genius for invective and vituperation.

It was therefore perfectly normal for Muhammad to include from time to time in his Koran releases little personal tidbits. When his planned marriage to Zeinab caused such a sensation and so much unfavorable comment around Medina where he was then living, he felt he should issue a divine revelation on the approaching wedding. The

Medina ladies just couldn't understand why Allah should allow
Muhammad to marry his own daughter-in-law when he already had
nearly three times his quota of wives. The order came straight down
from Allah, through Gabriel as usual. "Oh Prophet! Why hast thou forbidden thyself that which God hath made lawful to thee, seeking the
good pleasure of thy wives? . . . God has ordained for you the absolu-
tion of your oaths. . . . God is your protector." So "the grotesque utter-
ance," as Muir has styled it, duly appeared in the Koran's sura 66.
Muhammad dutifully obeyed Allah, the Medina ladies stopped grum-
bling, and Zeinab joined the harem. There was another Zeinab already
there, so she became Zeinab II.

Unlike the later harems of the Abbasid caliphs in Baghdad, or the
splendid seraglio of the Ottoman Empire by the shores of the Bosporus, there was nothing luxurious or picturesque about Muhammad's
harem in old Medina. It was simple. Each of the wives lived in her own
little one-room house, and they were grouped around a main yard. To
satisfy the requirements of his own Islamic custom, Muhammad slept
with a different wife each night. It was understood that each wife
would keep out of the others' bedrooms, but one day one of the wives,
Hafsa, found Muhammad on her bed with Mary, his Coptic concubine.
Hafsa and the other wives were so incensed at this betrayal that the
Angel Gabriel had to intervene again with a message from Allah for
the wives, through the Koran: "If he divorces you, his Lord will give
him in exchange wives better than you." To quell the incipient harem
mutiny, Muhammad summoned all the wives to a meeting and gave
them the message he had received. He informed them that unless their
behavior improved he would leave them and, to show he meant what
he said, he slept by himself for several weeks.

To inspire such devotion in his wives and followers, Muhammad
obviously must have had both charisma and political sense. He was
indeed a very different man from the one whom the Muslims revere as
the Prophet of God. The Muhammad of history is a man who was
loved at home and feared in war. The Muhammad of the Muslim
psyche is a man who was simply loved, revered and respected at home
and among his own people.

The violence of Muhammad's life as a warrior and chief of state
deeply marked the religion that he created at the same time he was
fashioning the Arab nation. The two, the spiritual and the temporal,
continually blended into each other, and the Muslim psyche has remained ossified ever since. "Give unto Caesar the things that are

Caesar's and to God the things that are God's," Jesus Christ said. For the Christians, and the Jews, and the Buddhists, and nearly everyone except the warlike Muslims and the peaceful Tibetans, the State and the Church are two separate institutions. For the Muslims they are one, governed by the rules of the eternal and uncreated Koran.

One country, Saudi Arabia, has even enshrined the Koran as its constitution. On the eve of the twenty-first century, several Muslim countries have reintroduced the sharia as the law of the land. It is as if Britain discarded more than 1,300 years of jurisprudence and constitutional law to take itself, in the name of God, back to the time and the laws of the Anglo-Saxon King Ethelbert, 250 years before King Alfred. This would no longer be considered piety, but insanity. Yet that is what has happened in several Muslim countries (Iran, Pakistan, and Sudan among others). There are tens of thousands, perhaps more, of Muslims ready to die or kill to bring the Islamic community, all 690 million or more of them, back to the days when the Koran was being inscribed on palm leaves and on the shoulder blade bones of camels and sheep; back to the days when, in Europe, Ethelbert ruled over the kingdom of Kent and King Dagobert (famous in French nursery rhymes), a couple of hundred years before Charlemagne, ruled over the ancient kingdoms of Neustria and Austrasia, in the land we call France.

5

WHEN THE KILLING HAD TO STOP

I N MECCA, AFTER THEIR DEFEAT at Badr, the local pagans were mulling revenge. Two young Muslims from Medina happened to fall in their hands. One they promptly killed; the other, Khubyah, was urged to recant and return to the gods of the Kaaba. He refused and was crucified. A mob gathered to watch his agony. A boy whose father had died at Badr prodded him with a spear, but Khubyah was firm in his Muslim faith and cried out to Allah to avenge him. "Allah count them well," he shouted to heaven, sweeping with his eyes the smirking spectators who stood around watching him die. "Count them well, Allah," he shouted. "Kill them one by one and do not let one of them escape."

Two of the bystanders who did escape his curse were Abu Sufyan and his little boy Muawiya, future caliph and empire builder. The prudent Abu Sufyan, when he heard the curse, pushed his son to the ground with his face down so that Allah could not recognize him. Perhaps Abu Sufyan also found a good hiding place for himself, for Allah didn't kill him either. On the contrary, he became richer then ever. Soon afterward, in 625, the year after Badr, he raised and sent a large army to Medina in search of revenge and victory. They had the greatest soldier of the Arab world as deputy commander of the Meccan army, Khalid ibn al-Walid, Khalid for short, later to be known as "the Sword of God." Khalid was one of the great soldiers of history and had he been a Frenchman at the time of Napoleon he might well have become one of the emperor's most famous marshals.

Two hundred cavalrymen and three thousand foot soldiers, seven hundred of them wearing mail armor, rode and marched out of Mecca, Medina-bound, to the shouts and screams of the delighted locals and the shrill, traditional ululations of the women. Sixteen women went along, all of them wives, daughters, or mothers of men killed at Badr. They included Hind, who had lost her father and a son in the battle, one of them killed by Muhammad's uncle Hamza. To show that their war was holy, too, the Meccans carried with them the statues of Hobal and Lat, two favorite Kaaba deities. The Meccan army was largely one of professionals. Many of the soldiers were Abyssinian mercenaries and Bedouin desert warriors.

Muhammad, with an army of one thousand men which included his former landlord Abu Ayub, awaited the attackers at the foot of Mount Ohud, a few miles north of Medina, confident of victory and perhaps awaiting the reinforcement of 3,500 invisible (except to him) fighting angels whose presence at Badr had given him victory. This time there was dissent in the Muslim ranks and three hundred Medinese decided to go home before the battle started, leaving the cause of Allah to another day. Gabriel and his angels also failed to turn up. Undaunted, the Muslims took the offensive and Ali, Muhammad's son-in-law, led the first charge against the enemy. One of the first casualties was Muhammad's uncle Hamza, who fell transfixed by a spear thrust from one of the Abyssinians. Abu Sufyan's wife, Hind, shrieking her delight and disregarding the danger invaded the battlefield, slit Hamza's body open, pulled out the liver and ate it raw on the spot. Her husband, outraged at her display of bad manners, struck her across her bloody mouth and ordered her to drop the liver at once and go back and join the other women who, more refined, had only cut off the ears and noses of the fallen enemy and were making little bracelets out of them. Muhammad, hit in the face by a stone that cut his lip and broke two front teeth (which are now on display in Istanbul), left the battlefield, his face covered in blood. His men, thinking he was dying, lost heart, panicked, and gave the victory to Abu Sufyan.

The annihilation of Muhammad and Islam were within the grasp of the Meccans that day, but instead of pressing on and taking the town, Abu Sufyan unexplainably ordered his army to turn around and march back to Mecca. He came back to the attack two years later, but in the meantime Muhammad had ordered a deep and wide ditch to be built around Medina which the attackers were unable to cross. Thwarted of an anticipated victory, the Meccans went back home again.

Muhammad entered the last years of his life, his authority not only over Medina but over most of the Arabian tribes now well established. He began to take an active interest in international affairs and, as head of what was now a de facto Arabian state, sent messages to the Persian sovereign, to the Negus in Abyssinia, and to Emperor Heraclius in Constantinople, urging them to convert to Islam. It is about this time that he ordered the slaughter of the Jewish Beni Qoreiga tribe, after they had rebelled against him and his rule at the instigation of Abu Sufyan.

Muhammad's rule was no more savage than that of other rulers of that distant epoch, whatever their beliefs, but at least the others did not invent a new religion. Muhammad the massacrer and Muhammad the man of God are very incompatible people. However, the banality of spirituality and cruelty side by side was an accepted part of daily life, and Muhammad was no different from anyone else. After the torture and death of Kinana, already described in chapter 4, Muhammad took the murdered man's seventeen-year-old bride, Safiya, to his tent for the night. In the morning Muhammad heard a noise outside and went out to investigate. It was Abu Ayub, his former Medina landlord and now his devoted follower, who had "kept watch there all night with his drawn sword." According to Muir, at the question "What has brought thee here?" asked by the Prophet "surprised at the inopportune presence of his friend," Abu Ayub replied, "O Prophet, I bethought me that the damsel is young. It is but yesterday she was married to Kinana, whom thou hast slain. And thus distrusting her, I said to myself, I will watch by the tent and be close at hand in case she attempts anything against thee." Muhammad, Muir added, "blessed Abu Ayub for his careful though ill-timed vigilance and desired him to withdraw in peace."

The practice of murder was also normal. Muhammad desired to have his implacable Umayyad enemy Abu Sufyan assassinated. The task was assigned to a disciple, a semi-professional part-time executioner whom Muhammad sent to Mecca to carry out the killing. He was recognized as he lurked around the Kaaba waiting for his intended victim and forced to flee; but, as he explained later, his journey had not been all a waste of time. He may have missed his main target, but he was able to kill three other people while in Mecca and had brought a fourth as a prisoner to Medina.

Killing seems to have been a normal form of professional activity among both devotees of Allah and their foes, just as it was among

Hejaz tribesmen, often in the most barbarous circumstances. Zeid, Muhammad's adopted son, was sent to avenge the hijacking of a Medina caravan by some robbers from the Beni Fezara tribe. He captured a member of the gang, a middle-aged woman named Um Kirfa, the aunt of one of the robber chiefs, along with her daughter. Her legs were tied to two camels and, Muir said, "the camels were driven asunder and thus she was torn to pieces." For good measure, her two young sons were also killed. On Zeid's return, Muhammad congratulated him on a job well done, embraced him and gave the woman's daughter to Aisha to serve as her maid.

So life continued in slaughter, battles, raids, and conversions in the desert, villages, and oases until a large part of Arabia, including Yemen and Oman, became Muslim and, eighteen years after the Hegira, Muhammad and Abu Sufyan decided to make their peace. The Prophet returned to his birthplace in triumph, and Abu Sufyan was converted to Islam as was his wife, Hind, and the bulk of the population of Mecca. Muhammad walked the ritualistic seven times around the Kaaba, just as they still do during the pilgrimage, but now under the aegis of Muslim practices, and had four of his enemies executed. The victims did not include anyone who counted in Meccan society. A minor poet was ("inevitably," one is tempted to add) executed, and so was some unfortunate, small-time girl singer whose ditties had displeased the Prophet. They were unimportant and expendable. Hind was spared even though she had devoured Muhammad's uncle's raw liver. Muhammad the politician was well aware that it was important to secure peace with Mecca by not antagonizing the powerful ex-opposition. In fact, to strengthen his new alliance, Muhammad married Abu Sufyan's daughter Habiba and became his former enemy's son-in-law.

6

A MAN OF HIS TIME

I AM WELL AWARE OF the often uncritical devotion with which most Muslims regard their Prophet Muhammad. He is, for them, the man nearest to God. He was not only the Prophet of God, he was also the wisest of rulers, the charismatic leader of the Arab people, a great Arab patriot, a brave warrior, a devoted husband to his eleven wives, and the most loving of fathers. More intelligent and enterprising than most, he was a man of his time and place—but seventh-century Arabia, like Europe, was a brutal place in a cruel time; and so were Arabs, so were the people of Europe, and so was Muhammad.

Arabs are very aware of Muhammad's good qualities, but seem unaware of his faults. We have noted earlier Malise Ruthven's judgment that "the Muhammad lodged in the Muslim psyche is not the same as the Muhammad of history." There is an extra problem with the personality of Muhammad. He is the founder and leader of one of the world's great accredited religions. It makes any objective examination of the person particularly difficult, because any adverse criticism of him, of any facet of his personality, still evokes, more than a thousand years after his death, a great deal of emotion, passion and, sometimes, fury.

To the Muslim world, Muhammad is a man of love and mercy. To the modern West's jaded eye, Muhammad appears as a man of unlimited prurience, as well as of cruelty and brutality, not as a man of God at all. One event symbolizes the dark side of the historical Muhammad.

In one long day and night of slaughter in Medina, he had six hundred (perhaps more) captive Jews beheaded and, during the massacre, took one of the youngest and prettiest recent widows to his couch for the night.

Says his Victorian biographer, William Muir, who often judges Muhammad harshly, moderating his condemnation with the euphemisms of the times: "Magnanimity and moderation are nowhere discernible as features of the conduct of Muhammad toward such as his enemies as failed to tender a timely allegiance." There is even an individual entry into the 1885 *Dictionary of Islam,* still on sale in London's Muslim bookshops, to describe "the cruelty of Muhammad's character" for resorting often to murder in dealing with his enemies. "He is guilty, even more than once, of conniving at the assassination of inveterate opponents," it states in the *Dictionary.* Enemies sometimes had their hands and feet cut off and their eyes gouged out. We read of torture and of enemies impaled. These events, little known to most Muslims, are inscribed in the early writings of Islam (notably of al-Bukhari). He ordered political opponents, even young women who wrote mockingly about him, to be executed. He particularly disliked poets and had four of them killed, three in Medina and one after his return to Mecca. By modern standards, Muhammad's life was "unedifying" wrote the historian H. G. Wells in his *Short History of the World,* describing the Prophet as a man "of very considerable vanity, greed, cunning, self-deception and quite sincere religious passion. . . . A shifty character."

The Muslim holy books recount several tales of murder and mayhem. There had always been a tradition of fighting and raids in pre-Islamic Arabia, which Islam took over. The Jihad, as it became, turned into one of the mainstays of Muslim faith, having been conveyed to Muhammad, Muslims believe, directly from Allah through the Angel Gabriel. "When you meet the unbelievers strike off their heads until you have massacred them," says the Koran. "Fight in the cause of Allah! . . . Kill them wherever you find them. Until they surrender. Then if they give over there shall be no enmity."

History judges Muhammad as one of its most famous leaders and lawmakers. Muhammad believed in Arab unity and fought for it all his life. It was his patriotism, his love of his people, and his pride in them that created Islam and made a nation of the Arabs. In the seventh century, Arabs were simply the people who lived in the Arabian peninsula; many of them rough and tough Bedouins, considered a coarse and ignorant bunch of semi-civilized creatures by their more sophisticated Greek, Persian, Ethiopian, and Egyptian neighbors. They were despised by these monotheist peoples as worshipers of many gods and were widely condemned for the widely known infanticide of baby girls. Muhammad hankered for the betterment of the Arab people and saw himself as their leader. He strove for Arab adherence to a more godly way of life through the worship of only one God instead of the thousands of deities—including idols, stones, and stars—that thronged their pagan pantheon. And he outlawed infanticide. Muhammad brought a new concept of law to the Arabs. It became the sharia.

The law as it was practiced in Medina and Mecca thirteen centuries ago continues to be the point of reference in many Muslim countries. Stoning to death is still the practice in some countries of Islam. Muslim purists can claim the example comes from on high. Muhammad personally took part in the stoning of Ghamdiyah, a woman who "had confessed whoredom." After ordering a hole to be dug as deep as the woman's waist as "decency was thus effectively preserved," Muhammad threw the first stone at her, a small one, not larger than a bean we are told. The sharia still flourishes today, but it is being called more and more into question in a number of Muslim countries by many followers of the Prophet who, however devout, claim that the sharia is no longer relevant to our age, and that cutting off the hand of a thief and stoning an adulterer (or more usually an adulteress) to death are no longer acceptable methods of punishment. There are plenty of imams and mullahs and ayatollahs who insist that the sharia must still be obeyed and that, since the Koran is God's will and a divine part of God himself, we can change nothing in it. That, they say, is the will of Allah. Therein resides, perhaps, the greatest challenge facing Islam as the twenty-first century looms.

If Muhammad seems to us a hard man, let us not forget that the Arab leader, in addition to being a lawmaker, statesman, and occasional executioner, was also a tough warrior who had fought on the battlefields of Arabia and killed those who fought against him. "Muhammad, unlike Christ, was a man of violence, he bore arms, was wounded in battle and preached holy war, Jihad, against those who defied the will of God as revealed to him," John Keegan reminds his readers in *A History of Warfare*. This description of the Prophet may be psychologically unacceptable to many devout Muslims but it is in line with historical reality. Killing became part of the routine of the life of Muhammad the warrior after he moved from Mecca to Medina in 622 and became a fighter in

the cause of Allah. "Mahomet established a religion by putting his enemies to death, Jesus Christ by commanding his followers to lay down
their lives," was the Christian explanation of the seventeenth-century
French philosopher Blaise Pascal, in his *Pensées*.

Muhammad, as well as being a fighting warrior, was responsible
for the deaths of thousands not only in battle but through execution and
assassination. Not many are aware of the massive execution by beheading of 600 to 800 men of the Jewish Beni Qoreiga tribe in Medina,
who had withheld their support from him after his takeover of the city.
He had the executions carried out in the market place, where trenches
previously had been dug to receive the corpses. The carnage started in
the morning and went on all day and into the night by torchlight.
Muhammad left the scene early in the evening to enjoy the charms of
Reihana, the young widow of one of the victims, a beautiful Jewish girl
who had been set aside for the Prophet's pleasure. She refused to
become his wife but was enrolled into his harem as a concubine
instead. The other women of the tribe as well as the children, about a
thousand in all, were sold into slavery.

The slaughter of the Beni Qoreiga tribe was also a highly profitable business operation for Muhammad. In addition to the slaves, the
spoils included a rich haul of livestock (camels, goats, sheep, and
horses), and of land, date trees, houses, furniture, jewelry, and money.
The booty was divided into 3,072 parts, of which one fifth went to the
Prophet and made him a rich man overnight. The Muslims also took
from the slain Jews a large number of weapons, including 1,500
swords and scimitars, a similar number of shields, 1,000 spears, and
300 coats of mail that all went to furbish the Prophet's recently created
army. The Koran (sura 33, verse 25) praised God for the killings and
Muhammad became a foe to be feared. The Jihad had been born in a
deluge of blood.

7

OF BONES AND STONES

USLIMS HAVE A NATURAL TENDENCY to attribute their victories to divine guidance, sometimes even to the support given by thousands of unseen angels who fought on their behalf on the battlefields; and also, of course, the righteousness of their cause. Others are now more skeptical. According to the Islamic expert, Italian Professor Francisco Gabrieli, the Arabs were anxious to prove to the Persians and the Byzantines, who had always despised them, that the Arabs were as good as they were, better in fact; and, Gabrieli maintains, love of loot rather than the love of God was their main motivation. Indeed, many Arab tribes who were not Muslims also took part in these first assaults. Later, seeing how lucrative Islam could be, they became Muslims themselves, much as a person today may join a political party, or perhaps the Freemasons or the Rotary, for the advantages it may bring him.

When the Muslim Arabs erupted from their peninsula of sand, stone, and oil (underground, and then still unknown), other Arab clans who had migrated north generations before joined them in their attack on the Byzantine and Persian empires, which had been greatly weakened by their recent war. These were the Arab Christian tribes south of the Dead Sea and the Arab pagan tribes on the Euphrates. These Arabs were certainly not interested in Allah or Muhammad. They were after plunder. The same urgency, whatever the demands of their faith, spurred the tribesmen from the peninsula. Those from the Hejaz, the sandy and stony wasteland of western Arabia, Muhammad's birth-place, were probably the most motivated for Allah, since the Prophet came from their midst; but for the majority, the first priority was win-ning loot, slaves, and women. In fact, when the second of Muham-mad's successors, the caliph Omar (634–644), was first asked by his governor at Damascus for permission to cross the sea and attack the islands of Greece, Omar forbade the expedition as he feared the dan-gers of the deep. "The safety of my people is dearer to me than all the treasures of Greece," he explained. "Treasure" in this instance did not mean infidels to be converted to Islam, but loot to be plundered. It meant gold, jewels, and beautiful things. The caliph's order of priori-ties was quite clear: treasure, not Islam, was uppermost in his mind. The cancellation of the religious mission of his troops was not even mentioned. Omar's Jihad was, at least in part, a front for treasure hunting and looting.

For most, the Jihad was no fraud; the majority simply accepted the Koran as the direct word of God. No one had any difficulty in recon-ciling religiosity and rapacity. Muhammad had not only made it easy for them to do so, he had made it a virtue by presenting plunder and war as righteous paths to Paradise. In his ten years in Medina he organized no fewer than 65 military campaigns, and personally led 27, although we should note that the traditionalist al-Bukhari placed the number at between 15 and 19. Even Napoleon Bonaparte could not better that numerical record, although his battles were, of course, of greater emi-nence. The Koran, anyway, urges the Muslims always to battle.

The Muslim must accept every word of the Koran as coming from God in person, in fact, as being part of God and therefore beyond query. It was God who spoke the words of the Koran through Gabriel to Muhammad. After receiving the message, Muhammad dictated it to various friends, mainly his secretary, the fifteen-year-old Zeid ibn Thabit, who wrote it all down (it represents 120,000 words, the equiv-alent of a book of about three hundred pages) on bones and stones that lay around the living quarters of Muhammad and his wives.

Although Muhammad supposedly could neither read nor write, he could listen and he could talk and shortly before his death he told his followers he would dictate an addition to the Koran before he died—presumably Allah had told him he would come round again to bring him the new message—to prevent his disciples from lapsing into error. But that final message was never given. What errors had he in mind? That is a question that has long troubled some Muslims.

The final version of the Koran (in ancient times four different transcriptions of it were in circulation), accepted and revered by the Muslims as the uncreated and eternal truth, may in fact contain a number of inaccuracies. Unscrupulous scribes inserted their own verses into the suras. One of the more famous Koran falsifiers, Abdallah ibn Saad, who later became an admiral and commanded the Muslim expedition to Cyprus in 649, when a young man wrote his own verses into the revelations that Muhammad was dictating to him, perhaps to enliven the text. Muhammad didn't even notice the changes and Abdallah was unwise enough to tell his friends in Medina the story of his misdeed as if it were a great joke. The story of his indiscretion was repeated to an enraged Muhammad and the Prophet, who was not a man to forgive an offense lightly, particularly if it made him look ridiculous, tried to have the indiscreet young man murdered. A very scared Abdallah moved faster than his employer and fled to Mecca, where he remained in hiding for a considerable time until his foster-brother, Othman, Muhammad's son-in-law, managed to win him a pardon.

Much of the Koran is meaningless anyway to Westerners. Some of the verses, apparently beautiful and very inspiring when chanted in Arabic, do not make sense in any other language. "The impact of words and form counted far more than the transmission of ideas," explained Bernard Lewis in his account of the literature and history of the Arabic people. Koranic passages we might consider obscure would not be out of place in the company of the *Centuries* of Nostradamus or the Book of Yin and Yang. Still others are instructions on decorum and etiquette. Similar passages occur in the Bible and are accepted as part of its educational value. The Book of Leviticus, for instance, reminds us that we should bathe regularly and inspired John Wesley to write that "cleanliness is next to godliness" and that "neatness of apparel is a duty not a sin." Norman Davies neatly summed up the Koran in his history of Europe as "a source of law, a manual of science and philosophy, a collection of myths and stories, and an ethical textbook."

The thoughts expressed in the Koran may be sonorously inspiring in Arabic, but their meaning is often hard to deduce when they are translated into English or French. Some Western scholars have judged the Koran very harshly. Thomas Carlyle described it 150 years ago as "a wearisome, confused jumble, crude, incondite, endless iterations, long-windedness and entanglement." More recently, H. G. Wells saw it as "a book of injunctions and expositions" and, he added, "unworthy of its alleged Divine authorship whether read as literature or philosophy" (*A*

Short History of the World, p. 177). East is East and West is West; it is not true to say the two never meet, but often they don't!

When they are clear, many of the verses in the 114 suras (or chapters) of the Koran often contradict one another; but devout Muslims insist that Islamic principles have always existed and always been part of the essence of God. They cannot be changed and the injunctions, penalties, and admonitions in the Koran and Hadiths (or Traditions), the second Muslim sacred book, with its huge collection of thousands of anecdotes about the Prophet's life and teachings, must be as strictly applied today as they were in 630. This includes amputation for thieves, polygamy for brides and bridegrooms, stoning to death for adulterers, the lash for drinkers, the rope for homosexuals, and slavery for captives. All in the name of Allah.

There is, to be correct, no mention in the Koran of stoning for adultery. One hundred lashes is the indicated punishment. Stoning to death is a later addition to the sharia. Aisha, Muhammad's child bride, may be responsible for its inclusion among capital punishments. She told an enquirer years later she once saw in her room a sura calling for the death penalty by stoning for adulterers. The verses were inscribed on a palm leaf which had been left lying on the floor, but a frisky young goat trotted into the room, spotted the leaf and ate it, thus saving many future adulterers from death until the ultimate penalty was reinstated thanks to Aisha.

Not all Muslims are convinced about the eternal, uncreated, and nonchangeable nature of the Koran. As early as 757, less than a century and a half after Muhammad's death, the Mutazilites, a group of theologians, denied that the Koran was eternal and asserted that when its contents went against reason and common sense, it should be read symbolically only. This thesis was tolerated for nearly a hundred years, but in 847 the caliph who from his palace in Baghdad ruled over the vast Muslim empire declared this belief heretical and that the eternal existence of the Koran was the law of the land. Many Muslims, particularly those who were not Arab, were still not convinced that God spoke in Arabic and had a face and hands and feet. They queried both the Koran and Hadiths or Traditions.

In the Middle Ages, in the Spanish Muslim Kingdom of Granada, the physician Ibn al-Khatib, author of *On the Plague,* a 1360 medical treatise on the Black Death then ravaging Europe, heretically urged that the Traditions "undergo modification when thy are in manifest contradiction with the evidence of the senses." Contrary to the widely held belief that the Black Death was a punishment by God for man's sins, Ibn al-Khatib taught that the plague was an infectious disease and that the sick should be quarantined. His teaching was rejected as contrary to the truths of the Koran.

More recently and more prosaically, in December 1991, Hamid, a Muslim resident of Algiers, criticizing some of his fundamentalist neighbors, complained to a reporter of the Paris newspaper *Libération* that they appeared to have "forgotten that the Prophet lived a long time ago and that his recommendations are no longer suited to these modern times." Some of his neighbors were so attached to the Prophet, Mr. Hamid added more earthily, "that if he told them to shove a stick up their arse, they would do so."

The Koran is the most authoritative source on Muhammad, but it is actually very sketchy on details about the Prophet's life. There is much more information to be found in the Hadiths, or Traditions, information gathered a hundred or so years after his death by a special group of collectors who traveled around talking to people who had known people who, at some time, had known people who knew the Prophet.It was a lifetime job for several of them. Al-Bukhari, the most famous of these researchers, more than two hundred years after Muhammad's death, studied no less than 600,000 stories concerning the Prophet and threw out some 593,000 of them. The surviving 7,275 anecdotes were gathered in a book which he called *The Correct Book.* Other collectors were less scrupulous or demanding than al-Bukhari. Although they disregarded as frauds most of the stories told to them, there are probably thousands of dubious entries that made their way into the collectors' books. One gentleman called Ibn Abi al-Awja, who was put to death in Iraq in 772, confessed before his execution that he had made up no fewer than four thousand Traditions. How many were inscribed in the collectors' volumes and are now venerated as part of the Islamic truth was not made clear, but for the last 1,300 years most accounts of Muhammad's life and deeds—and even misdeeds—have depended largely on these Hadiths.

8

A PARADISE FOR WARRIORS

B<small>Y 622 MUHAMMAD, THEN FIFTY-TWO</small> years old, had migrated with his followers to Medina for safety from the people of his native city of Mecca, who were at the time very hostile to him and his creed. Let us remind ourselves in passing that the Muslim calendar and the founding of Islam date from that event. Ten years later Muhammad died in the arms of his beloved Aisha, a toothpick clenched tightly in his jaws. In the intervening years he had conquered half of the Arabian peninsula, including of course his own province of Hejaz in the west, bordering on the Red Sea, the province of Yemen to the south, and Persian-ruled Oman to the southeast. During the next thirty years, under the leadership of the first four caliphs, Muhammad's Arab armies shouting "Allah is great and Muhammad is his Prophet" rode out of the desert and began to conquer the known world.

Few in numbers but great in courage, they went to war against the Byzantine and Persian empires, which were exhausted after fighting each other for the past twenty-six years, defeating both; invaded the Near and Middle East and North Africa; captured Jerusalem, Antioch, Aleppo, Caesarea, Gaza, Tripoli, Babylon, Alexandria, and the islands of Rhodes and Cyprus; plundered Sicily; took and then lost Kabul in Afghanistan; laid siege to Constantinople; and reached Sind and the Indus river valley in India.

If there was a recipe for these immediate and immense victories, no one, not even the most respected military analysts, is sure what it was. The Arab invaders were usually outnumbered and underequipped, armed only with swords, spears, and bows and arrows; but they rode fast camels and horses, and were ferocious and enthusiastic followers of their Prophet, while the Christians were torn apart by religious disputes and heresies. The Arabs, it seemed, had launched their Jihad at a particularly opportune moment. There were other explanations for their successes. Some say it was the Arab warriors' fanatical belief in the Muslim Paradise that was awaiting them that opened the way to victory for Islam.

Even more than Allah, the prime motive for fighting that inspired the Arabs were plunder, slaves, women, and eagerness for death fighting for Islam, which meant immediate entry into Paradise with all joys and pleasures for those who died in battle. Dying for Islam made them "martyrs" (it still does) and an eternity of sexual pleasure awaited them. Hence, death in action was a highly sought privilege and the best way to die in battle was to charge and fight fearlessly. It made the Arabs the most terrifying of enemies, eager for death, like the kamikaze pilots during World War II.

For the Muslim dying and killing can both be acts of great religiosity, either as a warrior of Allah, one of the Mujahidin, or as a martyr if he is killed. He is then assured an instant place in Paradise without having to wait, as lesser mortals have to do, until the Day of Judgment. Being killed in a war against the infidels was the surest passport for a rapid arrival in Paradise; and Paradise, for the Muslim warrior, was truly heaven! First of all, it was a place of unending sexual activity. From the moment he arrived, the fallen warrior was provided with seventy-two wide-eyed "houris" for his sensual pleasure, reclining on silk-lined couches, all lovely as rubies, beautiful as coral, with renewable virginities, and with complexions like diamonds and pearls. "Therein shall they delight themselves, lying on green cushions and beautiful carpets," says the Koran. Those who like riding "will get a ruby horse with two wings" which will carry the rider wherever he wishes. The sex scene must have been particularly exhilarating to these hardy warriors of the desert. In the Muslim Paradise, orgasms last a thousand years and are intensified a hundred times "to render him [the beneficiary] worthy of his felicity," explains British historian Edward Gibbon. Another book mercifully reduces the duration of the orgasm to a more manageable twenty-four years. The Koran does not indicate how a lady Muslim spends her time in this male-dominated macho Paradise. Everybody in Paradise is under thirty. No infants and no old people are admitted; they have to change their age first—and, of course, only Muslims can enter.

Prophets, like martyrs, also have priority for entry into Paradise. Abraham, Enoch, Moses, Joseph, and Jesus, all considered to be prophets in Muslim theology, are also in the Muslim Paradise. In fact, Muhammad met them there when he visited Heaven on the famous Night Journey he took on the twelfth year of his mission, after the Angel Gabriel had cut him open from his chest to his navel to take out his heart and wash it in the local Zam Zam well water.

Muhammad's journey to Paradise and back took only one night. He rode all the way on a buraq, the only animal of its kind in the world, with the head of a woman, the body of a mule, the tail of a peacock, and two wings. The journey, which is mentioned briefly in the seventeenth sura of the Koran, started in Mecca and included a stopover in Jerusalem, a Muslim holy place since then. The first person Muhammad met on arrival in Paradise was Adam. Muhammad did not recognize him and it was Gabriel who introduced Adam to the visitor. He met a number of prophets, including Jesus, who said to him, "Welcome, good brother," and Moses, who wept because, thanks to Muhammad, more Muslims would now go to Paradise than Jews. On earth, no one had noticed Muhammad's absence (he was staying at his cousin's at Mecca at the time) and he was back in his bed by early morning. Christians, as could be expected, have derided these teachings. Blaise Pascal, the French philosopher, commented in his *Pensées* that "Paradise and such like scenes" in the Koran made the Prophet "appear ridiculous."

The stopover in Jerusalem was probably the only occasion during his life that Muhammad ever visited the city, previously sacred only to Christians and Jews. After the Night Journey it also joined Mecca and Medina as holy cities of Islam. The Dome of the Rock mosque stands on the spot from where the buraq, with Muhammad and the Angel Gabriel astride, took off for the direct flight to Paradise. Some Muslim theologians believe, however, that Muhammad changed there from the buraq to a very long ladder for the final lap to Paradise.

Paradise is reserved for Muslims. Christians, Jews, Buddhists, Hindus and other non-Muslims don't go to Paradise. They presumably go to hell. From Paradise there is a splendid view of hell, and the dwellers in the heavens (there are seven heavens) can watch the people down there being roasted in eternal fires and drinking boiling water to quench their thirst. In Paradise only vintage wines are served and fine liqueurs that have the additional distinction of never intoxicating the drinker, for eating and drinking are also among the pleasures of Paradise. Each resident in Paradise has three hundred servants to wait on him at table, each bearing on a gold plate a different dish for his meal. They must be very different from the usual Bedouin diet of dates, barley bread, and camel milk, broken occasionally by a snack of dried camel meat. Three hundred dishes a day per person normally would represent a big problem of human waste disposal, but no toilets are necessary in Paradise. Meals once digested are vaporized through the pores as musk-scented perfume. The Muslim mystic and poet Jalal al-Din al-Suya, who lived in Persia in medieval times, was quite explicit. "Dwellers in Paradise do not have an anus. Anuses were made for defecating and in Paradise there is no defecation," he wrote in his poem "Kitabal Anwar."

The anticipated presence of the houris in Paradise naturally had a very stimulating effect on Muslim warriors. Their commanders used to shout at them before they went into battle, "The houris are waiting for you!" and the warriors of Islam, eager to die, would rush into the fray determined to earn immediate entry into Paradise. The expectancy of the delights ahead drove them to prodigies of valor. But let us not scoff at what appears to Westerners as the bizarre inspirations of the Muslim warriors. It helped them to conquer half the known world in less than one hundred years. Once again it's a case of *cherchez la femme* to explain their victories. Or rather *cherchez les femmes,* except that in this case the "femmes" didn't exist. At least, not on earth.

PART TWO

BEYOND ARABIA

9

ONWARD MUSLIM SOLDIERS: BYZANTIUM AND PERSIA 632–640

O N MUHAMMAD'S DEATH IN 632, his friend and father-in-law, Aisha's father, Abu Bakr was elected Islam's first caliph, and Aisha, from being one of Muhammad's eleven queens, became the princess of Medina, from where her father ruled the realm of Islam.

Muhammad's son-in-law Ali, husband of Fatima and father of Muhammad's grandsons, Hasan and Husain, had expected the title for himself and his descendants, but loyally pledged his allegiance to the new head of Islam. On Abu Bakr's death two years later, Omar was elected to the Muslim headship and, although disappointed for the second time, Ali loyally supported him as caliph. Omar was also the Prophet's father-in-law; his daughter Hafsa was the Prophet's third wife. Omar's caliphate, also exercised from Medina, was to last ten years, until he was murdered by a Persian slave.

This time Ali's partisans all expected Fatima's husband to step into the caliphate. He was the Prophet's nearest male kin and his followers considered it outrageous that he had been overlooked in the previous elections, but another disappointment awaited them. Instead of Ali, Othman, the dandified young man of Islam's early days and a close relative of Abu Sufyan, was chosen third caliph. Othman and Ali were, at any rate, related in an Arab Muslim sort of way. Othman had married two of Muhammad's daughters, Ruqyah and Ummu Kulsum, which made Fatima his sister-in-law and made him and Ali brothers-in-law.

The rejected Ali overcame his disappointment again and swore allegiance to Othman, but strains were already apparent in the fabric of the new creed. They culminated in the murder of Othman by the first caliph's son in 656. The new religion was tearing itself and its followers apart. Two main rival groups emerged: the majority Sunnis, who backed Yazid, grandson of Abu Sufyan; and the rebellious minority Shiites, who backed Hasan, grandson of Muhammad. Finally the descendants of Abu Sufyan, the Umayyad businessman who had tried to throttle Islam in its infancy and to kill Muhammad, were to defeat the descendants of the Prophet and rule over the Muslim empire Abu Sufyan had tried so hard to destroy. Of such ironies is history made. The contest between Sunnis and Shiites is still part of the reality of life in Islam today, thirteen centuries later. More than any other single person it was one of Abu Sufyan's sons, Muawiya, who turned Islam into a great international political force; but that epic tale is for our next chapter.

The internationalization of Islam had, in fact, begun two years before Muhammad died, in the early days of the reconciliation between himself and Abu Sufyan. Islam had begun to spread outside of the Arabian peninsula. Two years before, at Mutah, south of the Dead Sea in present-day Jordan, a Muslim army first met the Christian Greeks of the Byzantine emperor in battle, and lost. The real purpose of the Arab raid, the acquisition of the beautiful—and sharp, very sharp—Mashrafujah swords made in Mutah and nearby towns, was achieved. They helped the Arabs to carve their way into Spain eighty years later.

Zeid, the Prophet's black adopted son, the first husband of Muhammad's wife Zeinab, who led the Muslim troops, was killed in the early stages of the battle of Mutah. Khalid, who had once been Abu Sufyan's trusted commander in the Meccan army, had converted to Islam and, now a soldier of Allah, took command of the Muslim army. He distinguished himself by extricating his dwindled force from the battlefield and bringing his troops back to Medina. In the last year of Muhammad's life, Khalid also had helped to keep the Arabian peninsula loyal to the Prophet.

Just before his death Muhammad had ordered Zeid's half-Ethiopian black son, Usama, whose mother was a former slave, to lead a Muslim army back north and defeat the Christian dogs who had killed his father. Usama, obeying the Prophet's last military instructions, set out two weeks after the Prophet's death for the Land of War to the north. Khalid, ordered to conquer Iraq, set out originally with five hundred men, won the battle of the River of Blood and, near Baghdad, captured a few dozen terrified Christian seminarians hiding in a church, who chose apostasy into Islam rather than decapitation into eternity. One of them, a young Yemenite, was to become the father of Musa, governor of North Africa, who launched the first Muslim invasion force from Tangiers across the Mediterranean into Spain.

All the fighting in the first decades of Islam was, for geographically obvious reasons, either in Arabia itself or in the Near and Middle East. The success of Muslim arms in those regions and in those years was due in a large part to Arab military ability: Arab cavalry was swifter and more enterprising than that of their Persian and Byzantine foes. The Arab warriors frightened the Greeks and the Persians with hideous battle cries and, for tactical reasons, always chose to fight on flat, level ground, ideal for charging horses and camels. The Arabs, most importantly, knew what they wanted. Allah, Muhammad, and Islam were the battle cries. Plunder, however, was most probably the primary target; or, for some, the houris in Paradise. The Greeks and Persians, on the other hand, were completely unmotivated.

As they progressed, the Arabs' courage and military capacities only partly explained their victories. Another obvious factor was the Persian and Byzantine empires' exhaustion after more than a quarter century of warfare against each other. Perhaps more importantly, at least in Heraclius's empire, were the religious disputes between his Christian subjects over obscure points of theology concerning Christ's nature, which led to incredible persecutions and dissensions. The Monophysites insisted that there was only one nature in Christ, partly divine and partly human. The human was of course subordinate to the divine. Nestorians insisted that these two natures, divine and human, were quite distinct and separate and that Mary was only the mother of the "human" Jesus Christ, not of the "divine" one. These dogmatic differences may not appear unduly important to the layman, but they turned out to be historically disastrous to the Christians; indeed, they helped to lose them the Middle East and Egypt to the Muslims.

An unsophisticated observer cannot help wondering why the much more ferociously fought differences between Sunnis and Shiites—and there were also other warring sects among the Muslims—did not paralyze the Islamic war effort as it did the Christian. Perhaps it is because mass plunder and rape are great incentives which the Christians lacked. The Jihad, to the Muslim warrior, was a wonderful sexual holiday: if he lived, lots of young and pretty women captives were available to him on earth; if he died, seventy-two houris with pearls and diamonds and renewable virginities were waiting for him in heaven lying on green satin couches. Live or die, either way the Muslim warrior won.

There are contradictory accounts about these early Jihad campaigns, about who fought where and when. One fact remains abundantly clear: the Greeks and the Persians lost, and the Arabs won. In addition to the great fighting quality of Khalid, who towers above all by his courage and military skills (and, alas, ferocity and savagery), these sheiks of Araby and these Bedouin proved the fighting quality of the men of the desert. Dates and camel milk were obviously a diet well suited to the valorous: Amr, who conquered Egypt; Obeida, who marched into Syria; Buthanna, who invaded Persia; Saad, who gave the final blow to Persian domination; Abu Sufyan's son Yazid, who with his brother Muawiya riding by his side bearing his standard, conquered Syria with the participation of Khalid in the campaign. Yazid and Muawiya captured Beirut, a name that has often figured in the news in more recent fighting. Muawiya was one of the three signatories to the treaty by which Jerusalem was surrendered to the Arabs, the beginning of a long tussle among various national and religious factions over the city which is not yet over.

It is interesting to read the surrender terms 1,350 years later: "There will be no constraint in the matter of religion, nor the least annoyance. The Jews will inhabit [Jerusalem] conjointly with the Christians." Tolerance, alas, was not to last long. Damascus had fallen to the Arabs in 635 and Antioch in 636. Two years after the fall of Jerusalem, Muawiya and his brother captured Caesarea by storm after a long siege. The carnage was prodigious, Muir tells us: four thousand captives, many of them "women of gentle birth degraded now to menial office or, if young and fair to look upon, reserved for a worse fate" were sent to Medina as part of the booty to be sold as slaves. It is probably around this time that Khalid died in exile and disgrace, and that Muawiya's brother Yazid died of the plague.

Omar had taken away Khalid's command, allegedly for corruption, and the humiliated and broken-hearted warrior died in misery and want in some forlorn Arab village in 639; but, by the time of his death, Islam was set on its course of imperial conquest. By 640 Greek Christian Syria was becoming Arab Muslim. By 641 Persia and Egypt were also being taken over by Islam. Muhammad had only been dead nine years and already much of the Middle and Near East were the property of his heirs. Alexandria was now the main Arab naval base of the desert tribes of the Hejaz. The Jihad had now become the main instrument of Islamic polity.

The conquered populations were given three choices: Islam, the sword, or tribute. A few, usually from the middle classes, chose martyrdom; many, particularly from the rich upper class, chose tribute; and only a few, at first, and usually from the poorer classes, converted to Islam. But mass conversions to the cause of Allah were in the offing among the Christian peoples of the Middle East, Asia Minor, and North Africa. Christians were tolerated as an unpleasant fact of life outside Arabia, but within it they no longer had their place. All Jews and Christians were expelled. They have never been allowed since to set foot in Mecca or Medina.

The rising star in the Muslim firmament was Muawiya. When the caliph Omar visited Damascus in 640, he appointed Muawiya governor of Syria. Perhaps it was on this occasion that to seal his alliance with the caliph, Muawiya married Omar's divorced wife Koreiba. Passing one's wife on to a worthy interested party was an admitted practice among the Muslim dignitaries of the age. We have seen how Muhammad had set the example by marrying Zeinab, his adopted son's wife.

A brilliant administrator and a born imperialist, Muawyia made Damascus the springboard to greater things for himself and Islam. He was the first great Muslim statesman, the first Muslim conqueror of Europe, and the first Muslim to send the sailors and soldiers of Islam west over the Mediterranean and north through the Dardanelles in conquest of Europe. After he became caliph, by depriving Ali of the title, he was to establish the Umayyad dynasty as rulers of the whole Islamic world for nearly a century, and in Spain for three centuries. But how many Europeans have even heard of his name? William the Conqueror, a tough Norman lord, is famous because he conquered England. His feat is really just a bit of local history. Compared to Muawiya, William the Conqueror is just a roughneck who made good, a minor figure of European history. Muawiya was a giant of world history.

10

THE ISLAND CAMPAIGN: CYPRUS, RHODES, AND CRETE 649–668

I T IS NOT THE PURPOSE of this book to describe the dynastic dissensions and rivalries that tore the ruling Muslim families apart, of which the Ali/Muawiya confrontation was the first big warning. Nor do I want to chronicle the expansion of Islam in regions other than Europe: east into Persia, India, Afghanistan, Transoxiana, Turkestan, and to the borders of China; west into Egypt and North Africa all the way to Morocco; and north into Mesopotamia and the Caucasus. They are not part of our story. Europe is.

Nevertheless, we cannot bypass them altogether, for the Arab offensive was exploding almost simultaneously in all directions except south into Africa (which came later) during a period that lasted over a century, in one of the most dazzling displays of military conquests that the world has ever witnessed. Dynastic quarrels between families, just as much as these invasions across continents, are an essential element of the Islamic saga. They form part of the general background of early Muslim history of which we have to know at least a little if we want to place the European Jihad in its proper historical perspective.

The Ali/Muawiya quarrel is one of the essential landmarks of early Muslim history, and it finally resulted in two major Islamic developments: one was the first invasion of Europe, the other was the birth of the powerful Shiite faction within Islam. It would not be wrong in fact to say that Muawiya is the man who deprived Muhammad's descendants of what they considered their hereditary right to the caliphate and passed it on instead to his own Umayyad dynasty that, in the early days of Islam, originally had been, through Abu Sufyan, the most bitter enemy of Muhammad and Islam. Although neither of these events occurred in Muawiya's lifetime, they were spawned then. Before we pass on to the European campaigns of Islam, let's investigate the clash between Ali, Muhammad's son-in-law, and Muawiya, Abu Sufyan's son. They set the course Islam has followed ever since.

Three of the first four caliphs were murdered. They all had been disciples and personal friends of Muhammad, and they are known in Muslim history as "the rightly guided." Their assassinations set a pattern for Islamic ideological, political, and even religious development that has never diverged and still continues today. To check, read your daily newspaper. After the assassination in 654 of Caliph Othman, Muhammad's roly-poly son-in-law Ali, who was considered by many to be responsible for Othman's murder, was at last selected to become the next caliph. His nomination to the caliphate did not go unchallenged. Ali was a poor organizer, sometimes weak, who failed to stir his countrymen sufficiently in spite of the huge prestige he enjoyed as Muhammad's son-in-law and the husband of Fatima, Muhammad's well-loved daughter. His contemporaries recognized his failures of character, which would explain why he was rejected so many times in the caliphate elections, in spite of his family connection to the Prophet. Ali, moreover, was a henpecked husband and didn't even have the consolation of the pleasure of the permitted three other wives. The Prophet, anxious for Fatima's happiness, had forbidden Ali to have more than one wife. There was no harem for Ali, at least not until the Prophet died.

Ali took over Islam, basing his capital near Basra in Iraq; but Muawiya, as Othman's nearest and most belligerent relative, challenged Ali as the man responsible for his uncle's death and with a Syrian army invaded Iraq. At Siffin, in 657, Ali's troops refused to fight their fellow Muslims, who all went into battle carrying the Koran at the tip of their lances; and the quarrel between Ali and Muawiya went into arbitration. Ali lost and three years later Muawiya took over the caliphate, basing it in Damascus where he had been ruling for seventeen years as emir of Syria. Ali was subsequently murdered by a fanatic while plotting a comeback, and Muawiya ruled Islam until 680, a total of twenty-three years, as the founder of the Umayyad dynasty. The dynasty was to be in power until 749, the year the Umayyads were overthrown by the

Abbasids, vague descendants of Muhammad's uncle Abbas, with a good admixture of Persian blood. The Abbasids were then to rule all Islam (except Spain and Portugal) from Baghdad for the next five hundred years and to give the world *The Thousand and One Nights*.

There was a long period during the Abbasid caliphate, which lasted until 1258, when any favorable mention of Muawiya—or of any of the Umayyads for that matter—could result in the speaker's or writer's immediate execution. Life was cheap in the land of Islam. No judgment, or even explanation, was necessary. Executions in Baghdad were a very expeditious matter. The reigning caliph always had his executioner in attendance by the throne and could order any visitor who displeased him to be beheaded on the spot. The execution block stood on a leather mat so as not to spoil the Persian carpets in the throne room; hence the discretion of many of the Abbasid Hadith collectors who valued the truth but who valued their lives even more. In their commentaries and compilations, they either ignored or reviled the more controversial early companions of Muhammad in Medina and Mecca and their descendants. The boycott included Muawiya and the other Umayyad caliphs.

Abu Sufyan and his descendants were for several hundred years the most *personae non gratae* in the Muslim establishment. The understandable fear of Muslim writers and historians for their lives may explain in part the widespread ignorance that exists over the personality of Muawiya, one of the great names of Arabian history. As an Umayyad his name was too dangerous to recall in Abbasidian times. Moreover, because of his role in Ali's death, the Shiites have no place for him in their hearts. He is one of the greatest men Arabia ever produced, but to the West he remains largely unknown.

We do know that Muawiya, when still a young man, became what has been called "secretary" to Muhammad after the conversion of the Meccans to Islam. Aide-de-camp, in modern terms, might be the more suitable word. During his subsequent career as a soldier and as emir (governor) of Syria, he was in charge of one of the most important countries of the nascent Arab empire under three subsequently assassinated caliphs (Omar, Othman, and Ali), all of whom governed from Medina.

Muawiya was an intelligent youth who became an intelligent ruler. He liked to attain his aims without violence. "I never apply my sword when the lash suffices, nor the lash when my tongue is enough," he liked to tell the people around him. He preferred bribery and corruption to war. In any case, a bribe cost considerably less than a battle. Muawiya was a ruler whom Machiavelli would have appreciated.

One cannot say that Muawiya ever had a specific plan to invade Europe. The conception of Europe as a separate geographical continent did not exist then. Anatolia, most of what is now called Turkey, was separated by the narrow Dardanelles strait, the sea of Marmara, and the Bosporus from Constantinople and its inland region of Rumelia. During Omar's caliphate, Muawiya was already interested in crossing the seas and attacking the islands beyond, along with Constantinople. Omar, like most of the Arabs of the Hejaz, was frightened of the sea, to him a totally unknown and terrifying element. "The isles of the Levant are close to the Syrian shores. You might almost hear the barking of dogs and the cackling of hens. Give me leave to attack them," Muawiya had pleaded to the caliph. Another man, one whose murder Muhammad had once planned, was also anxious to lead the Muslims to new glories overseas: Abdallah ibn Saad, no longer a scoffing youth falsifying Muhammad's cherished Koranic verses but a seasoned warrior, one of the finest cavalry leaders in the Arab armies, and conqueror of what is today Tunisia.

To Omar, who lived in a city surrounded by the emptiness of the desert, the sea was like the vast plains of the Hejaz, except that he considered it far more dangerous. You can drown at sea; you can't in the desert. He sought the advice of one of his soldiers. "The sea is a boundless expanse whereon great ships look like tiny specks. Trust it little, fear it much. Man at sea is an insect on a splinter, now engulfed, now scared to death," the soldier explained. So Omar had said no to Muawiya's proposed expedition. "The Syrian sea, they tell me, is longer and broader than the dry land, seeking to swallow it up. How should I trust my people on its accursed bosom?"

Omar was perhaps made even more cautious by the recent loss of an Arab Red Sea expedition during a raid on an unfriendly Abyssinian shore and had, Muir tells us, vowed that "he would never again permit troops to embark upon an element so treacherous." He ordered his generals to attack and occupy only places which were within reach of his camel. The treasures of Greece, he had added, were less important to him than the safety of his people. So during all his reign, which lasted until 644, the Arabs kept to dry land.

At Omar's death, Muawiya renewed his request to the new caliph, Othman. He specifically again asked for permission to attack Cyprus. Othman, who happened to be Muawiya's uncle, was ready to help his nephew in any way he could and, for that matter, any relative who required assistance. Soon also to be included among the future benefi-

ciaries of Othman's benevolence would be his foster-brother Abdallah
ibn Saad (who was therefore a sort of uncle also to Muawiya), another
relative very keen to raid Cyprus and its riches. Nepotism had now
been added to the usual Muslim incentive of plunder.

These piratical schemes were always, of course, presented to the
participants and to the people at home—who were excitedly awaiting
their share of the loot, the slaves, and the profits—as religious expeditions in the name of Allah the Merciful. These early followers of the
Prophet found it impossible to tell the difference between religion and
robbery; as did the Crusaders a few hundred years later, when they
attacked the Holy Land.

Cyprus was, in 649, the first European island invaded by the
Arabs. Cyprus has only a borderline claim to call itself European. Geographically it is as much Asian as European. Some atlases, however,
see it as part of the Near East. Politically it is and was mainly European by population and by inclinations. The Greeks, who form the bulk
of its population, are a European people. Anyway, Cyprus is as European as Rhodes, Crete, Sicily, Malta, Corsica, or Sardinia, which were
all also under Muslim rule once, as were the more distant Balearics.

Two expeditions headed for Cyprus. One, under Admiral Abu
Keis, set out from Saida, in present-day Lebanon, in 649. It was joined
by a second expedition from Alexandria commanded by Abdallah ibn
Saad. The total force consisted of 1,700 ships. The raiders took and
sacked the town of Constantia and massacred most of the population.
Cyprus, part of the Byzantine dominions, was taken "easily," we are
told: the booty filled seventy ships, and a great multitude of unfortunate weeping captives were taken away to be sold on the slave markets
of Damascus and other Muslim cities.

The Cyprus expedition was not only the first major Arab naval
enterprise. It was also the first of these raids by what Americans, more
than a thousand years later, were to call "the Barbary Coast pirates";
those who haunted and terrorized Mediterranean Europe until the
French took Algiers in 1830 and ended the flourishing enterprise of
slave raiding in the Mediterranean.

The Arabs remained in Cyprus until it became known that a Byzantine relief force was coming from Constantinople to fight the invaders.
After the Cypriots had agreed to pay annual tribute to the Syrian governor, the Arabs sailed away and Muawiya, back in Damascus, planned
to carry out the next raid, against Crete this time. It was a relatively
minor affair, in the year 651, two years after the Cyprus landing. A

historian tells us "the inhabitants were treated with mildness as it was the policy of the caliph at this time to conciliate the good opinions of the Christians in order to pave the way for future conquests."

The Jihad raids were lucrative, and so the Arabs returned to Cyprus for a second time in 653 with five hundred ships. After this raid the Cypriots decided to seek safety in the mountains, where they built several castles at St. Hilarion, Kantara, and Buffavento, from where they could defend themselves against the Muslim raiders.

The most spectacular Jihad raid, also in 653, was on the island of Rhodes, where the fallen bronze Colossus of Rhodes, one of the Seven Wonders of the ancient world, was taken apart and shipped back to Syria for sale as junk metal to a Jewish scrap merchant at Homs. Built around 290 B.C.E. and representing the sun god Apollo, the Colossus was a hundred feet high and stood near the harbor until it collapsed about sixty years later during an earthquake. The people of Rhodes, still proud of their statue, had left it lying there for nearly nine hundred years until Muawiya's fleet sailed in and took its bits and pieces away in 73 ships to Syria. The Saracens, as the Muslim invaders were beginning to be universally called in the lands they raided, seem to have remained on the island for at least five years.

Sicily, in 668, was the next major Mediterranean island to be attacked by Muawiya's sea rovers. In the evocative language of the Victorians, Arthur Gilman tells us in *The Saracens* how the Arab fleets "ravaged Sicily and Sardinia, sacking cities and carrying off booty, prisoners, and beautiful maidens," the latter to suffer the inevitable fate worse than death. The same fate, let it be said in passing, also befell quite a few of the boy captives. Sicily had become well aware of the Muslim peril some years before, around 642, when the Arabs were threatening Tripoli in the land they called Ifriqiya, of which Libya is now part. Terrified refugees fleeing from the invaders had reached Sicily with horrifying tales of the sword-wielding followers of Muhammad.

By this time Muawiya was no longer emir of Syria but caliph, the No. 1 man of the Muslim hierarchy and empire. To attain Islam's supreme post Muawiya had had to outwit and outfight Othman's successor, the unlucky Ali, and had done so, as we read earlier, with considerable cunning and supreme intelligence. When Ali was murdered by the local rebels known as Kharajites, his son Hasan, the grandson of Muhammad, became caliph. Muawiya, anxious to be the ruler of Islam, offered him a large pension in Medina, to which Ali's son retired, handed over his empire to Muawiya, and married a hundred women. (This was one account. Another claims Hasan was poisoned by one of his wives, Jadah, who murdered him to please Muawiya's son Yezid, who had promised to marry her if she did, but then didn't.)

Muawiya's rightful place in the timetable of history would have been more properly in Renaissance Italy, that era of refinement, art, and political acumen, than among his barbarian compatriots of the desert. With his sharp diplomacy and subtleties, he outwitted all his competitors to take power from the Muhammad clan, whose Muslim teachings his father had originally fought so hard against. Unlike the majority of his companions, and his foes, he was never a religious or political fanatic. It has been said, in fact, that he did not believe in Islam and that he used it only as the most appropriate road to the power to which he felt entitled. Muawiya was an aristocrat by conviction and vocation who believed he had a natural right to rule.

Muawiya remains an enigmatic character whose motivations, outside of the sheer love of power—which he rarely abused—remain obscure unless he was concerned, like Muhammad, with advancing the place of the Arabs in the world. Such was certainly his intention when he sent out a fleet from Alexandria and Syria, through the Aegean Sea and the Dardanelles, north to the very gates of Constantinople, capital of the Byzantine empire, the new Rome. Islam now stood on the soil of continental Europe. The siege of Constantinople, carried on intermittently during the summer months only, was to last six years.

11

CHECKMATE ON THE BOSPORUS: CONSTANTINOPLE 668–673

ONSTANTINOPLE MUST HAVE SEEMED TO an Arab boy of 668 C.E. rather like Paris in the fair land of France in the sixteenth century did to a farm boy from the backlands of central Europe: a wondrous, distant place that no one he knew had ever seen; a city of light, knowledge, and power; where kings in magnificent costumes, with crowns on their heads, reigned in fabulous palaces; and high-born ladies in tall domed coiffures savored costly sherbets; where fortunes flourished and poor peasants like himself had no place. To Muhammad, Constantinople, the capital of the new Roman Empire, however Greek it might have become, was an inescapable lure to conquest; a city to be enriched with the teachings of the Prophet and the words of Allah, an inevitable target for the Jihad if it resisted the Koran.

In his desert outpost of Medina, acknowledged as the messenger of God, the Prophet had visualized Constantinople as the strong point of his Christian rivals which could one day threaten Islam. He demanded from the emperor Heraclius submission to Islam, failed to obtain it, and determined to win it by force of arms. Early in its career, Muhammad quite obviously had already great ambitions for the Arab nation and a vision of Islam as more than just a religion for date-chewing camel drivers and Bedouin nomads. But Muhammad died and it was Muawiya who inherited the dream forty years later and who ordered his Arab armies and liegemen to capture the Rome of the East.

83

There was no lack of volunteers, for Muhammad had decreed shortly before his death that all who took part in the attack on the Christian capital would be forgiven their sins, and those who died in the campaign would go straight to Paradise. It was a situation made to order for a political genius like Muawiya, with his imperialist vision of Islam. The winds of change were blowing in the eastern Mediterranean, and Muawiya was determined to make sure they blew the Arabs' and Islam's way.

The first problem for the Arabs was how to get to Constantinople. The vast land mass of Byzantine-ruled Anatolia, most of present day Turkey, stood between Muawiya's warriors and the Byzantine capital, safe and snug on the other side of the Bosporus. Instead of marching through hundreds of miles of hostile territory, the expedition would have to go by sea. In 668 or thereabouts, for the dates in the history books vary with the author (Gilman puts it at 670 or 672, to the unexplainable exclusion of 671; the Frenchman Paul Lemerle settles for 673; Muir says 672; others fluctuate around these dates), a vast expedition sailed from Syria. It was commanded by one of the lesser military lights of Islam, a general named Khale, described, however, as "the most valiant and the hardiest of the Saracens." His expeditionary force must have consisted of around fifty thousand men. It included the aged stalwart Abu Ayub, Muhammad's former landlord from Medina, a veteran of many battles against the infidel and loyal friend of the Prophet, and now probably well into his seventies. His aged presence in the besieging force has made him one of the unforgotten historical heroes of Islam.

This first Arab attack against Constantinople should have come down as one of the epics of warfare. Unfortunately history has passed it by. Virtually nothing has ever been written on it or, if it was, it has been lost. This was, anyway, a strangely organized operation. The Arabs established their headquarters on the island of Cyzicus, in the straits a few miles south of Constantinople, and decided to spend the winter there, sailing only during the spring and summer months to the enemy battlements to lay siege to the capital. The siege lasted, intermittently, seven years. Abu Ayab was one of the early casualties. He died under the walls and a mosque was built over his tomb.

The besieging force was joined by Muawiya's son Yezid, a funloving and irresponsible young man who most reluctantly abandoned his hunting lodge in Syria for the less comfortable, bleak headquarters of the besieging Muslim force in Cyzicus. Ali's second son, Hosain,

also turned up to do a spot of fighting against the enemy and, hopefully, obtain a pardon for his sins and a guarantee for, at some more
distant date, quick entry in Paradise. A few years later he was to die
fighting in southern Iraq against Yezid's army at Kerbala and was
made a Shiite saint. His death caused a breach between Shiite and
Sunni Muslims which has never healed to this day.

The Byzantines were never conquered by the Arabs. The defenders
of Constantinople had a secret weapon. The Saracens called it "Greek
fire": it consisted of a burning liquid, probably made from naphtha
mixed with sulphur and pitch, which they poured down in huge vats
from their battlements or fired from tubes on the approaching enemy
ships. It obliterated many of the attackers and their ships as well. The
Arabs were terrified of it, and they had every reason to be. It was the
napalm of the seventh century. The fires it provoked could not be put
out. It burned on water, burned through the skin and flesh all the way
to the bone.

It became obvious to Muawiya, after a few years of the intermit-
tent siege of Constantinople, that the operation was a no-win proposi-
tion for the Arabs. The position of the city was its first major defense,
built as it was at the tip of a peninsula jutting into the sea, surrounded
by water on three sides by the Bosporus, the Golden Horn, and the Sea
of Marmara. Its battlements were too strong and remained untaken and
unshaken through all the various sieges. After a seven-year standoff,
with no progress in its attacks nor hope of any, the Arabs reconciled
themselves to the obvious: they could not take Constantinople. A
return to Syria was indicated. But how to get back? The campaign had
been conducted for several years already—six or seven—and many of
the Arab ships, drenched in Greek fire, had been burned and completely destroyed, often with many of the sailors and soldiers aboard.
As many fighting men as possible were loaded aboard the ships that
still remained afloat. Thirty thousand shipless soldiers were left. The
ships sailed away and the remaining soldiers began the long overland
march across Anatolia back to Damascus. Disaster by land and sea
overtook both groups of the defeated expedition. The fleet was overwhelmed in a storm, and most of the ships were sunk or smashed on
the rocks. As for the weary Arab infantry, they were continually
attacked and harried by the pursuing Byzantine army as they plodded
heavily toward home.

To save the few survivors who remained, Muawiya sent emissaries
to the Byzantine Emperor Constans, who had succeeded Heraclius, and

asked for peace. Constans was magnanimous. In return for a yearly payment of three thousand pounds of gold, fifty slaves, and fifty Arab
horses, the Emperor allowed the Muslims to make their way back home
unimpeded. The first Jihad against continental Europe had failed.

The Arabs were to return some forty years later, in 717, to lay siege
to the Byzantine capital once again. But before this new attack, Obei-
dallah to the east had killed Hosain at the battle of Kerbala and sent his
decapitated head to Muawiya's son Yezid, who had succeeded his
father as caliph; the Persians had founded their own Shiite branch of
Islam and refused to acknowledge the suzerainty of the Umayyads. To
the west, the Arabs had founded the holy city of Kairouan in Tunisia
and swept to the Atlantic Ocean, first defeating and then converting the
Christian Berbers of North Africa. The Arabs and the islamized
Berbers, usually known as Moors, had invaded and occupied a large
part of Spain and Portugal.

PART THREE

THE IBERIAN VENTURE

12

THE TOLEDO WHORE:
SPAIN 710

HERE IS ALWAYS AN EXPLANATION for most deeds of history; one particular reason, sometimes no stronger than the others, why certain events occur at certain moments and others don't. Usually it is a concatenation of disjointed circumstances which, in the wake of each other, finally shape the course of events and find a place in our history books. Taken singly, these events seem unimportant, often unconnected. Yet, joined together they can change the fate of nations. The invasion of Spain by the Muslims was the culmination of such a sequence of events, one is tempted to say, even of accidents, with a dash, in the middle, of the inexorable French dictum *cherchez la femme* once again. For somehow there's always a pretty woman lurking around somewhere. History would be very dull if it were concerned only with kings, treaties, and statesmen. Romance, intermingled with the clash of arms, is far more exciting.

If, according to legend or history, King Rodrigo of Spain hadn't seduced a young lady, his country might never have been invaded by the Moors, and Spain might have escaped eight hundred years of Muslim occupation. The lady in question was called Florinda. The Spaniards, rigid and intolerant, who consider her responsible for the Arab conquest of their country, called her La Cava (The Whore). The insult is unjust. She wasn't. In fact, no one is sure whether Florinda ever existed; or whether the Florinda lodged in the Spanish psyche, like the Muhammad lodged in the Muslim psyche, is a totally different person to a creature of flesh and blood who once upon a time walked this earth, lived, loved, suffered, and died.

By the early 700s, the Arab invaders in North Africa had reached the northwestern extremity of Morocco, with only a vast stretch of ocean ahead of them to the west. So where could they go next? They could stay where they were, consolidate and meditate. Inaction is a great force but it was not one to inspire conquering eighth-century Arabs. They had two other choices: to go south, or to go north. They could turn south toward the Atlas mountains and the Sahara desert, familiar enough types of terrain to the Arabs from their peninsula on the Red Sea. Or they could turn north, cross the narrow straits that divide the Mediterranean from the Atlantic, and Africa from Europe, to invade Spain, then ruled by the Visigoths who had taken the country from the Romans almost three hundred years before. The Arabs chose to go north to cross the narrow sea into Spain, the legend says, because of a teenaged Greek girl in Toledo who had been perhaps raped, certainly forcefully seduced, by Don Rodrigo, king of the Visigoths, a few months previously. Florinda had a father in Morocco who wanted to avenge his daughter.

It is here that Florinda appears in history. She was the Orthodox Christian daughter of Count Julian, governor of the city of Ceuta, then a Byzantine colony located a few miles from Tangiers along the Mediterranean coast of Morocco. With his name and title, Count Julian sounds like someone out of a light and witty Sheridan or Beaumarchais play, all froth and bubble and banter. Instead, he suddenly appears in our story as the Dark Ages heavy, justice-seeking outraged father determined to avenge his daughter's lost honor.

Florinda had been sent, at King Rodrigo's invitation, to learn the craft of lady-in-waiting at the royal Visigothic court in Toledo, then the capital of Spain. The king had spotted Florinda one day swimming in Toledo's Tagus River and, smitten by her Greek beauty, had invited her to visit him in his royal apartments, where the inevitable had happened. The distressed young lady, aware that she had only been what in modern parlance is called "a one-night stand" (since Rodrigo was married) had weepingly written to her father confessing her shame and asking him to come and fetch her. Count Julian had hurried to Toledo. King Roderick had undoubtedly been guilty of a grave breach of the knightly code of honor, but he was a king, and Julian, being only a count, could seek no redress. Muttering obscure threats of "loosening a flight of hawks" on Spain, he returned to Ceuta with Florinda. Soon afterward, he visited the emir Musa who ruled North Africa from Kairouan in Tunisia, to suggest the Muslims invade Spain which, with his help, he maintained, could not withstand a determined attack.

Count Julian was right. Spain, under the heavy-handed Visigoth rule of Rodrigo, who was anyway an usurper, was groaning in misery. Most of the original native Iberian population were serfs working as underpaid farm laborers for the ruling Visigoth families and, Count Julian said, the Muslims would have no problem defeating the forces sent against them. The peasants, who would provide the bulk of the Visigoth armies, armed only with sticks and spears and hating their rulers, would not fight. The Jews, ruthlessly persecuted, would welcome and help these new Islamic entrants on the Spanish scene. Count Julian, who had many friends on the other side of the Mediterranean, promised Musa his whole-hearted cooperation. The Muslims would find aid and support not only from the bulk of the downtrodden peasantry and from the persecuted Jews but also, most importantly, from the sons of the previous king, Witiza, who had been excluded from power by the usurper Rodrigo upon their father's death. Using whatever was the expression of his times, invading Spain would be a piece of cake, Count Julian said. He had properties on the other side of the Mediterranean near Gibraltar, he knew the country well, and he could greatly facilitate their invasion. There was much loot to be had and as an added inducement, he must have added with a sly wink, many pretty girls for the harems of the Emir Musa in Kairouan and of the caliph al-Walid Yezid in Damascus.

There was nothing holy about this Jihad. It was just a magnificent illustration of implacable Mediterranean revenge (on the part of Count Julian), and of planned mass abduction and mass robbery (on the part of the Muslims). The Jihad, throughout these ages, inspired from its pre-Islamic tradition of Arabian tribal raids, was already a mighty instrument of what in the twentieth century we could bluntly call white slave traffic. At that moment Muhammad had been dead only eighty years. There were still men and women alive in Medina and Mecca who had known the Prophet and sat on his lap as children. Yet we are already at the beginning of the Islamic onslaught on Europe. The teachings of the Prophet have spread far beyond the worship of Allah to Muhammad's own political and imperial vision which has been given, in the Koran, the divine imprimatur. Islam was already more than a religion. It was already an international political force, as it still is today, of many hues, diversions, and heresies, but still a fairly compact and cohesive whole centered on one tenet of faith to which all Muslims adhere: Allah is great and Muhammad is his Prophet.

Musa had another project of conquest already germinating in his mind. To invade Spain, yes, but also to advance north though Spain and well beyond it, into the land of the Franks beyond the Pyrenees, deep into the Dar-al-Harb, the Land of War; to turn to the right through lands unknown and advance on and on until Constantinople and Damascus were reached; and to perhaps overthrow the pope on the way, take over the Vatican, and form the whole Mediterranean into a closed Muslim lake.

It was a magnificent scheme of imperial domination, grandiose in its scope and imagination; had it come off, we might today all be prostrating ourselves on the ground and praying to Mecca several times a day instead of attending (or not attending) mass or evensong in the subdued quiet of our Gothic churches.

We are inevitably reminded at this moment of General Bonaparte who, during his 1798 Egyptian expedition, was similarly motivated by measureless dreams of conquest of the Middle East and India. To Madame de Remusat, the Empress Josephine's friend, he once described his eighteen months in Egypt as "the most beautiful time of my life because it was the most ideal. I saw myself marching into Asia, riding an elephant, a turban on my head, attacking the power of England in India." Muhammad was also a great military leader—but at a lesser level than Napoleon Bonaparte, and we can only be grateful that the Emperor of the French nation, unlike the founder of the Arab nation, never saw himself as the messenger of God, nor his writings as the words of God himself whose truth and values were for all times and must never be changed. The seventh century lacked the questing and questioning spirit, the intellectual and philosophical ferment, of the eighteenth. History calls it the Dark Ages. It is the age to which the Muslim fundamentalists, or at least some of them, want Islam to return.

13

THE MOUNTAIN OF TARIK: SPAIN 711

ALL THAT WAS REQUIRED NOW to invade Spain was the authorization of al-Walid, the caliph who, from his palace in Damascus, supervised the government and administration of the Muslim empire and an expedition commander to be appointed from among the Muslim warriors in North Africa.

By this time the caliphs were less reluctant than their early predecessors to allow their warriors to face the perils of the sea, and al-Walid sent a message to Musa giving him permission to cross the Mediterranean and attack Spain, as long as the voyage did not place the life of his Muslim charges in danger. Musa chose as their commander a Berber, Tarik, a former Algerian slave who had long proved his talents as a soldier and his loyalty to Islam. The Berbers, formerly Christian, after some fierce fighting against the Arab invaders had massively converted to Islam. Now, under Musa, the men of the Atlas mountains and of the plains were Muslims. Tough soldiers, like Tarik, were the norm. They swore by the Koran and by the sword.

They sent a small strike force of a few hundred men on a raid across the straits; they returned loaded with booty and pretty girls and much impressed Musa with the riches, human and material, of the land beyond. Tarik assembled in Tangier a force of some seven thousand men, most of whom were Berbers like himself, only recently converted to Islam. With Count Julian at Tarik's side to act as adviser, the Muslim fleet sailed for Europe in April 711. Western Europe first encountered the Muslim invaders from the south on one of those lovely Mediterranean spring days when the sea is blue, the sky cloudless, and all is right with the world. They landed at a spot undoubtedly suggested by Count Julian, who knew the region, at the foot of a mountain jutting out into the sea; later generations called it Jabel Tarik, the Mountain of Tarik. We have Europeanized the name into Gibraltar. Centuries later, the rock of Gibraltar was to become the imperial symbol of Britain, then a wild, distant, and rain-pelted island to the north where a monk from Durham, known to us as the Venerable Bede, was then preparing his ecclesiastical history of the English people, one of the earliest classics on Britain.

It is through Gibraltar that the Jihad entered Europe. The point of entry was very fitting. Gibraltar has always been a place for clash, conflict, and conquest. It still is, in recent years in more muted form, and no longer between Christian and Muslim, but between Spaniard and Briton who have been fighting over it for three hundred years.

The Visigoth king, Don Rodrigo, was in Cordova when the news of the Muslim landing reached him. "We do not know who these invaders are, we do not know whether they are from heaven or from hell," the exhausted messenger, sent to warn the king about the invasion, gasped out to Rodrigo. They were most fitting words to announce, without even knowing anything about it, the arrival of the Jihad; for the Muslims must have considered themselves envoys from heaven, since Muhammad was the messenger of God, while the Jihad was to the Christians a blasphemous demonic intrusion into a land that worshiped Christ.

The Christians even resented the presence of Jews in their midst. Although they already had been in Spain for several centuries, well before the arrival of the Roman and later the Visigoth invaders, Jews were mercilessly persecuted. One of the most recent edicts forbade Jewish parents to bring up their children and took their offspring away from them unless they converted to Christianity. In Spain, unlike Arabia, all the conditions existed for Jews and Arabs to be friends and allies. The Visigoth enemy, anyway, was no longer a fearsome foe. "Secluded from the world by the Pyrenean mountains, the successors of Alaric had slumbered in a long peace; the walls of the city were mouldered into dust and the youth had abandoned the exercise of arms," affirmed Edward Gibbon.

The setting was right for a Muslim victory, and for the Visigoths the moment of truth was about to appear. It bore on its banner the star and the crescent, and at its sword tip the desert message of the Jihad: "God is great and Muhammad is his Prophet." So corrupt had the Visigoth kingdom become that even Oppas, the bishop of Toledo, primate of all Spain, was ready to go over to the enemy and secretly sent word to the Muslim invaders that he would support them when they attacked King Rodrigo. Understandably so, perhaps, for Oppas was the brother of the former king Witiza and therefore the uncle of Witiza's two sons, who had been excluded from power. They also secretly contacted the invaders, while the Jews prepared to welcome their liberators. Don Rodrigo, totally unaware that his seduction of Florinda a couple of years ago was—so the legend says—the cause of these calamitous ills, prepared to do battle.

The first, and decisive, battle between Muslim Moors and Christian Spaniards was fought on the banks of the Guadelete river to the northwest of Gibraltar, in the land of Xeres (where sherry, a delightful lunchtime apéritif for men and women of good taste, comes from). It is not far from Cadiz and in the territory of Medina Sidonia, where, nine hundred years later, the miscast Duke of Medina Sidonia, leader of the expedition known as The Spanish Armada set out in a singular internecine Christian-style (Catholic vs. Protestant) repeat of holy war to invade England—and failed to do so. Tarik, however, did not fail in his invasion of Spain. As they prepared for battle, they were bringing 1,300 years of conflict into Europe with them, all in the name of Allah the Merciful.

Don Rodrigo rode, or rather was driven, into the first battle of the Jihad, the Battle of Rio Barbate as it is sometimes called, at the head of an army of 100,000 men. Some chroniclers say 40,000. No one really knew at the time, and certainly no one knows now. The Muslims, reinforced by five thousand men sent by Musa at Tarik's request, numbered perhaps twelve thousand men. King Rodrigo "sustaining on his head a diadem of pearls, encumbered with a flowing robe of gold and silken embroidery, and reclining on a litter of ivory drawn by two white mules" led the army into battle, the traitorous Bishop Oppas at his side. The knights on their horses wore armor; the infantry, dragged from their fields and dressed in rags, carried spears, scythes, and hoes.

"My brethren, the enemy is before you, the sea is behind; whither would ye fly," Tarik extolled his men, urging them into battle. Muslim casualties were heavy. Gibbon tells us that the plains of Xeres were strewn with the bodies of sixteen thousand Muslim dead, which is remarkable as only a reported twelve thousand of them went into battle. Confusion is always rampant in the figures of these medieval battles. The fighting apparently lasted several days. What is meant by "battle" is not clear. By its duration (Waterloo only lasted eight hours) it must have included scouting expeditions spread over several days, skirmishes, and perhaps a parley or two. Witiza's sons and Bishop Oppas deserted to the Muslim enemy. Rodrigo fled from the battlefield on his fleetest horse and apparently drowned. His horse, his robes, and his diadem were found on the river bank—a slipper recognized from its pattern as belonging to him. An unrecognizable corpse was lying nearby, and to satisfy Muslim requirements it was decided that the body was the dead monarch's. Its head was ceremoniously cut off, perfumed, packed in camphor, soaked in brine, and urgently sent off by special messenger to the caliph in Damascus for his contemplation and delectation.

So the Jihad reached the West in 711. During the next few years after the battle of Rio Barbate, the Arabs went on to conquer Spain and Portugal. In these first campaigns, their role was more that of liberator than conqueror. The population was happy to see the end of Visigothic rule. The invaders, too, were delighted; plunder, the first objective of any self-respecting war, was abundant. Count Julian worriedly began to wonder when his allies would go away; perhaps he had royal ambitions for himself. But it soon became clear that the Muslims would not go. They were in Spain and in Portugal; they stayed for eight hundred years. They called the peninsula al-Andalus, the Land of the Vandals. Perhaps they confused the Visigoths with the Vandals, barbarians were all much alike. More and more Muslims, Arabs as well as Moors, began to arrive, and the cry of the muezzin was heard in the land, calling the people to pray to Allah. The conquest began, striking out in all directions at once. It was to take the invaders three years to reach the Pyrenees and cross into adjoining France.

14

A CONQUEROR'S FATE:
SPAIN 711–715

"THERE IS A TIDE IN the affairs of men which taken at the flood leads on to fortune," Shakespeare once wrote. What he wrote was equally true for Tarik when he invaded Spain. Rodrigo, the king of the Visigoths, was dead and all Spain was at Tarik's mercy. Now was the time to take Spain and to turn it into a fiefdom of Allah. More importantly, now was the moment in the affairs of Tarik which could lead him to fortune as well as to fame and power.

Musa, who wanted the glory for the Conquest to be his alone, had given orders to Tarik before the expedition left Tangiers that, after he had defeated Rodrigo, he should await Musa's arrival with reinforcements before seeking new conquests. After Tarik's victory and Rodrigo's death, the renegade Count Julian was at hand with inflammatory advice to Tarik, which must have been very much as Gibbon wrote it. "The King of the Goths is slain. Their princes have fled before you. Their army is routed. The nation is astonished. In person and without delay march to the royal city of Toledo." Toledo was then the capital of Spain and the advice was sound, both militarily and politically.

After diverting part of his army under the command of one of his lieutenants, Mugaith, to the attack and capture of Cordova, Tarik, following Count Julian's advice, marched north to Toledo, which he captured without a fight, as most of the inhabitants, headed by their archbishop, had fled. The booty, according to the chroniclers of the epoch, was fabulous, and included a gold and emerald table said to have come from the Temple of Solomon. Within three to four years the entire Visigoth domain, except for the Asturias in the northwest and a corner of France then called Septimania and centered on Narbonne, was to be in the hands of the Muslims.

Musa, furious at his underling for disobeying his orders, particularly for upstaging him by winning battles, capturing cities, and occupying already a large part of Spain, landed at Algeciras in the autumn of 712 with about eighteen thousand Arab and Berber troops. An old man well into his seventies and perhaps his eighties, with long white hair and a long white beard, Musa was very conscious of his role as the defender of the Muslim faith. He was also in a towering rage against Tarik, so the accounts of the period say. He was afraid that his second-in-command, by his victories, would upstage him in the eyes of Caliph al-Walid in Damascus.

Before marching to Toledo, Musa darted hither and thither with his vast host in tow in search of victories and cities to take. He captured several: Carmona, Medina Sidonia and, after a siege of a few months, Seville, the city of a thousand dreams where the large, long-throttled Jewish population welcomed him as a liberator and joined the Muslim army. Merida, once also the capital of Spain, was the next town to fall to Musa. There the Moors captured Rodrigo's widow Egilona, and Musa's affable son Abd el-Aziz promptly found a place for the lonely widowed queen in his tent.

She accompanied him on his next campaigns, in which he captured Malaga and Granada. He then was dispatched to Murcia, where the ruling Christian Duke Theodemir agreed to surrender to the Muslims on condition that he could continue to reign over his duchy, which included the city of Alicante, and that the Christians could continue to worship in their churches. In return they had to pay yearly tribute to their conquerors: one dinar, four measures of wheat, two pitchers of olive oil, and two pitchers of honey for each freeman. They could worship as they willed so long as they agreed not to revolt. These were generous conditions, but they didn't last. The Muslims began cutting down the concessions they made to the Christians, greatly increased the tribute they had to pay, and often simply canceled the treaties. They did so sixty years later with the agreement they signed with Theodemir.

The war elsewhere in Spain was continuing. Details on the campaign are few. Records of these campaigns once existed, but most of them were destroyed in a fire which, hundreds of years later, ravaged the Escurial in Madrid in 1671. We know that Musa met Tarik in Toledo, struck him across the face with a whip for daring to disregard his original orders and, it is said, considered whether to have him beheaded for his disobedience. Decapitation, an ancient Arab custom, was a popular way among Muslim leaders of showing their authority. "Why did you disobey me?" the angry old man shouted at his subordinate. "To serve Islam," Tarik replied. His only desire, he stressed, had been to serve Allah. "Allah has been well served," said Musa tactfully, at loss for words. So Tarik kept his head.

The war continued until 715, by which year nearly the whole of Spain was under Muslim occupation. Musa and Tarik marched north together and took Saragossa, where they diverged, Tarik to the northeast where he captured Lerida, Tarragona, and perhaps Barcelona; Musa to the the Ebro valley; and his son Abd el-Aziz to Lisbon and the Algarve, today one of the popular playgrounds of Europe. Spain vanished under the mantle of Islam and the Jihad was triumphant everywhere except in the Asturias.

When the conquest of Spain was virtually over, Musa left his son behind in Seville to reign as his personal representative. But Abd el-Aziz, under the influence of his new wife Egilona, had abandoned the simple ways of the desert, according to Arab critics, in favor of the elaborate ritual of the Visigoth court. Queen Egilona, to make courtiers bow in her presence, a practice unknown among the unsophisticated Arab tribesmen, had installed a very low door into the palace reception room, so that all visitors had to bend to the waist on coming into the presence of the couple.

Musa returned to Damascus on a long overland journey through what is now Morocco, Algeria, Tunisia, Libya, Egypt Israel, Palestine, Lebanon, and Syria, taking with him several tons of booty, many Visigoth dignitaries as prisoners and, so the story goes, three thousand Spanish virgins for Caliph al-Walid's harem. They would be a particularly welcome gift, for the old caliph enjoyed young girls. He had at one time been "accused of tampering with his predecessor's harem. Even darker vices were bruited abroad" about him. Musa, whose advanced years protected him from the temptations of the flesh, anticipated a grand welcome from the uxorious caliph in Damascus. But when he arrived, al-Walid was dead and Musa had three thousand virgins on his hands. The new caliph, Suleiman, was less interested in the Spanish virgins than in Musa himself.

Suleiman paranoiacally regarded Musa as a dangerous rival,

perhaps out to bribe the entire Damascus leadership with his three thousand virgins. The two men also obviously disliked each other on sight and, alas for Musa, Suleiman was the man in power. His command was law. The old general was arrested and made to stand in the sun for several hours until he fainted from dehydration. Suleiman called the executioner and ordered him to behead Musa, but then changed his mind and ordered him instead to take the old man into one of his deepest and darkest dungeons.

Finally Caliph Suleiman decided neither to imprison Musa nor to behead him. Instead, he banished Musa back to Arabia, to the Yemen, from where many decades earlier his father, a Catholic seminarian, had left home to study for the priesthood in Iraq. There, as we read earlier, his father had been captured by Khalid, the Sword of Allah, in the old, pure, early days of the Jihad when the Infidel faced two options: death or Islam. Musa's father had chosen Islam.

Musa was now going back to the land of his ancestors; but before he left, Suleiman had one last surprise for him. He called the old general before him and presented him with the decapitated head of his son Abd el-Aziz, assassinated in a Seville mosque on the caliph's order for allegedly plotting to secede from the caliphate. In the head, preserved in brine, the dead eyes of his son were dolorously staring at his father. Musa received the head and bowed to the caliph. "Give me leave to close the eyes of my son," the old soldier asked the caliph. He was graciously permitted to do so and returned to his native village, with the head of his son in a basket, to live out his life as a beggar in the street. Thus ended Musa, conqueror of Spain and dreamer of an Islamic trans-European empire stretching from Gibraltar, north to France, east to Baghdad and beyond, then south to the Red Sea—an empire that was never to be.

History does not tell us how Tarik, the other early conqueror of Spain, the man who gave his name to Gibraltar, died. Perhaps he died a beggar, too, or decapitated in a Damascus courtyard, or of thirst and hunger in a Syrian cell. If he had ended his days in glory, history would surely have told us. Suleiman was a suspicious, paranoid man, erratic and unbalanced. The worst could have happened to Tarik—or the best.

PART FOUR

ISLAM UNFOLDS

15

THE FORGOTTEN ISAURIAN: CONSTANTINOPLE 717–718

T HE WEST HAS FORGOTTEN ONE of its great heroes, who in the year 717 shattered what would have been the first major Muslim onslaught into and across Europe, but from the east this time, and heading west. Europe's savior was a soldier and emperor of the Byzantine Empire. He saved the Balkans and Eastern Europe from the Jihad for another 650 years and perhaps, in the totally confused situation of Europe at the time, he saved the whole of Europe from an Islamic invasion, for there would have been no one to stop the Muslims between the Balkans and the Alps. He helped to make Europe what it became, or at least prevented it from becoming something which it did not wish to become. Christian Europe had no wish to replace Christ with Muhammad.

Leo the Isaurian was an Anatolian, born somewhere along the Turkish-Syrian border when that region was one of the Christian bastions of Asia Minor. He was seeped in Christianity, even in some of its most obscure doctrines, and he believed in the vocation of Constantinople as the heir of Rome, to save the empire from what he regarded as these new barbarians. He repelled the Arab invaders when, for the second time, they appeared under the walls of Constantinople, intent not only on capturing the capital of the eastern Roman Empire, but also perhaps planning to launch from there an attack across Europe to link up with their provinces of Spain and southern France, where they were already established in what we call today the Languedoc.

Leo took over the throne in the year 717. It was mainly the threat of the Arabs from the south that brought him to power. The Bulgarians to the north were also a frequent threat, but for the moment they were quiescent. The main enemy was the Arab. A large part of the known world seemed to be submitting to Muslim Arab domination. Spain in the west had just succumbed to Islam. In the east Transoxiana, on the fringes of China, was now acknowledging Allah as its god and Muhammad as his Prophet. Islam ruled the world from the Mongol desert to the Atlantic ocean. It had all been conquered in less than sixty years.

A Greek envoy to Damascus had returned to Constantinople in 715 with the alarming news that Suleiman, the new caliph, the one who had so ill-treated Musa, was preparing a vast new expedition by land and sea. Its target: Constantinople.

The new Byzantine emperor, Anastasius, seemed unable to control his army, which was in a state of constant near mutiny. He was replaced on the throne by a colorless bureaucrat, Theodosius. The new monarch appeared equally incapable of organizing any resistance to the oncoming onslaught, which could only be a year or two away. Leo the Isaurian took over, with the support of his troops. He was a very professional type of officer and he knew he had reached the moment where the main purpose of his life had become clear: to defeat the Jihad. Leo was neither a courtier nor a nobleman. His father was a grazier who owned five hundred sheep, and Leo had started life as a peddler who sold his paltry goods from a donkey's back at country fairs. But he was a born soldier and organizer. After joining the army he rose rapidly through the ranks until he was given the command of the Anatolian legion that dethroned Theodosius and made Leo the Isaurian emperor.

An army of 120,000 Arabs and Persians, under the command of Moslemah, brother of the caliph, was advancing on Constantinople, many of them mounted on horses or camels. They crossed the Hellespont from Asia to Europe. Moslemah marched on Constantinople, wheeled his army around and, surrounding his camp with a ditch and rampart, prepared to wait out the Byzantine army in the besieged city. All the citizens inside who did not have the means or the subsistence—mainly corn—to hold out for three years had already been evacuated, and the city's granaries were full. Leo was confident he could outwait the besiegers. Another force of 100,000 Muslim warriors and sailors on 1,800 galleys sailed from Syria and Egypt and joined the blockading force. Leo lured them in into the Bosporus by removing the heavy chain thrown across the harbor to prevent the entry of enemy ships.

Then, when they were all assembled and helpless, he ordered in his fireships, loaded with their dreaded Greek fire. They destroyed a large number of the vessels and the men and supplies in them. "It came flying through the air like a winged long-tailed dragon, about the thickness of a hogshead, with the report of thunder and the velocity of lightning," reported a victim of one of these Greek fire attacks.

The Arabs had relied more on starving the Christians than on taking their city by storm but, after the devastating attack by the fireships, the Arab blockade never really materialized. In fact, it was the Arabs and their Persian allies who began to starve, not the besieged Byzantine Greeks. When winter came, it was the Muslims, unused to the cold weather and neither dressed nor equipped for it, who froze to death. Snow and ice lay on the ground for nearly four months. Men died of the cold in the tens of thousands, as well as their horses and camels. Then dysentery appeared among the weakened men and killed a few thousand more. The Byzantines, in the comfort of their homes in the city, huddling in their warmest clothes around a fire, would occasionally step outside and, from the top of the battlements, call down mocking messages to their shivering attackers trying to survive in the cold shelter of their unheated tents.

The situation for the Arabs and the Persians improved temporarily in the spring, when reinforcements arrived from Egypt in four hundred ships. Leo took care of them with his fireships again, while sorties by armed parties from the besieged city cut the weakened Arab troops to pieces. To add to the Arabs' woes, the Bulgarians, usually unfriendly to the Greeks, now came over to their side and routed a large Muslim force near Adrianopolis. Twenty thousand Muslims fled or were captured. Then famine struck. Moslemah, like his predecessors in the 668 siege, bowed to the inevitable, ordered what remained of his troops, some thirty thousand survivors, to march back to Tarsus. The remnants of his fleet sailed away, most of the ships to founder and sink in a storm in the Aegean. Only five galleys returned to Syria undamaged.

The Jihad had failed. Constantinople was not for the taking, and Caliph Suleiman, who had been ready to join the besieging army, now compensated for his defeat by going into a huge eating spree during which he consumed, we are told, two baskets of eggs and figs, and several plates of marrow and sugar. Suleiman was, anyway, a man of both unbalanced reactions and gargantuan appetite. During a recent pilgrimage to Mecca, to demonstrate his attachment to the Prophet, he had consumed at one sitting a young goat, six chickens, a basket of grapes,

and seventy pomegranates. Perhaps thanks to the nearby inspiring presence of the Kaaba, he had digested the lot nicely. This time the disap-
pointing failure at Constantinople was too much for his overburdened
stomach. The caliph Suleiman died of indigestion a few hours later. His
courtiers claimed he died of a broken heart. The new caliph, presumably
to persuade himself that the Jihad was still operative, ordered all Christians within his domain who refused to convert to Islam to be put to
death immediately. The order was quickly countermanded, but not
before an unknown number of dhimmis had been executed.

After those two crushing rebuffs in the Bosporus, the first forty-
five years before, the Arabs never tried again seriously to capture the
Byzantine capital. It remained in Christian hands for another seven
hundred years and for all those centuries stood as a bastion of Christian defense and defiance against the Jihad.

16

THE DHIMMIS:
DAR-AL-ISLAM FROM THE
SEVENTH CENTURY ONWARD

SPAIN, MEANWHILE, WAS SETTLING IN for what was to be 777 years of Muslim rule in which the original inhabitants, Christians and Jews, became legally the inferior citizens inside the country, subject to the imposition of special taxes and to a lifetime of humiliations. Here let us take a short pause in our account of the Jihad to ponder the fate of those who lived in the lands occupied and conquered by the Muslims, not only in Spain, but also in the Near and Middle East, Christians mainly but also Jews.

The Christians and Jews were called "dhimmis" (in the east European and Balkan lands later conquered by the Turks, they were known as "rayahs") and they had to acknowledge the superiority of the Muslims in their daily life, which was to become one of constant humiliations. They could not carry a weapon or ride a horse, only a donkey. They were not allowed to wear shoes but had to walk barefoot. A Christian who claimed Jesus was divine was automatically executed. A Muslim who became a Christian or a Jew was also executed. The ringing of church bells was forbidden. Christian religious processions were banned. Non-Muslims had to stand aside if a Muslim passed them in the street. They could not wear anything which had green in it, as that was the color of Islam. If a Muslim assaulted them, they were not allowed to fight back but were only permitted to ask their aggressor to stop hitting them. Their status in many ways resembled that of the

Untouchables in Hindu society. The dhimmis were the dregs, the people at the bottom of the pile. If they failed to pay the tribute due their conquerors, they were enslaved or executed.

Nowhere, however, were the defeated subjects of al-Andalus, as the Muslim-ruled part of Spain came to be known, forced to abjure their faith and go over to Islam. As Jews and Christians they were the people of "The Book," as Muhammad respectfully referred to the Scriptures, and as such entitled to consideration as men who adored God and revered his prophets. But, through the centuries of servitude that lay ahead of them, the official respect tendered to them as people of "The Book" had very little relationship to the indignities to which they were often subjected. I say "often" rather than "always," for there were epochs when and places where the treatment was better; but usually it was bad, particularly for the poor. Finally, for many, conversion to Islam became the only possible way of ensuring a tolerable life for themselves and their children.

It soon became obvious, however, that the Muslim conquerors were not anxious to win too many converts. Converting infidels meant losing taxpayers or potential slaves, both valuable commodities. The non-Muslim citizens of these new Muslim lands were setting the pattern for the future lucrative Islamic rule in conquered territories: some of the conquered, usually through self-interest, sometimes through a genuine change of faith, sometimes for reasons of sheer survival, would convert to Islam and no longer pay tribute; the majority of the Christians and Jews continued in their faith, paid tribute and enriched the Muslim state; a few would choose martyrdom. If conversions to Islam were not actively discouraged, they certainly were not encouraged either. Although many Muslims would have denied it, and probably still do, more money, more slaves, and more tax-payers were more important to the Islamic rulers than more Muslims.

The Dutchman Reinhart Dozy, in his classical nineteenth-century work on *Spanish Islam,* presented the situation in elegant and pertinent terms:

> The Law provided that Christians and Jews who came under Mo-
> hammedan rule, and who embraced islamism, were exempted from
> payment to the Treasury of the poll-tax exacted from those who
> adhered to the faith of their ancestors (Christianity or Judaism).
> Thanks to this bait offered to avarice, the Mohammedan Church
> daily received into her bosom a multitude of converts who, without

being entirely convinced of the truth of her doctrines, were devoted to the pursuit of wealth and worldly advantages. Divines rejoiced at this rapid spread of the faith and the Exchequer lost heavily.

The Muslim rulers needed money more than they needed converts. Dozy's quote makes the Jihad, on which Islam relied for its expansion, seem more like a method for gathering taxpayers than for converting infidels, but there were some men of good faith among the Muslim rulers. Not all conquerors looked upon the conquered as future tax-payers rather than future Muslims. One caliph rejoiced when told by a distraught official that the conversions from Egypt were causing a tremendous loss of revenue to the treasury. "Allah sent his Prophet to be an apostle, not a tax-collector," the caliph said. But he was the exception. The Jihad was largely a fraud. It fought for the Treasury as much as for Allah. Throughout the centuries it was one of the great triumphs of hypocrisy.

The writer Elmer Bendiner, in his *Rise and Fall of Paradise,* called the Jihad a game, "the supreme game for rich and poor, for slave and free . . . war in the name of Allah, war against the infidel, glorious holy war that might bring wealth to a poor man, emancipation to a slave, a wife to a bachelor, a concubine to a family man. All this and salvation too." The Jihad was great. The Jihad was fun; but for the faithful, not for the dhimmis.

The Jihad has often been a fraud of staggering proportions, except perhaps in its very early days; but then, when the choice for the infidels was only Islam or the sword, for many Christians it meant apostasy to Islam or death. The third option, tribute, was the gift of life. Fraud is better than death, both for the victim and for the aggressor. The victim survives and pays; the victor pockets the money and can rob or tax his victim again and again. The victim becomes a valuable investment, a valuable property. For hundreds of years, this was to be the individual fate of millions of Spaniards who lived in al-Andalus.

The Arab conquest of Spain had been one of history's blitzkriegs. It was over by 715 and three years later the Spaniards began the long reconquest of their country. Spain was not the only Arab objective in Europe. Their 717 attack, at the other end of the Mediterranean, where Europe and Asia merge, was the Jihad's second front in Europe, and it had so far failed.

17

FORAYS INTO FRANCE: THE LANGUEDOC 718–732

T HE ARABS GAVE UP TRYING to take Constantinople in 718. That was also the year when, at the other end of Europe, only three years after losing the whole of their country to the Muslims, the Spaniards began La Reconquista, the liberation of Spain from the Arabs and the Moors. Their military campaign lasted until 1492, 774 years. Compared to it the Hundred Years' War between England and France, from 1337 to 1453, ranks as a minor skirmish.

The whole episode, nearly eight centuries long, is one of the most stupendous sagas in history, unique, full of sound and fury, of love of God and cruelty to man, of hopes vanished and reborn; an epic of exaltation, pride and despair marked by the clash of arms, by battles, forays and sieges; and, above all, by the stubborn courage of a defeated but unvanquished nation. We recall a few names here and there in the turmoil, lost in a haze of confusion of swirling swords and scimitars, of battles unheard of and of heroes who don't seem real. Some of them perhaps never existed but—like the Muhammad of the Muslim psyche to the Muslims—they are real to the Spaniards, who needed heroes and who gave form and substance to those who maybe were only figures of legend and of campfire stories.

Pelayo was the first of these resistance fighters. He is more than a myth, but how much more is an enigma. He lived, and is mentioned in an ancient document dated 812, and also by various Arab writers; one of whom describes him as "a despicable barbarian" who had fled with forty followers, ten of them women, to the vastness of the Asturias mountains, where he and his group fed on honey, berries, and wild plants.

Pelayo was the son of a Visigoth nobleman, one Fafila, and he was born in these mountains of northeastern Spain. He was a member of King Rodrigo's bodyguard and perhaps fought alongside his king in that first fatal Jihad encounter near Xeres where Rodrigo was slain. Perhaps Pelayo escaped from the battlefield and made his way back north to his birthplace and there founded the first resistance movement against the Muslim occupation of his country. Perhaps he even had to collaborate at first with the enemy. The Asturias in these early days of Arab occupation were ruled by a Moor, Munuza, who had married Pelayo's sister and who had, according to some reports, sent his brother-in-law as hostage to Cordova. Pelayo escaped, returned to his native mountains, and was there chosen as leader by the local Christians. These Christians were not only Asturians but also refugee Visigoths and a scattering of exiles from other points in Spain, all fleeing from the Moors.

Pelayo defied the Muslims and mocked the Jihad. The occupiers launched an expedition against him, but at the battle of Covadonga, near a cave on Mount Aseuva, he defeated his pursuers, many of whom were killed in their flight by an avalanche. Others drowned in the river Deva while trying to flee across to the other side. Pelayo, after this victory, was acclaimed king, and established his capital in the small town of Cangas de Oni where, perhaps fighting an occasional skirmish against the Muslims, he remained until he died in 737. Like Leo the Isaurian, Pelayo is one of the forgotten heroes who first stemmed the Jihad onslaught when it surged out of the desert into Europe. But Pelayo is less forgotten than Leo the Isaurian because in his own country he is remembered as one of the early patriots of Spain and as the King of the Asturias.

Kingdom is too exalted a word to describe the domain over which Pelayo reigned. The French, during World War II, might have called it a "maquis," a territory which he controlled and from where he attacked the foreign occupiers. There were many such "kingdoms" right across Europe in these unruly Dark Ages, when all law and order had broken down and the only safety lay in the protection of a heavily armed lord with a large army of retainers. Pelayo's domain obviously grew, expanding north toward the coast, then south. He kept up a form of diplomatic relations with other similar "kingdoms" which were growing around him, one such kingdom was Cantabria, the son of whose ruling duke, Pedro, married Pelayo's daughter, Ermesinda.

In 739 Pelayo's own son, called Fafila like his grandfather, was killed by a bear while hunting. A son-in-law, Alfonso I, became the leading prince in the Christian region and, after civil war broke out between the Arabs and Moors, he led raiding parties of Christian knights all the way south to Avila, Segovia, and Salamanca, greatly expanding his kingdom. It gradually grew, through the next two centuries, into the kingdom of Leon which in the thirteenth century became part of Castile. The kingdom of the Asturias was thus the seed of Spanish nationhood. Since the inspiration, the drive, and the muscle for the Reconquest came from Castile, we can rightfully consider Pelayo as the founder, or at least the originator, of modern Spain.

For several centuries Spain must in many ways have been like the American Wild West, in the early days of the white settlers and the Comanche and Sioux raiding parties. The land that separated the two parts of Spain (al-Andalus, as the Muslims called Islamic Spain in the south; and the Christian kingdoms of the north) was a sort of no-man's land. In places it was several dozen miles wide where a few farmers lived dangerous lives (much as the settlers in Arizona or the Dakotas in the early days of white settlement lived in continual fear of Indian attacks), as prey for wandering bands of Muslim or Christian outlaws. The no-man's land, all though those centuries, however, was moving inexorably south as the Reconquista nibbled deeper and deeper into the lands of the faltering Islamic stronghold, and Christian crusades were supplanting the Jihad.

In Spain the Jihad also spread north beyond the Pyrenees. We have already mentioned the penetration by the invaders into the Narbonne region, into a corner of France then known as Septimania because it was once the stomping ground of the seventh Roman Legion. Like Spain, it was part of the Visigoth Kingdom at the time of the Arab invasions, and fell naturally under their domination.

Musa, whom today we might call an imperialist, is said to have crossed the Pyrenees to gaze at this furthest northern acquisition of Islam and seen it not only as the gateway to the lands of the Franks, the people we call today the French, but beyond it as the first stage to Italy and Greece and Constantinople, all the way to Damascus, where the caliph ruled, and onward to the eastern Muslim empire. This would have meant the ultimate triumph of the Jihad and the Islamization of Europe. Fortunately, or unfortunately, according to your point of view, this was not to be. The conquest of what we call France was planned by the Muslim invaders of Spain, and it came very near to success.

Al-Semah was the leader of this first invasion across the Pyrenees, a gentleman about whom little is known except that he had distinguished himself as a soldier and administrator in Spain and was a zealous Muslim, anxious to lead the Jihad to the land of the unbelievers. He crossed the border into Septimania, the Catalan province of France, in 721, with a large army which took Narbonne, killed every male in the city and enslaved all the woman and children. Because of its position near the sea, al-Semah made Narbonne his capital and the springboard for a military campaign across France. He then marched west to Toulouse, where he was killed fighting against the duke of Aquitaine, Eudes, who had rushed from Bordeaux to its defense. Abderaman, the second-in-command, took over and led the survivors back to Spain. Abderaman is usually known as Abd al-Rahman, but there are several more people of that name coming into these Spanish chapters, so we will give this one the simpler spelling of Abderaman, since it also can be so written. It means Servant of the Merciful and is still a popular name in Islam.

The Muslims continued to occupy Narbonne and from there they carried out many raids. A new Muslim army, led by the new emir of Spain, Ambissa, arrived in 724, took Carcassone and Nimes, but returned to Spain when Ambissa was killed. The Muslims' preferred targets in France were usually the monasteries and churches which they cheerfully plundered of all their holy objects, enslaving or killing the monks. They marched up the Rhone, plundered Lyon, Macon, Chalons, Beaune, and Dijon.

Both Eudes, the duke of Aquitaine, and the warrior Charles Martel, "mayor of the palace" (it was a sort of hereditary prime ministership) as he was called under the Merovingian kings of the Franks, were strangely inactive in the face of these incursions in the south. They were personal enemies and each feared that the other might take advantage of him while he was fighting the Muslims. Charles Martel advised his followers to wait. Eudes, playing a strangely lonely game, had allied himself with the Muslim Munuza, former ruler of the Asturias, who had fought and lost to Pelayo.

Munuza, a Moor from North Africa, was waging his own private war against the Arabs and, as a token of his esteem, Eudes had given him his daughter Lampegia in marriage, perhaps to join Pelayo's sister in his harem. Yet Munuza was notorious for his anti-Christian attitudes, and when in power he had ordered a Spanish bishop called Anambadus to be burned alive. Anambadus died as Joan of Arc did, hundreds of years before she did, but she made history and he didn't.

The Jihad around the Pyrenees region was faltering badly. In the meantime, another Jihad foray into France led to an attack against Arles and, while the Saracens were plundering this old Roman city on the Rhone, another force, led by Abderaman, who was now emir of Spain, with fifteen thousand Berber horsemen in the van, came across the Pyrenees from Pamplona to attack Aquitaine. Munuza, the renegade Moor, tried to warn his father-in-law Duke Eudes, but he was cut off by his old Arab friends and, rather than fall into their hands, he jumped to his death from a high cliff. The Arabs, in their traditional style, cut off his head, packed it in camphor and brine, and sent it to the caliph in Damascus along with Munuza's pretty and very alive French wife, Eudes's daughter who, we are told, went to garnish the caliph's harem and vanished from history.

Abderaman and his troops first headed for Bordeaux. Beyond lay Poitiers and Tours and their rich abbeys and basilicas, ripe for plunder. The Jihad could be a lucrative investment as well as a great game. The stage was now set for one of the most renowned battles of Christendom. It has been listed as one of the fifteen most decisive battles ever fought. It changed the course of world history. Yet so little is known about it that historians do not even agree as to where it took place and give a different place name for the battle according to whether they are French or British.

French historians have placed it near Poitiers and call it the battle of Poitiers. British historians, perhaps anxious not to have it confused with the British victory over the French at Poitiers several hundred years later, locate the approximate site of the battle near Tours and call it the battle of Tours. The battle certainly was fought somewhere between the two towns, and one name is a good as the other. Arab historians don't help at all. They simply describe the site of the battle as "the roadway of martyrs," presumably because it was fought near the old Roman paved road and many Muslim soldiers were killed there and, as martyrs, went away to Paradise on that same day.

It is not known either how many men took part in the battle. One French ecclesiastical source gave the number of Arabs—actually most of the Muslim fighters were Moors—as 385,000, which seems impossible. Another source adds that there were 15,000 horsemen among the Moors, armed with lances and swords. David Eggenberger's *Dictionary of Battles* informs us that the Muslim general "pressed on toward the Loire River at the head of more than 60,000 hard-riding cavalrymen." No one can know the precise number of combatants. Perhaps they didn't know even on the day the battle was engaged. Numbers can be so easily and gloriously inflated or deflated, according to whether you win or lose. We do know that the Franks, most of them foot soldiers, blond and bewhiskered, fought mainly with battle-axes. We do not know how long the battle lasted. Two days, according to Arab sources; the Franks say one week. We do know that the Christians won, that the Muslims lost, and that France was saved for Christianity on that day.

Before the battle, Abderaman, as he was cantering north at the head of his vast host, and Charles, not yet known as Charles the Hammerer, as he hurried south after putting down some obscure rebellion in his German fiefdom, had no idea what a formidable judgment of history was awaiting them.

18

THE HAMMER OF THE FRANKS:
TOURS 732–759

I T IS EXTREMELY UNLIKELY THAT Charles Martel, as he rode south to
meet the Arabs and Moors in battle, had the slightest idea that he
was now committed to a Holy War, albeit a Muslim one. In spite of
papal conflicts, the notion of holy wars was still foreign to Christian
minds. The first Crusades were still nearly four hundred years away.

In the eighth century, to the Frankish soldier Charles Martel, the
Muslim attack must not yet have appeared so menacing. These
invaders were just a new, unpleasant bunch of outsiders from foreign
parts, with a strange religion, to be thrown out of the land of the Franks
as quickly as possible. Dangerous perhaps, but no more so than their
other enemies. There had been threats galore to the Franks since they
had conquered the land we know as France from the Gallo-Romans in
the year 431, forced the Visigoths out of Aquitaine and into Spain,
taken over Burgundy, and made Paris their capital.

Charles Martel, as mayor of the palace, was theoretically the No. 2
man in the kingdom of the do-nothing Merovingian king Theuderich IV
(I doubt, as I write these words, whether he is remembered by anyone in
the world today). Theuderich, however, was the son of the more famous
King Dagobert, known to every schoolchild in France through he
nursery rhyme they sing about him and his pants, which he wore inside
out. Abderaman, for his part, was well aware that he was engaged in a
holy war, just as when he had saved the Muslim army near Toulouse a

few years previously. He had next been named emir of Spain by the caliph in Damascus. Abderaman was particularly venerated by his Muslim subjects because in his youth he had been a friend of one of the sons of Omar, the second caliph, and had therefore, so to speak, a closer relationship to the Prophet than any other person in Spain. His subjects revered the emir for another very good reason. Abderaman was totally uninterested in the spoils of war and gave his share to his soldiers. At the same time, like Musa, Abderaman had his imperialist side. He regarded the conquest of France and all the lands of Europe as his Muslim duty. Muslim settlers from the rugged lands of North Africa and the more distant territories of the Near and Middle East (we used to refer to that part of the world as Asia Minor) were pouring into green and fertile Spain at the time. On arrival, these new inhabitants were immediately taken in hand and taught how to ride a horse, if they didn't know already, and how to use a sword to best advantage when called upon to fight. The Jihad, even if a rip-roaring adventure for some, was taken seriously by most. There's nothing like a little loot to foster piety. The cause of Allah was obviously a just one since it brought so many material rewards, reasoned the warriors of Islam.

Preparations for the French expedition had taken two years. The invaders set out from Cordova, where Abderaman had his seat of government, and, recruiting volunteers on the way, marched to Pamplona from where they advanced through the valleys of Navarre at the western end of the Pyrenees, near the Atlantic Ocean, into the land of the Franks. They had maintained all these years their conquered territory of Septimania, capital of Narbonne, at the Mediterranean end of the Pyrenees. This new invasion in the west was totally independent of the Arab army to the east, which was busily carrying on warfare in the Rhone valley.

Abderaman's army, once over the Pyrenees, headed for Bordeaux (not yet famous for its vintage clarets), killing or enslaving all who opposed them and burning or plundering every church and monastery on the way north. Their reasons were excellent and were not motivated by religious fanaticism. The churches were then the repositories of wealth, money, and jewels; rather like banks today. The Arab invaders were not only the pious knights of Islam they claimed to be, they were the equivalent of our bank robbers as well. I take my imagery from Richard Fletchers, who adds in his *Moorish Spain* (p. 76), "There is no reason to suppose that the religious convictions or observances of the staff of the bank were of any interest to the raiders." So much—sometimes—for the Jihad!

Bordeaux went into a panic when told that the Saracens were coming. Rather than face destruction, the city surrendered immediately. Eudes, the duke of Aquitaine, was as worried (almost) over the fate of his Bordeaux subjects as he was over the fate of his daughter Lampegia. He need not have been. Munuza's widow was a little homesick perhaps, but quite happy cavorting with Abderaman's other wives and concubines in the caliph's harem in Damascus.

Eudes sent a message to Charles Martel pleading for his immediate aid, to which he mayor of the palace responded as quickly as he could. He was on the other side of the Rhine at the time, Bordeaux was far away, and his army of foot soldiers moved slowly. Eudes tried to prevent the Muslims from crossing the Dordogne river, but was decisively beaten by the Saracens, who killed so many Christians that, said a chronicle of the epoch, "only God could count their numbers." Unable to stem the Islamic tide, Eudes reportedly dashed north to link up with Charles Martel while the Moors plundered on, loaded down with chasubles and chalices stolen from Christian churches and "topazes, hyacinths and emeralds" taken from the properties and estates looted along the way. Holy wars invite unholiness, and burned churches marked the advance of the invading army. Arab historians like to compare their warriors to "a storm which overturns all and everything."

The basilica of St. Martin in Tours became the magnet that drew the Saracens on. It was rumored to be so overflowing with riches that Abderaman feared his soldiers' love of loot might cause the army to break apart. He mulled over an order forcing the men to abandon their plunder but decided it might provoke a mutiny. So he just soldiered on and, somewhere between Poitiers and Tours, in October 732, Christendom and Islam met in battle and Christendom won. "The men of the north stood as motionless as statues, they were like a belt of frozen ice together and not to be dissolved as they slew the Arabs with sword," wrote a chronicler of the time. The Franks fought in the square formations which later, as Frenchmen, they have always favored in battle throughout their history. They stood, battle-axes in their hands, waiting for the onrush of the Berber cavalry.

The battle of Poitiers (or Tours, if you prefer the British version) is one of the few instances in medieval and premedieval history when infantry triumphed over cavalry. Shouting "Allah is great," the Muslim cavalry on their sturdy Spanish horses charged time and time again the squares of the Franks, who brought their battle-axes crashing down on horses and Muslims with impartial ferocity. Fighting continued until

Abderaman was killed and the Muslims retired in disorder, and during the night melted away back to their camp.

The next morning scouts from Charles Martel's army cautiously crept into the enemy camp, and found the tents empty and the soldiers gone. The Saracens had left the bulk of their loot behind. Charles, that day, became known to the Franks as "The Hammerer," and it is as Charles Martel that he has taken his place among the saviors of western civilization and the great soldiers of world history. The French are naturally pleased to have contributed this illustrious figure to world history, although the Germans also claim him as one of their own, as the territory of the Franks bestrode both present-day France and Germany.

As Edward Gibbon reminds us in *The Decline and Fall of the Roman Empire*, published in the late eighteenth century, "a victorious line of march had been prolonged (by the Muslim invaders) above a thousand miles from the Rock of Gibraltar to the banks of the Loire: the repetition of an equal space would have carried the Saracens to the confines of Poland and the Highlands of Scotland; the Rhine is not more impassible than the Nile or the Euphrates and the Arabian fleet might have sailed without a naval combat into the mouth of the Thames." Gibbon added in words that are still remembered and often quoted today, "Perhaps the interpretation of the Koran would now be taught in the schools of Oxford and her pulpits might demonstrate to a circumcised people the sanctity and truth of the revelation of Mahomet."

So many Muslims were killed on the plains of Poitiers/Tours that for years afterwards, the locals said, you could hear the soft, silky rustle of angels' wings as they flew reverently at night over this holy spot where the enemies of Christianity had met the fate that awaits the ungodly. The battle of Poitiers/Tours has remained for the past twelve centuries a symbol of Christian victory over the infidel invaders. It has acquired in recent years racist connotations in a France grappling with the enormous problem caused by an immigrant population of over two million Muslim workers, mostly Arabs and Moors from North Africa, whose cultural adaptation into French life is still far from assured.

Charles Martel did not pursue the beaten enemy. Perhaps he felt an operation in the dense forests that then covered France might imperil his whole force through an ambush. Anyway, he still had to impose his will in Burgundy. To make sure of the soldiers' loyalty, and to the great anger of the Church, he distributed among his men the ecclesiastical property he recovered instead of returning it to its former owners.

The Muslims, after fleeing all the way back to Spain, started a few months later to make their way back into France after a new governor, Abd al-Malik, was sent from Africa to take over the emirate of Spain and carry the Jihad back over the Pyrenees. They remained in France for another quarter of a century, ravaging the south and finding many allies among the regional leaders who feared the growing power of both Charles Martel and the duke of Aquitaine. One of the Arabs' staunchest allies was Mauronte, the duke of Marseille, who asked the Muslims of Septimania to help him impose his rule in Provence. Yousouf, emir of Septimania, crossed the Rhone, took Arles, where he plundered a few tombs and churches, captured Saint-Rémy-de-Provence, went on to Avignon, and occupied that part of Provence for four years.

To the west, Abd al-Malik crossed the Pyrenees and occupied much of Languedoc, all the way to the Rhone river, where the invaders linked up with their compatriots from Septimania. A Muslim force marched up the Rhone valley all the way to Lyons, while another group diverted east and invaded Piedmont, in Italy. In view of all the help the Muslims were receiving from their Christian allies, the Jihad was only partly a true Jihad. It was just blood-and-guts war, unadorned with lofty principles and with the minimum of calls to Allah; enough, though, to guarantee heaven for any Muslim fighters who might fall in battle.

In about 737 Charles Martel sent his brother Childebrand to lay siege to Avignon, which he took by storm, putting every one of its Muslim defenders to the sword. Next he attacked the main Saracen bases north of the Pyrenees and, in turn, took Narbonne, Béziers, Montpellier, and Nimes. In 739 he captured Marseille, at a time when, in other parts of Mediterranean France, the coastal region began to endure the first of those Arab slave raids from the sea which turned the northern Mediterranean shore into a danger zone for Christians for the next thousand years. Holiday makers in Cannes today can gaze from the beach on the Croisette across to the Lerins island, site of a famous Benedictine monastery which was attacked in 739 by Arab raiders who massacred all but four of the five hundred monks there. The four survivors, all young men, were being taken to Spain, but managed to escape after their captors put into the local port of Aguay for supplies. Frequent Muslim sea raids were also carried out against Sardinia, Sicily, and Corsica, where the port of Bonifacio was founded as a stronghold against the pirates.

During this period of European history, dissensions and disputes among the Muslims in Spain and elsewhere helped the Christian population to survive. Berbers and Arabs loathed each other. The Moors considered, quite rightly, that they had done the bulk of the fighting in Spain and France and had been rewarded only with arid mountain lands, while the Arabs had kept the most fertile lands on the plains and along the coast for themselves. There was no solidarity among the Arabs either. The two main purely Arab groups among the invaders came from Syria and from the Arabian peninsula, and they were both influenced by ancient tribal rivalries which continued in Spain for hundreds of years after their origins in the Hejaz, or elsewhere, had long been forgotten. The Arabs from the Yemen were at odds with those from other parts of Arabia. All of them were always ready to slaughter one another instead of the Christians. The Jihad, when they marched together against the Christians, was often the only link of solidarity between the tribes who professed Islam.

The death of Charles Martel in 741 changed also the rivalry between the Christian princes of France. Charles Martel was succeeded by his son Pepin the Short, who was as tough as his father. Pepin, who was the father of a son later to be known as Charlemagne, acquired a great ascendancy in the Languedoc region, and a local Visigoth chieftain handed over to him the cities of Nimes, Agde, Montpellier, and Béziers. The inhabitants of Narbonne, who were nearly all Christian and Visigoth, also decided to rally to Pepin the Short. They massacred their Saracen neighbors and overlords, and suddenly there were no Saracens left north of the Pyrenees. The Muslim rule over France, Jihad and all, was over; at least for the moment. A new self-made Umayyad ruler, Abd al-Rahman, who a few years earlier had survived a massacre by his fellow Muslims in Basra with his life and little else, came to power in Cordova.

19

THE UMAYYAD TAKEOVER:
SPAIN 756–852

I N MUSLIM SPAIN, AFTER DECADES of incessant misrule, chaos, and an unending parade of passing and usually incompetent rulers— twenty-four in forty-five years, one of whom irritated the local citizenry so much that they crucified him between a dog and a pig—order was installed in the 750s. A new self-made Umayyad ruler, Abd al-Rahman, took over Muslim Spain from its quarreling chieftains in 756.

The last of the Damascus Umayyads came over the straits from North Africa, landed near Gibraltar, and established himself and his dynasty in Spain. All the other Umayyads had disappeared in the previous few years in a great massacre of the family in Syria, Iraq, and Arabia. The Umayyads were to be replaced by a new dynasty of caliphs, the Abbasids, who moved their capital to Baghdad. The name under which this last Spanish representative of the Umayyads has come down in history is Abd al-Rahman. We've just had another Abd al-Rahman in this story, whose name we spelled Abderaman, the one who was killed at the battle of Poitiers. But this new Abd al-Rahman was a winner.

Abd al-Rahman I had been a titleless prince on the run, pursued by a posse of aspiring murderers, when he arrived in Spain to become the ruler of Islam's furthest western possession. Spain's role in this cataclysmic period was rather like that India was destined to play in the nineteenth-century British Empire. It was an exciting place and everyone seemed to be fighting, but no one had a clear explanation why. Perhaps it was because the Jihad has many ramifications and every Muslim in that epoch, when he was fighting for whatever the reason, liked to feel that his was a holy war and would inevitably provide him if he died with a short cut to Paradise.

Abd al-Rahman I was familiar from personal experience with the art of killing on a mass scale. He had recently escaped a massacre with just his life and his determination to keep it and enjoy it for as long as possible. If he was still alive, it was thanks to his decision not to attend a banquet given by the new Abbasid caliph who had just broken the power of the Umayyads and taken over the Muslim empire for himself and the descendants of Abbas, Muhammad's uncle.

The Abbasids believed that as descendants of the Prophet's family, they had more right to the Muslim throne than the descendants of the Prophet's long and stubborn enemy Abu Sufyan. At the same time they also disregarded whatever right the descendants of Muhammad's daughter Fatima and Muhammad's son-in-law Ali might have had. Heredity is a fine principle, but before it can become self-serving it must be selective.

This book is about the Jihad, not about dynastic quarrels among Muslim pretendants, nor about massacres and murders, although inevitably these figure largely in the operations of the Jihad. It is not possible to disassociate the Jihad from its political environment, for politics and religion form one in Islamic life. So at this point we have to linger, if only briefly, on the passing of the century-old Umayyad caliphate (651–750) in Damascus to the Abbasids in Baghdad. It was an operation which was carried out in a massive blood bath by the first Abbasid ruler, Abu al-Abbas who prided himself on his sobriquets "The Shedder of Blood" and "The Butcher." He overthrew the last Umayyad caliph, Marwan II, whose corpse was discovered after a battle near Saida by a seller of pomegranates, who cut off the caliph's head and presented it to the victorious Abbasid general. The brain and other organs in Marwan's head were removed, his tongue was fed to a passing weasel, and the head was embalmed and shipped off in a jeweled box to the new caliph. It's all a bit ghoulish, but very interesting. One does often wonder, however, what all this has to do with religion, with the love of God and man. One is sometimes aghast at the ferocious overtones that religions can sometimes take, and none has done so more than Islam for many centuries, and it is still continuing today, notably in Algeria. The new caliph was, after all, the head of Islam, the deputy on earth of Allah the Merciful. He also happened to be a sadistic mass murderer. Fearing that one of the surviving Umayyads scattered throughout his dominions might lead a revolt against him, al-Abbas had every single Umayyad tracked down and exterminated.

Many of the Umayyads lived in Basra and were easy to locate and kill, and their bodies were afterwards dumped in a field outside the town to be eaten by wolves and wild dogs. Ninety of them, however, managed to evade their executioners. Abbas knew how to deal with them. He claimed the executions were all a terrible mistake, carried out by people who misunderstood his orders, and invited the survivors to a banquet to plead in person for their pardon. All of them came except the future emir of al-Andalus. When all the guests were comfortably ensconced around the table, Abbas summoned his soldiers and executioners, who surrounded the ninety guests and flogged every one of them to death. Carpets were then rolled over the dead or dying victims and Abbas invited his followers to gorge themselves on the uneaten food which was thus served while the guests reclined on the bodies of the last of the Umayyads.

The last of the Umayyads but one, for Abd al-Rahman was not there. Abbas sent his troops to find him and meanwhile in Damascus opened the tombs of every one of the former Umayyad caliphs, and had their bones burned and the ashes scattered to the wind. One, whose body had not yet reached the required state of decomposition, was crucified and exposed to the mockery and taunts of the multitude. Thus the descendants of Abu Sufyan disappeared from the face of the earth. All but Abd al-Rahman. He fled from his farm by the banks of the Euphrates, escaped from his pursuers through Egypt and North Africa, appeared in Spain in 756, met the emir of Cordova in battle, defeated him, claimed all of Islamic Spain as his, and was accepted by the Muslims of al-Andalus as their new emir. "It was like the arrival of the Young Pretender in Scotland in 1745," wrote Stanley Lane-Poole in his *Moors in Spain* (1887).

The new emir naturally broke away from the far-away Abbasid rule in Baghdad, while at first diplomatically recognizing their suzerainty over Islam. In fact, his purpose was to tear Muslim Spain gradually away from the colonial rule of the caliph. The Abbasids sent an expedition to overthrow him. Abd al-Rahman I destroyed their army, executed their leaders, packed their decapitated heads in a large bag with notes attached to their ears identifying each head, and sent the package to the caliph in Baghdad. From then on al-Andalus was safe from the Abbasids.

Abd al-Rahman I started to make Cordova into what became, two or three centuries later, probably the most sophisticated city in Europe. He began to turn Muslim al-Andalus from the western outpost of Islam into what was to become a center of civilization where the representatives of three great Mediterranean cultures—Muslim, Jewish, and Christian—gathered together, sometimes in conviviality, living well together and prospering, sometimes in hostility, clashing to the death in a bizarre Holy War ritual of massacre, assassination, and decapitation.

As Richard Fletcher reminds us, "Moorish Spain was more often a land of turmoil than it was a land of tranquility." Cordova, as large as Constantinople, enjoyed its cultural eminence for only about a century, during a period of tolerance that started with Abd al-Rahman III's accession to power in 912. The city acquired a library of four hundred thousand volumes and a prestigious reputation for scholarship. Students, including a future pope, came from all over the Christian empire to study in this Muslim haven; however, it didn't last. In the end, religious antagonism proved too strong.

During these years that had followed the establishment of the Asturian Christian kingdoms and the arrival of Abd al-Rahman in Spain, Berbers and Arabs had been too busy fighting against each other in ferocious wars to fight the Christians. Abd al-Rahman's arrival in al-Andalus didn't only provoke the threat of the Abbasids from the East, it also brought new threats from the Christian north. The Franks, or the French if you prefer a more modern name, who had defeated the Muslims on the other side of the Pyrenees, were now arriving in Spain as the allies of the Spanish Christian kingdoms. Charlemagne appeared in 778, supposedly as the friend of the Muslim governor of Saragossa who wanted a strong ally to help him against Abd al-Rahman; but when Charlemagne appeared at the gates of Saragossa, they remained closed to him. Charlemagne considered taking Gerona and Barcelona, but decided instead to go back north and fight against his German subjects in Saxony who had rebelled against his rule.

The revered Charlemagne could be as barbaric against his enemies as his Muslim foes were against theirs, and after putting down the Saxon rebellion, he had 4,500 of his disloyal Germanic subjects executed. But in Spain, his march north is mainly remembered for the annihilation of his rear guard, led by the brave Breton knight Roland, in the mountain pass of Roncevalles, probably by a mixed force of Muslims, Basques, Navarese, and Gascons, none of whom had any cause to love the Franks. *The Song of Roland* remains the epic tale of the Spanish adventure of Charlemagne.

Instead of Charlemagne seizing Saragossa, it was Abd al-Rahman who captured Pamplona. From this period on, and for much of the next few centuries, French knights fought alongside the Christian kings of Spain against the Muslims. Fighting Moors and Arabs in Spain became a Christian pastime. The Muslims in Spain, for their part, were often far more occupied in fighting against one another—Arabs against Berbers, Syrians against Yemenites, Arabs against everyone in turn— than fighting against the infidels. This propensity for infighting, which still characterizes the Arabs even today, probably saved Christendom.

Abd al-Rahman I realized that, apart from the mighty Charlemagne, the Christians represented a far smaller threat to Muslim Spain than his own erratic Muslim brothers in the peninsula, each one of whom, such as the governor of Saragossa, was more intent on founding his own little kingdom than in accepting unity under the Umayyad ruler in Cordova. He managed little by little to impose himself on the other Muslim rulers. The *Encyclopaedia Britannica* sums up in a few lines the overall accomplishment of Abd al-Rahman I during his 32-year rule (756–788): "Abd al-Rahman I secured his realm against external attack by defeating armies sent by Charlemagne and the Abbasid caliph. Although he faced a series of rebellions by Muslim Spaniards, Berbers from the mountainous areas, and various Arab clans, his dynasty and authority remained firmly in power." It was left to his successors to carry on the Jihad, but the conquest of Spain by the Muslims was slowly turning into the Reconquest of their land by the Spaniards.

The first of Abd al-Rahman's successors, Hisham I (788–796), was a kind, saintly but lecherous man who became a father at the age of fourteen, helped the poor, and prayed much to Allah. He believed in Islam's divine mission of conquest, and in 792 called for a Holy War against the infidels in the Asturias and in France. One hundred thousand Muslim warriors flocked to his standard, many of them from as far afield as Syria, Arabia, and Algeria. They invaded France, set fire to Narbonne, and marched on Carcassone where they met the Christians in battle, after which, unable to proceed further, they returned to Cordova where Hisham I, with the proceeds of the plunder brought back by his army, built a mosque to the glory of Allah.

The second Umayyad successor, al-Hakam (796–822), was as satanic as his predecessor had been saintly. Only fourteen years younger than his father, al-Hakam kept the Jihad against the Christians on hold during his reign but launched something very similar to it against his Muslim subjects. Aghast at whispers of rebellion among the more sophisticated and intellectual recent converts of Allah in Toledo, he invited them all to a reception in a large new building consisting of four high walls and a large splendid entrance leading into a narrow corridor that turned and twisted and ended in a huge ditch. The eager guests were invited to proceed one by one to the room where the emir's son awaited them. As they reached the ditch they were promptly seized and decapitated.

"Strange, no one has come out yet," remarked a bystander waiting for a friend at the exit gate, which had inexplicably remained closed all day. Suddenly he understood that the strange odor in the air was not from the blood of bullocks slaughtered for roasting. "Woe is me!" the bystander exclaimed. He was a physician and he knew the smell of blood. "That reek ascendeth not from the baked meats of the feast, but from the blood of your murdered brethren," quoted Dozy, or rather his translator, in his best Victorian prose. A blank stupor, he added, fell upon Toledo.

Total tally for the day, according to some sources: five thousand headless Toledans. The estimate seems excessively high. At the rate of five executions a minute, which already sounds like an overestimate, it would have taken nearly sixteen hours, a hard day's work, at that smart rate and without any breaks, to cut off five thousand heads. The executions were carried out singly, one beheading after another, as each guest arrived, anxious to salute the emir's son. The lowest number of appraised victims is given as seven hundred. Whatever the number, "to the converted Christians (to Islam), prominent among those slain, it was a reminder of the fragility of their safety under Islam," wryly comments author Elmer Bendiner. The massacre does have something of the Jihad about it, even if all the victims were converts to Islam, since because of their recent allegiance to Christianity they were undoubtedly regarded with suspicion by the old Muslim establishment. For hundreds of years thereafter the massacre was known in Spanish history as "The Day of the Ditch."

It was just one massacre among many. Al-Hakam's reign flowed with blood. Crucifixion was rife in his realm, and the dying or rotting corpses of dissidents, hanging from their crosses, dotted the Spanish landscape. The leaders of a demonstration protesting against the high price of food in Cordova were crucified. Guards crucified on the spot ten other citizens who were demonstrating against the crucifixions. A few days later three hundred more demonstrators from a Cordova suburb were also crucified and the rest of the population shipped off to Egypt, from where they subsequently colonized Crete and became pirates. The caliph, meanwhile, turned his attention to two uncles whose ambitions he distrusted and had them strangled in a jail cell. Having made Spain safe for the Umayyad dynasty and for the worship of Allah, al-Hakam retired to his harem, where for the rest of his life he wrote poetry and enjoyed the pleasures of procreation. During his reign the Jihad went into reverse, at least in northern Spain, along the frontiers of the Christian kingdoms. In the year 801 Louis I, Charlemagne's son, led armies from Provence, Languedoc, and Burgundy into Catalonia and captured Barcelona after a siege of several months.

For the next two or three hundred years Barcelona became a frontier town, sometimes held by the Christians, sometimes by the Muslims. It did not become a permanent Christian possession until the late eleventh century. In another battle nearby the Muslims defeated a French contingent, sliced off the heads of the living and dead enemy, stacked them into a high pile, and from the top of this makeshift minaret of stinking, rotting French skulls, a muezzin called the faithful to prayers and gave thanks to Allah. There have been moments in Islam's long and eventful history when the religion of the Prophet did seem very close to the Hindu worship of Kali, goddess of death and destruction.

Quiet almost reigned on the northwest Jihad front, near the junction of the Pyrenees and the Atlantic. The Basques, as restless and rebellious in 799 as they are today, killed the Muslim governor of Pamplona and selected in his stead a local man, their compatriot Velasco. With admirable impartiality, the Basques in 816 rose once more in revolt, with the support of the Moors, against the Franks when Louis I threw out the Basque governor of Gascony, Count Jimeno.

Back in Cordova, the French intrusions into Catalonia and points south were not high on al-Hakam's list of priorities. His harem was. Sex was his main pastime, well ahead of the Jihad. It was also the main occupation of his immediate successor, Abd al-Rahman II (822-852), who fathered 97 children, 45 sons and 42 daughters. His biographer says of Abd al-Rahman II that "he loved women," quite obviously, in the light of these figures. In addition to his wives and concubines, he patronized poets, musicians, and men of religion, lived a fulfilling family life in his splendid palace at Cordova among his many wives and children, and enjoyed the quiet and unimportance of his reign. Abd al-Rahman II was probably a very happy man. If he wasn't, he should have been.

This uneventful reign is marred, however, by the strange martyrdom of a dozen or so young Christians of Cordova who deliberately sought, and found, death by insulting the Prophet, an offense punished by decapitation (it still is) in Muslim law. They were all inspired by a priest, Eulogius, who, according to the writer Stanley Lane-Poole in *The Moors in Spain,* "had reduced himself to the ecstatic condition which leads to acts of misguided but heroic devotion." His ultimate aim was to make Muslim Spain part of Christian Spain. One of his early disciples was Flora, the daughter of a mixed Christian-Muslim marriage who was theoretically a Muslim but at heart a Christian. She and another girl, Mary by name, whose brother, a priest, had already been executed, were brought before the local judge, where they reviled Islam as "the work of the devil." After spending a few months in a prison cell, the two young women were executed. So was, among several others, a priest, Perfectus, who had secretly told a group of Muslim acquaintances his views on Muhammad. His head was publicly sliced off as part of the end of the Ramadam festivities. Eleven Christians were executed in the summer of 851. Eulogius managed to survive until 859 when, asked to retract the unpleasant comments he had made on Muhammad, he refused to do so and was condemned to lose his head.

Disregarding the Cordova martyrs, if the Jihad was temporarily stalled in Spain, it had found a new outlet in the Mediterranean. This was on the island of Sicily off the toe of Italy, now destined to become for nearly three hundred years another Muslim fiefdom in Europe, second in importance only to Spain.

20

THE LONG RESISTANCE: SICILY 827–902

THE CONQUEST OF SICILY BY the Arabs began in 827, but the Mediterranean island had by then already been raided numerous times. As we read in an earlier chapter, the first two Arab attacks on Sicily had been launched from Tunisia in 652 and 667. In this last Jihad the Arabs had plundered a huge booty of gold and silver icons studded with precious stones and pearls from the local churches. Unwilling to allow these infidel symbols of worship on holy Muslim ground, the Arabs had shipped the lot to India for the titillation of local Hindu rajahs quite willing, as always, to pay a high price for the precious wares of the West. This was a boom time for the Jihad and many more raids took place in the eighth century against Sicily, which was only weakly defended by the Byzantine emperors. The emperors were themselves busily trying to cope on their home ground of Anatolia, Rumelia, and Italy against the invasions of motley barbarians: Bulgars, Slavs, Khazars, and Lombards, as well as Arabs. In those trying times Sicily did not usually have priority in the defensive strategy of Constantinople.

Most of these raids started from Tunisia, Ifriqiya as it was then called (in due course it gave its name to the continent of Africa), but a few originated from other spots of the Muslim world. One in the year 700 started out from the small island of Pantelleria, another in 730 from Syria. Sicily was for decades the happy hunting ground of Arab raiders who came and went more or less as they pleased. The Byzantines were not always helpless. Once, in fact, in the 660s, they even used Sicily as a base against the Arab dominions. The energetic emperor Constans II, grandson of Heraclius, determined to check the Arab incursions into Italy and Sicily (he also dreamed of making Rome capital of the world again), established his headquarters in the Sicilian city of Syracuse. Another of his aims was, from this nearby base, to prevent the Arabs landing in Greece, which would have meant the encirclement of the heart of his empire on the Bosporus. It availed him little. The Lombards went on occupying large chunks of Italy and founded the duchy of Beneventum in the south of the peninsula, while the Arabs devastated big areas of Anatolia. To crown this series of misfortunes, Constans II was finally murdered by rebellious soldiers while visiting Sicily, but his defense of the island had at least delayed the occupation of Greece by the Muslims until a few hundred years later. (The Muslims who were to overrun Greece in the mid-1300s were not Arabs but Turks, who were second to none in their loyalty to the Prophet.)

It was in 827 that the isolated Arab raids into Sicily ended and turned instead into a massive Jihad. As in Spain, the invasion of Sicily took place with the participation of a renegade Christian nobleman largely motivated by the love of a woman. Unlike Count Julian in Tangiers who was a soldier, the Sicilian rebel Euphemius was a sailor. Moreover, he was not inspired by concern for his daughter, but rather by love for a young nun.

Euphemius, the Byzantine naval commander in Sicily, had apparently fallen madly in love with Sister (as I suppose we can call her) Omoniza, and eloped with her, much to the chagrin of the local ecclesiastical dignitaries who, appalled at the violation of her vow of chastity, complained to the Byzantine emperor, Michael II. The emperor, a stickler for the proprieties of life, ordered Admiral Euphemius to have his nose (Gibbon says his tongue) cut off, a fairly usual punishment of those times, unpleasant but still less drastic for Euphemius than the loss of the offending portion of his anatomy would have been. Admiral Euphemius, who had no intention of losing even his nose, summoned his crews to mutiny against the Emperor. The rebellious sailors met and defeated in battle the armies of the governor of Sicily. The fat was, so to speak, now in the fire.

The Admiral realized that he could not take on the Byzantine empire single-handed, so he dashed over to Ifriqiya and offered Sicily to the local emir on condition that he was given the title of emperor of Sicily (but paying tribute to the Muslims of course). The understanding

Arabs offered him the support of a large army; the muezzins called from the top of their minarets for a Holy War, and the conquest of Sicily was now prepared amidst the chants and the prayers of the holy men of Islam. As in Spain, behind the Muslim Jihad also lurked the image of a wronged Christian woman. Wronged by a Christian man. It was a case once again of *cherchez la femme.*

The Muslim expeditionary force, ten thousand men in all, sailed in a considerably larger armada than Tarik's had been—between seventy and a hundred ships. To stress the Holy War character of this new campaign against the infidels, command was given to one al-Furat, a noted religious leader and Koranic expert who, however, had little experience of military affairs. The Sword, at least in theory, was to take second place to the Book. The invading force, heavily armed and ready to slay and pray and rob and rape was largely made up of the usual Berbers and Arabs but also included some Persian volunteers and numerous Andalusian warriors who had been thrown out of Cordova and had finally settled in Crete. A few scholars were recruited for the probable purpose of explaining the Koran to the foreigners awaiting conversion to Islam on the other side of the straits. Admiral Euphemius's dissenting fleet came under the overall Muslim command.

One early summer day, in June 827, the invaders landed at Mazara, a Euphemius stronghold on the south coast of Sicily. The soldiers of Islam—aided by Admiral Euphemius' troubled Christian sailors who were wondering why they were fighting against their own folk—defeated the Byzantine army led by one Balata. The conquest of Sicily by the Arabs had begun. One of its first casualties was the confused Admiral Euphemius. Perhaps appalled by his act of treachery, he deserted his Arab allies and returned to the Byzantine Greek cause, urged the Sicilians to resist the invaders, and made his way to Castrogiovanni where he hopefully expected the local Sicilian population would hail him as their new emperor. Instead, they killed him.

Unlike the Spanish invasion, the Sicilian campaign was a slow occupation, marked by much fighting and many massacres. It took the Saracens seventy-five years to conquer the island. There were no Jews, no exploited peasants as there had been in Spain who, persecuted by their rulers, would help the invaders. Fighting was hard and bitter. Sieges lasted months. In the mountains, villages were turned into fortresses. The Arabs took Palermo in 831, made it their Sicilian capital and, it is said, built five hundred mosques to mark their victory and honor the Prophet. They took Castrogiovanni, the present-day Enna, where they massacred eight thousand people in 859. Nearby Malta was raided in 869. Syracuse was taken in 870 after a siege of nearly a month. The defenders of Syracuse were expecting a Byzantine fleet to come to their relief, but the naval commander decided the best way to fight the Jihad would be to build a church in honor of the Virgin Mary instead of going to sea. So he ordered his crews to disembark their ships and start building and by the time the church was finished, Syracuse had been taken by the Muslims. One after another, spread over half a century, the Sicilian towns fell to the Arab invaders. Taormina, now the most famed resort in Sicily, was one of the last in 902.

Islamic piety and love of Allah sometimes took strange forms. Edward Gibbon, who had a definite taste for the salacious anecdote, recalls one such instance in the south Italian town of Salerno, where the leader of an Arab invasion force gave an ecclesiastical twist to his instinct for rape.

> It was to the amusement of the Saracens to profane, as well as to pillage, the monasteries and churches. At the siege of Salerno a Musulman chief spread his couch on the communion table, and on that altar sacrificed each night the virginity of a Christian nun. As he wrestled with a reluctant maid, a beam on the roof was accidentally or dexterously thrown down on his head: and the death of the lustful emir was imputed to the wrath of Christ. (*Decline and Fall of the Roman Empire,* vol. 5, chap. 46)

Islam provided suitable motives to its soldiers for the pursuit of the Jihad, plunder and travel among them. The Muslims were great travelers, as their far-flung conquests indicate. The Jihad also had much to offer those who loved power and adventure. The islands of Corsica, Malta, Sardinia, Pantelleria (where the Arabs kidnapped three hundred monks), and the Baleares, and among the towns and cities Bari, Ancona, Naples, Genoa, Ravenna, Ostia, and even Rome itself were all for a time pillaged or occupied by the Saracens. Human beings became a cheap and abundant commodity. In Rome, in 846, the Jihad reached its climax. There the Muslims even looted the churches of St. Peter and St. Paul, and the pope had to buy off the invaders with the promised tribute of 25,000 silver coins a year. Pope Leo IV then ordered the construction of the Leonine Wall around the city to protect St. Peter's from further assault.

In Sicily itself the Arab occupation lasted 264 years, and Islam was firmly implanted among the population, although some regions of the island, Jihad or no Jihad, never relinquished their Christian faith. The Arabs contributed greatly to Sicilian life, arts, and culture. Some people maintain the Mafia arose as a movement of resistance and of protection against the Muslim despoilers (others say later Norman or French invaders) who, year in and year out, went on looting the island people until many of them were reduced to beggary. The Arabs introduced oranges and lemons, cotton, mulberry trees and the silk worm, sugar cane, hemp, and the date palm. In 1091, after a thirty-year war, another warrior race defeated the Saracens and took over the island— the Normans. Their cousins, some twenty-seven years previously, in 1066, had invaded and occupied another island on the other, and colder, side of Europe. It was called England.

21

THE FRENCH RIVIERA CAMPAIGN:
ST. TROPEZ 898–973

IN THE LATE NINTH CENTURY a small party of Arab raiders—originally there were about twenty of them—suddenly appeared again in France, from the sea. They landed at an entirely unexpected spot, near St. Tropez, famous in more recent years for Brigitte Bardot, its yachts, and its nude beaches. These first Arabs discovered St. Tropez by accident. They were on a looting operation and were blown ashore by wind and waves. For the next few decades they raided, plundered, and raped their way from St. Tropez inland all the way north to Switzerland, perhaps even into Germany, and east into Piedmont in Italy.

St. Tropez, or a village very near it, was not then known by the name that has made it famous in our time, but has come down in history under the name of Fraxinetum, perhaps the name of some former Roman hamlet in the vicinity. It is believed Fraxinetum itself was on the hill site where the village of Garde-Freinet stands today, with its few scattered remains of ramparts and deep trenches in the ground that may once have been a moat. According to accounts of the period, which are few and not usually reliable, some twenty Saracen warriors and sailors from Islamic Spain, hoodlums described as pirates, were caught in a boat by a storm and made for the nearest shelter, a wide bay where St. Tropez now welcomes its international jet-setting guests, millionaire yachtsmen, or penniless backtrackers.

From the reports that have come down to us about these freebooters, it seems unlikely that they were animated by the religious spirit of the Jihad. Plunder and robbery were probably solely on their minds, but they undoubtedly did not forget their daily prayers to Mecca. They looked around them, the heavily forested landscape seemed attractive, the trees running all the way north toward a distant line of blue mountains a dozen or so miles away. The sky was as deep blue as in al-Andalus and the scent of flowers and wild plants was in the air. The raiders promptly massacred the bewildered inhabitants of a nearby village and went off into the mountains to explore.

The names of these early visitors to the French Riviera have not come down to us, but we know that their short journey on foot into the interior and to the top of the nearest hill, and the glimpse it gave them of the surrounding countryside, convinced them that here was Paradise on earth and that they should establish their base right there by the seashore. To the north, east, and west lay rolling forests, hills and mountains, free of towns with just a few scattered small and defenseless villages here and there, like the one they had already destroyed. Beyond, they knew, lay towns and churches to be plundered, maybe for the glory of Allah, but certainly for the enrichment of themselves. To the south lay the sea, a highway to conquest. They were now the lords of the land, but they were too few to take it and hold it. The call went out to other Muslims along the Mediterranean rim, to North Africa, Spain, Syria, Egypt, and Sicily: "Come and join us." Soon their compatriots converged on St. Tropez from all over the Mediterranean, ready to take over this empty land. They were just like the Pilgrim Fathers who landed in Cape Cod in 1620, except that there were no Indians around. Provence was their fief. It remained so for nearly a century. The Muslims took it over and terrified the locals. "One of them can put a thousand men to flight, two more than two thousand," muttered the terrorized local peasants and fishermen about the new arrivals.

The Saracens were everywhere. There seemed to be no pattern in their career of conquest. The Alps, beyond the hills to the east, and the gorges of the Dauphine were their first targets. In due course their armed bands roamed further afield, plundered Piedmont, took Turin, burned the churches, the convents, the monasteries and libraries, chased the population back toward the mountains, and slaughtered the Christians in such numbers that a book published in Turin described one place where the Christians died as "the Field of Martyrs."

By 911 the Arabs had closed all the passes across the Alps and cut off France from Italy, so that the archbishop of Narbonne had to cancel his trip to the pope in Rome. Another Saracen group was ravaging the coast of Languedoc, to the west of the Rhone. The main church in Marseille was destroyed by a roving band of ne'er-do-wells who went on to Aix-en-Provence where, enraged by the resistance of a few brave students, they flayed them all alive. The bishop of Aix wisely took refuge in flight and did not stop running until he reached Reims, where he begged for hospitality from his brother bishop. The rich people of Avignon fled to Burgundy for safety. In the Alps, Sisteron and Gap were set on fire and destroyed. At Embrun the archbishop and most of the inhabitants were casually slaughtered. The Italian coast around Genoa was not spared the Saracen visits. In Genoa itself, hundreds of men who had tried to resist were tortured and killed after they had surrendered, and the woman and children were enslaved. Next it was Switzerland's turn. Bands of raiders ravaged the valleys of the Grisons and of the Valais, turned west toward Lake Geneva, where they founded a village they called Fraxinetum, later renamed Ferney, later still renamed Ferney-Voltaire in honor of the French philosopher and writer who made his home there. The Jura mountains were their next target. Terrified, the Queen of Burgundy, of which the Jura then formed part, fled to the safety of a fortress in nearby Neuchatel.

Back south on the Mediterranean, in 940, the inhabitants of Toulon and Fréjus, attacked by an army from Fraxinetum, fled for their lives into the mountains. The Moors in the St. Tropez bay found an unexpected ally in Hugues, count of Provence, who gave them his protection if, in return, they kept the Alps passes closed to his rival, Berenger, king of Lombardy. One of the few writers of this epoch whose works have survived, Liutprand, severely admonished the count of Provence for his alliance with the invaders and castigated him in powerful words of reproof, particularly from a commoner to a nobleman. "You dare to let our pious men perish and offer shelter to the Moorish rogues! Hugues, you wretch, do you not blush to lend your shadow to those who shed human blood and live from plunder? What can I say? May you be consumed by lightning, or broken into a thousand pieces and plunged into eternal chaos!"

After fifty years in France many of the Moors, particularly those who lived on the Côte d'Azur, had begun to forget about the Jihad, had settled down on the Riviera and married local women, under whose influence they started going to mass and were even beginning to till the soil, an occupation always previously considered utterly contemptible by Arabs. But not all were turning to these domestic tasks. Up in the mountains, more attuned to the Bedouin code of plunder, many more lived by "demanding tribute" from (i.e., robbing) travelers making their way between France and Italy. Those who did not have money to pay were murdered on the spot. "The number of Christians they killed is so great that only he who has written their names in the Book of Life can know of the number," wrote Liutprand.

From their original bastion at Fraxinetum, the Muslims had spread all over southeastern France and over much of Italy and Switzerland. An Arab army corps was stationed in Nice, Grenoble was also in their hands, and in the Piedmont they had even given the (seemingly popular) name of Fraxinetum to a village near Casal, by the Po River. In Switzerland they reached the town of Saint Gall, near Lake Constance, and from there they may have spread into what is now Germany. From Germany, the Holy Roman Emperor Otto I (called "The Great") in 956 sent an envoy to Abd al-Rahman III, who was considered (at least by Liutprand) to have placed Fraxinetum under his protection, and asked him to put an end to the Jihad raids on France and Italy. Tantalizingly, we do not know what the answer was, for Liutprand's account of the meeting ends right there, in the middle of a sentence. At least one other Muslim base of operations was closed down a few years later when the Saracens were chased out of Mount Saint-Bernard.

The presence of the Arabs and the Moors in these cold and snowy Alpine regions, so far from the hot desert and the warm Mediterranean, seems an anachronism. There is no doubt that in the tenth century they were a great threat to western Europe, not so much by their numbers, which were never excessive, but by their ubiquity and by the divisions in the ranks of the Italian and French Christian realms—exactly as in Spain—who opposed them. Inexorably, the Muslims were being pushed out of their recently and superficially conquered lands. In 965 they were forced to abandon Grenoble, in 972 the Muslim chief in charge of the Sisteron district surrendered to the Christians and asked to be baptized. The same year also saw the liberation of Gap. William, Count of Provence, after a first battle near Draguignan, laid siege to a nearby castle which surrendered after a few days, and most of its defenders again were converted to Christianity. The harsh code of Islam failed to fit into the balmy air of Provence. Even the Muslim conquerors found Christianity more congenial, and they must have decided that the the Côte d'Azur was well worth a mass.

William of Provence, to thank one of his most able lieutenants, Grimaldi, a Genoese, offered him a tract of land near St. Tropez which is still in the family's hands and is called Port Grimaud. The Grimaldi family also later acquired another tract a few miles further east along the coast. They called it Monaco. Subsequently the first lord of Monaco married a young Genoese lady, presumably of good birth and fortune, called Pomela Fregosi, who, several hundred years before Grace Kelly, became the first Princess of Monaco. The Grimaldis, the oldest existing reigning house in Europe, are still Princes of Monaco, but the Fregosi girl has, alas, long been forgotten.

PART FIVE

FOR SPAIN,
MY HUMBLE DUTY

22

THE CORPSES OF SIMANCAS:
SPAIN 912–961

INTERESTING AS THESE JIHAD INTERLUDES in France, Switzerland, and
Italy may be, they are only peripheral in these Dark Ages to the
main European struggle between Islam and Christendom which was
taking place in Spain, and continued to do so for several more centuries. After the battle of Poitiers/Tours, it is in Spain that, finally, the
religious future of Europe—the Crescent or the Cross—was fought.
The conflict sometimes did lapse into ambiguity, when Christian kings
allied themselves to Moorish rulers to fight against rival Christian sovereigns and similarly Muslims went into battle side by side with Christian to fight against their Muslim brothers who had become political
enemies.

To the combatants, however murky the contest might often have
appeared when they fought on the side of their enemies against their
own kinsmen, their ultimate war aim was always clear: the triumph of
Christianity on one side, the triumph of Islam for the other. In many
ways the Jihad, as it was to the Muslims, and La Reconquista, as it was
to the Christians, was also an immense and confused civil war in which
Christian fought against Muslim, Spaniard against Spaniard, Spaniard
(whether Christian or Muslim) against Arab and Moor, Moor against
Arab, and Arab (of one tribe back in Arabia) against Arab (of another
tribe back in Arabia).

For a couple of centuries, particularly at the time of the

Almoravids and the Almohads, the Reconquista turned into what was largely a European-African war; but the religious contest—Muhammad versus Jesus Christ—was always present. In the end, because the Christians won, Spain and most of Europe, unlike the Muslim-ruled Near East and North Africa, remain to the Muslims Dar-al-Harb, the Land of War. In the days of the Reconquista, Spain was already so known to the Moors of Morocco and Algeria, where pious young Muslims eager for the martyr's crown went to fight and die to gain in Paradise what the *Encyclopedia of Islam* prudishly describes as "the peculiar privileges" awaiting the martyrs of Islam.

Disunity has been a frequent Arabian hallmark and we must ventilate, but not too much, these inter-Muslim and inter-Christian wars which were frequent and which finally had nothing to do with the Jihad except to distract our attention from it. One example, from Reinhart Dozy's masterly work on Islamic Spain, first published in 1861, shows all that need be said on these diversionary wars among the Muslims. In 903, we read, the Moorish Sultan's army fighting against fellow Moors and Arabs "captured Jaen; in 905 it won the battle of Guadalbollon against Ibn Hafsun and Ibn Mastana; in 906 it took Canete from the Beni al-Khali; in 907 it compelled Archidona to pay tribute; in 909 it deprived Ibn Mastana of Luque; in 910 it captured Baeza, while in the following year the inhabitants of Iznajar revolted against their lord, Fadl ibn Salama, Ibn Mastana's son-in-law, and slaying him, sent his head to the Sultan."

In Spain, however clear cut the final objectives of the Reconquest, the motives of the immediate fighting were often obscure. For centuries the Christian kingdoms of Castile, Navarre, Leon, and Aragon, led by rough-neck pretendants, more gang leaders than princes, fought just as violently against one another as they did against the Muslims. Similarly, the Muslims' violent wars against one another worked to the immense benefit of the Christian realms to the north, whose kings were always ready to do battle anew for God, Spain, and Saint James. La Reconquista, in its own way, was as holy (or unholy) as the Jihad, because Spain, for those who fought for it, was a holy cause for which it was fitting for a Spanish soldier to die.

This was not an exceptional period of troubles, only an average one. Civil wars interspersed among the campaigns of the Jihad raged up and down the Iberian peninsula for centuries. We read, for instance, that one Lope, whose father, Mohammed ibn Lope, had been killed in the siege of Muslim-held Saragossa, "employed his troops in ceaseless wars with his neighbors including the lord of Huesca, the King of Leon, the Count of Barcelona, the Count of Pallars and the King of Navarre—until he was killed in an encounter with the last in 907." In early medieval Europe, war was a way of life for hundreds of years.

It is in this Spain of intemperate, haphazard, and incoherent warfare that the greatest of all its Umayyad rulers, the short, fair-haired, blue-eyed, and bow-legged Abd al-Rahman III (912–961), decided at the age of thirty-one to bring sanity into the political life of his country before plunging into the Jihad. Within ten days of his accession to the emirate, Abd al-Rahman III had his first decapitated head of a foe nailed to the door of his palace as a warning to local troublemakers. There was a rebellious mood in al-Andalus at the time of his takeover which had to be mastered. Abd al-Rahman III had followed as emir the particularly loathsome Abdallah (882–912) who, fearing their influence, had poisoned two of his brothers, murdered a third, and even killed two of his own sons who, he feared, were planning to take over al-Andalus. Abdallah was, of course, even more cruel to his Christian enemies. When the Castle of Polei, defended by Spanish soldiers, some Muslim and some Christian, had surrendered, he recruited the Muslims into his own army and ordered the Christians, about a thousand in number, to all be decapitated unless they converted to Islam. Only one did; all the others were killed.

Abd al-Rahman's first objective was to restore the authority of Cordova over his mutually squabbling and fighting underlings, princes and lesser emirs, who had turned the Muslim emirate of al-Andalus into an untidy mosaic of tiny states, each calling for the Jihad against the enemy to the north, but all fighting against each other instead. The Spanish landscape was dotted with mountain forts in the Sierras where independent lords, more brigands then noblemen, defied the world around them, fought savage campaigns, and ravaged the land. Abd al-Rahman tackled the man he considered his greatest enemy, the rebel Ibn Hafsun, the most powerful of the insurgents, who, from his fiefdom of Bobastro in southern Spain in the mountains behind Marbella, controlled seventy fortresses scattered among the provinces of Elvira, Granada, and Jaen.

Ibn Hafsun claimed to have returned to the Christian faith of his Spanish forbears, so the campaign waged against him had a little bit of the Jihad about it—not too much, because many of Ibn Hafsun's lieutenants remained Muslim. It was essentially a movement of patriotic Spaniards, some Christian and some Muslim, against the foreign dom-

ination of their country by Arabs and Berbers. Ibn Hafsun's rebellion
ended soon after his death, unbeaten, in 928. As a lapsed Muslim, his
body was taken out of its tomb by the victorious Moors and publicly
nailed to a stake. Other rebel forces were also attacked and beaten one
by one. Abd al-Rahman III captured the mutinous cities of Seville,
Algeciras, Sidonia, and Carmona. In 929, he transformed his emirate,
then still under the authority of the Baghdad Abbasid caliphate, into an
independent caliphate with him as caliph and the title of "He Who
Fights Victoriously for the Religion of Allah."

For along with his campaigns against insurgent cities and mountain lords, Abd al-Rahman III had already led a few years previously
the Jihad against the Christian kingdoms of northern Spain. The first
enemy had been the kingdom of Leon whose king, Ordono II, had in
913 taken and sacked Talavera and massacred the Muslim population
of the city. The anti-Jihad was frequently as violent and inhumane as
the Jihad itself.

Ordono II, an admirable but ruthless soldier, liked to lead forays
into Muslim territory and come back with a lot of booty and a few heads
to nail to the church doors of Leon. In retaliation, Abd al-Rahman III
had sent an army to take the fortress of San Estevan de Gormaz under
the command of an old general by the name of Ibn Abi Abda, who was
killed when his soldiers were routed. "The hills, the forests and the
plains from the Douro to Atienza were strewn with the corpses" of the
Muslim soldiers who had been cut down in their flight by the pursuing
Christians. Not discouraged, Abd al-Rahman III sent more expeditions
to the north, secured some minor victories, and in 920 defeated the
combined armies of Leon and Navarre and sacked Pamplona. During a
large part of his reign, the Umayyad sovereign was frustrated on his
northern, Christian frontier by the fear that he might be attacked, while
fighting in the north, by his co-religionists from Africa in the south. So
his Jihad, to the great relief of his northern enemies, was invariably a
half-hearted affair. He feared too much a stab in the back from his
fellow Muslims from the other side of the Mediterranean.

The culmination of Ordono's dithering policy was the catastrophic
defeat of the caliphate army at the battle of Simancas, a few miles from
Valladolid, when the cavalry of the new Leonese king, Ramiro II,
trounced the Arab infantry. The Arab general Nadja (actually he was
not an Arab at all, but a Slav) was killed, the viceroy of Saragossa was
taken prisoner, and the caliph barely managed to decamp with an
escort of forty-nine loyal followers. Shaken by this near-capture, Abd

al-Rahman III decided there and then never to appear again in person on a battlefield. Almost unbelievably, Simancas was the first important victory by the Christians in Spain since Covadonga, nearly 220 years earlier. The Conquest by the Arabs had been a three-year series of quick victories. The Reconquest by the Spaniards was a slow grinding process which was to go on for another 460 years.

Historians usually agree that Spain could have rapidly liberated itself from its uninvited Berber and Arab guests after Simancas, but the Spaniards were too busy fighting and quarreling among themselves to spare more than a passing thought for La Reconquista. Eastern Leon, soon to be transformed into the kingdom of Castile, was trying to free itself from central Leonese suzerainty. Navarre was also engaged in some obscure conflict with Leon. When Ramiro II died, his two sons began fighting over the succession to the throne of Leon, and the Reconquista was temporarily shelved again.

For the Christian, the reconquest of their country now turned into an absurd farce while Sancho the Fat, one of the pretenders to the Leon throne, decided he must go with his grandmother Theuda to Cordova for his health. Sancho was so fat he couldn't get on a horse and, even to walk, had to be supported by a male nurse. Abd al-Rahman III had suggested that he come to al-Andalus for treatment. So, accompanied by his grandmother, Sancho the Fat made the 500-mile journey to the al-Andalus capital where, on arrival, he paid personal homage to the caliph who in return graciously put his personal Jewish physician, Hasdai ibn Ciprut, at the service of the overweight Christian prince. Hasdai ibn Ciprut was the most renowned physician of his epoch. During the reign of Abd al-Rahman III, Cordova had become not only the intellectual but also the scientific capital of Europe, where the great minds of the Muslim, Jewish, and Christian worlds could meet in easy discussion and conferences, whatever their differences in the religious field might be. It is also under Abd al-Rahman III that the magnificent royal palace of Medina az-Zahra, with its 4,300 marbled columns, its fountains, its flowers and gardens, and its arcades and walls encrusted with jewels and precious stones, was built outside Cordova as a testimonial to the glory of the Spanish Umayyad dynasty.

More prosaically, for the time being, in these wondrous surroundings, Sancho the Fat had to get rid of his surplus blubber. After six months of treatment, the roly-poly monarch, although still not exactly sylph-like, was able to climb onto a horse again; and with his grandmother and his retinue of courtiers and soldiers, he rode back to Pamplona. Thankful for his new figure, he repaid his Muslim hosts by accompanying the Arab army to the siege and the taking of Zamora. The following year, in 960, the Muslims captured the capital city of Leon and ceremoniously installed Sancho on the throne of his kingdom. The Christian king now felt uncomfortably indebted to his Muslim partner; however, Abd al-Rahman III eased the situation by dying the next year. The men of the Jihad and of the Reconquista sharpened their weapons and awaited in watchful serenity the future, whatever it might be.

23

AURORA'S LOVER: SANTIAGO DE COMPOSTELA 967–1002

A N UNSCRUPULOUS YOUNG ROGUE'S SEDUCTION of the prettiest wife of the homosexual caliph Hakam II, the lovely young Basque girl, Aurora, paved the seducer's way to power and to the subsequent bloodiest campaigns of the Jihad. The persuasive villain who won his way to Queen Aurora's heart and bed was Ibn Abi Amir, known to the world as Almanzor, the terror of the Christian kingdoms, future vizier, future prefect, future general, future political and military leader of al-Andalus, future conqueror of Santiago de Compostela, of Barcelona, and of Pamplona, protector of philosophers and, with Abd al-Rahman III, the greatest leader Islamic Spain ever produced.

After taking the town of Zamora from the Christians in 981, putting four thousand Christian captives to death, destroying a thousand villages and hamlets in the region, and besieging the town of Leon, Ibn Abi Amir styled himself, until the day he died, Almanzor, "Victorious by the Grace of God," victorious against the enemies of his caliph, of Muhammad, and of Islam. The Christians called him Almanzor.

From the youngest recruits to the most honored generals, the Jihad was always the inspiration of every Muslim male yearning for fame, power, honors, plunder, slaves, and virgins. Sex, if he survived, was the warrior's reward in his tent after battle, or even right there on the field. Sex, if he was killed, awaited him immediately in Paradise. It was an all-round no-lose situation for every Muslim man of spirit who was capable

149

of bearing arms, fighting, and worshiping Allah. With this promise of felicity, Almanzor, like all great Arab war leaders, was never short of recruits ready to fight and die. For the Muslim warrior was always a winner. He always got the girl in the end, whether he was alive or dead.

Almanzor was always a winner, too. His distinguished ancestor, a Yemenite he claimed, had landed in Spain two centuries earlier with Tarik. This was a high distinction in Islamic Spain, rather like nowadays having a convict ancestor in Australia, preferably one who came out with the First Fleet. Almanzor first earned his living by preparing letters to the caliph for illiterate petitioners. He next worked as a clerk in the Cordova law court, then moved on to the stewardship of a property belonging to the 5-year-old son of the caliph and of Aurora, his favorite wife. The year was 967 and Almanzor was then twenty-six years old. From then on, the career of the young man moved steadily up. He took on the management of Aurora's properties and she did all that was necessary to further his career. "The intimacy between them grew so close that it provided food for scandal," Dozy discreetly tells us. The gay caliph cared not a whit what his wife did. With Aurora's backing, Almanzor became Master of the Mint and steward to the young future caliph al-Hisham II, then was sent to Morocco as chief justice with orders to see that the generals stopped their swindling on the side. Back in al-Andalus, Almanzor became vizier, theoretically the second most important man in the caliphate but in fact the most. The new caliph, al-Hisham II, Aurora's son, was persuaded to sign away most of his rights to Almanzor and retire to his harem while Almanzor took over the running of the state.

To pretend a religious fervor which he did not feel, but which was necessary to obtain the support of the mullahs, Almanzor copied out the whole of the Koran and ostentatiously carried it around with him on all the military campaigns which he now undertook against the Christians. The Jihad was booming once again, and to the north the Christian kings and counts of Aragon, Castile, Leon, and Navarre prepared once again to meet the Muslim onrush. Ramiro III, king of Leon, Garcia Fernandez, count of Castile, and the king of Navarre uneasily drew together to try to stem the approaching avalanche. They failed. The Saracens, led by Almanzor in person, defeated the Christians at Rueda, southwest of Simancas, and every Christian soldier of the four thousand who surrendered, with the exception of one who abjured his faith, had his head cut off. Almanzor next pushed on to the capital city of Leon, but the arrival of winter put an end to the fighting, and he returned to Cordova.

La Reconquista and the Jihad, when political necessities arose, were often overlooked in favor of internecine warfare. The kingdom of Leon split into two camps, one favoring Ramiro III, the other his cousin Bermudo. Almanzor, as cunning as a fox, helped both sides to destroy each other and Leon became—at least for a while—a tributary of al-Andalus. Catalonia was next on the Muslim hit list. Muslims in the past had been very wary of attacking Catalonia because of its close connection with powerful neighboring France. No such concern hindered Almanzor's thinking. He knew France was at that time in a state of disorder bordering on anarchy and would not interfere in Catalonia. He was right. Accompanied by a troupe of artists and poets, Almanzor set forth on the conquest of Catalonia and laid siege to Barcelona on July 5, 984. It lasted five days. The usual massacre followed. Most of the leading citizens and soldiers were summarily executed, the survivors enslaved, and the city plundered and burned. Almanzor enjoyed a leisurely return to Cordova through Murcia, where, in the home of one of the great estate owners of the region, he soaked himself in a bath of rose water and, to show his gratitude, reduced his host's taxes. Back in Cordova, to show his piety to the credulous Muslim multitudes, the mighty Almanzor, pickaxe and trowel in hand, slaved in the sun like a bricklayer on the new mosque that was going up in the city. The deceitful art of public relations was already flourishing in those distant times. The Jihad called him again north where King Bermudo II of Leon had recently expelled a Muslim garrison. The campaign was deadly for the Leonese. The kingdom was devastated. The capital, protected by its 20-foot thick walls, withstood the Muslim siege at first; but, when a breach was made near one of the gates, the Muslim soldiery poured in and the massacre in the name of Allah began.

Back home among his own, Almanzor discovered that one of his nearest (his son, 22-year-old Abdallah), but not dearest (he suspected that he was not the father of the boy), was involved in a plot against him. Anxious to put as much distance as possible between himself and his father, young Abdallah fled to the court of Castile where he remained, a refugee in silk robes, for a year. Anxious not to provoke Abdallah's powerful father, the Castilian ruler sent him back to al-Andalus. Abdallah's Muslim guards beheaded him on the way home. The young man, his biographers say, showed no fear in his last moments. "He leaped lightly from his mule and with a tranquil mien, yielded his neck, without a tremor, to the fatal stroke." Anything but a grieving father, Almanzor marched north again on a couple of Jihads,

one against Castile for sheltering his son, and one against Leon for har-
boring a fellow plotter of Abdallah. The victory, once again, went to
Islam. Soon afterward Aurora came back into Almanzor's life, but no
longer as his paramour. On the contrary, appalled at her son's decline,
she urged him to assert himself as caliph against Almanzor; al-Hisham
was more interested in copulation than combat and preferred the com-
forts of his harem to the rigors of a military campaign.

Almanzor, to show his true blue mettle, went north again, this time
to the most revered western shrine of Christendom, Santiago de Compostela, where the apostle Saint James is reputed to be buried. Of all
Almanzor's campaigns, this has remained the most famous and retains,
even to this day, the full flavor of the power of the Jihad. To quote a
Muslim scholar, Compostela was to the Christians what the Kaaba is
to the Muslims. The Muslim crusaders marched out of Cordova on July
3, 997, advanced north through Portugal, reached Compostela on
August 11, found the town empty and all the inhabitants gone save for
an old priest kneeling by the tomb of St. James. "What dost thou
here?" asked Almanzor, puzzled. "I am praying to St. James," replied
the old man, not at all impressed by the Muslim soldiery. "Pray on,"
said Almanzor, who ordered his soldiers to leave the old priest alone
and to respect the shrine, but to burn the town.

Almanzor The Victorious marched back to Cordova with thousands of captured Christians, who were made to carry the bells of
Compostela all the way to the Umayyad capital, where they were ceremoniously installed in the mosque to be used, suspended from the
ceiling, as lamps. Another Jihad campaign followed. Like so many of
Almanzor's military adventures, it combined political and religious
purposes. Almanzor marched with his army as far as the Rioja region,
from where so many fine wines come, reached Caneles, destroyed a
monastery or two here and there, then, ill, started on the journey home
in a litter. "Of the 20,000 soldiers in my army, not one suffers like I
do," he cried out in pain and anguish. On the way home, on August 12,
1002, at the age of 61, he died. "Almanzor has died and was buried in
hell," wrote a delighted Christian monk when he heard the news of his
death. But the priest may have been wrong. A rejuvenated Almanzor
may instead be frolicking in the Muslim paradise with his houris,
although unbridled copulation hardly seems Almanzor's style. Hopefully, he and Aurora are friends again.

24

EXEUNT THE UMAYYADS: SPAIN 1085

T HE BEGINNING OF THE ELEVENTH century, just after the death of the formidable Almanzor, might be the right moment to cast a quick look at the Muslim empire, of which the Spanish Umayyad caliphate was then one of the brightest jewels. Islamic Spain was also a de facto colonial power ruling from Cordova over much of what is today Morocco and the western part of Algeria, where Almanzor had once been sent to curb the corruption of the Umayyad generals. The dominant Abbasid caliphate in Baghdad was split in two, the pro-Shiite Buhaywids in Iraq and Persia, and the Damanids further east on the borders of China. In Syria, Egypt, and much of North Africa, a new caliphate had arisen, the Fatimids. Sicily and the Hejaz were also in their domain. The Fatimids claimed, as descendants of Fatima, Muhammad's daughter, to have a better right to lead Islam than the Abbasids, who were only descended from Muhammad's obscure cousin, Abbas. Islam was in shambles, disunity reigned. Islam had almost ceased to be a religion and instead had become a battlefield for competing, power-hungry dynasties.

Within Muslim Spain the seeds of disunity were also sprouting more strongly than ever and the Umayyad dynasty was approaching its total and final collapse, which was to occur in 1031, to be replaced for the next fifty-five years with the so-called "taifas," a disparate collection of some thirty little Muslim states, each with its own king, each centered on some important (or even unimportant) city. Within Christian Spain the seeds of unity were beginning to sprout. Navarre and Castile joined forces, conquered Leon, and Ferdinand I of Castile became, in addition to his own realm, King of Leon as well. Thus, slowly, Christian Spain was becoming one country, although Aragon and Catalonia to the east still lived on as separate entities; and, in the west, the Portuguese, after taking Coimbra, were gradually creating their own country.

For those, Muslim or Christian, who were motivated above all else by the Jihad or its Spanish Catholic corollary, the Reconquest, these were not great times for either the aggressive Jihad or the expanding Reconquista. Aggressiveness and expansionism were directed inward against their own kinsmen rather than outward against the enemy. Within al-Andalus, chaos was king. The Umayyad caliphs, with Hisham II, had become became mere figureheads, and various rivals were trying to wrest power from one another. For some twenty years outright civil war raged through the Muslim realm. Names of caliphs, pseudo-caliphs, and official and unofficial leaders appeared and disappeared in indescribable clashes and confusion: Muzzafar (Almanzor's oldest son); his brother Abd al-Rahman IV (who traveled to battle accompanied by his harem of seventy wives); the sinister Mahdi who decapitated him and had the embalmed corpse nailed to a cross near a gate of the palace; Sulaiman, the great Abd al-Rahman III's grandson; Zawai; Wadhih; and more still. We mention only these names, almost accidentally, in passing. Their passion was power, or survival if power proved unattainable. Their interest in the Jihad was nonexistent. Sulaiman, in fact, in 1009 called in the help of Sancho, count of Castile, who supplied the Berber army in Spain with 1,000 cattle, 5,000 sheep, and 1,000 food-laden wagons during their march on Cordova. In return, two hundred fortresses taken by the Muslims in previous campaigns were returned to Castile. At the battle of Cantich, ten thousand Arabs were killed by the Castilians or drowned in the river Guadalquivir while trying to flee. At Akaba-al-Bakar, some twenty miles from Cordova, 9,000 Catalans, called in by Sulaiman, defeated 30,000 Moors. A couple of years later, in this barely comprehensible fury of death and destruction where everyone was killing everyone else, the Slav army in Muslim service killed Wadhih, stuck his head at the end of a pole, and paraded it through the streets of Cordova. Two years later the it was the Moors who attacked Cordova. This last conflict, although of Muslim against Muslim, was a true Jihad because the mullahs of Cordova declared it so; but their Jihad against their fellow Muslims failed. The Berbers took the city and the palace, massacred thousands, and went on a rampage of destruction. The ruins of Cordova, which date from those events, are a monument to the savagery of those times, as Dresden is of ours.

It was not until 1031 that the last of the Umayyads, Hisham III, was banished from the city and sent into exile. Cordova was in revolt. Hisham III, his wives, and his children had been held in a prison where, Dozy tells us, the fallen caliph "shivered in the damp and chilly air of a noisome dungeon" holding his only daughter, a small child, to his bosom to try to keep her warm. She was also almost dying from hunger, for the prisoners had not been fed for several days. "Let me have a morsel of bread for this poor child," pleaded the last of the Umayyad when his jailers came to tell him he was to be transferred to another fortress in Lerida. Hisham III escaped and died, a forgotten man, in 1036. Thus Abu Sufyan's dynasty from the old city of Mecca vanished from history. It had lasted four hundred years. For the next half-century al-Andalus lapsed into the petty tyranny of the weak and helpless taifa kings.

The Jihad petered out during these decades, but La Reconquista came to life again. With victory after victory, the frontier of Christian conquest nibbled its way southward. The capture of the old Visigoth capital of Toledo, now a taifa kingdom, by Alfonso VI of Castile in 1085 was the culmination of the advance. The Castilian southern frontier shifted from the Douro River to the Tagus, and what for centuries had been a semi no-man's land between the two rivers was taken over completely by the Christians. Salamanca, Avila, and Segovia started to become the cities they are today. Two giants appeared on the scene: for the Christians (most of the time), the knight Rodrigo Diaz de Vivar, immortalized as El Cid; for the Muslims, the dour Berber chief from the Sahara, Yusuf ibn Tashufin, leader of the austere Almoravid empire, conqueror of Ghana and Senegal, founder of Marrakech, the terror of all those who loved the good things of life.

In answer to a call for help from the Seville taifa, Yusuf crossed the narrow neck of sea between Tangiers and Gibraltar with his armies of Negroes, Touaregs and Berbers, with his war drums and tents and goats and camels. It was first at Zalaca, then in Valencia, that the Reconquest and the Jihad met again in bitter battle. The clash this time was no longer just between Christian and Muslim or between Arab and Spaniard. It was also the first confrontation between Europe and Africa since Hannibal.

25

THE DESERT WARRIOR:
ZALACA 1085–1086

The Christian capture of Toledo suddenly made the taifa kings very aware of their vulnerability. Weak, divided, and mutually warring, they were at the mercy of the Christians, and particularly of Castile, which was now the most powerful kingdom in the north. In fact, since the surrender of Toledo to Alfonso VI, the northern Christian realm of Castile seemed to have acquired a very southern extension, right into the middle of the taifas. Alfonso VI now titled himself "King of the Two Religions" and had graciously granted the kingship of Valencia to Kady, the former Muslim king of Toledo, on condition that the new monarch maintain and pay an army of six hundred Castilians on his territory.

Alfonso VI was also besieging Saragossa with the intention of adding it to his realm and, in the south, in the very heart of al-Andalus, one of his lieutenants, Garcia Ximenez, had occupied with a troop of cavalry the castle of Aledo, from which he was carrying out frequent raids against the nearby kingdom of Almeria. All in all, the taifa kings had much cause for concern.

None had more reason to worry than Mutamid, king of Seville, who only recently had crucified King Alfonso's envoy, the Jew Ben-Shalib, for refusing to accept the counterfeit money Mutamid had offered him as tribute to Alfonso VI. Mutamid had a peculiar hobby which had made him many enemies. The way some people today collect stamps, he collected the heads of decapitated foes and criminals and adorned his garden with these grim relics of his power. He knew he could expect no favored treatment from Alfonso VI, who was the most powerful sovereign, Christian or Muslim, in the peninsula. There seemed only one possible counterweight to the Castilian threat: Yusuf ibn Tashufin, the ruler of the puritan Muslim Almoravid creed that had become an empire and taken over a large part of northern Africa from Algiers to Senegal.

The Almoravids were a recent addition to the panoply of the multi-faceted Muslim theology. They had started as a small group of camel breeders in the Sahara, ancestors of the modern-day Tuaregs, who had gone on a pilgrimage to Mecca and on their way back had stopped in Kairouan, in Tunisia, one of the great intellectual centers of Islam. There they had reverently listened to the teachings of a jurist, a disciple of Malik, an eighth century Muslim luminary who was one of the most respected interpreters of the Koran and of the Hadith. It was an ultra-conservative creed, with a very moralistic approach to life and, before passing judgement on an action, decided first of all whether the motive behind it was good or bad. It is still the most widely practiced form of the Islamic faith in north and west Africa, Egypt, and the Sudan. The Muslim law, as propounded by the Maliki school, is one of the four still active in Islam, the others being the Hanafi, the Shafii, and the Hanbali. They all contradict one another in major or minor points, which perhaps helps to explain why the Muslim world always seems to be in the process of tearing itself apart.

Yusuf, a small, dark-skinned, dried-up old man, was now the leader in North Africa of the sect that has come down to us under the name of Almoravid. Yusuf's passions revolved around Malaki Islam. He had no interest whatsoever in the finer things of life. He was definitely not a gentleman, spoke some uncouth Saharan dialect, had great difficulty expressing himself in Arabic, and, we are told, smelled like a camel. His meals consisted of bread and camel milk, his clothes were made of rough skins, and his face was always hidden behind a blue veil, like those the Touaregs of the Sahara still wear today. He was a warrior, and he was anxious to launch a Holy War against the Christian kingdoms of Spain. He had the reputation of being a military genius and his soldiers of being the best and the toughest of Islam. The Almoravids fought in phalanx formations, the soldiers of the front rank kneeling behind their tall shields of hippopotamus hide with their long spears held horizontally forward, and the rear ranks throwing spears at the enemy advancing toward them. The Almoravid cavalry was organized tactically. The horsemen attacked in formation instead of the usual haphazard method of that period when each horseman attacked individually, each seeking his enemy to fight in single combat. The Almoravid cavalrymen, in addition to their horses, had 30,000 camels at their disposal. They were formidable hosts, but Yusuf's main *force de frappe* consisted of four thousand fearsome and feared black horsemen from Senegal and Mali whose mere presence on the battle-field often paralyzed the enemy. They went into battle beating huge war drums, shouting strange oaths and singing fearsome songs. For their European enemies, it was their first glimpse of unknown black Africa. For most, it was terrifying.

The invitation to Yusuf was accompanied by a huge risk for the hosts. The guests might stay and take over the small and weak taifas of Muslim Spain—including Mutamid's Seville—and turn them into satellites of Morocco. Yusuf could prove to be more dangerous than the enemy Christian kingdoms. "If I have to choose, I prefer to be a camel-driver in Africa rather than a swineherd in Castile," Mutami told the kings of Granada and Badajoz, who had come to Seville to advise him. Presumably they agreed. It was an important decision, for it demon-strated that, in al-Andalus, Islam had precedence over Spain. Mutamid was not quite yet a Spaniard. Neither were his Muslim fellow mon-archs. It was one of those decisions which, taken perhaps without suf-ficient consideration, postponed the unification of Spain for four hun-dred years. Who knows, had Mutamid been willing to accept the suzerainty of Castile, Spain with a then large Muslim population might well have become in due course a country of two tolerant faiths. The Jihad would have expired and perhaps the Inquisition might never been born. History is full of lost opportunities. Under different influences Muslim Spain might have turned into something other than what it subsequently became.

Mutamid must have had second thoughts after his request to Yusuf for aid, for his first message was soon followed by a second one informing the Almoravid leader that the invitation had been extended to him on condition he would swear not to take over the Muslim king-doms. Yusuf swore as requested, landed in Spain, and in Algeciras met the kings of Seville, Malaga, Badajoz, and Granada soon after his arrival, to reassure these taifa rulers of the purity of his intentions, and also to plan secretly how to take possession of those kingdoms.

Yusuf, austere and somber, a holy warrior who revered puritanism, had little in common with his fun-loving Hispanic Muslim colleagues.

It was near Badajoz, at the Battle of Zalaca, or Sagrajas as it is also sometimes called, a few months later, that he made his feelings quite clear—and won an immense victory in what was one of the very few big battles of the Spanish Jihad.

Many of the Muslim Andalusian regiments fled at the first attack by Alfonso VI, who had come down from the siege of Saragossa with his Castilian and Aragonese troops and his coterie of French knights. But one soldier was not with him, a man who alone was worth a thousand men: Rodrigo Diaz de Bivar, el Cid Campeador the Spaniards called him, the Challenger, Mio Cid, a man who has inspired a nation for nearly a thousand years and who represents all that is fine and all that is best among the men of Spain, the pride of a nation, a man before whom all other men seemed puny. He and Alfonso VI had quarreled and in a monumental sulk, the privilege of greatness, he had gone to the other side of Spain, to the Levante, the East, to offer his sword to his Muslim friend the King of Saragossa, al-Mutamin ibn Hud, who was at war with the kings of Lerida and Aragon and the count of Barcelona. Although El Cid was absent from Zalaca, his friend Alvar Fanez, the knight whom El Cid called "my strong right arm" and who always went into battle by his side, was charging the warriors of Islam at Zalaca that day.

Yusuf, the Almoravid leader, watched with a sneer the troops of most of the taifa kingdoms of al-Andalus fleeing at the first Christian charge. He made no effort to intercept Alfonso's soldiers, who were pursuing and cutting down the Andalusian Muslims. "It does not matter to me if these people are slaughtered," he said. To Yusuf, these fleeing Andalusian troops were a disgrace to Islam. With their lax, pleasure-loving ways, their poetry, their love of music, the Andalusian Muslims, as far as he was concerned, were no better than the Christians, and it did not disturb him to watch them being killed. On the battlefield Alfonso VI launched a frontal attack on the Almoravids. Yusuf sent a Moroccan regiment to shore up those under attack and in support of Mutamid whose troops, unlike the bulk of the Andalusians, had remained steady at their posts. Mutamid was wounded six times. While the Spaniards were engaged in the front, Yusuf led a regiment of Sahara desert nomads to the rear and caught the Christians between his two attacking forces. The cunning Almoravid leader then sent in his black African guards to complete the carnage. Alfonso VI managed to escape with his guard of five hundred men.

Three thousand of their own were killed in the battle, the Muslim victors said afterward, but the Christian casualties were far heavier. The Muslims stopped counting the the numbers of enemy dead after reaching the figure of 24,000. They then began to cut the heads off the corpses and piled them up to make a sort of minaret for the muezzins who, standing on the piles of headless cadavers, sang the praises of Allah and called the faithful to prayer.

To show what a great victory it really was, Yusuf ordered the heads to be packed and shipped to all the main towns of al-Andalus and North Africa. Seville, Granada, Cordova, Murcia, Saragossa, and Valencia each received its quota, and a message with each cartload telling the faithful they had nothing more to fear from these Christian dogs. It was a great day for the men of the Jihad but a dismal one for the Spaniards of the Reconquest. The Christian survivors prayed for their dead comrades and hoped that Alfonso VI would call into his service the greatest warrior in Castile, El Cid, with whom he had recently parted company and who was now pitted against the count of Barcelona. This was no time for Christians to be fighting against one another.

26

MIO CID:
VALENCIA 1080–1108

O F ALL THE HEROES OF the Reconquest, El Cid is the only one
who is known to the world at large. By his defense of Valencia
against the Almoravids, he assured the long-term triumph of Christian
Spain over Muslim Spain. Of all of his country's warriors, he was the
only one whom Yusuf, the Almoravid conqueror from Morocco,
feared. He was a born soldier, an incredibly brave fighter on the field,
a tactician without peer, a strategist of genius in an age when military
science barely existed. In that brutal age he was not, perhaps, quite like
Bayard, "a knight without fear and without reproach." Certainly
"without fear," but not "without reproach," for he had a few dirty deeds
to his name; but the warmth of his person still reaches us across the
centuries, and he remains an inspiration for those who have the privilege of breathing today the same Spanish air that he once breathed.

Perhaps he was a legend, as some say, half fiction and only half
fact. His victory at Cuenca, outside Valencia, was a fact. It was a
classic of tactical flair. He, more than any other man, prepared the final
defeat of the Almoravids more than half a century before it came about.
Their failure to capture Valencia ended their progress north. It was outside the walls of El Cid's Valencia that victory for the Jihad turned into
defeat. Beyond Valencia, rich Barcelona and Catalonia stayed out of
the reach of the Moroccan and Saharan soldiery. Al-Andalus never
became African. The camels returned to Morocco and the Sahel. Spain

remained Spanish. "One Rodrigo lost Spain and another Rodrigo will recover it," he said, recalling the loss of Spain to the Moors by the Visigoth king Rodrigo in 711. Rodrigo Diaz de Bivar, alias El Cid, had faith in his destiny.

We are not concerned in this book with the career of El Cid, only his role in the defeat of the Jihad and in the Reconquest. He married Ximena, the Castilian king's cousin, and was given the command of the army. Then he insulted some of the greatest notables in the kingdom and was banished. In 1081 the king of Castile gave him nine days to depart or die. El Cid was forty-one years old. He had to abandon Ximena and his daughters. Another man who was to become a king, Alfonso the Learned, later described El Cid's departure in *The Chronicle of the Cid.*

> Dona Ximena came up and her daughters with her, each of them borne in arms, and she knelt down on both her knees before her husband, weeping bitterly, and she would have kissed his hand; and she said to him, Lo, now you are banished from the land by mischief-making men, and here I am with your daughters, who are little ones and of tender years, and we and you must be parted, even in your lifetime. For the love of Saint Mary tell me now what we shall do. And the Cid took the children in his arms, and held them to his heart and wept, for he dearly loved them. Please God and Saint Mary, said he, I shall yet live to give these my daughters in marriage with my own hands, and to do your service yet, my honored wife, whom I have ever loved even as my own soul. The knights with whom he had served also came to him and Alvar Fanez,who was his cousin-german, came forward and said, Cid, we will go with you through desert and through peopled country, and never fail you. In your service will we spend our mules and horses, our wealth and our garments, and ever while we live be unto you loyal friends and vassals. And they all confirmed what Alvar Fanez had said.

In our age of wimpish men and macho women, when love, friendship and loyalty cannot compete against money, we wonder if we can still find men and women who cherish such sentiments and can express them with such simple dignity.

During the next five years Alfonso VI and El Cid remained estranged. The Islamic days of al-Andalus seemed already to be ending—the Almoravids had not yet made their appearance. King Alfonso had taken over, or threatened to do so, one taifa kingdom after another:

Toledo, Valencia, Seville, Granada, Saragossa, and several of the lesser principalities. To the east El Cid was engaged in other fighting. Fighting, it seemed, on any side, Muslim or Christian. He was fighting for Saragossa's Muslim king Mutamin against al-Hayib, the Muslim lord of Lerida, against Sancho, the Christian King of Aragon and Navarre, and his ally the count of Barcelona, with his train of knights from France and Catalonia. El Cid defeated them all.

In the Muslim south, in Seville, King Mutamid was awaiting his prospective allies, the Almoravids, whom he had called to his aid to protect him from Alfonso VI. The king of Castile had swept through his kingdom on horseback, galloped south right through Mutamid's realm, from Toledo all the way down south to the sea near Gibraltar, where he rode his horse into the waves and shouted through the spray, "Behold the furthest limits of Andalusia which I have trampled underfoot."

In Seville, his capital, Mutamid, awaiting the arrival of his ally, Yusuf, would not yield. The Almoravids came, and defeat awaited Alfonso VI at Zalaca. The beaten monarch escaped from the battlefield back to Toledo. Now he called for El Cid; he needed his troublesome vassal. He needed the Cid's sword and his courage to defeat Yusuf and his desert Moors, his Tuaregs, and his black warriors from the Sudan. After his victory at Zalaca, Yusuf was on the rampage. In spite of his earlier undertaking to respect the sovereignty of the taifas, he was taking them over, one after another, and becoming their rightful sovereign, insofar as might makes right. Al-Andalus was becoming an African colony, ruled from Morocco.

In the midst of all the fears and confusion, El Cid rode out with his knights to carve a country for himself, a sort of taifa, but a Christian one. He chose Valencia, a Muslim city. After a twenty-month siege, one of the longest of the Reconquista, and to the sound of trumpets and under the waving banners of the king of Castile, Valencia fell in 904. El Cid entered the town as the conqueror. "How great was the rejoicing when my Cid won Valencia," wrote Alfonso the Learned in his *Chronicle of the Cid.* "Those who were on foot are now mounted on horses, and who can count the wealth that is theirs." Savagery and violence were also rampant in Spanish ranks. El Cid was not an untainted hero. The vanquished Muslim ruler of Valencia, Ibn Jahhap, was burned alive by a vengeful Cid. Men were brutal in that brutal age.

The fighting for Valencia had been, on both sides, up to now solely between men of Spain: the Muslim knights of al-Andalus against the Christian knights of Leon and Castile. Yusuf and his Almoravid

Saharan horde with their smelly camels, their desert tents, their goatskin waterbags, their curved daggers, and their war drums had temporarily returned to North Africa, but El Cid knew they would be back in Spain and that he would have to battle them soon. First he wanted Ximena and his daughters by his side.

He sent Alvar Fanez and a hundred knights to the monastery at San Pedro de Cardena, where his wife was staying with their daughters, to escort his family to their new home among the orange groves of Valencia. We can feel, in the words of a poet of those times, the emotion of Alvar Fanez as he greeted the women whose safety and honor had been placed in his care. "He rode to San Pedro where the ladies were," wrote the poet.

> How great was their joy when they saw him. Alvar Fanez dismounted and went to say a prayer in Saint Peter's church. The prayer done, he turned to the ladies and said: "My humble duty, Dona Ximena, and may God preserve both you and your noble daughters. My Cid sends you his greetings. The King in his grace has given me leave to escort you hence to Valencia, which has now fallen to our inheritance. If my Cid sees you safe and sound, then all his sorrow will be turned to joy." "May God Almighty grant it," said Dona Ximena.

These sentiments were deeply felt by the people who expressed them. In our permissive age of TV violence, instant pornography for the masses, shattered families, organized obscenity, feminists without femininity, children without innocence, men without guts, street gang warfare between uncultured louts, and magnates and moguls whose only passions are money and power and, sometimes, sex, can such sentiments still be found somewhere? Recounting in this book yesterday's unspeakable excesses of Holy War and of brutalities and atrocities almost as bad as those of our own century, we can only hope that all the sleaze around us today, like the shit it is, will fertilize more courtly and more noble tomorrows.

Nobility and the Almoravids were as far apart in the eleventh century as nobility and ourselves are in this one. Emptiness and obscenity may be our forte, but hatred and fanaticism were theirs. The Andalusian Muslims were, perhaps, different. They were men with an underlying sense of honor, their natural heritage from the soil on which they strode every day and from the pure, crystal air of Spain which they breathed every day. In faraway, alien Mexico and Peru, six centuries later, the men of Spain forgot honor and nobility, but the Spain of the Reconquista was a land of hidalgos and heroes.

The Moor Abengalbon (Ibn Galbun) met, we are told, a party of horsemen led by the Castilian knight Mano Gustioz, sent by the Cid to meet his wife and daughter and their escort in his Muslim-held territory through which they had to pass on their way to Valencia. The Muslim governor, we read,

> when he received word of their coming rode out to meet them with great joy. Mano Gustioz straightaway addressed him: "The Cid salutes you and begs the favor of a hundred knights to ride with us at once. His wife and daughters are nearby and he would have you escort them hither and not leave them until they reach Valencia." 'Gladly will I do this,' said Abengalbon. That night he feasted them well and the next morning they set out. A hundred had been asked of him, but he mustered two hundred. . . . Alvar Fanez, like a prudent captain, sent out scouts to see who these armed men might be, and was reassured to learn they were his own comrades-at-arms, riding in the company of Abengalbon. . . . When Abelgabon caught sight of him, he rode forward and embraced him. . . . 'Well met Alvar Fanez. You do us honor by bringing with you these ladies, the wife and daughters of the warrior Cid. It is only meet that we should all show you our respect, for such is his fortune that even though we might have no love for him we could do him no hurt. What is ours is his too, either by peace or war.' . . . They entered Molina, a rich and goodly place. The Moor Abengalbon did not fail to serve them well. There was no lack of anything they might desire. He even saw that their horses were reshod. The next morning they mounted again and rode on. The Moor attended them faithfully as far as Valencia and would accept nothing from them. And so, with joy and honor they journeyed on.

When they reached the outskirts of Valencia, El Cid rode out to greet his wife and daughters. "He took them in his arms, mother and daughters, tears of joy flowing from his eyes. . . . Hear now what he said, who in good hour girded on his sword: 'Dona Ximena, my dear and honored wife, and you daughters of my heart and soul, come with me into Valencia, the town which I have won to be your home.' . . . The Cid and all his company now have their heart's desire. Winter is over and March is come again."

The Almoravids were also coming again and, unlike Abengalbon, Yusuf was no gentleman. He was closer to being a monster. From Marrakech, which he had founded and where he had gone to supervise his Moroccan realm, he sent a message that if the Cid refused to evacuate Valencia, Ximena, his children, and the Cid himself would be tortured to death in such a way that "no Christian would ever forget it." The Jihad, the Muslim Holy War, was back, in its raw and unholy garb.

The Almoravids landed from Morocco near the beaches of Valencia with Yusuf at the head of an army of fifty thousand men, countless camels and countless war drums. They camped at Cuarte, outside the besieged city. Their plan was to starve Valencia into capitulation, but to await surrender was not El Cid's style. On his charger, Babieca, he led a sortie of four thousand horsemen outside the city walls. "My Cid yields the lance, then draws the sword. Countless are the Moors he slays, the blood dripping from his elbow. He struck three blows at Yusuf, who fled at full gallop and took shelter in Cullera, where stands a noble castle." The Almoravids fled. For the Christians it was a vital, victorious moment in the Reconquista.

Cuarte, fought in 1094, eight years after Zalaca, was the first Christian victory against the Almoravids. Only 104 of the fifty thousand Berbers escaped, says a chronicle of the epoch, but the casualty figure is certainly grossly exaggerated. The Cid's tactics, as well as the dash of his attack and the inspiration of his presence and of his unquenchable courage, gave the Spaniards victory that day. El Cid's master stroke was to send part of his force to attack the Almoravid rear while their van was attacking him frontally, thus forcing them to fight on two fronts and sowing confusion and panic (the two often go together) in their ranks. After this victory, El Cid began to consider a plan to land an expeditionary force in Morocco and to attack the Almoravid enemy right in his lair. It was then that he was first heard to mutter that one Rodrigo (the Visigoth king) had lost Spain and another Rodrigo (himself) would regain it.

He never did because he never left Valencia again. He remained to the end of his days the ruler of his Mediterranean province, though he won a second battle against the Almoravids at Bairen. When Yusuf threatened Toledo, El Cid, unable to come to the aid of Alfonso VI, sent a party of knights who included his only son Diego and his kinsman Alvar Fanez. Alfonso VI was defeated but Toledo remained untaken. Alvar Fanez was also defeated fighting in a small skirmish against Yusuf's son, and Diego was killed in his first battle.

The Almoravids invaded El Cid's principality and defeated a detachment of his troops in an affray at Alcira, not far from Valencia. Then the town of Sagunto, with the support of the Almoravids, the Muslim ruler of Albaraccin, and the count of Barcelona, revolted against El Cid's rule. The Cid led his troops in person against the mutinous town, and at his approach the town immediately surrendered. That was El Cid's last battle and his last victory. He died the following year, on July 10, 1099. One of his last thoughts was for his horse Babieca. He willed that he be looked after until he died a natural death and that he should then be buried like the warrior he was.

Three years after El Cid's death Valencia fell to an Almoravid army commanded by Yusuf's nephew, whom the Spaniards called King Bucar. He lacked Yusuf's drive, and Valencia never became a springboard to further Muslim conquests, as had been feared. Ximena returned to San Pedro de Cardena, the Cid's daughters married the princes of Navarre and of Aragon, Alfonso VI lived on for another ten years and his old age was saddened by the death of his son Sancho in battle against the Moors at Ucles in 1108. Alvar Fanez, El Cid's strong right arm, defended Toledo against the Almoravids and died, a few years later, fighting for the rights of Alfonso's daughter Uracca to her father's inheritance. The Reconquista still had a long ordeal ahead for the Spaniards. It took nearly another four hundred years to deliver Spain from the aliens who were occupying the country.

PART SIX

DEFLECTION IN THE SOUTH

27

LIBERATION IN LUSITANIA: PORTUGAL 1079–1147

T HE RECONQUEST IN IBERIA DIDN'T concern only Spain. The Jihad in Iberia wasn't only an operation against Spain. As well as France, Spain had another neighbor, Portugal, hewn out of the turmoil, the confusion, and the blood of the unforgiving conflict between Christian and Moor. Portugal, then a county attached to Castile, known in previous centuries as Lusitania even before it became part of the Roman Empire, found its way to independence in the twelfth century when it was occupied partly by the Moors and partly by the Castilians. Its fight for independence was cruel and bitter. It is a tale of greed, intrigue, and blood that began when a young French knight, a descendant of kings, Henry of Burgundy, rode into Saragossa one morning and placed his sword at the service of King Alfonso VI of Castile and Leon, and soon afterward married the king's (illegitimate) daughter, Theresa.

The presence of Henry of Burgundy in Castile was not a fortuitous event. French knights were in the van of the Crusaders who went to fight in the Holy Land. Jerusalem was not always the only destination available to these Christian warriors. Spain, much nearer to France, was also occupied by the infidel Moors, and Castile and Aragon were also thronged with French adventurers of noble lineage, lured south of the Pyrenees by the pathetic appeals from the pontiff in Rome calling for volunteers to save Spain from the Saracens. The young men of France flocked over the Pyrenees to the side of their embattled Spanish

Catholic kinsmen, not only out of a sense of Christian brotherliness but also, it must be said, by the lure of adventure and the hope of great rewards. Restless, ambitious, and enterprising, some hoped to carve out of the chaos of war a kingdom for themselves and their children. Henry of Burgundy was such a man.

The great-grandson of King Robert the Pious of France, Henry of Burgundy was one of those knights of royal blood roaming over the disputed and troubled lands of Europe and the Near East, sword in hand, in search of a cause for which to fight and a throne on which to climb. He arrived in Castile with the best references possible: he was the nephew of the recently deceased Queen of Castile, Constance, formerly of Burgundy, former wife of King Alfonso VI of Castile and Leon. Perhaps King Alfonso hoped that Henry of Burgundy might turn out to be another Cid. He was of royal blood and had to be fit, by his ascendancy, to join the royal Castilian family. So the king gave the Burgundian knight the hand of his daughter and, as dowry, the county of Portugal, which was then Spanish and part of the Castilian domain but largely occupied by the Muslims.

Alas for Alfonso VI, Henry was no Cid. In fact, he was a useless general, probably lost Santarem for Castile in 1095 and, by his negligence, was considered responsible for the death of a Castilian prince in a later battle against the Almoravids. He had a flaming row with his father-in-law and angrily flounced off to France, where he tried to find support in the quarrel he had initiated against the Castilian crown. He found no backers, returned to his Portuguese fiefdom, fought for Aragon against Castile, and demanded a large slice of territory as his reward. He was allotted two towns in Leon as bounty, and died, unregretted, while visiting one of them (Astorga) in 1112.

His contribution in the war against the Moors and for Portugal had been minimal, but he did leave a three-year-old son, Alfonso Henriques, who became the founder of the kingdom of Portugal. As for his widow, Theresa, she took over the regency of Portugal but could never make up her mind whether she should call herself queen of Portugal, infanta or countess. She found herself a powerful lover, Fernando Peres, lord of Coimbra and Oporto, who found her preferable to his wife. Theresa and Fernando Peres had a baby daughter and lived happily, if not ever after, at least for a number of years.

Portugal was soon at war, not against the Moors but against the neighboring kingdom of Castile. Too weak and without support or desire to fight against her own country, Theresa accepted Castilian overlordship of Portugal.

Alfonso Henriques, as Henry's son became known, is the man who freed Portugal from the Saracens—and the Spaniards—and created the kingdom of Portugal. He made it not only by fighting against the Muslims, whom he immediately recognized as his country's main enemies, but also by fighting against Castile, disavowing Castilian rule, and sending his supine mother and her lover back to Spain. The year was 1128. His first major battle against the Moors was not fought (and won) until eleven years later in southwest Portugal, where he crushed the Almoravid enemy in their fortress of Ourique. Actually, Ourique is rather an obscure battle in which fact and fiction seem to blend in equal proportions. No one is even too sure where it was fought. It may have been fought near Santarem. God is alleged to have intervened on the Christian side; but, whatever the doubts about the nature of this action, it remains the battle in Portuguese history that heralded the coming of age of Portugal as an independent country. After his victory Alfonso Henriques proclaimed himself Alfonso I, King of Portugal and in due course signed a border agreement with Castile. Portugal, although largely occupied by the Moors, now existed as an independent state.

Alfonso I's own Reconquest of Portugal culminated in 1147, eight years after Ourique. That spring he marched from Coimbra at the head of a force of Knights Templar and took and occupied Santarem. A few months later, in a spectacular attack by land and sea, he besieged and captured Lisbon from the Almoravids. It was an international operation, one of the most remarkable military actions of the Reconquista, in which hundreds of crusaders from France, England, Flanders and Germany, sailors and soldiers, were involved, and it all began in Oporto with the arrival of an English fleet of 164 vessels from Dartmouth, with thirteen thousand men aboard, crusaders and sailors, bound for the Holy Land.

They put into the Douro River estuary (site of Oporto) for supplies. The local bishop, Pedro Pitoes, promised them money if they would help him to rid Lisbon of the Moors. They enthusiastically agreed and sailed to the Tagus estuary (site of Lisbon), where they were joined by the Portuguese king, who came marching in from overland. "A great meeting was held to discuss the collective contract," H. V. Livermore tells us in his history of Portugal. King Alfonso promised them money and land (after the Muslims had been thrown out) if, instead of going to the Holy Land, they stayed and fought with him in Portugal against the Moors. After the Moors had been ejected from Lisbon, any man who wanted to stay and live in Portugal would be welcome to remain.

They all voted to remain. They sailed to Lisbon and laid siege to the city.

From the top of their battlements the Moors taunted the besieging Christians with the infidelity of their wives back home and with the babies that were awaiting them on their return. The enraged crusaders retaliated by decapitating eighty unfortunate Muslim prisoners and lining up their heads outside the walls of the capital. The siege lasted four months. The desperate and hungry Arab defenders agreed to capitulate, abandon all their possessions, and return to their own lands. Guarded by 140 Englishmen and 1600 Germans and Flemings, the survivors of the siege began to stream out of Lisbon through three of its gates. It took four days to evacuate the city. According to a second version of the taking of Lisbon, the Christian warriors executed, without orders and contrary to the terms of the capitulation, most of the captured Muslims. The practice of mass murder is not a Muslim monopoly; the Christians have also been excellent at it on various occasions. The capture of Lisbon was probably one of them.

The surrender of Lisbon was a resounding victory for Alfonso and a major setback for the Jihad. It is from that day that Lisbon became the capital of Portugal. The allied crusaders and seamen of the Lisbon siege liked the city so much that most of them decided to just stay and settle there. One of these migrants was the English priest Gilbert of Hastings, who was promoted to Bishop of Lisbon on the spot.

But before Portugal became independent, there was still considerable fighting ahead for Alfonso. His last battle against the Muslims was fought and won at Santarem nearly a quarter of a century later, in 1171. He was a man of sixty-two by then, proud to be a Portuguese and equally proud to be a man of Burgundy. His wife Matilda was also a Burgundian. Being a Burgundian means loving good wine, and let us hope he was able to enjoy the splendid wines—particularly the red— of the country his father had made his own and where the founder of Portugal died in 1185, at the age of seventy-six, having turned most of his country into a Muslimless land.

28

WHENCE THE
GREEKS AND NORMANS:
SICILY 1025–1091

I F YOU WERE A NORMAN and you wanted action in the eleventh century, one of the best places to go was Sicily and nearby southern
Italy. You also were able to enjoy a very good climate, lots of sunshine,
luscious fruit, and the best lobsters in the Mediterranean. Not unexpectedly, it was a place full of visitors; but they hadn't gone there for
the good life. They'd gone there to fight, a motley bunch, mainly Lombards, Franks, Byzantine Greeks, Spaniards, Egyptians, Syrians,
Tunisians, and Italians and Sicilians too, naturally. After all, it was
their country. There were also a scattering of Norwegians and Russians, Varangians they were called, mercenaries in the pay of the
Byzantine empire, big fellows with blond hair and ruddy faces, who
drank too much and made fun of the locals. One of the biggest foreign
contingents was made up of Normans from France, mercenaries
mainly also, but who were far more interested in fighting for themselves than for the local counts and princes and kings who had hired
them. Originally they had come to Rome, where a gentleman from Bari
by the name of Melo invited them to help him free his native city from
its Byzantine rulers.

This was a time when the Byzantine empire, often considered
moribund, was flexing its muscles against its enemies, who were
many. In fact, it was surrounded by enemies on all sides and for the last
few previous decades had been shrinking considerably, particularly in

its Italian domains. One of its favorite colonies, Sicily, had been in Arab hands for over two centuries and was now part of the Tunisian-based Fatimid caliphate; Naples and Amalfi, Catholic instead of Orthodox, were both semi-independent and flourishing little city states; the Lombards, who had once dominated only northern Italy, now also ruled part of Calabria and Apulia. In fact, the only bit of Italy that the Byzantines could still call their own was the foot and the heel of the peninsula.

Outside Italy, the Byzantine Greeks had recently conquered the Crimea, chased the Bulgarians away, made the Serbs their vassals, and taken over Armenia. Now was the time, the Byzantines felt, to recoup their Italian dominions, particularly the flourishing island of Sicily, where Islam had humiliatingly crushed Christianity. Crete had been retaken a few decades previously and now was really the time to carry out again a similar exploit in Sicily.

Some sixty years previously, in 961, under the then famed general Nicephorus Phocas, the Byzantines had reconquered the island of Crete, which was occupied by the descendants of the Cordova Muslim rebels. Phocas, one of the military geniuses of that epoch and author of a handbook on the organization of armies (which professional soldiers were still studying several centuries later) had led the invasion of Crete in a fleet said to have numbered thousands of vessels. The whole campaign had lasted only a few months; the Cretans had all been expelled or been converted to Christianity, and Phocas had taken the emir of the island to Constantinople in chains, plus an immense amount of booty. That had not been his only success. He had also conquered Cyprus, captured Tarsus and Adana, invaded northern Syria, threatened Damascus, and occupied Antioch and Aleppo. His victories might have continued had not his ambitious nephew, the Armenian John Zimisces, led a coup against him in which the old general, a regent on behalf of the infant Emperor Basil II, was killed. Phocas had also married the widowed empress Theophano, who found him too old and cranky. On promise of marriage she agreed to help Zimisces kill her husband. The plotters broke into his bedroom at night and the old soldier died with the words "Oh God, grant me thy mercy" on his lips.

As for John Zimisces, he reneged on his promise to marry the ageing Empress. Instead, the treacherous scoundrel obliged her to enter a nunnery while he, like the man he had murdered, went on to become a famous and successful general who defeated the Russians in Bulgaria, captured Damascus and Beirut, and met with no reverses until an

Arab army fighting the Holy War brought his exploits to an end outside Jerusalem in 976. He died suddenly and unexpectedly that same
year at the age of fifty-one.

In the 1030s a new general entered the Byzantine firmament, Gior-
gios Maniakes, with ambitions to start a holy war of his own and wrest
from the Muslims some of the territories—Sicily in particular—they
had, through the centuries, appropriated from the Byzantines. He had
recently saved an imperial army, led by Emperor Romanus III, from
certain defeat at the hands of the Arabs in Syria. On the advice of
Harold Hardrada, a Norwegian mercenary who had become his chief
military adviser and who, being a Viking, knew all about the ocean,
Maniakes decided to launch a campaign across the sea and attack Sicily.

Harold Hardrada was the brother of St. Olaf, king of Norway, who
had been killed fighting against King Canute (the one who ordered in
vain the waves to stop lapping his feet) in 1030. After his brother's
death at the battle of Stiklestad, he had made his way south through
Russia to Constantinople, and being of royal blood he had been given
the command of the Varangians in Byzantine service. He served
mainly at sea, fighting Muslim pirates off the Anatolian coast and
raiding the North African shores. The landing in Sicily in 1035 was
largely an extension of these naval raids.

The Byzantine soldiers, who were mainly a mixed force of Italians
and Norwegians, won a victory at Rametta (1038) and, two years later,
at Dragina. But no permanent landing was made on the Sicilian shore,
perhaps because the Byzantines were also engaged at the same time in
another war in southern Italy, against the Normans, whom Maniakes
defeated at the battle of Monopoli, near Naples, in 1042. Or perhaps it
was because of confusing intrigues against Emperor Michael V in the
Byzantine court by the thrice-married Empress Zoe, an old Mae West
harridan type, who was loved by the mobs of Constantinople but who
hated her husband, the emperor. He wanted to be sole ruler of the
empire and tried to have his wife put away in a convent. Instead she
had him put away in a monastery after first asking Harold Hardrada to
gouge his eyes out.

Somehow the Viking warrior got involved in many of the ongoing
scandals in Constantinople. He amassed a huge fortune, was accused
of massive corruption, and kidnapped Zoe's niece, Maria. Perhaps his
old friend Georgios Maniakes turned against him. In revolt against the
debasement of public life, General Maniakes landed in Albania, presumably from southern Italy, and was preparing to march at the head

of his rebellious troops against the capital when he was accidentally killed. So he and Harold Hardrada vanished from Byzantine history, the Muslims remained undisturbed in Sicily for a few more decades, and it was not the Byzantine Greeks but the Normans who finally expelled them.

It's worth noting in passing that after his exploits in the Mediterranean, Harold Hardrada appears again prominently in history, this time in the British Isles where, after the death of the English sovereign Edward the Confessor, he nearly became king of England in 1066, following a series of events in which the Normans were again closely involved. On Edward the Confessor's death, another Harold, the earl of Wessex, immediately grabbed the English crown. His claim to the kingship was promptly challenged by two men: William, duke of Normandy, and Harold Hardrada, king of Norway. Harold Hardrada, in the company of Tostig, earl of Northumbria, landed in the north of England and began to march south to fight Harold for the English throne. Harold rushed north to meet them in battle, and offered the 51-year-old Harold Hardrada, who was a huge man, "seven feet of good English earth" under the ground for his kingdom. Their two armies clashed at the battle of Stamford Bridge, where Harold Hardrada was defeated and killed and was given the seven feet of English earth underground he had been promised.

The English earl was celebrating his victory over his Norwegian rival when he heard that the other claimant to the English throne, William of Normandy, had landed in the south of England. Harold immediately hurried south to meet the intruder, but this time the gods of luck and of war failed him. William the Conqueror, as he became known in history, defeated and killed Harold at the Battle of Hastings on October 14, 1066, and the duke of Normandy became King William I of England. This is the one date everyone in England knows.

Meanwhile, in southern Italy, William's Norman compatriots were also in the process of taking over other realms and kingdoms, of which Sicily was the most important. This time the Saracen Arabs and the Byzantine Greeks were the enemy. It was a triangular contest as Muslims and Orthodox were also at war against each other in an unending Holy War that could end only with the annihilation of one of them.

Southern Italy was at that time divided into lots of little states, rather like the taifas of Spain, and mercenaries were in great demand. The Normans, tough fighters, impressed their employers. After Melo's invitation to Bari, the next call for their services probably came from

Guiamar IV, prince of Salerno. The Normans were quick to recognize the opportunity that had come their way. Hundreds of them began to make their way from Normandy south across France to the Alpine passes. All they had to offer were their heavy swords, their strong right arms, and sometimes a coat of mail and a horse. They offered their services to whoever would hire them. The rulers of Capua, Naples, Bari, and Beneventum soon had their contingents of Norman fighting men. Presumably they occasionally had to fight against each other, but they made a point of treating each other lightly, for many of them were related, descendants of the prominent Norman family of Tancred de Hauteville.

The first leader of the Normans in Apulia and Calabria was one William of the Iron Arm, who died in 1048. His brother Drogo then took over the leadership until he was murdered; then his brother Robert Guiscard, joined by his other brother Roger, rose to the top of this rough and tough Norman hierarchy. Robert Guiscard has been described as a brigand who shrank from no violence. Nothing was sacred to him; he respected neither old people, nor women, nor children, and "on occasion he spared neither church nor monastery," writes Aziz Ahmad in his book on Islamic Sicily. There was nothing very holy about the Norman presence in southern Italy. They were rogues and outlaws who lived violent lives. Like the Arabs, they were in the fighting business for the loot; but at least they never claimed they were fighting a Holy War for God. In fact, Pope Leo IX condemned and excommunicated the Guiscard brothers, but they captured him while he was visiting Bari and refused to free him until he gave in to their demands. Leo IX died and five years later his successor, Nicholas II, gave Robert Guiscard the right to rule over Calabria and Apulia, fiefdoms of the Orthodox Byzantine empire, and over Sicily, ruled by the Muslims. There was nothing godly about the war the Guiscards now undertook.

Robert Guiscard was too involved in the campaigns against the Byzantines on the mainland to go to Sicily, and sent his brother Roger to fight the Muslims. Roger landed near Masara in 1061 at the head of an army of two thousand men and occupied the city. In retaliation the Muslims called for a Jihad against the infidel. A peculiarly convoluted marital situation seems to have inspired the Norman landing, at least at the time it did. The Arab governor of Syracuse, one Ibn al-Thumna, because of a dispute with his wife Maymuna (the ex-wife of Ibn Maklati, ruler of Catania, whom Ibn al-Thumna had killed in battle), is reported to have called the Normans for their help against Maymuna's powerful brother, Ibn al-Hawwas, governor of Castrogiovanni. Marriage is never simple, even with just one wife. With four, as with the Muslims, it is considerably more complicated. So in Sicily we find once again a shadowy feminine presence at least partly responsible for one more war.

The enigmatic Ibn al-Thumna was Roger Guiscard's main ally after the arrival of the Normans in Sicily, while Ibn al-Hawwas, holed up un his fortress of Castrogiovanni, proved to be their main enemy. Both Moors were of only passing concern in the Norman conquest of the island, as they did not survive long. Ibn al-Thumna was killed in a skirmish in 1062, and Ibn al-Hawwas lost his life around 1064 fighting his own ally, Ayyub. The struggle for the island continued for more than thirty years. Roger headed the combat against the Moors until he was over seventy. It was essentially at first a war to the death between rival gangs of Christians and Muslims, adventurous rogues all of them, rather than real crusaders or Jihad devotees. In 1084, however, the Sicilian campaign took on a stronger religious overtone for the Christians after the Moors in southern Italy burned down the churches of Reggio and enslaved all the monks of the Rocca d'Asino monastery.

For Roger Guiscard the Sicilian campaign was almost a lifetime career. He led it in person from its very beginnings in 1061 right to the end in 1091, when the last Muslim-held stronghold, Noto, surrendered. A comparison is in order at this point. In 1066 it took the Normans in England one battle and a few weeks to conquer the English; but it took the Normans thirty years to defeat the Arabs in Sicily. One can only assume that the Arabs were more motivated fighters than the English. Perhaps the Jihad inspired the Muslims more than Harold inspired his English subjects. About one-third of William the Conqueror's invading army in England was made up of Normans; the rest were other Frenchmen from Poitou, Anjou, and Brittany. The officers of Roger Guiscard's Norman army in Sicily were Normans, but many of the rank and file were Italians and Greeks. After the conquest by the Normans, Sicily came back into the mainstream of European life, from which it had been cut off by more than two centuries of Muslim occupation.

Once conquered, the Muslim population of Sicily proved remarkably amenable and cooperative. In fact, a large part of the army which Roger led against Amalfi and Capua in 1098 was made up of Muslims, and there was only one minor local rebellion against the Norman's rule before his death in 1101, at the age of seventy. A few more outbreaks of rebellion followed in the course of the twelfth century, some Arabs were massacred in Palermo, and toward the end of the century many Muslims fled to the hills for safety. The Jihad was long forgotten as the Muslims struggled to maintain their identity and religious freedom. Under a later king, Frederick II, Muslims still formed an important part of the population of Cefalu, and many of the shepherds in southern Sicily were still Muslims. The last Muslims were deported from Sicily to the town of Lucera, in Apulia, where the remnants of the old Islamic kingdom of Sicily were all forcibly converted to Christianity in 1300.

29

THE AFRICAN TAKEOVER: SPAIN 1104–1212

ALONG WITH HIS CAMELS AND his Tuaregs, Yusuf brought in his wake a century and a half of North African rule to Muslim Spain. Al-Andalus became a European colony of Africa, and in due course it also became a secondary target fought over by two rival Berber Muslim empires (one with its capital in Marrakech, the other in Fez) spread across Algeria, Morocco, and Mauretania: the Almoravids and the Almohads.

Spain was important to these two sects, of course, but it was not their country. Spain was a de facto Moroccan colony over which each side claimed authority and over which they fought and killed each other by the tens of thousands. Morocco was the heart of their empire. Spain was one of its limbs. The campaign in Spain was a colonial campaign, rather as Libya was to the British and Germans during World War II: important but not the main theater of war. To the Almoravids and the Almohads the main war zones were elsewhere, in the desert and plains of North Africa and in the Atlas mountains. The inter-Islamic conflict was a Jihad just the same, in which each Muslim empire fought a holy war against the other, sometimes against the Spanish Muslims, and occasionally against the Spanish Christians also.

That word "holy," as applied to war, is misleading. It conveys a picture of Christian knights in armor kneeling and praying before battle, of standards waving in the wind, of tonsured friars in brown

robes and sandals holding aloft crosses; of fierce bearded Arab warriors waving their scimitars, shouting "Allah is Great" and, after victory, exhorting their captives to conversion. In fact these holy wars in
Spain were ferocious orgies of carnage and decapitation. Each side
massacred its prisoners or, more lucratively, enslaved them. After a
battle, the Muslims, when victorious, would wander around the battlefield cutting off heads by the hundreds, and at times thousands.

The Jihad was just as ferocious when it was Muslim fighting
against Muslim. In fact often even more so. When the Almoravids took
Tlemcen in Algeria from the Almohads (more about them later) in
1145, their leader Abd el-Mumen, according to Condé's not always
reliable book, "avenged himself by causing all the living souls that
appeared before the eyes of his ferocious soldiery to be put to the
sword. The carnage was of a truth most frightful; nay, it is affirmed by
Isa Ben Ahmed Musa that 100,000 creatures of Allah were slaughtered
on that day of horror." Even if the figures are largely inflated, it is clear
that all was not prayer and piety and thanksgiving after the battle.

By fighting so savagely against each other the Muslims finally
assured the victory of the Spaniards in Spain. They were more efficient
than the Christians at killing each other. The hostility of the Catholic
kingdoms in Spain toward each other was at least tempered by the
moderating advice of the pope and of the Spanish priests and bishops,
who restrained the bellicosity of their flocks. The unfortunate Moors
had no one to counsel them except their fanatical mullahs and imams
urging them on and on to more mutual destruction. It is during this
period that many of the Orders of Christian warriors were founded,
such as the Knights of Calatrava, the Knights of Santiago, the Knights
of Our Lady of Montjoie, and the Knights of St. Julian and Alcantara,
who placed their swords at the service of Spain and of their king and
who took such a large part in the liberation of Spain from the Moors,
particularly in the 1200s.

From the beginning of the twelfth century to the middle of the thirteenth, Spain represented a vast fresco in which the line dividing the
Moors from the Spanish inexorably moved south, with an occasional
northward lunge, taking over by nibbles and sometimes by gulps vast
territories which Tarik and Musa had occupied so rapidly in 711 and
for which the Spaniards now had to fight for every mile they reconquered.

If the response of Castile and Aragon to the Almoravids had been
less resolute, al-Andalus certainly, and the whole of Spain possibly,

would have become a North African colony. The North Africans in a few years occupied all taifas ruled by the Spanish Muslims—except at first the Balearic Islands. They were beginning to put heavy pressure on the Christian kingdoms although, besotted by the beauty of Spain and the beauty of Spanish women, their early drive began to falter. Toledo, so recently retaken by the Christians, was continually under threat. By 1114 they were putting pressure on Christian Catalonia. Christendom was aroused. French knights from Provence, Gascony, Béarn, and Languedoc mainly, but also some from Normandy, Burgundy, and the north of France, began to stream across the Pyrenees to help their Spanish comrades in what seemed to them more and more a holy war against Islam. The conflict was, in fact, becoming a crusade. Jerusalem had been retaken by the Crusaders in 1097, and many of the knights who were now riding into Spain to fight the Moors were veterans of the campaigns in the distant Holy Land.

The response from within Christian Spain itself to the Almoravid takeover in Muslim Spain was overwhelming in its patriotic intensity. For as well as a crusade, this was becoming a national war. The king of Aragon and Navarre, another Alfonso, but Alfonso I this time, took over from Alfonso VI, king of Leon and Castile. They called the king of Aragon "Battling Alfonso," and rightly so, because he won twenty-nine victories against the Moors, as Derek Lomax reminds us in *The Reconquest of Spain.* He roamed the Spanish countryside laying siege to cities, recapturing others, taking castles when he could, always on the attack. A few years after the Almoravids had captured the important city of Saragossa and were masters of al-Andalus, the pope, on a visit to Toulouse, proclaimed a crusade in 1118, and some six hundred French knights led by the famed prince of Béarn, Gaston the Crusader, just back from Jerusalem, set out for Spain and helped to retake Saragossa. Alfonso the Battler defeated an Almoravid force at Cutanda. In the face of one defeat after another, Almoravid rule was disintegrating. The Muslim city of Cordova rebelled in 1120 and five years later Alfonso I marched south all the way to Malaga, trailing his Aragonese army and his French knights behind him, then turned around and returned to Saragossa, taking with him ten thousand Christian families of Andalusia back to Christendom.

Raids and counterraids around Toledo and in Andalusia were the habitual type of warfare, sometimes carried out with incredible savagery by both sides. Gaston the Crusader was killed in 1131. His head was cut off and carried through the streets of Granada to the sound of trumpets and the beat of drums. When Tashufin, the Cordova emir's son, captured Escalona, he had all the men executed and the women enslaved. Christians were also engaged in slavery, but on a more modest scale than the Muslims, at least until the seventeenth century when the great slave trade to the Americas began in earnest as a commercial enterprise.

There is, and always has been, something shameful and repugnant about slavery to most Christian minds, which didn't stop them pursuing it assiduously when they had the opportunity. To the Muslims it had always been more stable. It has the approval of the Koran, and as Muslims consider that the injunctions of the Koran are as valid today as they were in 632, some Muslims argue that it is God's will that it should continue. In Mauretania, the country of the Almoravids, it was made illegal only in the 1960s. But the law can be helpless against custom. In Arabia, camouflaged for international public relations purposes, it continues disguised, but diminished, to this day.

Battling Alfonso I died in 1134, but the Reconquest continued, particularly as the Almoravid code, under the impact of Spanish life, so much brighter than the Moorish lifestyle in the North Africa of that period, was showing signs of wear and tear. But raiding by Christians and Muslims into each other's territory continued although Aragon, trying for some years to acquire large parts of French Languedoc, found itself fighting more and more north of the border and less and less against the Moors to the south. The French, for their part, were claiming Catalonia. It was finally a standoff, but for a few decades the quarrel slowed down Aragon's participation in the Reconquest, which became largely a Castilian near-monopoly. Aragon did acquire Catalonia, however, but peacefully, through a royal marriage.

The war against the Moors, on the Christian side, was being maintained by another Alfonso, Alfonso VII, king of Leon and Castille. There were no big battles, however, only quick raids, and gnawing and nibbling away at each other's territories. Then the Almoravids began to collapse, but not through Christian attacks. Another sect of North African Muslims destroyed them: the Almohads.

The Almohads invaded al-Andalus in 1146 and in this strictly Muslim internecine war trounced the Almoravids and restored Muslim unity in the country. The Almoravids fled to Mallorca, and by 1150 the Almohads were the recognized rulers of Muslim Spain; the victory was an ephemeral one. The followers of this ultra-austere sect were also in due course to come up against the natural desire of the Spanish Muslims to keep these North African aliens out. But for nearly a hundred years they were the masters of most of al-Andalus and the dreaded foes of Christian Spain.

There were many points in common between the conquering Almohads and the conquered Almoravids. W. Montgomery Watt, in his *History of Islamic Spain,* succinctly summarizes them: "Both came into existence in northwest Africa, and then later included al-Andalus in their territories. Both were ruled by a Berber dynasty and found their original supporters among Berber tribesmen. Both were in origin religious movements, or, perhaps rather had a religious basis. They were, however, largely political in purpose." There, of course, without delving further, Watt has come to the crux of the Islamic faith. As much as a religion, Islam is an ideological (or call it political) movement built on a religious foundation. The Jihad is there to spread the message, whatever it might be, with the aid of the sword.

Watt interestingly reminds us that the Almohads found their supporters, among the Berbers of North Africa, from among the old enemies of the tribesmen who supported the Almoravids. There was an old hostility at work there. The Almoravid movement came out of the Sahara desert. Its followers were nomads, like the Tuaregs. The Almohads were peasant farmers and pastoralists from the Atlas mountains. The two groups had little in common except their dislike of each other, their hatred of the infidels, and their love of Islam. The founder of the Almohads, Ibn Tumart, was born in 1082 in a village in the mountains. After studying in Spain, he decided to preach on the necessity of a united Islam, but by so doing he only added one more sect to the numerous ones that already existed! One day he harangued the emir's sister in Fez and pulled her off her horse for daring to appear in public without a veil over her face. He claimed to be the Madhi, the vanished leader whom Muslims await. There have been many of them in Islamic history and they often finish their days either killed in battle, hanged, beheaded, burned, impaled, or murdered. Being a highly placed Muslim can be a high-risk situation. Ibn Tumart, too, died violently, in battle in 1130.

In spite of their holy message, the Almohads favored the old method for getting rid of rivals: murder. Assassination for the potentially disloyal servants of the realm, massacre for the foe in battle, his wife and his children. One of the most famous Almohad kings, Abd el-Mumen, fearing a conspiracy by his vizier, slipped him a glass of milk laced with a good, strong poison before setting out on a Jihad against the Christian-held province of Algarve. He then left with a light heart and eighteen thousand mounted troops. One of his generals, Xeque Abu Mohamad Abdallah Ben Abi Hafaz (in view of his long and complicated name we shall make a point of not mentioning him again) took the fortress town of Atarnikes, near Badajoz, and put to death every Christian he captured, without sparing the life of a single man, we are told. The Castilian monarch, King Alfonso VIII, who had come to the throne three years previously, arrived just in time to gaze at the headless corpses and to lose a further six thousand men in the ensuing battle with the victorious Almohads. Many others were made prisoner and taken as slaves to Seville and Cordova.

Abd el-Mumen seems to have been a very peculiar sort of monarch, even by the bizarre standards then in vogue. We read in Condé that in 1152 he caused an unfortunate creature called Isaltin Coraib Ahmedhi to be brought to Marrakech in chains to be impaled before the gate of the city and before the king's eyes. The king went on to pray piously at the tomb of a famed imam, then journeyed to another city to distribute alms to the poor and to order the building of a "splendid" mosque. Abd el-Mumen died after reigning over the Almohads for thirty-three years. He left thirteen sons and two daughters and he moved his eyebrows up and down when he spoke. That is probably the nicest thing to be said about him.

In Spain the Jihad continued; Moors raided Castile and the Castilians raided al-Andalus. Abd el-Mumen's most distinguished successor was Yaquib Aben Juzef, who came to the Almohad throne in 1184 and called himself el-Mansur, meaning The Victorious, and it is by this name that we shall refer to him, carefully avoiding its other spelling, Almanzor, which we have used before for another victorious conqueror. We can thus hopefully avoid some of the confusion that these repetitious Arab names can cause to the reader (and to the indexer). El-Mansur's life of conquests was marked by intense piety, numerous massacres, the construction of many public buildings, and the ordering of many murders. He had his two brothers and an uncle murdered on suspicion they might be plotting against him, ordered the building of many mosques in North Africa and Spain, subjugated the region of Cabisa where "he made a fearful carnage among his rebellious subjects," undertook a new Jihad in Spain, "wholly devastated the land, killed or took prisoner the inhabitants, destroyed the villages, burned all the products, carried the devastation to such an extent that he left the Comarcas in the condition of a parched and sand-covered desert" and, returning to Morocco with thirteen thousand women and children for sale as slaves, he enjoyed the prosperity and good fortune which his God had granted him "in consideration of all his pious intentions and good words."

El-Mansur administered the Almohad realm, including his province of Spain, mainly from Marrakech, and it is there that he received in 1192 a message from King Alfonso VIII challenging him to battle. During the previous year the Castilians had fallen "upon the lands of the faithful as do wolves upon the sheep-fold, persecuting the true believers with cruel and fearful onslaughts, whereby the towns and fields were alike laid waste."

Outraged at the pretensions of the infidel monarch, el-Mansur loudly, clearly, and furiously called for a Jihad against the infidels and in 1195 assembled a vast army made up of all races and groups who made up his kingdom: Arabs, Zenetes, Masamudes, Gomaras, negroes from West Africa, volunteers from Mauritania, Kabiles, and Algiazazes. They gathered together in Tangiers and sailed for Algeciras. The Almohads were joined by detachments of Andalusian Muslims. El-Mansur gave the command of this vast host to his vizier, Abu Hafas. Then, chanting hymns in praise of Allah and the Prophet, they marched north to meet the Christian army of Castile. The two armies clashed just south of Alarcos, in southern Castile. The Christians—the Muslims claimed they numbered at least 300,000—were massed at the foot of a hill on which Alfonso VIII, astride his charger, stood like a statue.

The battle started in the early hours of the morning, a weak sun rising in the sky. It was the Christians who charged first, seven or eight thousand cavalrymen, according to Arab accounts, "the horses as well as their riders with defenses of iron, the breastplates, cuirasses and helmets of the cavaliers shone glittering in the sun." They came thundering onward, garbed in steel and heavily protected by chain mail. General Abu Hafas, watching the massed Castilian cavalry approach "with fearful clangor," steadied his troops with soothing words of hope and courage. "Ye fight in the service of Allah. . . . This is your first deed of arms. After it shall follow either a glorious martyrdom and the joys of Paradise, or victory and rich spoils."

The joys of Paradise. That was always the trump card that couldn't be overtrumped. Have no fear, men. If you die, seventy-two virgins on silk couches are waiting for you with their thousand-year-long orgasms. And three hundred waiters are waiting to serve you with three hundred dishes served on three hundred gold plates. How lucky you are, soldiers of Islam. You have nothing to lose. With such bounties awaiting them, dead or alive, the Muslim soldiers awaited serenely the onrush of the Castilian soldiers.

The Christian cavalry smashed into the first Muslim lines riding straight into the long Arab lances on which the horses impaled themselves. The Spanish cavalry moved back, charged again. Again they were repulsed. The cavalry prepared a third charge against the massed Arab infantry. "Allah supports you from his throne on high," shouted one of the generals to his troops to steady them. But this time the Muslim line broke. General Abu Hafas was killed trying to rally the fleeing Muslims to his standard. "He obtained the crown of martyrdom by dying for his Lord," a chronicler tells us. General Abu Hafaz now went to his reward, joined by many of his soldiers. The tribe of Henteta, from North Africa, was surrounded by the Christians and cut to pieces. "They entered that day the myriad joys of Paradise," says the chronicler.

But the swing of battle suddenly changed. The Moors were now attacking the Spaniards. The Christians, the Arab chronicles say, were now heavily outnumbered. "The dust and vapor which rose from the struggling masses in that mortal strife were at length such as to impede the light of the sun, and make the day appear to be night." The explanations are not clear. What is clear is that the Christians were going to lose. It was suddenly the turn of the men of al-Andalus to charge, straight up the hill where they believed—rightly—Alfonso VIII of Castile and Leon, on his horse, was watching, appalled; inevitable defeat replaced expected victory. The Spaniards broke and fled. The slaughter, we are told, was "very terrible," including ten thousand of the cavalrymen whose charges early in the battle had broken the Almohad line. The survivors of the Christian army were running up the hill, toward the safety they felt the presence of their defeated king would give them. The Arab crossbowmen intercepted them, "cutting them to pieces and grinding them to dust." They fled in another direction, trying to escape from the merciless weapons of their enemy. "So was the force of Alfonso VIII destroyed, and his cavalry in which he so much trusted brought to nought."

Alfonso VIII fled north, galloping in through the southern gate of the nearby town of Alarcos and galloping out through the northern gate, without stopping. The number of Christian dead was so great "that God who created them alone can know the answer." El-Mansur took twenty thousand prisoners in the town of Alarcos itself but, surprisingly and to the intense annoyance of the Muslim combatants who wanted their plunder, their slaves and their women, the Almohad leader released them all. The victorious Muslim warriors sensed the gesture was "one of the chivalrous extravagances proper to kings" and forgave him for giving up their booty.

The Muslim victory of Alarcos shook Christendom, particularly Spain's nearest neighbor, France, and England, ruled by Richard the Lion Hearted. The two countries felt so endangered by the new Islamic threat that had suddenly intensified only a few hundred miles from their homelands that they considered sending a joint expedition, under Richard and Philippe II, into Spain. But nothing came of it.

Fortunately for the Christians, the Church was now headed by Pope Celestine III, who had been the papal legate in Spain. He was therefore well aware of the immensity of the Muslim threat to western Europe. Celestine III, when cardinal, had helped in the founding of the Order of Santiago, one of the most powerful of the orders of Christian warriors whose role in resisting the Jihad became vital to the survival of Christian Spain and the downfall of Muslim Spain.

The pope's personal authority and his advocacy of Spanish unity brought sanity back on the Iberian stage where, after Alarcos, the kings of Leon and Navarre, in the hope of adding bits of defeated, weakened, and downcast Castile to their own realms, had meanly invaded Alfonso VIII's temporarily shattered kingdom. The odious Alfonso IX of Leon, in fact, recruited Muslim troops to invade Castile. Outraged at this lack of Christian solidarity on the part of the Leonese, King Pedro II of Aragon helped the king of Castile to drive the troops of the king of Leon out of his kingdom. The pope also now put in his word. He excommunicated the Leonese king and absolved the subjects of Leon and Navarre from all allegiance to their kings if they used Muslim troops against Christians. The pope's intervention was decisive. The kings of Castile, Aragon, and Portugal arranged for the king of Leon to marry the Castilian princess Berenguela, and the defense of the Iberian peninsula became not only a national matter but a family one. Spain was once again saved. So, with it, was Portugal.

To make sure there would be no backsliding by elusive monarchs, Pope Celestine ordered Sancho VII, king of Navarre, to end his flirtation with the Almohads and, instead, to support the king of Castile. He also made sure that Castile, in its struggle against el-Mansur, would receive help from north of the Pyrenees by granting permission to the knights of Aquitaine, who had taken a vow to go to the Holy Land as Crusaders, to fight for Spain instead of fighting for Jerusalem. The final combat was still several years away. Much of the fighting fell on the shoulders of the orders of knighthood who kept up the war against the Almohad strongholds in al-Andalus, while el-Mansur, for his part, continued his hit-and-miss raids and dashes into Christian territory. Toledo, Guadalara, Madrid, and Talavera figured on the Jihad hit list. So did Salamanca, where the Moors killed all the men and carried off all the women. So the war went wearily on for seventeen years after Alarcos.

On Trinity Sunday 1212, a year to remember, King Alfonso VIII of Castile called his vassals to Toledo. Now, he told them, was the time to strike deep into Almohad country and destroy these Muhammedan intruders who invaded our country five centuries ago. Soon we shall march into the land of al-Andalus and win it back for Spain.

Castilian ambassadors went to France and Rome to seek support. The French sent two thousand knights, ten thousand horsemen and fifty thousand foot soldiers. On arrival in Spain, some of the French, mistaking the enemy, began to massacre the Jews of Toledo until the Spanish knights rode between them and their intended victims and stopped them. Church bells rang. Te Deums were sung. Masses were celebrated. Religious processions circulated through the towns and villages. All over Europe people prayed, fasted, and offered donations to Christ and the Virgin Mary. As if in retaliation, the Muslims killed Alfonso's eldest son, Prince Fernando, who had vowed to spend his youth fighting Islam. The pope, well knowing with whom he had to deal, threatened to excommunicate King Alfonso IX of Leon if he dared to join the Almohads. Islam, everyone hoped, would soon vanish from Spain, and all the Christians would be able to sleep at night safe from the warriors of Islam. The year 1212 would indeed be one to remember. So everyone hoped.

30

THE YEAR OF DECISION: LAS NAVAS DE TOLOSA 1212

I T WAS NOT ONLY THE Castilian king's vassals who answered the call of the Crusades. The campaign that Alfonso VIII had now launched was recognized by all Christendom as a holy war, the Christian reply to the Jihad. King Sancho VIII of Navarre, Sancho the Strong they called him, and Pedro II of Aragon also rode into the Castilian capital, their knights and vassals riding behind them, to take part in the great crusade. The king of Leon, Alfonso IX, did not go over to the Almohads, but he didn't go to Toledo to join the gathering of Spanish kings and grandees either. Instead he launched a war against Portugal in an obscure quarrel over some vague territory somewhere, which history barely remembers. But the knights of Leon and Portugal, disregarding the nature of whatever quarrel divided their sovereigns, were present in Toledo, ready to fight side by side against the Muslim enemy. Eight fighting Spanish bishops and the masters and knights of three of the most famous fighting orders—the Templars, Santiago, and Calatrava —were part of the expedition. The militias of Segovia, Burgos, Medina, Avila, and Cuenca joined their Toledo comrades and waited, lounging in the grass of the apple orchards, for the order to march south toward the Moors and to defeat them.

It was the largest army ever assembled in Christian Spain, at least 100,000 men, with 60,000 mules to carry their train. The greatest names of Spain and its most haughty noblemen were present, going to mass and communion, shoulder to shoulder with the peasants from their estates, joined in the great adventure for "the glory of Spain and of Saint James."

The battle which was about to be fought changed the course not only of Spanish but of European history, far more than Formigny, Bleinheim, Waterloo, the Marne, or Stalingrad. Near Seville, awaiting the Christian army, ready to march toward it and engage it in battle, was the flower of Spanish Muslim chivalry, Andalusians as gallant as their Christian foes from the north, and the Almohad hordes that had come over from Africa in the hope of bringing first Spain, then perhaps all of Europe, into the fold of Allah.

On June 20 the Christian army, led by Alfonso VIII, marched out of Toledo and headed to the southeast to meet the Muhammedan foe, wherever they might be. By the side of the king rode Archbishop Rodrigo of Toledo, the warrior prelate who had pledged his life to the liberation of all of Spain from Moors and Arabs. One hundred thousand men followed them, grouped in three army corps: Castilian, French, and Aragonese. On June 22, the Muslims marched out of Seville and headed to the northeast toward Jaen. It was a huge army, several times larger than the Christians', and it was commanded by a man who considered victory and conquest his natural due: Mohammed I, son of el-Mansur, who remembered his father's victory at Alarcos, seventeen years before, and planned to repeat it.

Las Navas de Tolosa is the spot in southern Spain where the two armies finally were to meet. How many of us outside of Spain have ever heard the name of this battle, far more momentous than the one that Charles Martel had won at Poitiers 480 years before, the battle that saved Europe from the fate that Edward Gibbon so eloquently described for us? But before the slaughter came the marching. Before reaching, exhausted, this point of destiny, the army of Alfonso tramped for six weeks across the hot and dry summer landscape of Muslim Spain, fighting the odd skirmish and taking a castle or two on the way. It was the French contingent that led the way and initiated the fighting. On June 24 they attacked and captured the castle of Malagon. King Alfonso's Castilians arrived the next day. But the French knights, boiling in their armor and coats of mail, exhausted by the heat, pleaded to go home. They agreed to continue only when they were told more booty would await them at Calatrava. Calatrava capitulated to the French and to Sancho of Navarre on the 27th. After receiving their share of the plunder, the French, still complaining of the heat, said it was still too hot, they were going back home. Of the French force, originally perhaps the strongest in King Alfonso VIII's command, only 130 knights stayed on to continue the campaign. The others rode or marched back to France, taunted and pelted with garbage by the furious population of Toledo when, on reaching the city on their way back north, they stood outside its walls clamoring for food.

News of the French desertion reached the ears of the Almohad chief. He now felt surer than ever of victory. In the Christian camp, dispirited but undaunted and unafraid, Alfonso VIII marched on, his weary army straggling behind him across the hot, sunburned plain. He captured the town of Alarcos through which, seventeen years before, he had madly galloped as a defeated monarch fleeing the battlefield. For him it was an omen and a joy.

It is at Alarcos that news reached Alfonso VIII that Mohammed I's army was awaiting the Christians on the nearby plain of Las Navas de Tolosa. The Spaniards fell on their knees, prayed that the coming battle might be theirs, and then marched to meet the enemy. A large party of Moors stood massed at the narrow entrance of the Losa canyon, cutting the Spaniards from Mohammed's main force awaiting them on the other side. The Christians could go no further. An old shepherd then appeared, hat in hand, who humbly made himself known to the king. He was a Christian and a Spaniard who had known only Muslim rule all his life. He wanted to die in a Christian land. He knew, he said, of a path unknown to anyone except himself. The path would lead the Spaniards into the next canyon and they would come down to the west; from there they could attack the Muslim army. The shepherd then showed the king the way, kissed the king's hand and vanished, never to be seen again or to claim any reward. The Spaniards swore the shepherd was Saint Isidoro, patron saint of Madrid, and that he had now gone back to heaven.

The next day, by this secret path, the Spanish army simply went around the Muslim legions who, to their surprise, suddenly found themselves facing the army of King Alfonso VIII stretched across the plain of the Mesa del Rey. Alfonso VIII decided his tired troops should rest for a couple of days, until Monday, July 16. There was in those days a certain ceremonial ritual to battle that both sides had to observe, whatever massacres might occur afterward. War, however bloody and ferocious, was organized between gentlemen, even if they were Spaniards and Moors. The Christians were left undisturbed by the Muslims. Saturday was the time for confessions and, at midnight on

Sunday, the soldiers of the Christian army heard mass, went to communion, and lined up for battle afterward.

King Alfonso VIII and his Castilians stood in the center of the battle line, to his left Archbishop Rodrigo, not at all clerical-looking in his armor and with sword drawn, surrounded by the the knights of Santiago and Calatrava and the Templars, with Sancho's Navarrese massed alongside. To the right stood the men of Aragon and their king, Pedro. Far away in Toledo, another monarch, Leopold VI of Austria, was arriving too late for the battle. Opposite stood the might of Islam. Almohads from North Africa, negroes from West Africa, Andalusians. Mohammed I, in the rear, sat reading the Koran, the members of his personal negro guard, all chained one to the other to ensure they would not flee, stood shackled nearby,

The Spaniards attacked, overwhelming the first lines of light Muslim infantry. The heavily armored Christian knights pushed back the two wings of the Almohad army. Violent fighting raged, we are told. That short sentence means a long list of dead. Mohammed's center, mainly cavalry, which had held all day, broke when their counterattack failed. With cries of exultation the Spaniards rushed forward, infantry and cavalry mixed. Mohammed I fled all the way to Jaen. His chained negro bodyguards, helpless and unable to move, were killed where they stood. The rout turned into a massacre. The Christian horsemen pursued the fleeing enemy for twelve miles, cutting down the fugitives vainly seeking safety far behind the battlefield. One hundred fifty thousand Muslim warriors fell that day, so say the chronicles. Why had Allah and the Prophet given the infidels such a victory, the despairing faithful asked. The mullahs wrung their hands and had no answers. There were none.

In the Christian camp the victors sang hymns and praised the Lord. They rested for two days, using the enemy's abandoned bows and arrows and lances as firewood to cook their meals. When the news of Alfonso VIII of Castile's victory reached the scheming Alfonso IX of Leon, he interrupted his war against Portugal and agreed, in the future, to help the Castilian king against his erstwhile Moorish semi-allies. Everyone hoped the Almohads would soon be on their way back to Africa and that the Jihad would become only a memory. Half a million Muslims decided that their future in Spain no longer looked very bright and migrated to North Africa, but it took another fifty years to complete the Spanish campaign against the Almohads and for the Spaniards to free most of the soil of Spain from its alien invaders.

Mohammed I, the Almohad sovereign, shamed and anguished over his defeat, took to drink and, in spite of the Koranic injunctions against alcohol, gradually drank himself to death.

31

THE MUSLIM DEBACLE: SPAIN 1212–1250

A HISTORICAL MAP OF SPAIN and Portugal shows clearly how, during nearly eight hundred years, La Reconquista moved south across the peninsula in stages, sometimes slowly, sometimes very slowly. It was a very sluggardly war in terms of territorial conquest. It took the Spaniards and Portuguese three hundred years to retake their first one-third of Iberia, from the eighth-century beginning of the Reconquest by Pelayo in the Asturias to around 1080. To reoccupy the next one-third, Castile, Aragon, Leon, and Navarre, not forgetting Portugal, took one hundred thirty years, from around 1080 to 1210. It is during this period that four of the greatest cities of the peninsula became Christian again: Saragossa, Toledo, Lisbon, and Barcelona. We could add Madrid, but the present capital of Spain was then a fairly unimportant town. The last one-third, southern Spain (Granada excepted) was gobbled up by the Spanish far more quickly, in less than forty years, between 1210 and 1250.

This chapter and the next cover the thirteenth-century period. Islam and the Jihad were on the run, and they were running to the south, back toward Africa where Morocco and safety were only a few sea miles distant if you kept your eyes fixed on Tangiers as you sailed from Algeciras across the narrow straits of Gibraltar. Spanish Islam, al-Andalus, was shrinking so fast that it was disappearing.

This brisk summing-up, like all things short and quick, needs

197

expansion. Not all of Muslim al-Andalus vanished from Spain in the thirteenth century. One taifa lingered on. The Moorish kingdom of Granada kept its toehold in Spain, independent but a vassal of Castile, for another 242 years, to finally disappear from the Moslemah in 1492, a key date in Spanish history. It was also, of course, the year that Christopher Columbus sailed from Spain to discover America. The same year Spain expelled the Jews from its territory.

The Reconquest, from its eighth-century beginning to its fifteenth-century end, was always short on great battles, but there were a few, of which Simancas, Zalaca, Alarcos, and Las Navas de Tolosoa were probably the most important. But it was an epoch of Spanish history long in skirmishes and in massacres, raids, and sieges. Military activity was most intense in the decades between 1210 and 1250. During these forty years, from Toledo south, armed bands roamed the land, pious and savage freebooters praying to the Christian God or to Muhammad's Allah; fighting, raiding and taking towns and villages, massacring, capturing slaves, besieging, and sometimes taking castles. Christians and Muslims, Castilians and Moors, Arabs and Aragonese, Navarrese and Andalusians, they were all on the move, fighting for or against the Jihad; except that for the Muslims; this was now more a war of survival than a war for the faithful.

In the hope of avoiding expulsion from Spain, Muslims went to fight for the Christian kings against their Arab comrades. Condé recalls the feelings of the king of Granada after a campaign against his fellow Moors on behalf of the king of Castile: "More grieved than satisfied was the heart of Muhammad Alahmar as he thought of the advantages which his own army had aided the Christians to obtain, and he returned to his territories with a saddened spirit, well knowing that the aggrandizement and successes of the infidel could not but result in the ultimate extinction of the Moslemah power. . . . But the king had confidence in Allah and did not believe He would wholly abandon his people." Allah, however, was looking the other way. The slow war of sieges became unfashionable. The castles, built to withstand long sieges, started to fall to the ground; their ruins still litter the Spanish landscape. So many of these fortresses were built in central Spain that they gave the area its name, Castile, the Land of Castles.

Two royal names stand out among the Spanish leaders in this ardent phase of the Reconquista: Fernando III of Castile, who conquered Seville and Cordova; and Jaime I, king of Aragon, who captured the Cid's old Valencia fiefdom back from the Moors, conquered

Murcia and, with the help of the knights of France and Catalonia, took back the Balearic islands from the Almohads. The defeated Almohads skulked their way back to North Africa, where they hung on until 1296; then they vanished from history to be replaced by another dynasty, the Marinids, who were intelligent enough not to become too embroiled in Spanish affairs, at least at first.

As Spanish affairs continued to unravel themselves in favor of the Christians, much of the fighting was done by the warriors of their military orders with their tens of thousands of fighting knights and retainers, who now surpassed in religious fervor their Muslim enemies. Al-Andalus was dying; Islam was killing itself. It had become a shoddy system of murderous power politics. In the 1220s three men, each claiming to be the caliph, were fighting for power in Spain, each one striving to destroy the other two: al-Walid from Marrakech, al-Adil in Seville, and al-Bayassi in Cordova.

The Christians were no longer the primary enemy of these fighting Muslims; each one of the three caliphs called for a Jihad against the other two. Puzzled Muslims fought against one another, each faction hoping it was fighting for the rightful caliph. Fighting and dying for the wrong caliph perhaps meant hell instead of Paradise.

The Marrakech caliph al-Walid didn't last long. He was strangled by partisans of al-Adil, which at least reduced the number of claimants to the supreme headship of Islam in Spain to two. In fierce fighting between the two surviving rival factions, al-Adil conquered several cities belonging to al-Bayyasi, notably Ubeda, Jaen, and Cordova itself. The distraught al-Bayyasi, seeing his little empire withering away, called on his supreme Christian enemy Fernando III of Castile for help against al-Adil. As an inducement he promised to become the Christian king's vassal and to give him the city of Jaen after it had been reconquered. Months of confused fighting followed, with Fernando III employing fine diplomatic skill as well as lavish use of his Castilian troops; making his way through the maze of Muslim chicanery with all the aplomb, the elegance, and the brutality, when required, expected of a thirteenth century Spanish grandee.

The Spanish king became the de facto arbiter of the al-Andalus kinglets. He took the town of Loja and massacred all its Muslim inhabitants while his vassal al-Bayassi helplessly concurred but tried to look the other way. The king of Castile then took Granada by promising the inhabitants he would not destroy their orchards. Meanwhile Caliph al-Bayassi, backed by Fernando, had begun to make war against another Muslim petty king, Abul Ula. Abul Ula roused the Cordovans against al-Bayassi, defeated him in battle, cut off his head, and gave it as a present to al-Adil, who was now the sole survivor of the original trio of caliphate rivals. Al-Adil journeyed to Morocco, perhaps taking al-Bayassi's head with him, but on arrival in the Moroccan capital he too lost his head. The reasons for this monotonous series of executions are rather obscure. Haphazard decapitation was a sort of occupational hazard in the Muslim higher echelons.

All three of these recent rival caliphs were now decapitated, their headless corpses resting in their graves, two in Andalusia and one in Morocco. Other Jihad protagonists were now elbowing their way to the front, oblivious of the risk of further decapitations. Prominent among them was Abul Ula, after his victory over al-Bayassi. He now became caliph, called himself al-Mamun, and reigned over Seville. The other was a professional soldier of fortune, Ibn Hud, who appointed himself king of Murcia. Of course he and al-Mamun were soon busy fighting each other in a sturdy but meaningless Jihad of their own. Al-Mamun disengaged himself from this trivial, second-rate holy war to go to Morocco to lead an Almohad army from Meknes (the year was 1232) against a rebel army roused into revolt by al-Mamun's recent attack, as self-appointed caliph, on the infallibility of the Almohad founder Ibn Tumart, the Madhi. Al-Mamun had announced that there was "no other Madhi but Jesus, son of Mary." He was killed in battle soon after the proclamation of this unexpected dogma.

In Andalusia, just about this time, Ibn Hud began to manifest himself as a soldier of quality. The Spanish Muslims could expect no help from their brethren in North Africa, who were busily engaged in a civil war of their own. The Spanish Muslims were left to cope with the Spanish Christians by themselves. Ibn Hud may have been a Muslim, but he was also, perhaps first and foremost, a Spaniard, and a very ferocious one. "His real strength," writer Derek Lomax reminds us in *The Reconquest of Spain,* "lay in his expression of the pent-up hatred of the Andalusians for the Almohads. He beheaded the Almohad men, maimed their women, killed their children, ritually purified their mosques, condemned them as schismatics, and generally tried to implant a permanent hatred between Spanish and African Muslims."

More than a century of North African political occupation was now over. Muslim Spain was no longer a Moroccan dependency. The alien Almoravids had been expelled long ago and their rivals, the Almohads, were also being thrust back into Africa. By the 1230s al-Andalus was no longer a European annex of North Africa, but was becoming a Muslim annex of Christian Spain.

32

FIVE CITIES TO GO:
ANDALUSIA 1230–1248

A MONG THE MANY LOCALITIES STILL in Muslim hands after the expulsion of the Almohads, five large cities still remained to be liberated by the Christians: the old Umayyad capital Cordova, Seville, Granada, Jaen, and Valencia. Within ten years all except Granada were under Christian rule again. Granada was destined to coexist as a Muslim kingdom alongside the rest of Christian Spain for another two and a half centuries.

The first of these cities to fall to the Spaniards was Cordova, the old capital of al-Andalus, which had been perhaps the most splendid city of Europe in the days of Abd al-Rahman III, but which now was only the capital of a dying taifa, although still proud, tough, and belligerent. It had recently been ruled by Ibn al-Ahmar, who has been described as "perhaps the most skilful Spanish politician of the century." In the vanishing days of Spanish Islam, he managed somehow not only to survive but also to found a kingdom with the active help of the Castilian king Fernando III, who was no tenderfoot. While Ibn al-Ahmar—known universally as al-Ahmar, "The Red," by the color of his uniform—was desperately maneuvering to keep in Spain an Islamic presence (his own), Fernando was methodically pounding Islam into submission. His brother Alfonso destroyed a Muslim army at Jerez (the sherry country), killing all the prisoners he took; and Fernando criss-crossed the country at will, burning the crops and the villages, capturing mule trains, and battering castles into submission. Al-Ahmar and Ibn Hud were fighting their own inter-Muslim war, and Ibn Hud was now the boss of Cordova, although he was absent when the Castilians launched their final attack on the city.

King Fernando III assailed a city rent with dissensions and quarrels and treachery. A small band of Christian mercenaries had managed in January, 1236, to occupy a suburb which they had entered at night over a wall with the help of a bunch of citizens hostile to the present rulers. Fernando, at the head of two hundred noblemen, the flower of Castilian knighthood, rushed south from Toledo to give them support. More Spanish troops arrived to take part in the siege. Al-Ahmar, who disliked Cordova because he had once been expelled from the city, arrived to give advice to the Christian besiegers. Ibn Hud also came with an army from Seville, looked over the situation, and returned to Seville. In June, Cordova capitulated to Fernando after the king had agreed to let the citizens leave unharmed with all their valuables. He then dismantled from the great mosque the bells of Santiago de Compostela, which three hundred years earlier Almanzor had ordered his Christian captives to carry south hundreds of miles across Spain, to grace the mosque in Cordova. It was now the turn of Muslim slaves to carry them back to Compostela. Fernando III had a sense both of history and of the fitness of things. The Jihad had, so to speak, come a full circle.

Castile wasn't the only Spanish kingdom fighting the Moors. Almost as active, on the eastern seaboard of Spain, the kingdom of Aragon was determinedly breaking the Muslim hold over the region and replacing it with its own. King Jaime I faced an easy task at first, for the Almohad emir, Abu Sai, was anxious to give up his kingship and become a Christian. In 1236, Valencia, whose people were starving, fell to the Aragonese king. The province of Murcia to the south presented a more delicate problem. The Castilian king was encroaching on the territory that Jaime I of Aragon wanted to make his own. War between the two Christian kingdoms seemed likely to erupt. The discord, fortunately for the Spaniards, was settled by the 1244 Treaty of Almizra. Bivar, El Cid's original home, and a couple of other towns joined Aragon, which also kept Valencia; and Alicante went to Castile.

Over the next few years many towns and villages of al-Andalus fell into the Castilian net. In 1238 Ibn Hud was assassinated and two civil wars broke out in southern Spain. One was a meaningless conflict among Arab factions and tribes; the other was a war between Christianity and Islam. The Jihad was now a toothless, decrepit, snarling, and pitiful relic of the force it had so often been in the past.

During one of King Fernando III's absences north, al-Ahmar had taken over the city of Jaen and, moreover, had dared to fight—and defeat—the king's brother, Prince Rodrigo Alfonso. On his return to Toledo, Fernando engaged in a widespread scorched earth campaign and then laid siege to Jaen. Al-Ahmar was a realist. He knew Jaen was doomed; but his other domain, Granada, with its rugged, mountainous terrain and its villages built like fortresses on mountain tops, could hold out for years. He was also well aware that Granada, in the end, even if the final chapter was centuries away, would inevitably fall and become Spanish again. Geography, history, and demography were all on the Spaniards' side. Al-Ahmar wished to enjoy life rather than battle his way through it. He proposed a deal to the Christian king. Summarized, it went like this: "I'll let you take Jaen without fighting if you let me keep Granada. I'll be your vassal, I shall visit you at your court every year to present my respects, pay you a yearly tribute, and send my soldiers to serve alongside yours whenever you require them. But let me keep Granada!"

Muslim Granada was applying to become a satellite of Christian Castile and King Fernando agreed to the request. Now he turned his attention to Jaen and Seville, the two remaining important Muslim cities of Spain. Jaen gave in meekly, and a few days later Fernando entered the city and assisted at a solemn high mass. Seville remained the last city on his Reconquista agenda. For the Muslims who remained in Spain, the Jihad had become a meaningless word. La Reconquista had defeated the Jihad. That was the sole fact of life with which they could presently deal. Al-Andalus, Moorish and Muslim, was becoming Andalusia, Spanish and Christian.

It was said of Seville at the time, that it was the finest city in Europe. The same had been said of Cordova a couple of centuries before. Rome, Paris, and London were floundering out of the Dark Ages. The Renaissance was still a couple of hundred years away. Constantinople was no longer, for the time being, the capital of the Byzantine Empire, but the property of a young French knight of the Crusades, who raised money by selling off the city's antiques to the papacy and to the courts of Europe. That year, 1246, the people of Seville had distinguished themselves by assassinating one of their leading councillors, Omar ibn Jadd, for daring to suggest that Seville come to an understanding with the conquering Christians before it was too late. It was a wise counsel, defeatist perhaps, but certainly realistic. Like most good advice, it was rejected, and Ibn Jadd paid with his life for giving it. The cry went out across Seville: Fight the Christians! The Jihad was on again. Outraged at the Sevillian conduct, King Fernando III went on the attack, and by September 1246 his troops were already in the eastern outskirts of the city. His army included al-Ahmar and six hundred Muslim soldiers from Jaen fulfilling Granada's treaty obligations with the Castilian king. In the death throes of Muslim Spain, Muslim fought Muslim for Christian Spain.

Fernando III, who was a military thinker as well as a fighter, understood that the only way to overcome the city's resistance would be through a joint sea-and-land operation. Supplies could enter Seville too easily by ships coming up the broad river from the coast. On land, Fernando began the operation against Seville by attacking several of the small towns around it. Most surrendered easily. One, Cantillana, chose to fight. Fernando stormed the town and ordered those of its inhabitants who had not been slaughtered during the assault to be sold as slaves. The Sevillians fought back. "The besieged inhabitants of Seville were in possession of many wonderful engines," Condé tells us. "Some . . . there were the darts which were launched with such force that they were capable of transpiercing a horse from one side to the other, even though the animal were barded with iron."

In the summer of 1247, thirty Muslim galleys tried to intercept a convoy of thirteen vessels on the river carrying supplies, food, and weapons from Burgos to Fernando's besieging force. In spite of their superior numbers, the Muslims were beaten off and lost six ships. The wretched Sevillians, desperate at the risk of losing their beloved city (and possibly their lives), sent a message to the caliph, now in Tunis, imploring him to launch "the Jihad against the infidel enemies of God." Appeals in the name of Holy War rarely failed to be heard. The caliph sent several ships from North Africa loaded with relief supplies. Fernando's chief naval officer, Ramon Bonifez, a Burgos businessman, prevented them from entering the river.

More blood flowed along the banks of the Guadalquivir where fighting friars, knights in armor, and militiamen from the Christian cities sometimes met foraging parties from inside the hungry Muslim city looking for food and supplies. In Seville food was in such short supply that the starving citizens boiled their belts and shoes to make a meal. Seville at last surrendered at the end of November 1248. The siege had lasted two years and two months. The inhabitants were given a month to evacuate their city. They left in the hundreds of thousands. Many went to Morocco, others just moved a few miles to the coast and settled near Jerez. Many more made their way to al-Ahmar's kingdom of Granada, even though he had sent his knights to fight alongside the Christians besieging their city. Others left for Egypt. Some went no further west than to the Algarve, in the southwest corner of the Iberian peninsula. It is a territory that was contested between Castile and Portugal, but the Spaniards finally abandoned their claim to the Portuguese who, in this century, have made it one of Europe's fashionable playgrounds.

"So ended the empire of those princes in Seville who loved their city," sadly wrote a local man of letters, who watched the weeping Sevillians leave for an exile from which, for most of them, there was no return. "The Moslemah lost that beautiful city, the mosques and towers thereof were filled with crosses and idols, while the sepulchers were profaned." The Spanish Jihad, in the west of Europe, was over. The Ottoman Jihad, in eastern Europe, had been under way for more than a century and still had four more centuries to run.

PART SEVEN

ONSLAUGHT FROM THE EAST

33

THE OTTOMAN ADVENT: TURKEY MID-1200S

E VENTS IN THE MEANTIME WERE occurring elsewhere which would directly affect the course of the Jihad, not only in Europe but in the world. Within the ten years that followed the fall of Seville a new swarm of warriors was assembling in the east: the Turks. They were not yet Muslims, but pagans and animists. Within a few decades they were to discard their shamans and become enthusiastic followers of Allah. By the next century they would be battering their way across Europe, plundering, sacking, and massacring. They poured into eastern Europe and the Balkans to begin an occupation that lasted over five hundred years.

In 1250, only two years after the fall of Seville, Othman, the son of the Turkish tribal leader Ertogrul, was born, probably at Sugut, a little town near the Sea of Marmara. A band of a few hundred Turkish families, driven out of their ancestral homes in the central Asian territory of Khorassan by the advance and the terror of the Mongols under Genghis Khan, had made their way into Anatolia. Other Turkish tribesmen, among them a tribe called the Seljuks, had already settled in the unprotected and distant eastern limits of the empire of the Byzantines, after defeating them in the battle of Manzikert in 1071.

Othman's tribe had first settled near the site of present-day Erzerum, from where it had made its way west, under the protection of kinsmen from among the friendly Seljuk Turks, to the shores of the Sea of Marmara. There, within sight of the European coast on the other side of the Marmara, Othman's tribe stayed and stood guard against the encroachments of the Byzantine empire to the south, since the Byzantines were anxious to push the Turks out of Anatolia.

The Byzantines, however, were not the main threat to the Turks. It came from the east, where the Mongols, before whom Othman's tribe had fled a couple of generations earlier, were now sweeping across the plains of central Asia. Their main thrust, however, was not toward Anatolia, where the Turkish tribes were established, but further south into what is today Iraq and Iran. In 1258, Hulagu, the grandson of Genghis Khan, captured Baghdad, the capital of the Muslim empire. He then assembled the population in a field outside the city and massacred them all, then butchered al-Mustassim, the last of the Abbasid caliphs, and his family. Othman, whose father was probably a pagan, was only a child then, but when he reached adulthood he was converted to Islam and founded what became known, from his name, as the dynasty of the Ottoman Turks.

In Spain, in these mid-1200s, the star-and-crescent banners of the Jihad had nearly everywhere been furled; but, in Turkey, Othman was to unfurl them again and launch a new and even vaster expansion of Muslim imperialism through the Jihad. "Continuous Holy War was the fundamental principle of the state," Halil Inalcik, professor of Turkish history at the University of Ankara, asserted in his book on the Ottoman empire. Let us never underestimate the importance of piety as an instrument of politics and a cause of war. Islam was the inspiration of the later Ottoman onslaught on Europe; the Jihad was its instrument. The Turks, as the Arabs before them, had a very commonsense attitude toward war, particularly about their victories. "The fact that endless wars waged against their various neighbors had been vastly enriching was regarded as proof of God's approval, for plainly he would not have rewarded his servants so lavishly if he had not been pleased with their martial efforts on his behalf," explains the writer Antony Bridge. So the Turks continued what the Arabs had begun.

Within a century, Holy War was to penetrate and overwhelm most of southeastern Europe and transform it for centuries into the Land of Islam, the Dar-al-Islam. "Although the Turks went into battle for higher motives than mere loot, they expected to be allowed to pillage the places they captured and take their share of prisoners as slaves. This was a way of life which they greatly enjoyed, and which lasted for centuries," says Antony Bridge in *Suleiman the Magnificent*. We can query whether the Turks individually went into battle for any higher motive than plunder, slaves, and women, but there is no doubt about their enjoyment of this way of life which made them rich (if they didn't get killed).

Greece, by its very position across the narrow Dardanelles straits, was to be, in the mid-1300s, the first European victim of these conquering refugees from the steppes of central Asia. Other victims lined up to be sacrificed during the next few centuries. The Turks thus became the most powerful nation of Europe, a force at first almost impossible to stem. They were finally repulsed, twice, at the gates of Vienna. For their Holy War the Turks sometimes abandoned the Arabic term "Jihad" for the Turkish expression "Gaza." As Professor Inalcik reminds us, "the ideal of gaza, Holy War, was an important factor in the foundation and development of the Ottoman state. . . . Gaza was a religious duty, inspiring every kind of enterprise and sacrifice."

Southeastern Europe is still enduring the effects of this Turkish enterprise. The odious policy of "ethnic cleansing" of Bosnia's Muslim population and also, for that matter, of Croatia's Catholic population, by the Orthodox Serbs, is a latter-day sort of Holy War in reverse. These massacres, this confusion and disruption of life in the Balkans, is the most obvious modern reminder of centuries of alien rule in the region. On the part of the Serbs, hankering for a Greater Serbia, it is largely revenge. Until the nineteenth century the Muslims oppressed the Christians. Ninety percent of the big landlords of Bosnia were Muslims and 90 percent of the serfs were Christians, usually Serbs. They are all the victims of history, as were Bosko Brcik and Admira Ismic.

34

THE MONGOLIAN HORDE: RUSSIA 1340–1480

HE OTTOMANS WERE NOT THE only Muslim power threatening Europe from the east. The Mongols make a surprising appearance in Russia in the fourteenth century as unexpected adherents of the Muslim faith. They had been rampaging across the great land mass of Asia, from China in the east to Crimea in the west, for well over a century. But during all these decades they had been of no recognizable religion, practicing some vague form of shamanism all of their own. Russia itself did not exist as a name but purely as a huge territory the eastern part of which, from the Baltic to Moldavia, was ruled by Lithuania, bordering on the up-and-coming principality of Moscow to the east, while the famed Novgorod republic took in most of the land to the north, all the way from the Baltic to the Urals.

To the south, from the Crimea along the Don River to the Volga, stretching for about six hundred miles to the north and a thousand miles to the east from the Caspian Sea, lay the country recently conquered by Mongol invaders, the Golden Horde,* which had once been part of Genghis Khan's domain. This was now the land of the Mongols, who were the real rulers of Russia. The Russians had suffered mayhem at the

---

*So called because their royal robes were yellow. Horde was the nearest equivalent to Orgu, which in Mongol means "camp." Hence the appellation Golden Horde, a name which, however romantic it may sound, still has an underlying threatening evocation to it.

battle fought in 1223 by the river Kalka, a tributary of the Don. The captured Russian leaders had been made to lie on the ground and the Mongols, with the rough delicacy of a virile race, had built a wooden platform over them, over which the Mongols sprawled while they gorged themselves with red meat, drank gallons of fermented mare's milk and, shouting huge jokes, crushed their prisoners to death.

A few years later, in 1237, another Mongol army of 150,000 horsemen led by Batu Khan, son of Genghis, crossed the Volga from the east, rode north, and defeated all the Russian principalities one after another. The army then routed the Poles and the Hungarians. Batu was preparing to invade the rest of Europe when he suddenly turned back east on hearing of the death of the Great Khan, whose mantle he hoped to inherit. He founded a capital at Saray which, for the next few hundred years, remained the capital of the Golden Horde.

Batu demanded, and obtained, tribute from his Russian vassals which each Russian prince had to collect in his own domain. When he needed them to fight for him, Batu called the Russians into the ranks of his armies. We hear of Russians, under Mongol control, fighting in China in the thirteenth century. Little by little the barriers between Mongolians and Russians broke down and a new race came into being whose part-Mongol heritage is so obvious among the Russians of today.

So Russia went its own way, far from the currents agitating western Europe, where French and English rivalry finally erupted into the Hundred Years' War; where Muslim rule in the Iberian peninsula was gradually retreating before the Christian kings of Aragon, Castile, and Portugal; where Germany was trying to find itself between the Holy Roman Empire, the Hanseatic League, and the Teutonic Knights; and where Italy was soon to explode in the Renaissance in a haphazard medley of magnificent artistry, ignorant peasantry, and perpetually warring city states dominated by Venice, Genoa, and the papacy.

The Mongols formed the upper crust of the society of the Golden Horde. The bulk of the inhabitants were of Turkish stock, with a sprinkling of Armenians, Russians, Greeks, and various other Balkan folk. In the mid-thirteenth century we suddenly hear that the Mongols of the Golden Horde, perhaps under the influence of its Turkish minions who formed the bulk of the population of the territory, had become Muslims, led into the new religion by their khan Oz Beg, who died at 1341 at the age of twenty-eight.

The Mongol wars now acquired the holy tint of the Jihad as the Mongols reverently bowed toward Mecca in their five prayers a day to

Allah. Meanwhile the Grand Prince of Muscovy, Ivan I Kalita, or "Moneybag" as he was known to his contemporaries, had managed to persuade the Mongols to give him the right to collect tribute from the other Russian princes in their name. He took his cut, became very rich, and turned Moscow into the chief Russian principality. More and more he defied the Mongols until his successor, Dimitri Donskoy, with the support of the Orthodox Church, went to war against an army of two hundred thousand Muslim Mongols and at the battle of Kulikove Pole in 1380 sent them reeling back into their own territory.

But the Mongols, although down, were not out. Within two years they marched again in force against Moscow, while Dimitri was up north looking for allies in the Novgorod republic, and ravaged and destroyed the city. When Dimitri returned to Moscow he found more than twenty-four thousand Russian corpses lying in the streets. A new Mongol army erupted on the scene, laid waste the Khanate of Riazan just south of Moscow, and suddenly disappeared, leaving the Golden Horde to gradually disintegrate and break up into a number of rival Muslim territories. The most important became the Khanate of the Crimea, where the Mongols came to be known as Tartars. In due course they came to acknowledge the suzerainty of the Ottomans, then became independent for a while until the Crimea was annexed by Russia in the late eighteenth century. The Tartars remained in the Crimea until World War II when Stalin, accusing them of collaborating with the Germans, deported them all to some remote spot in Siberia, from where they have since been trying to return to their Black Sea home.

Russia in the fifteenth century was gradually becoming itself, an independent and sovereign country no longer a vassal of the Muslim Mongols and Tartars. The definite clash between Christian Russia and the Muslim Golden Horde came in 1480, during the reign of Ivan III. The ruler of the Russians refused to pay any more tribute to the Mongol overlords. Their two armies massed on either side of the river Ugra, each vowing to exterminate the other but both afraid to attack. The confrontation lasted several weeks, each side shouting insults to the other across the flowing waters. One morning, both armies vanished, each having gone back home in a fine example of discretion being the better part of valor.

Whether or not it was a holy war on the part of the Russians, it had been a victory for them since, without fighting, they had repudiated their obligation to pay tribute. Whether or not it was an officially proclaimed Jihad on the part of the Mongols, it was a defeat for them since on that day they lost the right to demand tribute from their Christian vassals to the north. But at least the decision had come about in peace and relative harmony. It lacked glory, but it was a victory of common sense for Russia, whose way was now open to greatness. But for the Golden Horde, the way was now open to oblivion. The final battle of the Mongols in Europe was at Zasalvi, in Poldavia, where a Polish army defeated a mixed Tartar-Turkish force in 1491.

35

JANISSARIES AHOY: THRACE 1301–1353

OTHMAN I, THE MAN WHO gave his name to the Ottoman Empire, did not leave much else to it. He certainly did not provide much territory to his imperial domain. His main contribution was the town of Bursa, close to the southern shore of the Sea of Marmara, famous for its blue porcelain. The siege of Bursa, then a Christian city, which began in 1317 and ended with its surrender to the Turks in 1326, is one of the minor episodes in the history of the Jihad. The whole operation took place in Asia Minor, therefore outside of the scope of our narrative, but we can view it as the inevitable prelude to the release of the Islamic avalanche which a quarter century later began to pour like a huge mud slide over unsuspecting and unready Europe. The capture of Bursa is important, anyway, because it was to become the first capital of the Ottoman Empire and to remain so for nearly forty years until the capital was moved to Europe, to Adrianople, in Thrace , northwest of Constantinople.

During the early fourteenth century several skirmishes and even minor battles had taken place in Anatolia when armed Turkish and Byzantine war parties, sometimes several thousand strong, met and clashed in the valleys of that mountainous region. As early as 1308, the Byzantines had beaten off an attack against Bursa by the Turks. Infiltration rather than conquest was Othman's style, and Turkish settlers moved into many areas unoccupied or sparsely populated by the Byzantines.

To this day Othman is considered a sort of remote founding father of the Turkish empire rather than its creator. That honor goes to his son, Orkhan I, who took over the tiny imperial domain in 1326 and made Bursa his capital. He is remembered by history as the first Turk to cross the Dardanelles into Europe, taking the Jihad with him. The first entry of the Ottomans into Europe dates from 1345, when the throne of Byzantium was the target of two rival claimants: John Cantacuzene, later to become John VI; and the child John V whose widowed mother, Anne of Savoy, was trying to defend her offspring's crown against all interlopers. John Cantacuzene called in the Turks to help him, and Orkhan cemented his providential alliance with the Byzantine pretendant by marrying his sixteen-year-old daughter Theodora. Presumably the young lady didn't object to being one of several wives in the harem of the multi-wedded Muslim ruler who was sixty years old. She could at least hope for an early widowhood.

In 1349 the Byzantines again asked for Ottoman help, this time against the Bulgarians. The Turks crossed the Dardanelles again, and this time stayed in Europe, where they have remained ever since. In 1353—one hundred years precisely before they captured Constantinople—the Turks established their first permanent European settlement in the Gallipoli peninsula, of later 1915 ANZAC fame for the Australians and New Zealanders who fought in World War I. The Turks called it Galipolu. The Turks have therefore been established in Europe for over six hundred years, two hundred years longer than Europeans have been in America. If part of the historical role of the Turks in Europe has sometimes been rather murky, they are not alone to merit castigation; the history of all European nations has some very blotchy passages that none of us has cause to feel proud about.

In addition to bringing his country into Europe and, in the long run, turning it into a European Muslim power, Orkhan I has another claim for our attention. He is remembered by history as the creator of the Janissaries corps, the most feared soldiers in the world. The Janissaries were for centuries the fer-de-lance of the Jihad. (The word *Janissaries* comes from the term Yani Sharis, which in Turkish means the New Soldiers.) Originally recruited by force, usually as teen-aged boys from the Christian villages of occupied Europe, they were forcibly (but often willingly) converted to Islam, cut off from all their roots and families, and turned into the finest fighting force of the age. One thousand of them were recruited every year and sent to Constantinople for training. They were heavily indoctrinated in the Muslim faith and ideology, and taught, above all, to be loyal to the sultan and to him alone. The Janissaries were the most formidable fighting force in Europe and Asia. They were considered by those who fought them, and those in whose service they fought, rather like the French Foreign Legion or the U.S. Marines; or, perhaps more fittingly, like the Waffen SS.

During the first three hundred years of the Janissaries' existence, they were not permitted to marry, and were expected to be instantly ready for whatever action the sultan demanded of them. But from the late sixteenth century, the rules and regulations concerning entry into the corps, and the terms and conditions of service began to ease. Janissaries were given the right to marry, membership to this elite corps was more widely opened, and it became less and less select. Fortunately for Christendom, its standards of fighting efficiency dropped also. The Jihad consequently began to falter. Other Muslim-born recruits were made eligible to join and political influence within the corps became rampant. The Janissaries became more interested in revolt than in battle, always ready to mutiny, but rarely ready for combat. The Ottomans began to lose regularly not only to their traditional Christian enemies in Europe, but also to their fellow Muslim foes, the Persians.

But for the first three centuries of the Ottoman Empire, the Janissaries were supreme on every battlefield where they fought, and they made it possible for the Ottomans to terrorize Europe until it seemed that one day all of Christendom would succumb to Islam. They were the elite of the elite, the men who could be depended upon at all times and in all circumstances, even the most suicidal ones. They were undoubtedly good at looting, massacring, and raping, but they were supreme at fighting. In their later years they became, like the praetorian guard of the ancient Roman Empire, the kingmakers. They made and unmade grand viziers and sometimes even sultans, and occasionally murdered them. To use colloquial language, they got too big for their boots which, incidentally, were beige in color, of fine, flexible leather with pointed toes, which looked as comfortable as slippers.

36

THE GAY REVOLT:
THRACE 1376–1388

I T WAS ORKHAN WHO BROUGHT the Turks with their Jihad into
Europe. They took over Thrace, that seacoast part of Greece
between Constantinople and Salonika. The first European Ottoman
region was small, tight, and well organized, and Orkhan, a man who
liked order around him, had the first coins struck during his reign,
which lasted until 1359, six years after the Gallipoli landing.

European Islam was now present in Greece in the east as well as
in Spain in the west. Between these two outposts of the Moslemah,
perhaps the stepping stones to new conquests, Europe lay in its usual
state of disarray. In France, French and English had started their Hundred Years' War, while in Italy the two republics of Genoa and Venice
were on the threshold of a thirty-year war. In Spain the kingdoms of
Castile, Aragon, and Navarre were trying to establish which of the
three would take over the other two. In Germany the Black Death
raged; in eastern Europe Poles, Lithuanians, and Hungarians were
competing for a large slice of the Ukraine; in Russia the Mongols were
taking over; and King Louis the Great of Hungary had joined the
Italian conflict on the side of Genoa and imposed his authority over
Serbia, Wallachia, and Moldavia. The Ottomans could not have hoped
for a more divided Christendom.

It is during the reign of Orkhan's son, Murad I, that the Muslim
Holy War became a major fact of life in the Balkans. Murad can really

be considered the first of a long line of Turkish conquerors of Europe. The Balkans were already in a state of turmoil and chaos when the Turks arrived. It is still so. The long and disturbing presence of Islam has not helped. There are some who will say that Islam has been one of the main causes, if not *the* main cause, of the continued bedlam and murderous chaos that the name of the Balkans carries with it. For Murad, blood and conquest added to the zest of daily life. In his thirty-year reign, Murad not only led the first Turkish mass invasion force into the Balkans, he also tripled the size of the Ottoman empire. He made Islam, and the Jihad, a seemingly permanent political force on the European continent.

The sudden appearance of the Turks in eastern Europe did not pass unnoticed in western Europe. Murad I, although long forgotten and still virtually unknown to most Europeans today, was the terror of Christianity at the time. Pope Urban V blanched whenever reports from travelers of the Ottoman progress reached him in Rome. The pope was very aware that the Islamic threat to Christendom was now coming from two locations, from Iberia in the west, and from Thrace in the east. Rome lay between the two.

The Arabs and the Moors were in Andalusia where, although greatly weakened since the days of Fernando III's successful Reconquista, they might one day receive huge reinforcements from North Africa, overwhelm Spain, and come pouring across the Pyrenees into France and Italy as they had done three or four centuries previously. These other Muslims, these Turks, coming from the east, were already across the Hellespont in Greece where, with their lances and their curved scimitars, their huge turbans and their large, drooping mustaches, they were preparing in large numbers to invade the West. One day the Turks from the Hellespont could link up with the Arabs and the Moors from Spain. Rome could well be their meeting point. The Saracens, for that is the popular name by which all the Muslims were known, could one day stable their horses in St. Peter's, as they so often had threatened to do; Muhammad would replace Jesus Christ across Europe, and those fine Gothic cathedrals would become mosques. This was a threat that Pope Urban V took seriously, and he called upon the Catholic Hungarians and the Orthodox Serbs to stop the Turks.

In 1371 came the first important eastern European response to the Jihad threat. A mixed force of twenty thousand Serbians and Hungarians, led by three Balkan and Central European princes, marched east to meet the Muslim foe. Their target was Adrianople, the new Ottoman capital to the northwest of Constantinople. Their purpose was to smash Ottoman power in Europe and to send the Turks reeling over the straits and back into Asia.

On September 26, this Christian force, so far unopposed, reached a spot called Cenomen, on the Marizza River, a couple of days' journey from the capital. The Serbian leaders called a halt for the night. These medieval warriors had a great capacity for drinking, and the carousing went on until well into the night, when the revelry was suddenly broken by the sound of drums and fifes, the favorite musical instruments of the Ottoman Turks, who have since introduced them to much of the rest of the world. Before the Christians could wake properly to what was happening to them, the Turks, led by Murad in person, were among them, scimitars slashing through their bodies, lopping off arms and heads. Two of the three leaders, princes from Serbia, were among the thousands slain. The survivors fled haphazardly to whence they had come. Many drowned trying to swim across the river to the other shore. Murad returned to Adrianople in triumph.

It was at Marizza that the famed Janissaries, most of them Christian youths forced into the Islamic religion and Ottoman military service, first clashed heavily in battle against their former fellow Christians. The battle was the first major confrontation between the Turks and the Serbs and Hungarians, with whom war was to rage on and off for several hundred years. Five centuries of Muslim threats and occupation certainly helped to form the countries of that region into what they subsequently became.

The situation at the time was very confusing in the ex-Byzantine empire, often called the Eastern Roman Empire, but whose inhabitants are generally described as Greeks. Since their official language was Greek, we shall call them Greek from now on. Between 1341 and 1355 a civil war reigned in the Greek empire between two competing emperors. To add to the confusion, both were called John. One, John V, the deposed emperor, was of the Paleologus dynasty. The other, John VI, was a Cantacuzene. The Turks backed John VI, who had originally called them in to help him against the Serbs, giving them their first European toehold in Gallipoli; then they had switched their support to John V, John Palaeologus, about 1379.

John Palaeologus's imperial life had been anything but jolly. His capital was under attack from both Serbs and Bulgarians. Cringing in his imperial city, he trembled for both his throne and his life. Holed up in Constantinople, he was now surrounded and threatened by the Turks as well, with a Turkish army to the north based in their capital, Adrianople; another to the south, just over the Bosporus in Anatolia; and more Turks to the west in the Gallipoli peninsula. He and Murad, however, managed to keep an uneasy truce between them. Each, at least for the time being, needed the other.

The truce was nearly shattered by the sudden intrusion on the scene of two young gay lovers, not gay in the old, jolly, light-hearted, "let's-have-some-fun-chaps" sense, but gay in the modern, political, homosexual sense. These two young male lovers formed part of the local crème de la crème. One was a Greek, the other a Turk; both were of royal lineage. Andronicus was the son of the Greek emperor; the other, Sauzes, was the son of the sultan. Right from the top drawer, both of them, and what a scandal it was! "Andronicus, John's eldest son, had formed an intimate and guilty friendship with Sauzes, the son of Murad," Edward Gibbon tells us bluntly. It must have sent quite a few ripples of horror around the local Christian and Islamic courts where such happenings, although perhaps quite rife, carried a heavy whiff of shock, sin, and scandal.

This affair between the two young men was more than a sexual deviation, or even sexual revolution. It had strong undertones of politics, treason, and plain revolution, but just the same with an inevitable dash of sex to it. The two youths, who had just enjoyed a holiday together in Adrianople, were not interested in gay rights. They were interested in taking over the Greek and Turkish empires from their respective and respectable fathers. They were as much interested in making war as in making love. They were rebels and warriors, and they called on their armies to mutiny and to come over to their side. Each young man vowed to be the ally of the other and to fight to the finish in the cause of imperial sodomy, or whatever the reason for their revolt was—it certainly wasn't Holy War. They had the support of a number of young, aristocratic gays and hoped the Byzantine and Ottoman armies would overthrow their fathers and call them to power.

Unfortunately for the two young gay princes, their alliance miscarried. The two furious fathers conferred and each undertook to blind his own son when he fell into his hands. Murad captured Sauzes, ordered his executioner to gouge his eyes out, then went beyond the pledge he had made and ordered his son's head to be cut off. Emperor John was kinder. He had hot vinegar poured into Andronicus's eyes, leaving his sight seriously impaired but still a vestige of vision. Murad was now on the rampage. He captured a number of young Greek and

Turkish noblemen, friends of the two rebels, had them chained together in groups of two or three and thrown into the Marizza river, and just "sat by and smiled with grim satisfaction at the rapidity with which they sank beneath the waves," Creasy tells us in his *History of the Ottoman Turks,* still a classic work on the Ottoman Empire. Several fathers were ordered to cut the throats of their own sons. A couple who refused to kill their offspring were put to death on the spot.

Pleased at the skill with which he had put down the gay rebellion, Murad next launched a new invasion of Europe and captured Sofia in 1385. Shishman, king of the Bulgars, both mean-hearted and faint-hearted, gave his daughter in marriage to the Muslim sultan. She obtained the blessing of the local bishop, promised to remain a good Christian, and then went to join the sultan's other wives in his harem. A couple of years later the Turks took Salonika. Greece was largely no longer Greek—except for its soul that always remained so—but Turkish, and continued to be ruled by the Turks for another five centuries. Fear and greed are two great stimulators of respect. The Turks were conquerors and they were feared. The two powerful Mediterranean merchant republics, Genoa and Venice, with that uncanny flair of bankers to sense the future, decided the Turks were in Europe to stay and signed a treaty with the sultan, thus assuring profitable new investments and cash flows for the future.

37

THE FIELD OF BLACKBIRDS:
KOSOVO 1389

W E ARE ABOUT TO REACH the first of these early climaxes of the Turkish conquest of Europe: a battle and a date. The battle: Kosovo. The date: June 15, 1389. A battle and a day that are universally mourned throughout the Balkans even today, more than six centuries later, and that explains much of what is now happening in the ex-Yugoslavia.

By 1389, some thirty-five years after they had landed in Gallipoli, the Turks had already conquered and occupied a large part of the southeastern corner of Europe that ran north from the Aegean Sea all the way to south of the Danube near Varna, on the Black Sea coast; going west to near where Scutari, on the Adriatic, is located today. Most of this territory had once been within the Serbian empire. The reigning Serbian king, Lazar I, and his fellow rulers in the region felt intensely threatened by this alien race, and religion, that was advancing relentlessly on them, with its banners and its scimitars and its camels and its horses and its calls to Allah and Muhammad; and its merciless raids that massacred their men, women, and children or took them away to the slave markets of Anatolia.

Serbians, Wallachians, Bosnians, and Albanians, most of them men of ancient Slavonic stock, joined forces under King Lazar of Serbia and prepared to fight. Their purpose: throw the foreign invaders out. Whatever rivalries and clashes of interests separated these ancient peoples, they were now united against their common Turkish Muslim

224

1. Mahomet II, the sultan of the conquest of Constantinople in 1453. Gentile Bellini (1429-1507) was called to Constantinople as a court painter in 1479 and painted this portrait of the sultan shortly before the latter's death in 1481. National Gallery, London. Erich Lessing/Art Resource, NY.

2. Don John of Austria (left), who commanded the imperial fleet during the battle of Lepanto in 1572. Other commanders at Lepanto were Marc Antonio Colonna (center) and Sebastiano Veniero (right). Portraitgalerie, Schloss Ambras, Innsbruck, Austria. Erich Lessing/Art Resource, NY.

3. Franz Geffels. The relief of Vienna on September 12, 1683. The Turkish armies, under Kara Mustapha, had surrounded Vienna since July 14. Imperial armies, including Polish troops under John Sobieski III, delivered the city. Historisches Museum der Stadt Wien, Vienna, Austria. Erich Lessing/Art Resource, NY.

4. Jan Matejko. John Sobieski victorious over the Turks at the Gate of Vienna. Vatican Palace, Vatican State. Scala/Art Resource, NY.

5. Antoine Jean Gros (1771-1835). The battle of the Pyramids, 1798. Napoleon tried unsuccessfully to recruit Muhammad and Allah into the French camp. Chateau, Versailles, France. Giraudon/Art Resource, NY.

6. A photograph of the Grand Mufti of Jerusalem reviewing the Nazi "Handzar" S.S. division in Yugoslavia in 1944. In an address to the Muslim troops, the mufti put Islam and Nazism on the same level, claiming "there were considerable similarities between Islamic principles and National Socialism." Copyright © 1996 Topham Picturepoint.

7. The nose section of Pan Am 103, dubbed "The Maid of the Seas," lies in a field outside the village of Lockerbie, Scotland. The airliner was blown out of the sky on December 22, 1988, killing 259 passengers and crew and eleven more on the ground. Two Libyan nationals, suspected intelligence agents, were later accused in both the United States and Scotland of planting the bomb on board the plane. AP/Wide World Photos.

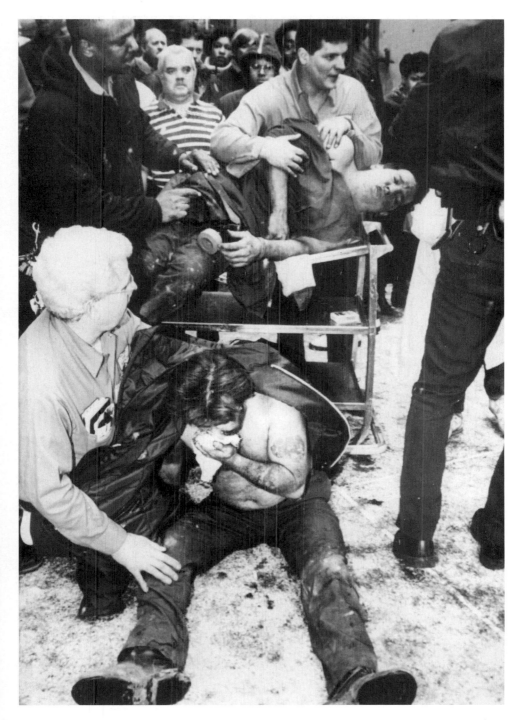

8. Victims being treated at the scene of the bombing of New York's World Trade Center on February 26, 1993. The bombing killed six and injured over a thousand. Six months after the blast, U.S. prosecutors obtained a massive indictment against the charismatic Muslim preacher Sheik Omar Abdel Rahman and fourteen followers. AP/Wide World Photos.

9. A view of the Yeni mosque in downtown Istanbul. Veiled women have become a common sight on western-looking Istanbul streets as Islamic fervor has increased among its people, including many recent migrants from the countryside. AP/Wide World Photos.

enemy. Near the frontier that separates Bosnia from Serbia, in what is today Montenegro, the armies of King Lazar met as the invading Turks of Sultan Murad halted under the mountains of Kosovo. The two sides faced each other over the tiny rivulet of Schinitza that separated the two camps, and Murad wondered whether he should attack the Christian armies that seemed so much larger than his.

As a pious Muslim fighting the Jihad for Allah, Murad spent much of the night in prayer, hoping that he would die fighting, "the only death that ensures the martyr's prize of eternal felicity" of love, feasting, and leisure. On the Christian side, King Lazar wondered whether he should attack during the night. Voices of caution urged him not to. The enemy could disperse and escape under cover of darkness, his generals said. In the Muslim camp, one prince suggested the Muslims line up all the camels, whose smell would cause the horses of the Serbian cavalry to flee from the scene in terror or, perhaps, in disgust. Prince Bajazet, Murad's eldest son, inspired by the holy mission of the Jihad, urged the Turks to have faith in Allah and not in camels. "The honor of our flag requires that those who march beneath the Crescent should meet their enemy face to face," he pleaded. General Timourtash, one of Murad's senior officers, was also opposed to the use of camels in the attack. He backed his arguments not with verses of the Koran but by his practical knowledge of camels. They would be frightened of the horses when the Christian cavalry charged, would rush back towards the Turkish lines, and would sow confusion and panic everywhere, he said. The camel strategy was dropped.

The grand vizier opened the Koran at random seeking inspiration. His eyes fell upon the verse that said, "Oh Prophet, fight the hypocrites and unbelievers." "These Christian dogs are unbelievers and hypocrites," he said. "We fight them." He opened the Koran a second time. This time he read, "A large host is often beaten by a weaker one." "They are the large host. We are the weak one," he said. "We fight them."

Christians and Muslims awaited the break of day. Dawn arrived and the light slowly spread over the landscape. The warriors in both camps stared at each other wearily and drew up for battle, horses nervously neighed and pawed the ground, camels were moved to the rear of the Turkish positions. The soldiers drew into lines, shouted insults at the enemy, and wondered who among them would die. Each man knew, of course, that it wouldn't be him. But it could be the man who stood by his side. Would Christ or Muhammad be the victor on the field of Kosovo? Would the victor be Serb or Turk?

We know the answer now but, at that moment, when the fate of
eastern Europe lay in the balance, probably none of those who were
taking part in the battle realized that they were standing on the edge of
one of the great moments of history. Historical prognostics usually
become clear only years, sometimes dozens of years, later when the
sequence of events has fallen into place. Prophecy is of only limited
import in historical narrative, except for the book of Nostradamus (and
no one can really understand him). The nervous soldier, sword in hand,
ready to kill, fearful of being killed, doesn't think beyond the next ten
minutes.

So, these valorous knights of Islam and Christendom stood poised,
facing and waiting to kill each other. As they drew up in lines of battle,
the Christians, between 20,000 and 30,000 strong, far outnumbered the
Turks. They were mainly Serbs, but there were many Bosnians and
Albanians among them, backed by contingents from Poland, Hungary,
and Wallachia (today a province of Rumania). It was, since Navas de
Tolosa nearly 180 years before, the most portentous clash between
Christians and Muslims. The outcome would fashion history for the
next six hundred years. It is still doing so.

The precise battle formations are not known for sure, but some
reports say that the Anatolian Ottomans were on the left of the Muslim
lines, led by Prince Bajazet. His brother, Prince Yakub, commanded
the right wing, composed of Murad's European vassals. Murad and his
Janissaries were in the center. On the Christian side the king of Serbia
was also in the center, the natural post for a commander-in-chief. The
king of Bosnia commanded the left wing. Lazar's nephew, Yuk
Bankowich, led the right wing, made up largely of Serbians and which
also included Albanians, who were led by a nobleman from their midst,
Teodor Musaka (or Musachi), who was killed in battle.

There is a gap of incomprehension that always separates us in our
irreligious, insensitive, and all-knowing century from those warriors of
another age. These fourteenth-century soldiers of Islam and these east
European warriors of Christianity, what sort of people were they really,
in their heavy mail armor and clutching their swords or scimitars as
they rushed forward praying and shouting to heaven? What thoughts
were running through their minds as they prepared for battle, to live or
to die? Where do Murad and Bajazet and Yakub find a place with us?
Or even King Lazar, a chivalrous Christian knight of noble presence?
Can they stir us, can their fates still move us over the gap of these
many centuries? Inevitably some of these distant figures have acquired

an almost legendary hue. But these men, soldiers of a Christian God or of a Muslim Allah, who seem so distant to us now, once upon a time swaggered across their kingdoms, swore, prayed, fought, killed, and died. These men made history, helped to shape our world of today or tried, and failed, to prevent its creation.

During the night, as they slept or prayed or kept vigil, the wind blew over the field of Kosovo, the field of blackbirds as it has come down to us, sweeping a lot of dust with it from the Christian side into the Muslim ranks. Early in the morning, while it was still dark, it began to rain; the rain settled the dust on the ground, and Murad thankfully took this meteorological incident as a sign of Allah's favor.

The battle opened in the early daylight. The two sides, aroused by the compulsion of their love for God or Allah and hatred for the foe opposite, charged at each other. Amid the clash of weapons, the shouted orders, the imprecations of the warriors, and the cries of the wounded and dying, the Serbians and the Albanians on the Christian right wing began to push the Anatolians back. The whole Muslim line was threatened with imminent collapse. Prince Bajazet, Murad's son, a heavy iron mace in his hand, rushed to the threatened Muslim left wing, knocking down with his flailing weapon all who stood in his way. Soon it became clear that the Ottomans were pushing back the Christians. Now was the time for personal sacrifice. From the Serbian ranks a knight in armor rode out toward the Turkish line, holding his right hand up and shouting words of peace. "I'm a friend, I'm a friend," he cried out. The Turks opened their ranks to let him through. The knight, Milosch Kabilovitch, King Lazar's son-in-law, rode to within a few yards from the sultan, was escorted into the presence of the sovereign, knelt as if in homage, bowed, whipped out a hidden knife, and stabbed Murad through the belly. He tried to rush back to his horse but was overtaken by the Janissaries and torn to pieces. So the sultan was murdered and so was his murderer slain. Murad, lying on the ground, began slowly to die from loss of blood, but he remained lucid enough to give the final order that gave the Turks victory.

"Send in the reserves," the dying sultan ordered. Rather like Napoleon 429 years later at Waterloo when, in a last desperate attempt to win the day, the French emperor ordered into battle—but too late—the immortal guards who had been kept in reserve all day. But at Kosovo, Murad was not too late, his order was well-timed and assured victory. King Lazar's nephew, Yuk Bankowich, fled the battlefield in panic at the upsurge in fighting and, they say, provoked the general rout of King Lazar's army. The Turkish victory was complete. King Lazar also was fleeing from the battlefield when his horse fell and, groggy from the tumble, the king was captured by the pursuing Turks and brought into the sultan's tent. "Cut off his head," the dying sultan ordered.

King Lazar's execution was the first of many that day, for thousands of Lazar's countrymen and allies were also captured fleeing from the battlefield, and the Turks were merciless to their beaten enemies. But the defeated Christians were not the only victims to fall to the executioner on that day. So also did the victorious Prince Yakub, who had led the Turkish left wing into battle. Within minutes of Murad's death, his eldest son, Bajazet, in the presence of the sultan's dead body, ordered his brother to be seized, held tight, and strangled on the spot with a bow string, a death without bloodshed because you do not shed the blood of a nobleman. "Unrest is worse than death," the Koran says. A rival to the throne means unrest and must be avoided whatever the cost. Allah may be merciful, but Yakub dead was one less pretender and rival to Bajazet for the Ottoman throne.

Bajazet had feared the popularity of Yakub and, with his death, hoped to forestall any potential threat of rivalry. For generations the killing of brothers became the religious duty of the new sultans when they came to the throne. Or so they claimed. Sometimes it was just a good excuse to get rid of an unloved relative, and one could always quote the Koran as the reason. Peace and quiet are preferable to strife and trouble, and killing a potential troublemaker is therefore an act of great piety. The universal good is more important than the life of one single creature. So Prince Yakub had to die. Even Machiavelli would have paled at the application of these principles.

With a collection of spouses and concubines, running sometimes into dozens, at his disposal a sultan sired his children from many different women, so the slaughtered brothers were usually only half-brothers. Thus were born the famous harem intrigues which tore apart the fabric of Muslim palace life. The inhabitants of the harem knew well what religious or political (the two were one) custom demanded. Desperate mothers schemed and plotted to save their doomed sons (and sometimes themselves as well), and tried to hide them in the dim recesses of the seraglio known only to them and to some faithful eunuch retainer. Daughters were spared, but every son except the heir could become a target for assassination the moment his father died. That day usually provoked frantic panic and activity in the harem, desperate searches for hiding places, even for baby sons, cries, pleading and sobbing, the comings and goings of grim-faced executioners, always deaf and dumb, holding tight to their bowstrings. Immense fear, despair, agonizing concern as to who might follow the dead sultan onto the mortuary slab: that was the reality of harem life in addition to the unbridled sex life of the sultan and the mutilation of hundreds of boys turned into eunuchs to become the servants of the sultan's playthings.

So the execution of Prince Yakub became an Ottoman precedent for the next two hundred years during which many of the Sultans, on coming to the throne, ordered the immediate executions of their brothers—and sometimes uncles and nephews—to nip in the bud, so to speak, any potential rivals. One sultan, more fraternal than most, Mahomet I, had his brother blinded instead of strangled. Selim I, in 1512, had two brothers and five nephews executed. The acme of atrocity was reached with Mahomet II who, when he became sultan in 1595, ordered his nineteen brothers to be immediately strangled; and three concubines, pregnant with his brothers' children, to be summarily decapitated and their bodies thrown into the Bosporus. Suleiman the Magnificent in the mid-1500s even ordered the strangulation of his own son who he feared—quite wrongly—was planning to overthrow him.

After the death of Murad, the silent battlefield of Kosovo turned into a slaughterhouse. Appalled at the Muslim losses, the new sultan decided to avenge his dead by killing all the Christian prisoners. They were tied together in groups of three or four and decapitated by professional executioners who formed part of the royal household. After some hours, their arms aching from the number of decapitations they had carried out, the exhausted executioners asked for permission to cut the throats of the victims with a dagger instead. For variety they cut off the hands and feet, easier to chop than the thicker necks of their captives, and the prisoners were simply allowed to lie on the spot and die from loss of blood.

In Jihad mythology, Kosovo ranks as the great Muslim victory it undoubtedly was. For the Serbs, it was a defeat of colossal proportions. The anniversary of the battle of Kosovo, even to this day, is one of Serbia's great days of mourning. Ever since, the locality of Kosovo has been remembered as the Field of Blackbirds. Blackbirds, in English, are birds of happy song. The better translation would be the Plain of Ravens, black also but birds of ill omen. Ravens evoke death, sadness, and the dark grey, cloudy skies of the massacre and mayhem of Kosovo, with its croaking, black birds, thousands of them, pecking away with their sharp, pointed beaks at the corpses of the decapitated warriors of Christendom, the heads heaped in pyramids, with the slain warriors of Islam lying strewn haphazardly over the battlefield where they fell. And everywhere, flying low over the ground, croaking, feeding off the corpses, thousands of black birds, the black ravens of death.

Kosovo opened up for the Ottoman Turks five centuries of victory. Serbia was their first far-reaching conquest in Europe. The Serbians, citizens now of a vassal state, were particularly vulnerable. But after Kosovo the first Serbian concern was survival, and that responsibility befell King Lazar's son, Stephen Lazarevitch, now king of Serbia. He did not have much choice; the very existence of his country now depended on Ottoman goodwill. As the leader of a vassal state, he became the supine—some have even called him loyal—friend and ally of the conquerors of his country and killers of his father. He remained so throughout his life. To consummate his thraldom he gave his sister Despoina as bride to Bajazet. She joined the sultan's harem and became the daughter-in-law of her father's killer. She became, in fact, Bajazet's favorite wife, and taught him to drink wine, a forbidden delight to the truly religious Muslim. She taught him to love wine so much that he turned into a drunken sot. Perhaps that was her way of avenging her father.

38

THE WILD KNIGHTS OF FRANCE: NICOPOLIS 1396

IT WAS KING SIGISMUND OF Hungary who alerted the French, and most of western Europe, to the danger of the new Islamic threat from the east. In the spring of 1395, Sigismund sent four knights and a bishop as his envoys to Paris to ask the French king to help him defend Hungary against the Turks. This was no longer the threat of a war between Christians factions, Catholics and Orthodox. This was no longer the mere presage of another Muslim invasion of another wearisome state such as Bulgaria and Serbia, clinging to the beliefs of Orthodoxy, hated by Catholic western Europe. Hungary was a Catholic country like France, looking to the pope for leadership and guidance, and the Turks were preparing to attack it with an army of forty thousand Muslim warriors and inflict their dominion over it. Sigismund, moreover, had studied in France, spoke French fluently, and was a scion of the House of Luxemburg. By his marriage to Mary of Anjou, he was related to the highest nobility of France. The cry for help from the east this time sounded much nearer. Sigismund's envoys called for help "in the name of kinship and the love of God." Could there be a greater cause for noble French knights to fight for?

The Hungarian envoys, Barbara Tuchman reminds us in *A Distant Mirror,* "told how the cruel Turks held Christians in dungeons, carried off children to be converted to Islam, despoiled maidens, spared no one and nothing from sacrilege." It was a cause bound to be heard by the chivalrous knights of France. The French, however insufferable they may appear sometimes, have an instinct for noble causes, for glory, for honor, and for great deeds that will resound to their own and to their country's renown.

But it was not the king of France who heard Sigismund's appeal. Charles VI was insane, loved and cared for by those around him, but unable to rule his kingdom; it was the dukedom of Burgundy, a state almost as powerful as France, to which it was attached, where the Hungarian appeal had the most impact. The Hundred Years' War with England was turning into a truce which would last twenty years. The warriors of France and Burgundy were eager to continue their fighting careers in a great cause. Catholic Hungary provided it. The infidel, the horrid Turks, loomed as the ideal enemy. The Muslims claimed they were "the sword of God who purifies the earth from the filth of polytheism." This filth was the Christians. Polytheism was the Trinity, the three persons in God of the Christian faith. The Muslims were outraged by this triangular deist conception and believed, moreover, that the Christians worshiped the Virgin Mary, who was part of this diabolical trio, a particularly demeaning thought for a Muslim attached to his male identity. The Christian knights of France and Burgundy prepared for distant battles.

The pope sent his blessing to these fighting men of old Gaul, some ten thousand of them, mounted knights, archers, and pikemen. The leadership was given to Jean de Nevers, the duke of Burgundy's son, an untrained 24-year-old soldier who came to the command by reason of his birth. Jean de Vienne, Admiral of France, and the Lord Enguennard de Coucy, old warriors with old heads on old shoulders, accompanied the expedition at the request of the duke of Burgundy and of his lady, largely to bolster with their advice their young and inexperienced commander. The cream of French knighthood were all present for the expedition. Among them, the young (thirty-two) Marshal Jean Boucicaut, small, slight, and intrepid, who had first tasted blood sixteen years before, at the age of sixteen, at the Battle of Roosebeke against the Flemings, and had fought with the Teutonic Knights in east Prussia against the pagan tribes of Lithuania, as well as against the Moors in Tunisia. Boucicaut, a soldier of high mettle, was respected as one of the noblest knights of his age by his peers.

The leaders knew, before their journey began, that the purpose of their expedition was to take back from the Turks the fortress city of Nicopolis, on the Bulgarian side of the banks of the Danube, recently captured by the Turks and turned into a strong point in their occupied territory. The objectives of the French were larger, more ambitious, but largely unspelled: to expel the Turks from Europe and force them back into Asia, to go to the relief of Constantinople, to liberate Palestine and the Holy Sepulcher. It was, in fact, a crusade. The pope had been preaching in favor of a crusade for the past two or three years, and all who took part in the expedition were given a plenary indulgence.

The main body of the French set out from the Burgundian capital of Dijon on April 30, 1396, headed for Strasbourg, crossed the Rhine, chaotically marched across Bavaria (pillaging and picking up volunteers and girlfriends on the way), and five months later crossed the Danube into Hungary, where King Sigismund, somewhat worried at the reports of rape and looting that had preceded their arrival, awaited his allies in his capital Buda, the first urban half of Budapest. It was a lavishly supplied expeditionary corps he greeted, whose aristocratic members had brought with them huge quantities of luxury foods and fine wines, silk garments of green and gold, porcelain dinnerware, musical instruments and of course girls, lots of them, living souvenirs of their journey across Germany. They had their swords and lances and the archers had their bows. But, Sigismund noted, they were short of heavy weaponry. They had brought no catapults, in fact, no siege weapons at all, although the first purpose of the expeditionary corps was to capture the citadel of Nicopolis. Questioned by Sigismund, Boucicaut explained that courage would be sufficient. They would make ladders and climb up and overwhelm the defendants of Nicopolis in hand-to-hand fighting.

Sigismund was disturbed at the French optimism. They boasted to a very worried Sigismund—for he knew from personal experience the fighting qualities of the Ottomans—that they would throw the Turks back to the Dardanelles at their first clash. The Turkish sultan, however, was equally boastful. He had recently informed Sigismund that he would soon throw Sigismund out of Hungary, march on to Rome, and feed and stable his horses in St. Peter's.

After a few skirmishes and the capture of the fortress of Rachowa where, unable to spare the men to guard them, they slaughtered their prisoners; the French and their allies went on to Nicopolis, arriving on September 12. Located high on a cliff, the town looked impregnable. The steep slopes on which the fortress was built also prevented the use of ladders. The governor refused to surrender. He was awaiting the arrival of Bajazet with his relief troops, who he knew would inevitably come. The French, without siege weapons, could not fight. When they were not carousing, they could only stand around, look up at the battlements, wait, and shout insults to the besieged Turks who were safe behind their high walls.

The vanguard of Bajazet's army arrived three weeks later. The French knights were having a feast when a party of Hungarian scouts brought the news that the Ottoman soldiers were seventy miles away. Coucy set off with a thousand mounted lancers and archers to intercept the approaching force, caught them by surprise, slaughtered a great many, then galloped back to join the main French body outside Nicopolis, where de Nevers had informed King Sigismund that honor demanded that he and his knights be allowed to be the first to attack the enemy. He clamored that the French had not come all the way across Europe to take second place in the fighting. The wiser de Coucy suggested to the young hotheads that they listen to the advice of King Sigismund who was experienced at fighting the Turks, but they didn't.

By the morning of September 25, the Turkish vanguard was drawn up for battle, facing the French camp. The Ottoman Islamic warriors had, until three weeks before, been part of the Muslim force besieging Constantinople. On hearing that Sigismund's Hungarians and the French had arrived at Nicopolis, Bajazet had raised the siege and marched west to fight this new bunch of infidels. The Jihad never rested. Circumstances and the exigencies of the French played in favor of the sultan. Sigismund was caught up in a situation that was beyond his power to control. Although he was the king of Hungary with fifty thousand men under his command, his authority over his French allies was nonexistent. The Hungarian king could not cope with his French underlings. Eager to go into battle, convinced they would overwhelm and defeat the Turks with their first assault, and unwilling to share the honor of victory with their Hungarian comrades, the French knights turned down Sigismund's protests and explanations. Jean de Nevers, whose experience in battle was as limited as his self-assurance was unlimited, complained that the Hungarian king wanted to keep the French back to make sure the victory would go to his troops rather than to the French. "The King of Hungary wishes to have the flower and honor of battle," a French count burst out angrily.

"Forward, in the name of God and St. George," cried one of the French knights, seizing a Christian banner and galloping ahead. Common sense and reason usually come a poor second and third to the call for courage and gallantry. It was the one great quality to which all knights aspired and for which they wished to be recognized. Heavily armored, the French charged the first Turkish lines, which they overwhelmed and scattered.

Exulting in their triumph, the French charged on. Ten thousand Janissaries tried in vain to stop them; they were pulverized. Five thousand cavalry, spahis they were called by the Turks, intercepted them; they were brushed aside. Fifteen hundred Turks had already been killed. Behind the French, Sigismund's Hungarians and German mercenaries were hurrying forward. The French charged up the hill under a deluge of arrows. Still they advanced. They then found themselves facing lines of sharp-pointed stakes planted upon the battlefield in close order. The knights had to dismount to avoid the stakes that stopped their horses and sometimes ripped open the horses' stomachs. From that moment, the knights were lost. There was no more helpless creature in the Middle Ages than an unhorsed knight, weighed down with armor, who, if he were knocked down to the ground could raise himself only with great difficulty. He was like an ox with its neck exposed to the killer's knife, a victim worthy only of having his throat cut. Nonetheless, the knights bravely stood their ground, expecting a clear battleground ahead of them, with a vision of victory and their banners high in the sky. The Hungarians and their allies were coming up behind them.

Alas for the knights of France, it was not a vision of victory that lay ahead; it was a vision of death. Thousands of Ottoman horsemen—the number has sometimes been given as forty thousand—awaited them. The flower of French chivalry was about to be decimated again, as it had been at Crécy and Poitiers. But this time, death was to come not from English knights and Welsh longbowmen, but from the dreaded Turk who, two centuries before, had come sweeping out of the central Asian steppes and was now threatening Rome. The Turks shouted "Allah is Great!" and charged. Allah, they always called to Allah, for this was after all the Jihad. Every war that the faithful fought against the infidel was a Jihad; that was the rule. The French could not escape it, any more than the Hungarians, or Serbs, or Bulgarians could. The French must die.

Here was the warning the French knights had ignored. Here was death and the end of the French dream of sweeping the Turks out of Europe, just as one day soon they would sweep the English out of France. It was a noble dream in the context of the times. Whatever the confused, muddle-headed, mingy-minded intellectuals of today may think, Christian Europe was a noble cause—however abominably it behaved towards the Jews—particularly when compared to that of its enemies. The French knights may have been a tiresome bunch of randy, roistering, and pretentious nitwits, but there was nothing ignoble about their cause. They were brave men, not afraid to die. It was certainly noble to fight for their country and Christendom in the distant Balkan marches of Europe, against alien invaders, ferocious and terrible. For in 1396 the Turks were so, as the Vandals had been in 409, as the Goths had been in 410, as the Huns had been in 451, as the Franks themselves had been in 486, as the Vikings had been in the ninth century, as the Mongols had been in 1237. So at Nicopolis, in Bulgaria, in 1396, some six thousand French warriors died for a country that has long forgotten them and their battle, and for a cause that seems totally unconnected to everything that exists today but isn't: honor, their country, their faith. The French died in the thousands. One of them was old Admiral Jean de Vienne (a cruiser was named after him in the French Navy in the 1930s), who fell holding aloft the banner of Our Lady.

But the Muslims had their Christian allies. An army of several thousand Serbs, the vassals of the Turks since Kosovo, now rushed into battle for their Muslim lord. The realistic Hungarians realized that this was the end. They fled. The Turks closed in on the French from in front and behind and hacked them to pieces. De Nevers surrendered. Their leader now in Turkish hands, the French survivors, perhaps three thousand in number, surrendered with him. Probably another three thousand lay dead on the battlefield around them. The Turkish losses were also enormous. The outnumbered French had fought as savagely as the victors. Despondent, Sigismund led his unengaged troops away from the lost battle. "We lost the day by the pride and vanity of the French," Sigismund moaned. He was right. The French had not heeded his advice and they had been vanquished. The Jihad may have been only a game, a game of pretense, but it was a game that had to be taken seriously. You played by the rules or you died. The French had fought bravely but stupidly. They had lost the game. Therefore they died.

For the French, the defeat of Nicopolis was the harbinger of such horrendous immediate consequences that the mind recoils from them. Bajazet toured the battlefield. Aghast at the numbers of his own dead, greater than the Christians, and incensed by the executions carried out by the Christians of their Rachowa prisoners, he ordered all his prisoners—perhaps three thousand in all—to be decapitated on the spot.

They were paraded before him in the morning, naked and tied together in bunches of three or four. The mass beheading ceremony started early in the morning and went on without a break until the late afternoon. The battlefield became a lake of blood. Only De Nevers and twenty-three other knights who could be expected to bring large ransoms were spared, but the sadistic and drunken Bajazet forced them to watch the execution of their comrades. Boucicaut was about to be decapitated when De Nevers stepped forward and pleaded for his life. De Coucy, a man of immense wealth, was also one of those whom the sultan kept as a prisoner. Jacques de Helly, a French knight, was dispatched by the sultan to France to acquaint the king, the duke of Burgundy, and the court with the news of France's defeat and to arrange for the ransom of the captives to be forwarded to the sultan.

For the Hungarians the defeat at Nicopolis meant the continued Turkish threat to their national existence. For the Bulgarians, on whose soil the battle had been fought, Nicopolis meant vassalage to the Turks—as Kosovo had meant to the Serbians—for nearly another five centuries, until the great uprising in the Balkans against Ottoman rule in the late nineteenth century and the Treaty of San Stephano in 1878.

Jean de Nevers, Jean-sans-Peur (it means John the Fearless), returned to France after three years of captivity, as did most of the other twenty-four French prisoners. De Coucy died in a cell in Bursa. De Nevers became duke of Burgundy in 1404 and a leading actor on the French political scene during the Hundred Years' War. He provoked a civil war in France, led the Burgundian party to power after the French defeat at Agincourt in 1415, and was murdered four years later while trying to wean his Burgundians away from their English alliance. Sigismund, undeterred by his defeat at Nicopolis, tried to make Bohemia part of his Hungarian domain and failed.

The indomitable Boucicaut appeared on the eastern scene again a few years later. He went back to fight the Turks once more. He offered his services to Manuel II, the emperor at Constantinople, whose city was continually under siege by Bajazet. Anxious for revenge, the French knight sailed from the Mediterranean port of Aigues-Mortes with a squadron of four ships and an army of over two thousand men, sixteen hundred of them archers and the remaining four hundred what we could call light infantrymen. He forced a passage into the Dardanelles through a defending force of seventeen Turkish galleys, and the fighting presence of his little army obliged the Turks to lift the blockade of Constantinople, both by land and by sea. He attacked and took from the Turks several castles and fortresses, but after a year of fighting he realized that his little force could not affect the long-range outcome of the conflict between the rising Ottoman empire and the dying Byzantine empire, and he returned home to fight for his country against the English in the Hundred Years' War.

Constantinople was, however, saved for another half century thanks to the intrusion into the region of another massacrer of men, women, and children even viler than Bajazet: the Mongol Timurlane, Muslim ruler of Samarkand, who on his career of conquest across Asia invaded and rampaged through Anatolia, leaving huge piles of decapitated heads as a memento of his visit. The Muslim world, however huge, was not big enough for two such potentates. Bajazet challenged Timurlane to battle, was defeated and captured at the Battle of Angora (or Ankara), famous for its cats and its wool, in 1402.

Bajazet's conqueror was even more loathsome than the man he had defeated. His wars were even more devastating, measuring by the immensity of suffering, death, and terror he inflicted on the people he conquered, but they had only touched the faraway fringes of Europe, notably in Georgia. He destroyed seven hundred towns and villages in that small country in the Caucasus and killed thousands of the Christian inhabitants after the Georgian prince had refused to appear before him when summoned to do so. When he captured the town of Sivas, in Asia Minor, he ordered four thousand of its Christian Armenian defenders to be buried alive. To make their agony as painful as possible, he had their heads bound down with ropes to their doubled-up legs. To make their agony last as long as possible, he then covered their mass graves with planking before throwing earth over it, so that they could go on breathing for a few minutes after their burial. There was something particularly unlovely about Timurlane. But he did not claim to be engaged in a Holy War, at least, not as far as is known. But, being a Muslim, perhaps he did.

To humiliate the captive Bajazet, Timurlane obliged Bajazet's favorite wife to serve him and his guests at table, quite naked. Timurlane was particularly proud of his victory over the powerful Ottoman sultan and to exhibit his prisoner he took him along on his travels in a sort of iron-barred prison on wheels, a strangely apt punishment for one who had conducted himself so ignobly toward those who had had the misfortune to fall into his hands. Unable to bear the abasement of his situation, Bajazet died of misery and shame within a year. He was followed to the grave within a couple of years, perhaps from the plague, by his Mongol conqueror. The reading of history would be a kinder experience if neither of these two creatures had ever existed.

After leaving Constantinople, Jean Boucicaut, faithful soldier and man of honor, returned to France, fought for his country against her old enemy, England, was captured at Agincourt in 1415, could not raise the ransom the English demanded, and died a prisoner in England after six years of captivity. If ever, when you are in Paris, you take the Metro, line 8 between Balard and Créteil, when your train stops at the "Boucicaut" station, spare a thought for that gallant French knight who six hundred years ago bravely fought for his country against England and for Europe and his faith against the Jihad.

Meanwhile, as Bajazet's four sons fought among themselves for dominance, Ottoman power appeared to disintegrate and, for a while, the Muslim empire and the Jihad both seemed doomed to vanish. In the West, Christian England went on destroying Christian France in the Hundred Years' War.

39

THE HUNGARIAN HERO:
VARNA 1444

THE DEFEAT AND DEATH OF Bajazet nearly brought about the end of the Ottoman empire, both in Europe and in Asia. In Asia Timurlane reinstated many of the former rulers in Anatolia who had been forced into Ottoman tutelage. In Europe the Turkish defeat gave a rebirth of energy and life to the old Byzantine empire, now more commonly called "Greek," since it was mainly Greek-speaking, and the neighboring kingdoms of Serbia, Wallachia, and Bulgaria all temporarily broke away from their subordination to the sultan. Within the Ottoman empire heavy fighting broke out among Bajazet's four sons, Soleiman, Issa, Musa, and Mahomet. Each aspired to the throne (in Musa's case, covertly), and their struggle against one another unwittingly pitted the European part of Turkey against the Asiatic part.

The Jihad had now turned not so much into a civil war as into a four-sided fraternal war of succession, with Allah on the inevitable side of the strongest and the most cunning of the four. Or perhaps the luckiest. Or maybe the most devout. The king of Serbia also became involved in this fratricidal conflict. He promised to help one of the brothers, Soleiman, who ruled in Adrianople, which by this time had acquired its new name of Edirne. Having thus made sure he would not be attacked from the rear, Soleiman crossed the Hellespont into Asia and captured Bursa and Ankara. Musa, escorting his father's body for burial in Bursa, found himself cut off from the cemetery, and joined forces with his brother Mahomet to fight his brother Soleiman. Musa, a sharp tactician, crossed over to Europe and attacked Edirne. Soleiman's army deserted en masse and went over to Musa and Soleiman was captured while trying to make his way, as a refugee, to Constantinople. His delighted captors, perhaps hoping for a bonus from their grateful sovereign, whoever he might turn out to be, strangled Soleiman with the inevitable bowstring reserved for noblemen, thus definitely removing one pretender to the Ottoman sultanate.

The victorious Musa then attacked Soleiman's servile ally Serbia, devastated the country, massacred three garrisons, spread the bodies of the slain tidily in a vast rectangle over the ground, laid planks on them, and invited his Janissaries to a huge outdoor banquet, all sitting crosslegged around this makeshift table and thinking what fun this picnic was and what a great idea of Musa's this had been. Feasting, killing, and jollification on a mass scale were routinely on par in these early Turkish carousals with all the gusto from their old nomadic days.

Musa next attacked Manuel, the emperor at Constantinople who had tended to side with Soleiman in the recent conflict. Manuel called to Musa's brother Mahomet for help. Mahomet was delighted to oblige, and the Asiatic Ottomans now entered the fray as allies of the European Greeks against the European Ottomans. Finally the two rival Ottoman armies met for battle just south of the Serbian border. By this time it is doubtful if anyone knew who he was supposed to be fighting for and who he was supposed to be fighting against, much less why, a typical Balkan situation which has persisted down the centuries.

One thing is certain. Musa by this time had become as unruly, cruel, and savage as his brother Soleiman had been. The confused Janissaries in his army refused to fight for him against the Janissaries in the other Ottoman army and scattered. Musa fled also and was later found dead, presumably with the assistance of a bowstring. The Muslim Holy War had become an unholy massacre of Muslim princes. Two aspirants to the throne were now dead, a third, already mentioned, Prince Issa, had also disappeared, never to be found again. As his rival brothers all seemed to have disappeared, in 1413 Mahomet became, by default so to speak, Mahomet I, Sultan of all the Ottoman Turks. It had taken nearly a dozen years of anarchy and fratricidal war for the Ottoman empire to come into its own again. But life didn't quite go on as before. Mahomet I was an exception to the majority who were to rule at the Sublime Porte, as the seat of Ottoman government came to be known. Recognized by all for his humanity, his sense of justice, his competence, and his energy, he was called "The Restorer" by his contemporaries and so has come down to us in history.

Mahomet was not a war lover but it is during his reign that the Turks clashed for the first time with the Venetians, in the first campaign of a long series of wars that went on for more than two hundred years. The Venetians destroyed a Turkish fleet off Gallipoli, after which the sultan decided to sign a treaty of friendship with them. He also made peace with the Greek emperor in Constantinople, and quietly and peacefully, with subtle pressures and arguments he reimposed indirect Turkish rule on his European vassals without recourse to the Jihad. When he died in 1421, one of his last requests, made to a trusted officer, was that his two infant sons should be taken secretly and hurriedly for safekeeping to the Greek emperor in Constantinople for protection from their elder brother, soon to be Murad II who, the dying sultan feared, would otherwise put them to death as potential rivals. The Koran can be and is merciless for those who wish to make it so. But he was wrong. Murad loved his little brothers and cherished them instead of murdering them.

It was during the reign of Murad II that, in 1444, Christian crusaders and Turkish ghazi met again in battle for the first big clash since Nicopolis, nearly fifty years before. The battlefield was at Varna, in what is today Rumania, at the mouth of the Danube, by the shores of the Black Sea. But well before Varna, Murad II had clashed many times with one of the gigantic figures of the war against Islam, the Hungarian warrior and captain-general Janos Hunyadi, a name virtually unknown outside his native country but who probably has done more than any other individual in history to stem the Muslim invasion that, in the fifteenth century, threatened to overwhelm Europe.

Another name stands out among the eastern European defenders of Europe: John Castriot of Albania, known to his and future generations as Skanderbeg, the Lord Alexander, perhaps because of the proximity of his birthplace to Alexander of Macedon's.

The Hungarian and Albanian heroes brought to a grinding halt the Muslim assault on Europe for a quarter century. But, however valorous, the action of these two lone leaders was finally as effective as King Canute by the English seashore bidding the waves to go back. The waves kept on coming in, and so did the Turks. But Hunyadi and Skanderbeg never gave up the struggle against the tidal Muslim onslaught. Their aim, each in his own country, was to throw the Turks out of Europe and back to the other side of the Bosporus.

Hungary, Albania, Wallachia, and Bosnia were now flirting uneasily with the idea of banding together to fight and expel their Turkish overlords. Liberation—had that word existed then—would have been the key word. Hunyadi was the inspiration behind these maneuvers for unity and war. He epitomized the fighting Hungarian knight, but to us in the West he remains a shadowy figure, heroic but unpalpable and unreal. Balkan and central European affairs have always seemed obscure to us anyway, the motives of their leaders lost in the labyrinth of our incomprehensions. Hunyadi was a combination of El Cid and Joan of Arc. It is somewhere between the two that his place in Hungarian history lies. We know that Hunyadi was a great soldier, a Hungarian patriot, a powerful lord guarding the approaches to the Hungarian frontier, perhaps the wealthiest lord in Hungary. We know that he was born perhaps in 1407, that he fought for the Visconti as a condottiere in Italy, and that he then returned home and raised an army at his own expense to fight against the Muslim invaders from the east. His soldiers were largely Hussite peasants from Bohemia and Germans for the heavy cavalry. His light cavalry were the origin of the first famous hussars, who have garnished every cavalry corps in the world. He fought for his country against the Turks until the day he died, always hoping in vain to push them out of Europe, but at least keeping them out of most of Hungary.

He was, so legend or rumor says, the illegitimate son of Sigismund, sovereign of Hungary and defeated warrior-king of Nicopolis, and of the fair and gracious Elizabeth Morsiney, of an old Aegean family whose forebears had perhaps once reigned in Constantinople as emperors. Hunyadi's career as a warrior had a much more cosmopolitan flavor than Skanderbeg's. Hunyadi spanned all the countries of the Balkans, leading international armies, negotiating with popes, kings, and emperors, fathering a future king of Hungary, fighting all over the Balkans. He was a man whose place resides in world history, not just Hungary's. By the fear he instilled in the enemy, even when he was defeated, he slowed down the Turkish advance to the west by three-quarters of a century. Perhaps by causing this delay he saved Europe. He did bestride the narrow world, yet he has no image in our world, certainly not one with the aura he deserves.

The other great Ottoman fighter of his time, Skanderbeg is much more of purely national character, a man, however great his stature, who found his role limited to the small nation which he led: Albania. He remained essentially a glorified guerrilla fighter in his native country all his life. Taken into Ottoman service when a child, converted to Islam, a friend of the sultan, he had rebelled against his condition after fighting for the Turks against the Hungarians in 1443. He had returned secretly to his native land and fought the Muslim conquerors for the rest of his life. Tito and Che Guevara are the likes in the recent past of Skanderbeg in the distant past. The Balkans today are unexplainable unless viewed against their Muslim background. Once the alien invader and ruler, now part of the local scenery, Islam is still widely resented by the Christians of that region.

In spite of the harsh and difficult terrain, the ungentle hills, precipitous mountains, and thick forests thronged with wolves, bears, and foxes, none as savage as man, the Balkans could not keep the invaders out. The Turks poured into the silent and pristine valleys proclaiming the greatness of Allah. Across a fearful Europe, the pope, cardinals, bishops, and priests prayed and trembled, and the faithful, if they had the knowledge or the imagination, shuddered at the advent of the Turks. Hunyadi didn't tremble; he fought. And sometimes he tortured and murdered and massacred, just like the Turks. In 1442 Hunyadi marched with his legion to the relief of Hermansdat, killing twenty thousand of the besieging troops. He took their general Mezid Bey and his sons prisoners and cut them up into little pieces, some of which he fed to the pigs. Then during the victory banquet afterwards, prisoners were brought in one by one before the feasting guests to be slaughtered as a sort of entertainment, since Hunyadi hadn't brought any minstrels or musicians along. It wasn't only the Jihad that was gruesome; Christian crimes were just as horrifying.

Timurlane, by defeating Bajazet, forcing the Jihad to the sidelines, had given Christendom a respite of many years. But Murad II was now anxious to regain the prestige, the territories, and the vassals lost in the Ankara debacle nearly twenty years earlier. Another Muslim expeditionary force marched against the White Knight of Hungary, as Hunyadi was known by the color of his armor, Christian and Turk met in battle at Vasag and the result, for the Turks, was even more disastrous than at Hermansdat. By this time Hunyadi had become the hero of the Balkans. The kings and princes of Serbia, Wallachia, and Bosnia became the allies of King Ladislaus of Hungary and Poland, and it was under Ladislaus that an allied force marched bravely into Turkish territory and prepared to battle the infidels. The year was 1443.

At the head of an international army of some twelve thousand men, remarkably few for such a vast purpose, made up of Hungarians, Serbians, Wallachians, Poles, Germans, and even a scattering of French volunteers, and with an Italian papal legate, Cardinal Julian Caesarini, dancing in attendance upon him, Hunyadi nobly went to war. It was no longer just a military campaign, it was now officially a crusade, a Jihad in reverse. A great Ottoman army marched to meet it and was soundly beaten at Nissa, by the Morava river. Thousands of Turks were killed, and four thousand were taken prisoner, including their general, Mahmoud Tchelebi, Murad II's own brother-in-law. Next along the way, Hunyadi took Sofia and accomplished the amazing feat of crossing with his army the Balkan mountains, of which at the time history recorded only two instances: one by Alexander the Great in 335 B.C.E., the other by Murad I in 1390. Hunyadi marched down the other side of the mountains to glory and to victory over the Turks.

Turkey, with its capital Edirne, lay open before him. The Turks were on their knees. But, incredibly, King Ladislaus, stopped where he was and signed at Segedin a totally unnecessary treaty of peace for ten years with Murad II. The sultan gave up Wallachia to Hungary, abandoned his claims to Serbia, and paid sixty thousand ducats ransom for his brother-in-law, whose wife, the sultan's sister, had been tearfully demanding from her brother the return of her husband, prisoner of the dreaded Hunyadi. Murad, the tired, defeated warrior, went back to Bursa for rest and recreation.

The Jihad had stalled temporarily, but only for a brief time. For does not Edward Gibbon remind us in his account of this campaign that, for the Turks, God and war marched together against the infidels and that "the scimitar was the only instrument of conversion"? But this time it was the Christians who were responsible for the renewal of war.

The Christian leaders facing the defeated Turks were appalled over the signature of the Segedin treaty between Ladislaus and Murad, signed at the moment of Hunyadi's triumph. The Hungarians and their allies should have crushed the Ottomans. "No oath can be kept with the unbelievers," Cardinal Caesarini kept on insisting. He made the Hungarian king swear he would break the treaty. This was the moment to do it, while Murad II was over on the other side of the Bosporus among his harem beauties, his mind far from thoughts of war. Treachery was in the air. Hunyadi's conscience began to bother him. The king of Hungary and the cardinal were determined to win him over. Ladislaus promised him the crown of Bulgaria. He would be king. Every one— or nearly—has his price. A kingdom, whatever Henry V may have said at Agincourt, is worth more than a horse. Or a broken treaty.

So the Christians broke the truce and began war again. Varna, a Bulgarian port on the Black Sea at the mouth of the Danube, was chosen as the target. The Hungarians arranged for a Venetian fleet to meet them offshore, bringing supplies and reinforcements. This was to be the last crusade. On September 1, the bewildered Turks heard that the Hungarian king was breaking the recently signed treaty with an army of ten thousand men. Murad II, in Bursa, hurried back across the straits to Europe. The Christian army crossed the Danube and continued the long march to Varna, massacring a few Turkish garrisons on the way. When they reached Varna, the Venetian fleet had not arrived (it never did). The allied army captured the seaport after a short siege and one day they heard the news: Murad II was no longer among the odalisques of his distant harem in Bursa, but back in Bulgaria among his Janissaries at the head of an army at least four times as large as that of the Hungarians and their allies. Hunyadi was not alarmed. He would not wait until the Turks attacked. He would attack first.

On November 10, 1444, came the clash. Young King Ladislaus, palefaced and all fire and fury, approved Hunyadi's decision. The Turks, from their side of the field, taunted the Hungarians with their breach of the treaty, displaying the broken document at the tip of a lance, which a mounted soldier held aloft in the front Muslim ranks. The Christians prepared for battle: the Wallachians in line on the left, the Hungarians on the right along with the French crusaders who were under the orders of Cardinal Caesarini. King Ladislaus, on his prancing charger, had taken his place in the center, the rightful place for a king.

Hunyadi took the immediate command of the Hungarian troops and ordered them to charge. The Asian troops in the Turkish ranks broke and fled from the battlefield. The Wallachians trounced the European Turkish troops. The Christian victory seemed assured. Murad was preparing to flee, but one of his generals begged him to fight on. He did, and in the renewed fighting that broke out King Ladislaus had his horse killed under him. The king fell to the ground in the middle of a melee, and a Janissary brought his scimitar down on the dazed monarch decapitating him on the spot. The Turks put his head at the tip of a long pike, along with the treaty he had signed, and brandished it toward the Poles and the Hungarians. "This is your king," they jeered. This was the moment of their revenge and victory. The Hungarians, sickened by the death of their king, fled. Cardinal Caesarini was killed. At Varna, the Jihad triumphed once again. The Turkish victory was total and absolute. Within a few months, the former Slavonic vassals of the Ottoman empire were back under their old Muslim master. But at least Hungary was able to hold out for nearly a century more as a Christian stronghold.

Four years after Varna, Hunyadi was still fighting. He took charge of a new army of twenty-four thousand men and fought the second battle of Kosovo, near the site of the first. Again, as at Varna, it was touch and go, but finally the Turks, far more numerous, more heavily mailed, and with better weapons, triumphed. The Janissary crossbows were particularly deadly. While Hunyadi was trying to maintain resistance to the Turks, and succeeded during his lifetime in doing so, Skanderbeg, in Albania, was similarly continuing his heroic but ultimately doomed resistance until he died after twenty-five years of unending warfare.

In this mid-fifteenth century the great cataclysm of the Jihad was about to seize the bastion of Christendom in the east: Constantinople. Constantinople sounded Roman, Christian, and imperial. It became Turkish and Muslim, but continued its imperial vocation for another five hundred years. In due course it changed its name to the much more eastern-sounding Istanbul. Istanbul is oriental, you can hear strange wailing music in its name: the East, heavy, thick, cloying, and sweet. Istanbul doesn't recall the Jihad at all but the carnality of desire, harems, the belly dance, and young women in transparent veils lying on silken couches, Topkapi, the seraglio, the Bosporus, and the Orient Express. Yet it is from this lovely city that the rest of Europe was once nearly overwhelmed by a Holy War that was anything but holy. The man who launched it and won it was Mahomet II, the Conqueror, sultan of the Ottoman empire.

40

THE LAST AGONY: CONSTANTINOPLE 1453

ONSTANTINOPLE BEGAN TO TURN INTO Istanbul in the year 1453. The fall of Constantinople is, after the Crucifixion, the greatest human calamity to have befallen Christianity. Poor theology, I know. The Crucifixion was the inevitable prelude to the Resurrection. But it's good imagery, and it conveys the feelings of Christians at the time. Today, more than half a millennium later, if one is a Western European, one can still cringe in shame when one remembers how this bastion, however flawed, of European civilization, religious tradition, and culture, in spite of its desperate calls to Christendom for help, was allowed by the rest of Europe to disappear into the maw of a then cruel nation while the West wrung its hands and twiddled its thumbs.

Only a few hundred foreign volunteers, mainly Genoese, went to fight for Constantinople. England and France had looked the other way. "The Western princes were involved in their endless and domestic quarrels," explains Gibbon. The French were afraid the English, after the Hundred Years' War, might once again descend upon them; the English were brooding at having been thrown out of France and plotting vengeance. Small as it was, the Republic of Genoa was the only country to send an expeditionary force to help defend Constantinople.

When news of the fall of Constantinople reached the outside world, Europe trembled and wept. Founded by the Roman emperor Constantine more than eleven hundred years before, Constantinople had been for many centuries the living proof of the continuity, ubiquity, and strength of Christian civilization. Now it was about to become instead the spearhead of those who, in the name of a strange, malevolent god— at least so Allah appeared to the Christians—wished to destroy the God Europe worshiped. Rome itself might be threatened next.

Theology, disputes over obscure points of doctrine, over the centuries, had turned into a political contest between the Catholics who followed the pope in Rome and the Orthodox who followed the patriarch in Constantinople. But it was more than points of theology that separated Christians from Muslims. It was civilization and religion itself. For considerably more than a thousand years the normal relationship between Christianity and Islam was war. After the fall of Constantinople and for the next 250 years Turkey was to become the most powerful state in Europe, not France, nor England, nor Spain, as the people of those countries each like to think about their own. In the 1500s, Suleiman the Magnificent was a far more powerful sovereign than Henry VIII or his daughter Elizabeth of England, or the emperor Charles V, or François I of France. They feared the Turks. The Turks did not fear them. The Turkish threat was for centuries the main concern of all the European nations, and every European man and woman lived in terror of the Turks. They feared the Muslim Turks much more than they ever feared the Nazi Germans or the Communist Russians, and for much, much longer. The Nazi peril lasted ten years. Soviet imperialism lasted seventy years. The Turkish threat lasted five hundred years.

The deeds of the various European armies do not always make pleasant reading. Our ancestors, too, were a violent lot. But what made fifteenth-century Turks so particularly abhorrent was the relish with which they displayed the savagery of their systems of government, of law, and of international relations. For practitioners of a religion that prides itself on its quality of mercy (Allah is, after all, "Allah the Merciful"), their way of life offered too many abominable contradictions to what they claimed it to be. There were, of course, the usual punishments of stoning to death for adultery and of amputation of the hand for stealing. The sultan was all-powerful; he could do what he wanted, however atrocious, and often did. So could his vizier and his generals. There was nothing unusual about the immediate execution of prisoners of war, the mass kidnapping and enslavement of subject populations, the lingering death by impalement, mass decapitation, burial, and burning alive, strangulation with bowstrings, the slave raids by the sultan's corsairs (they were not usually Turks but often Moors, Greeks, and Christian renegades) on distant shores, even as far away as Ireland and Denmark, the permanent presence of an executioner in the throne room to carry out the sultan's immediate bidding.

Only a couple of hundreds years ago, British navy personnel were particularly appalled by the beheading block fixed on the fo'c'sle of Turkish warships. One can understand Admiral Hood's comment, when Turkey was allied to Britain during the Napoleonic wars, that the Turks were "a horrid set of allies" and he was more concerned to save enemy French prisoners from the Turks than to fight the French. Hood, of course, apparently forgot that the Royal Navy had some horrid practices of its own, such as keelhauling and flogging through the fleet.

When he came to the Ottoman throne in 1451, the new sultan, Mahomet II, decided that in spite of its strong defenses, the time had come to take Constantinople, and that he was the man to do it. Besieging Constantinople had become, in recent decades, almost a permanent fixture of Ottoman political and military activity. Constantinople was, however, well protected. Its walls, thirteen miles of them, thick and high, surrounded the city. It was favorably located on the sea, at the juncture of the Sea of Marmara, the Golden Horn, and the Bosporus, with its entry into the adjoining Black Sea. Its main suppliers, Venice and Genoa, were competent maritime powers and, from the Ukraine, Constantinople received all the wheat it required from across the Black Sea. The enemy Ottoman fleet was useless and could not interfere. Small and incompetent, it presented no threat. Ships sailed in and out as in peacetime. The capital was not gravely perturbed by the threat of sieges. Anyway, sieges were traditionally a feature of Constantinople life. It had been besieged twenty-nine times since its founding under the name of Byzantium in 658 B.C.E. The Arabs tried seven times to capture it between 668 and 798. The Crusaders, who were Catholics, had taken it and plundered the Orthodox city "with unparalleled horrors" in 1204 on their way to the Holy Land. For Christianity, like Islam, has long been disunited and, like Islam, often at war with itself.

One of the great causes of the weakness of the eastern Roman Empire had always, in fact, been its dissensions. We mentioned them in an earlier chapter. The religious rivalries within the eastern Christian camp in the early days of Islam had been one of the main reasons for the first Arab victories. In the mid-fifteenth century, the Orthodox Christians were sometimes inclined to consider Catholicism an even greater abomination than Islam. Aware of the growing threat from his Ottoman neighbors, the emperor John VIII had traveled from Constantinople to confer with the pope, and at the Council of Florence in 1439 had agreed to union with Rome and to the pope's primacy. Although the agreement was technically in force, the people of the Greek empire repudiated it en masse. They seemed to hate the Christians of the West more than the Muslim neighbors at their doorstep. "Better the turban of the sultan than the red hat of a cardinal," said the Grand Duke Notaras, lay leader of the Greek Orthodox in Constantinople, who was known as a wit. He lived to regret his words. Even when the Turks were laying siege to the city the anti-papist citizens of the Greek empire, while clamoring for help from the rest of Christendom, accepted with neither grace nor gratitude the presence in their midst of those who came, at the risk of their lives, mainly from Italy, to try to save them from the Turks.

Unlike his predecessors, Mahomet II, who came to the throne on the death of his father, Murad II, was determined to take Constantinople and to put an end to what remained of the former Roman empire. Known throughout its 1,800 years of history by a variety of names (Byzantine, Roman, Latin, Eastern, and Greek), the empire had gradually disintegrated from a vast realm that had covered most of Asia Minor and a large part of south-eastern Europe into a tiny, fragmented little state of a few hundred square miles concentrated around Constantinople in the Greek province of Thrace. Its culture and its people were no longer predominantly Roman but Greek, as was their language. The territory of Salonica a few dozen miles to the east, an island or two in the Aegean, and a strip of territory in the Peloponnese completed this imperial domain in the early 1450s. That is all that was left of the old Roman Empire. Surrounding it on every side was the Ottoman empire. Constantinople was like a wart, an isolated blemish astride the center of his empire, an irritant to his sense of the righteousness of things. It was the capital (population: probably around 100,000) of an empire that had ceased to exist.

The 23-year-old Mahomet II, highly intelligent, ruthless, unscrupulous, and loathsome, so different from his kindly father, was the right man for this task of destruction. But in the usual fratricidal tradition of the sultanate, his first task was to eliminate his rival, his three-year-old brother. While the child's mother, a Serbian concubine of Murad, was congratulating the new sovereign on his accession to power, the new sultan ordered one of his officers to go to her quarters and drown his baby brother in his bath. He then ordered the officer to be strangled and the mother to be married off to a slave. The next problem on his agenda was Constantinople.

The new sultan didn't waste any time. In the spring of 1452, he sent five thousand workmen protected by a battalion of soldiers to build a fortress in his territory just north of Constantinople. They finished it in six months. Communications between Constantinople and the Black Sea ports of the Ukraine could now be cut off, and Constantinople be made to starve. The Greek emperor protested to the sultan. Mahomet replied with a declaration of war. Mahomet at first simply besieged the city without attacking it. He enrolled an army—probably of between 100,000 and 150,000 men—and waited. Time, always the ally of the one who knows how to use it, was on his side.

The Greek empire was then ruled by Constantine XI, a young man who was about to become the last emperor of what still called itself the Roman Empire. His first task, to meet the coming onslaught, was to repair the walls, the four-mile, 900-year-old wall of Theodosius facing the land to the east, and the nine-mile sea wall running along the three other sides of the city, facing the water, the Golden Horn, the Bosporus, and the Sea of Marmara. Next, he called all men who could bear arms to make themselves known and to prepare to fight for the city. Out of a population of 100,000, fewer than 5,000 answered the call. Courage was obviously not the forte of the men of Constantinople. Next, he called to the Christians of other lands for help. The Venetian patrician Gabriele Trevisano placed himself under Constantine's orders "for the honor of God and of all Christianity" and was given the command of sixteen ships. The papal legate, Cardinal Isidore, sailed in with two hundred soldiers in November. When he celebrated mass in the cathedral on his arrival the local population rioted and called for his death. They wanted no papist masses in their city. The next arrival was one of the greatest warriors of his time, the condottiere Giovanni Giustiniani, who led the Genoese contingent of seven hundred men in two ships, bringing with him a German gunnery officer, Johann Grant. Constantine appointed Giustiniani commander-in-chief of the forces defending Constantinople. The papacy sent a force of two hundred men. That was all the foreign aid Constantinople received.

Mahomet's preparations were far more intense and thorough. He obtained, we regret to say, a guarantee from Janos Hunyadi not to attack the Turks for three years. Hunyadi sent a gunnery expert to Mahomet to teach the Turk artillerymen how to break down the battlements by concentrating their fire on an imaginary triangular spot at the junction of two walls. It is said that Hunyadi was keen to destroy the Orthodox Church, then considered by Catholics as the ultimate heresy, because a local hermit had prophesied the Turks would only be driven out of Hungary after the heretics had been driven out of Constantinople.

Without neglecting important political and diplomatic measures, such as courting Hunyadi, Mahomet was naturally even busier on the military preparations. He had, and it would have been noticeable even today, a very modern and technical mind. He was particularly interested in logistics and artillery. The siege of Constantinople is one of the first sieges in which artillery was grandly used. Mahomet recruited a Hungarian renegade called Urban who, we are told, "cast a monster cannon for the Turks which was the object of both their admiration and terror." But one day, later in the siege, the cannon blew up and killed its inventor.

We shall not, in this book, go too deeply into the details of the siege. It has been covered by many writers already and does not require another version. I recommend, among others, Brigadier Fuller's 22-page account of it in his readily available *The Decisive Battles of the Western World,* as much for its felicitous style as for its accuracy and expertise. The siege of Constantinople is of particular interest to us within its Jihad framework, that is to say in the context of the Muslim Holy War. By the mid-1400s, the pretense in Muslim countries of waging a religious war when one went off on a campaign of rape and plunder was only upheld for the form of it. The Jihad acquired a very spurious quality very early in its history—in fact one is inclined to think that the Jihad was essentially an immense bit of humbug. Love of God was certainly not one of Mahomet II's outstanding traits, although he had been pious and priggish enough when a very young man. After talking with a Christian he would go and purify himself by washing his hands and face, but this practice seems to imply less a love of God than a sense of superiority of oneself and an excess of hygienic concern. And Gibbon moreover tells us of Mahomet II that "in his looser hours he presumed (it is said) to brand the prophet of Mecca as a robber and impostor." In addition he was an assiduous pederast, and the parents of his pages must have worried greatly about the morals of their children in his palace. He was also a sadistic monster, known to those around him as "The Drinker of Blood." Mahomet II fails totally to qualify for holiness and Holy War as a reason for the attack on Constantinople can readily be dismissed. The attack on Constantinople, if it had been carried out by Western European Christians against a Muslim city, would be considered outright imperialism. And rightly so, for that is what it was.

The Muslim attack on Constantinople had begun seven weeks before, on April 6, with a heavy bombardment against the Theodosius's wall, on the landward side of the city, and against the boom which lay across the Golden Horn where it flows into the Bosporus, preventing by its presence enemy ships from entering the Horn. Before attacking Constantinople, Mahomet had taken several small military posts outside, and had casually ordered their garrisons to be impaled. Now outside the city, day in and day out, the Turkish guns went on pounding the walls. They brought up tall movable towers up which the attackers scrambled, to be repulsed by the desperate defenders with maces, battle-axes, swords, pikes, and boiling oil. The emperor tirelessly went around to every defense post, encouraging the soldiers— most of whom were civilians fighting, in fact, in defense of their homes and families. Every post was undermanned; sometimes only three or four men would be defending a vital spot. Below the walls the Muslims milled around and jeered. Sometimes they would attack, shouting "Allah is Great" and "Let's sack the city."

More than a hundred thousand Janissaries and soldiers of every hue took part in the continual assault on the city. Most of the attacks were launched against Theodosius's wall, about the middle, where the heavily barricaded St. Romanus gate was tightly held as the most vulnerable defense post. As the Turks tired, fresh reinforcements poured in from the Asiatic side across the Dardanelles, and from the sultan's European domains to the north. Mahomet was everywhere, scanning the skies for changes in the weather and the sea in case expected reinforcements arrived from the West. At the end of March—some accounts say mid-April—four sails were sighted to the west. Mahomet was the first to spot them and he immediately sent out 145 of his galleys, under his admiral, Baltoglu, to intercept them and bring the crews in for questioning and perhaps for impalement as well. But there was no stopping the four alien ships, three Genoese galleases and an imperial grain ship. From the rooftops of Constantinople, thousands of Greeks watched the Italian vessels dauntlessly making their way toward the Horn, lying becalmed for awhile while the Ottoman sailors tried with grappling hooks and ropes to climb up their hulls and were cut down by the Genoese seamen. On the Asian side of the Bosporus, Mahomet too was watching, jumping up and down with excitement and shouting instructions to Baltoglu across the water. High on the water, commanded by three stalwart Genoese captains, Mauricio Cattaneo, Domenico of Navarra, and Baptisto de Feliciano, the galleases never faltered, never hesitated. They broke through the low-slung galleys, smashed their oars, stove in the Ottoman vessels that came too near and, as they passed, fired down on the Turkish crews with rocks, Greek fire, and swivel guns until they reached the safety of the inner harbor. Insane with rage, Mahomet ordered his admiral impaled, but the Turkish generals implored him not to do so. Mahomet beat him with a big stick instead. While four slaves held Baltoglu down, the frenzied and enraged sultan personally went on hitting his admiral until he fainted.

There was still hope in the Greek camp that the West might come to the rescue. Hope kept them fighting. Mahomet, unable to sail into the Golden Horn and threaten Constantinople and its fleet, had seventy of his ships dragged overland from the Bosporus across Galatia and into the Horn. He could now attack the city from a new, so far unused, side. The emperor's advisors begged him to leave the city secretly and live to fight another day. "Never, never will I leave you," he said, wept, and stayed. In the early part of May fifty thousand Turks attacked the Gate of St. Romanus. Led by Giustiniani, the Greeks beat them off. "What would I not give to win that man over to my service," sighed the sultan, watching his Janissaries being beaten back. Later that month the Turks tried to dig their way under the walls. Led by Johann Grant, the Greeks counterattacked and fought the invaders with knives and spears in the tunnel. But the end was near.

If there is a holy aspect to this unrelenting battle for the old Byzantine capital, it lies with the Christian defenders. Whatever their previous lapses, they were very conscious of their role before God, man, and history. There can have been only very few recorded moments that affect us as deeply as the last Christian service celebrated in St. Sophia. In the crowded church, in the dim light, the candle flames fluttering in the drafts; men, women, and children, entire families, crowded together, praying and sobbing and hugging one another and singing hymns to beseech mercy. "Crowns await you in heaven and on earth your names will be remembered with honor until the end of time," the emperor cried out to those around him. Thereupon, the chronicler Phrantzes, who was there, tells us, they all cried out, "Let us die for our faith and our fatherland, for the church of God and for thee, our emperor." It is the people of Constantinople who were the heroes and the holy ones, not their conquerors, waving their scimitars and tempesting outside in the fury of their attack. "The building was once more and for the last time crowded with Christian worshippers. . . . The empire was in its agony and it was fitting that the service for its departing spirit should thus be publicly said in its most beautiful church and before its last brave emperor." The emperor, the patriarch, all of Constantine's warriors who could be spared, and thousands of everyday citizens who all knew that the next day they would be facing rape, sodomy, slavery, or death, or all four, took part in what has been described as "this liturgy of death."

The end began at sunrise on October 29, in the wake of the previous night's ceremony in St. Sophia. The Turkish drums beat and the trumpets sounded. There came wave after wave of Turkish troops, the unruly bazi-bazouks in the lead, the sturdy Anatolians next, the disciplined Janissaries kept in line last for the final assault. Carrying ladders, scrambling over dead bodies, the Turks ignored their losses and came back time and again to the attack. Those who reached the top fought hand to hand against the Greeks, armed with swords, pikes, maces, and axes. However many Turks were killed, more and more kept arriving. Giustiniani fell, badly wounded and in great pain, and was taken to his ship anchored in the Golden Horn to die. With his disappearance from the scene the resistance weakened, but still the Greeks fought on. However, they were now too few against this brutal mass of murderous humanity that swarmed all over them. As Creasy recounts the story, "amid the tears and prayers of all who beheld him, the last of the Caesars went forth to die." With the Spanish knight Don Francesco of Toledo and his kinsman Theophilus Palaeologus on either side, Constantine XI rushed into the melee. Two Turks cut him down with their sabers and he fell dead among the corpses heaped around him. The last of the Caesars had known how to die. This was a tragedy of immense dimension. Only Shakespeare could have rendered it worthily.

Several thousand of the survivors had taken refuge in the cathedral: nobles, servants, ordinary citizens, their wives and children, priests and nuns. They locked the huge doors, prayed, and waited. Mahomet had given the troops free quarter. They raped, of course, the nuns being the first victims, and slaughtered. At least four thousand were killed before Mahomet stopped the massacre at noon. He ordered a muezzin to climb into the pulpit of St. Sophia and dedicate the building to Allah. It has remained a mosque ever since. Fifty thousand of the inhabitants, more than half the population, were rounded up and taken away as slaves. For months afterward, slaves were the cheapest commodity in the markets of Turkey. Mahomet asked that the body of the dead emperor be brought to him. Some Turkish soldiers found it in a pile of corpses and recognized Constantine by the golden eagles embroidered on his boots. The sultan ordered his head to be cut off and placed between the horse's legs under the equestrian bronze statue of the emperor Justinian. The head was later embalmed and sent around the chief cities of the Ottoman empire for the delectation of the citizens.

Next, Mahomet ordered the Grand Duke Notaras, who had survived, to be brought before him, asked him for the names and addresses of all the leading nobles, officials, and citizens, which Notaras gave him. He had them all arrested and decapitated. He sadistically bought from their owners high-ranking prisoners who had been enslaved, for the pleasure of having them beheaded in front of him. He then lined up their heads, counted them, meditated, and at one moment recited a verse by the Persian poet Firdusi:

> The spider's curtain hangs before the portal of Caesar's palace;
> And the owl stands sentinel on the watch-tower of Afrasiab.

If the poem is unclear, we must remember that the conqueror of Constantinople was also one of these pseudo-intellectuals who thrives on obscurity, and also a bit of a literary dilettante. Perhaps he visualized himself as being as wise as an owl. He certainly tried to be.

At the banquet that followed where, we are told, "he drank deeply of the wine" (Mahomet was fond of the bottle, in spite of the injunctions of the Koran against alcohol) and summoned the fourteen-year-old son of the Grand Duke Notaras to his room. Now, in the presence of this pederast and all-powerful ruthless ruler, the moment of truth had come for the Grand Duke Notaras, who had always managed to avoid such confrontations before. He sent a dignified and brave message to the sultan advising him that his son was not available to him and never would be. Mahomet II, conqueror of Constantinople, immediately ordered the entire Notaras family decapitated. The condemned nobleman enjoined the members of his family to die as good Christians and had to watch his wife and children being executed one by one first. Presumably suitably titillated, Mahomet II, protagonist of the Holy War, conqueror of Constantinople, then found another acceptable young boy for his couch.

But politics is the art of the possible, and Mahomet II was above all a shrewd politician. The Jihad, great for rousing his Janissaries and spahis to martial fury, had to take second place to the necessity of reconciliation and reconstruction when the rape and the bloodletting were over. The plain fact is that Constantinople was full of Christian survivors who did not want to be converted to Islam and, Jihad or no Jihad, they had to be included in the sultan's future calculations. Constantinople, or Istanbul as it was to be renamed, now needed stability. The sword of Islam had fulfilled its political and military purpose. It now had to be sheathed and replaced by the caresses of Islam.

A couple of days after the fall of the city, when the frenzy was over, Mahomet called on all the Christian clergy to come out of hiding under promise of their personal safety, and to elect a new patriarch to be the head of the Orthodox Church. Timidly at first, the Orthodox priests reappeared and for a new patriarch they chose one George Scholarios, whom they called Gennadios. After his election Gennadios was received with great honor by the sultan, who invested him with the authority of his new position, gave him a crozier of solid gold studded with precious stones, accompanied him to his horse, and sent him forth under the protection of his top officials to the Church of the Apostles, which replaced St. Sophia, now a mosque, as the principal place of worship for the Christians.

The Muslim sultan and caliph, the recognized protector of the holy lands of Islam, the successor of the Apostle of God, the ruler of the faithful, king and chief, was now also the accepted protector of the Christian church with which Islam was in a state of permanent warfare. However, the post of patriarch was never to be a sinecure, any more than it had been under the Christian emperors. During more than nineteen centuries of the patriarchate, from the year 36 to 1884, only 137 patriarchs stayed in office until its normal expiry date: 141 were deposed and banished, 41 resigned, five were murdered (two of them by poisoning), one was decapitated, one was blinded, one was drowned, and one was strangled (presumably with a bowstring). Banishment was a frequent fate "as soon as a competitor offers to gratify the Grand Vizier with a larger present, or annual tribute, than the predecessor," wrote a chronicler in 1784. Christianity, whether as a religious entity to be protected within the Ottoman empire or as a religious entity to be assailed outside the empire, was always first and foremost a cow to be milked. The Muslim protection of the Ottoman Christian subjects was always as ambiguous as was the holiness of the Muslim Holy War.

Fortunately for the sultan, his loyal Islamic subjects never asked any questions. Some perhaps wondered whether the Jihad was not simply a vast freebooting enterprise, but the human race being what it is, most were happy to keep quiet, praise Allah, and count the loot as it came pouring in.

41

THE ROAD TO ROME: BELGRADE 1456

NOW THAT CONSTANTINOPLE HAD BEEN taken, Rome was the next inevitable Muslim target. The papacy, the see of St. Peter where more than two hundred popes had reigned, now stood as the main bastion against gradual world-wide submission to the rule of Allah and of his prophet Muhammad. Rome had to be taken.

After Constantinople, the Vatican seemed within reach to the Turks. Sultan Mahomet II visualized his Janissaries stabling their horses by the high altar in St. Peter's. This was to be the ultimate victory of the Jihad, Muhammad triumphant, the whole Christian world now Dar-al-Islam, the Land of Islam; no more Land of War; the Koran intoned in the mosques of an empire upon which—the expression had not yet come into favor—the sun never set. St. Peter's, Canterbury, Chartres, Notre Dame, Cologne—the great cathedrals, like St. Sophia, would all become mosques, the cry of the muezzin to resound to the sky. It was to Mecca that the whole world would soon bow. After the fall of Constantinople, there seemed to be no sovereign powerful enough to stop the progress of Islam through Europe. But first Sultan Mahomet would have to destroy the enemies of Islam right at his doorstep in the Balkans. But, alas for the sultan, and fortunately for Christian Europe, it is right there in the Balkans that his plan for European conquest was shattered. It is in south-eastern Europe that he met both his Waterloo and his Wellington. Belgrade was the Waterloo, Hunyadi was the Wellington.

Just the same, the fall of Constantinople inevitably inaugurated the start of a gigantic game of skittles across the Balkans as the Ottoman blitzkrieg swept through the region once again. The Jihad, sums up a historical atlas, "subjugated twelve kingdoms and two hundred cities" in the next few years. The Peloponnese, in Greece, the last remnant of the Greek empire, was the first to fall. Constantinople, its capital, now renamed Istanbul, was in Turkish hands, and there was no point to any resistance on its part. The next two states to be bagged in the Turkish net, after a brief renewed fling at freedom, were Serbia and Bosnia. Stephen, king of Bosnia, and his sons surrendered to Mahomet II according to terms which granted them their lives. But Mahomet found the Christian king of Bosnia and his offspring tiresome, wished to be rid of them, and consulted the supreme spiritual authority of the empire, the Grand Mufti, who assured him that agreements with unbelievers were null and void. "Kill him" was the mufti's recommendation, and he volunteered to carry out the execution himself. The Bosnian monarch was summoned to the sultan's presence and ordered to surrender his sword to the Grand Mufti, who promptly severed his head from his body with it. "It is a good deed to slay such infidels," the Grand Mufti observed. The king's sons were similarly disposed of by the devout Mufti, who went to Bosnia for that purpose. Perhaps acting on the principle that Islam was just too strong, many Bosnians, most of them followers of the Bogomil Christian sect, became followers of the Prophet. They still are today. Their Serb Orthodox Christian neighbors have never forgiven them or their descendants. We see the consequences in Bosnia today.

But some cities and countries did not surrender to the Islamic wave, at least not for many years. Albania, where Skanderbeg was still holding out, was one of them. The Albanian leader even forced the sultan to sign a treaty acknowledging Skanderbeg as Lord of Albania and Epirus. Skanderbeg remained fighting until he died in 1468. Hungary, led by Janos Hunyadi, also continued to oppose the sultan's imperial designs. Hunyadi found a staunch ally in the Spanish Franciscan friar Juan de Capistrano, who came to Hungary to preach a crusade against the infidels. The Jihad had met its match. Capistrano's honey-tongued oratory and eloquence, the vigor of his faith, his martial spirit, and his charisma drew tens of thousands of volunteers, often poor peasants, to the banners that Hunyadi held aloft. Saint John of Capistrano—for he was later canonized—joined his own crusade, and when the Turks marched to Belgrade, then part of the Hungarian kingdom, Capistrano, Hunyadi, and the crusaders, traveling overland as fast as they could, reached the threatened city to join in its defense well ahead of the Turks.

The Ottoman army was led by Mahomet II in person. The Turkish guns, which three years previously had smashed the Theodosius Wall of Constantinople, this time smashed the walls of Belgrade. The Turks launched a general attack on the city on July 21, 1456. The Janissaries in the van carried the forward trenches and fought their way into the lower part of the town. Capistrano, a crucifix held aloft, singing hymns, praising the Lord and promising heaven to anyone who might fall in the defense of the faith, led the counterattack by one thousand crusaders, calling on Jesus Christ for help. The Turks fled, panic stricken, calling on Allah for help. Mahomet, furiously striking out at any of his fleeing soldiers he could reach with his sword, was wounded in the thigh and carried off from the field of battle screaming and shouting and insulting his general Hassan, who commanded the Janissaries and was later killed in the battle. Hassan was one of many Turkish casualties; twenty-five thousand were reported killed on that day. The Muslim casualties occurred in two waves: first while trying to take Belgrade, and secondly while fleeing from the city after failing to capture it. Hunyadi captured the Turkish guns, all three hundred of them, and all the stores which the Turks had brought with them from occupied Serbia. They also captured hundreds of camels and the carts which had been used to bring up guns and ammunition. All in all, it was a splendid victory for Janos Hunyadi. It was also his last battle, and a stirring way of closing his mission in life: fighting for Hungary. Hunyadi, national hero, soldier, crusader, and occasionally brutal massacrer of men, died three weeks later of the plague. He remains one of the greatest names of Hungarian history and deserves to be one of the greatest names of European history.

Mahomet II's defeat at Belgrade did not discourage the Muslim emperor from more Jihad ventures. But after his victory at Constantinople and his defeat at Belgrade, his later expeditions were all rather anti-climactic, including a largely naval campaign he carried out against Venetian outposts in Albania and on the Dalmatian coast in 1463. This war, which went on in a desultory fashion for fifteen years, was the first of many that pitted the Venetian Republic against the Ottoman empire.

When in his fifties and still hale and hearty, the conqueror of Constantinople decided that the moment had come to conquer Rome. Only the capture of the former capital of the Roman Empire, now capital of Christendom, could add to his fame as conqueror of the world and defender of Islam. The campaign would have to be a southern one, and also a sea-borne one, over the Mediterranean sea and through Italy. The longer overland route through the Balkans and eastern Europe was too dangerous. The terrain was difficult and although Jancs Hunyadi was dead, his son Mathias Corvinus, king of Hungary, seemed as if he might be equally troublesome.

Mahomet launched two campaigns in the Mediterranean, one in southern Italy, the other against the coastal towns of Anatolia and the island of Rhodes, held by the Knights of Saint John and a perpetual threat to Ottoman trade and shipping. In the first campaign, in April 1480, the Turks smashed the walls of the citadel and were all set to seize and occupy the island when the Janissaries went on strike. Their general had just issued a general order outlawing pillage by the troops, a recognized form of reward in the Middle Ages when a town was captured after it had refused to surrender and was taken by assault. The troops were entitled to four-fifths of the loot, and one fifth was reserved for the sultan, but this time Mahomet wanted all of it for himself.

Deprived of their cherished plunder, the Janissaries refused to attack. They were very polite to the sultan over their decision but, bluntly put, their argument was simple and direct. They loved fighting for Allah and the Prophet, and for the sultan, too, of course; but the Jihad should bring its proper reward—loot, women, and slaves—to those risking their lives for the faith. No plunder, no assault. So the warriors of Allah sailed back to Istanbul, and Rhodes was saved for Christendom for another few decades.

The second of Mahomet's late Mediterranean campaigns, in August of that year, was nearer Rome itself. The Turks landed in Otranto, in the heel of Italy, then regarded as they key to the whole of the peninsula. They sawed the archbishop in half, killed half the population, and those they didn't kill they shipped back home to be sold in the local slave markets.

The Rhodes setback and the unreliability shown by the Janissaries obliged the sultan to consider anew his Roman expedition. He decided to set out for Asia Minor instead. He did not travel very far. On May 3, 1481, he suddenly died of a heart attack while on the march among his soldiers. The Janissaries returned to Istanbul with the sultan's body and his two sons, Prince Bayazid, aged thirty-five, and his younger brother, Prince Djem, aged twenty-two. Each tried to seize the throne for himself.

Meanwhile the pope had called for a crusade against the Turks in southern Italy. The archbishop of Genoa, Cardinal Paolo Fregoso, former sailor, soldier, and doge, determined to avenge his fellow archbishop who had been so cruelly tortured and killed, took command of the papal forces, sailed off to battle the Turks and, on September 10, 1481, recaptured Otranto.

PART EIGHT

BY LAND AND SEA

42

THE SIGH OF THE MOOR:
GRANADA 1492

HE CONFLICT BETWEEN THE TWO warring brothers is perhaps the
outstanding feature of Bayazid's unexciting reign, which covered thirty-one boring years unmarked by any events of great military
importance in Europe. Djem, the loser, was exiled to France and Italy,
where he died in 1495, some say murdered by Pope Alexander VI, the
infamous Rodrigo Borgia, presumably at the request of Bayazid. In
Europe the reign of Bayazid did, however, achieve one distinction: it
marked the entry of the Ottoman navy as a power of the Jihad, under
the command of the first well-known admiral of the Turkish navy,
Kemal Reis. He provides us with a link between the Ottoman empire
in the east and the original Muslim domain in western Europe, Spain.
Kemal Reis raided the coast of Spain at the request of the local Moors
who, faced with the assault on the kingdom of Granada by Ferdinand
of Aragon and Isabella of Castile, had asked Sultan Bayazid II for his
help "as lord of the two seas and of the two continents" against the
Spaniards.

In this chapter we therefore return to Spain, where the war between
Islam and Christianity had entered its final phase. Of the Muslim conquests there remained in the fifteenth century only the kingdom of
Granada (population: 1 million, compared to Castile's 6 million) and a
few very small taifas, some of them vassals to the Christian kings, that
had somehow managed to endure through the upheavals that had

swamped the Moslemah of Spain since the fall of Seville in 1248. The most important were Algeciras, Gibraltar, and Tarifa, all ports on the southern coast, through which Granada was provisioned in warriors, weapons, and supplies from the Marinid kingdom of Morocco. If it were not for this North African aid, these last minor remnants of the Muslim presence in Spain would probably have vanished much sooner.

The war on the southern frontiers of Spain had become, as Derek Lomax writes, "a jousting ground for idle European noblemen who wanted something more exotic than the tourneys of Windsor and less dangerous than the Balkan crusades." Spain, for most of Europe, had acquired a low priority compared to the struggle underway in the Balkans between Turks and Christians. There were, however, a couple of important battles fought in the Iberian peninsula during these decades.

The first was at the Rio Salado, near Tarifa, in 1340, where Alfonso XI of Castile, aided by Alfonso IV of Portugal, routed a considerably larger force of Muslim warriors, many of whom had recently arrived from Morocco. There was never a shortage of volunteers in Morocco for fighting on what one could call the Spanish front. The Moroccans considered Spain the natural site for Holy War because of all the Christians there, and the Marinid armies never lacked recruits: Berbers from the Atlas mountains and Arabs from the coast. They were all anxious to sail across to the other side of the strait of Gibraltar to find either booty and the women of Spain, or martyrdom and the houris of Paradise.

Spain, to the men of Morocco, was known as the land of the Jihad. Algeciras was their usual entry point. The Spaniards were anxious to keep these Moroccan warriors out. Algeciras thus became their next target. The Castilians naturally called in their allies to help them.

The strategic implication of that campaign, four years after Salado, had been clear right from the beginning, particularly to the papacy, which was always concerned with the inroads of Islam into Europe. The Genoese were among Alfonso XI's allies at the siege, as was a Catalan fleet from Barcelona and King Philippe III of Navarre, who came down with an army to aid the Spaniards, as did some valorous English knights, among them the earls of Derby and Salisbury. The capture of the Atlantic port of Algeciras by the Spaniards, more than any other action, by virtually blocking Moroccan entry into Europe, should have brought to an end the huge support the North Africans had been able to give to their fellow Muslims in Spain. The Spaniards even hoped that their capture of the Moorish gateway into the peninsula might end the Jihad offensive in Spain once and for all.

The Muslim surrender of Algeciras should certainly have resulted in the rapid extinction of Moorish power in Spain and the end of the kingdom of Granada. But instead of continuing to fight the Moroccans, Castile became involved in the Hundred Years' War between France and England. A French army under the constable Bertrand du Guesclin and an English army led by the Black Prince came to fight on Spanish soil in support of two rival Spanish claimants to the throne of Castile. The French backed Henry II, the English aided Pedro the Cruel.

The war against the Moors became a secondary matter and the anti-Muslim front in the south became a sideshow. The Castilians, taken up with the events on their northern border, neglected the south. Local Andalusian Christian lords did most of the fighting against the Muslims, notably the marquess of Cadiz, Rodrigo Ponce de Leon (whose conquistador grandson was to try in vain to find the fountain of eternal youth in Florida), and the duke of Medina Sidonia (whose descendant was to lead the Spanish Armada against England a couple hundred years later). The two men, rivals for local power and land, loathed each other and spent as much time between mass, compline, and vespers fighting each other as they did fighting the Moors. Ponce de Leon used to refer to Medina Sidonia as "my enemy incarnate." Their cooperation against the Moors was usually quite ineffective.

But we must not linger too long over this last half-hearted phase of the Reconquista and, instead, leap over more than a century, across the names of the thirteen kings of Granada who rapidly followed one another in their isolated and disintegrating kingdom. Innumerable sieges, skirmishes, countersieges, raids, and affrays followed each other over the next century and a half as the Muslim kingdom moved inexorably toward its inevitable demise: Antequera, Zahara, Ayamonte, Priego, Ubeda, Cordova, Matrera, Rute, and many others. Innumerable participants with little-known identities: Abul Hassan Ali, Gonzalo Martinez, Abul Hassan's son Yusuf I, Juan Manuel, and Uthman ibn Abil Ula fought and killed one another with gusto. The list of names is long and many valorous deeds have been lost in the murk of these half-forgotten campaigns. Then we come to the year 1469, and we begin to see a little light. It is an important year, the year when Ferdinand, heir to King Juan II of Aragon, and Isabella, heiress of Enrique IV, king of Castile, married in Segovia. He was eighteen years old, she was nineteen. Their marriage united Christian Spain. The wedding bells that noble guests were hearing were announcing the approaching birth of Christian Spain, whole and entire. They were also sounding the death knell of Muslim Spain.

Ferdinand and Isabella brought modern Spain into existence. The unification of Spain was the main achievement of the royal couple. It was accomplished through the defeat of the Jihad. The human toll of this victory was horrendous, but in view of the divisive nature of Islam, to battle it was the only course acceptable to the Spanish nation. There would have been, perhaps, one other route to unity: the Islamization of Spain. That was the Jihad way. But Spain would no longer have been itself; another country would have emerged, perhaps flourished, as a European extension of North Africa. The wailing cry of the muezzin resounding from the minaret would have been its symbol. Picturesque, yes. Spanish, no. Europe did not want to be North African, any more than North Africa has wanted to be Spanish, French, Italian, or British and has, understandably so, shown it. Anti-imperialism is a sentiment that has to be respected, even admired, whatever its source. The people of Spain and Portugal showed it from the eighth through the fifteenth century fighting against the Moors and the Arabs. The people of North Africa showed it in the nineteenth and twentieth centuries fighting against the French, the Spaniards, the Italians, and the British.

It was eleven years after the marriage of Isabella and Ferdinand that Islam's—and the Jihad's—final process of disintegration began in Spain. In 1480, Isabella had been on the Castilian throne six years, Ferdinand had been king of Aragon one year. They both wanted, and felt they now had the power to do so, to bring the Muslim kingdom of Granada to an end, to eliminate it from Spain, to make Granada part of Spain. The king of Granada, Mulay Abu al-Hassan, gave them the opportunity. First, the story says, he refused to pay them the usual yearly tribute, sending instead a message that "the coffers of Granada contain no more gold, but they contain steel," a foolish threat from a small and weak neighbor to a strong and large one. In a surprise midnight attack on nearby Zahara in 1481, the Moors killed all but one of the men defending the fortress, captured 150 Christian men, women, and children, and marched them in chains to Ronda. Incensed, King Ferdinand told a high official in Galicia, "We now intend to put ourselves in readiness to toil with all our strength for the time when we shall conquer the kingdom of Granada and expel from all Spain the enemies of the Catholic faith and dedicate Spain to the service of God." The aim was clear: it was the destruction of the Moorish kingdom of

Granada, the destruction of all Muslim Spain. It was the Christian anti-Jihad in action. The policy that Ferdinand followed toward Granada during the next few years showed he meant exactly what he said.

The first target, partly in retaliation for the Muslim raid on Zahara, was the fortress of Alhama, about thirty miles from the capital of Granada, built on a rocky crest rising sheer out of a river valley and therefore considered impregnable by the Moors. But it was weakly defended and could be taken easily, reported Juan de Ortega, a captain of *escaladores,* a special team of army mountain scalers. Ferdinand gave the command of an army of 3,500 men to Don Rodrigo Ponce de Leon, who put aside his feud with the duke of Medina Sidonia and marched off to the attack in the heart of winter. Juan de Ortega's men, in the middle of a cold December night, crept into the fortress, killed the watchmen and opened the gates to the Spanish troops below, who after a few hours of fighting occupied the town, looted it thoroughly, killed some of the inhabitants, and enslaved most of them. The Spaniards found and released many Christian captives in the fortress and hanged a Christian renegade from the battlements. "The report of this disaster fell like the knell of their own doom on the ears of the inhabitants of Granada," Prescott tells us in his history of Ferdinand and Isabella. The doom was not far off.

Confusion reigned in Granada in the highest circles. King Mulay Hassan was thrown out by his rebellious subjects and took refuge in Malaga. His son, nineteen-year-old Boabdil, young, energetic, and inexperienced, took over the kingship in 1483. Confusion also reigned among the Castilians who, determined to keep their Alhama prize, wasted much effort trying to take the nearby town of Lorca also, the possession of which, they felt, would help them to defend Alhama. Boabdil, a somewhat disorganized youth, was captured by the Spaniards when he went to fight them at Lucena. The Spaniards released him on condition he swore an oath of vassalage to Castile. Then he agreed to share his kingdom with his half-brother el-Zagal, whose father Mulay Hassan abdicated in his favor. The Spaniards captured Boabdil a second time, captured Loja, and for the next few years went on ceaselessly attacking the kingdom of Granada, taking it slowly, one small slice of the country at a time. The most prominent of the Spanish military leaders was Gonzalo de Cordoba, the Great Captain, whose infantry went into battle armed with individual firearms against the Muslims' bows and arrows and pikes.

In 1487 the Spaniards captured Malaga, adding its valuable port to their possessions. Marbella, now so fashionable, became the main Castilian naval base. Almeria, in recent years a favorite place for shooting Italian "spaghetti" westerns, fell to King Ferdinand's forces soon afterward. The king himself commanded the army—some eighty thousand foot soldiers and fifteen thousand horsemen. Queen Isabella was a sort of quartermaster general, modest, unassuming, but of great presence. She started the first medical service in military history, setting up tents for the sick and wounded. Among those commanders and generals she never gave her advice unless it was requested and on one occasion, when she did so, she prefaced her counsel with a modest remark which some feminists of today would excoriate, "May Your Lordship pardon me for speaking of things which I do not understand," when she probably understood them better than her husband or any of the men around him. But, like most intelligent people, either male or female, she felt no need to boast or assert herself. Her very presence sufficed to earn her respect. When she wasn't organizing the administration and supplies for the army, she liked to knit. She was loyal and faithful to her husband, financed Christopher Columbus, raised money to ransom captives in Muslim hands, was an admirable woman, intellectually far above her contemporaries, men and women alike. She was strong but she was feminine and she would not have liked the graceless modern feminist macho women of today. She was beautiful, she had her feet firmly planted on the ground, and she a mind that soared. She is one of the truly great figures of history.

The Spanish army laid siege to the Granadan capital and built in three months a satellite city just outside the walls in order to house and provide shelter to the besiegers. The troops wanted to call the town Isabella, but the Queen asked that it be named Santa Fe, as that was the only locality in Granada that, according to a Spanish writer, "had never been contaminated by the Muslim heresy." The town still exists today. Inside the besieged city of Granada, the Muslim population awaited every day a relief force from North Africa which Boabdil knew would never come. The future, for the Muslims, was without hope. There was no solution, no recourse, except defeat and honorable capitulation. Negotiations between Muslim and Christian representatives were secretly conducted at night. They were ratified by the two monarchs at the end of November 1491. The date of capitulation was fixed for January 2, 1492. The Jihad was now over in Spain, but the Moors of Granada were to be allowed to keep their mosques and their religion, a condition which the Spaniards were later to ignore completely.

Boabdil was allotted a small kingdom to govern in the nearby Alpujarras mountains, just to the south, as vassal to Castile.

The capitulation ceremony was largely religious rather than military, as befitted a war that, to both sides, had probably had a far more enforced, embattled holy character than any other in which they had taken part. A cardinal led the Spanish forces to the ceremony. Ferdinand stood by a mosque, later consecrated to St. Sebastian a symbol of the Jihad that had failed. The cardinal greeted Boabdil as, glum-faced, he rode out of Granada with his family around him, and escorted him toward the king, who embraced him and accepted the keys to the city from him. "These keys are thine, O King, since Allah so decrees it," humbly said the deposed king. Allah had been present during the 780 years of the Muslim occupation of Granada. It was fitting he should not be forgotten as the occupation was ending. One of the people present at the ceremony was a Genoese navigator by the name of Christopher Columbus, who was seeking aid from Queen Isabella for a voyage he wished to make west, across the Atlantic to the Indies.

As King Ferdinand, crucifix in hand, advanced on his horse toward the surrendered Muslim city he was perhaps thinking of another city, a Christian one this time, Constantinople, which had been lost thirty-nine years earlier to the Muslims amid scenes of unparalleled horror. It was cold in Granada that morning, but the sky was blue. The banners of Castile and of St. James were waving in the sky. A choir was singing a Te Deum. The whole army was on its knees to honor "this last and glorious triumph of the Cross," Prescott tells us. The Jihad in Spain was no more. Thanks to Ferdinand and Isabella Spain, whole and entire, was now a nation.

A few miles away, Boabdil, his mother riding alongside him, reached a high spot on the road to the Alpujarras from which he could look down on Granada, his city until yesterday. Far below he could see it, red against the winter dullness of the countryside, a city of beauty and joy which he would see no more. Although he did not know it, he was a Spaniard after all, who was born and had lived all his life under Andalusian skies. He gave a deep sigh of despair and burst into tears. "Alas," he cried out, covering his eyes with his hand, "when were woes ever equal to mine!" His mother, who had once been a slave in a harem, did not extend a word of sympathy to her distraught son. Her rancor overwhelmed her. "You do well to weep like a woman for what you could not defend like a man," she shouted at him.

Boabdil tragically moves out of our history. After a few months, he gave up his Andalusian domain in the mountains and went to Fez, in Morocco, where he died fighting in one of the many internecine Islamic conflicts, far from the Granada which he had loved and lost. They call the spot from which Boabdil gazed for the last time at Granada "the Last Sigh of the Moor." It is a memorable moment in history, and an important one, not only symbolically, because it marked the end of the Arab military penetration of western Europe and its rejection by the people it had tried to conquer. It is also a moment of immense personal pathos and drama. The tragedy of Boabdil is a universal one. But it was a necessary moment in European history. A triumphant, intolerant Islam had no place on that continent. The Jihad, by its very nature, would have destroyed Europe. Europe must be Europe. It could not have remained itself under a militant, intolerant, dominant Islam. Muslims know equally well that Dar-al-Islam, the Land of Islam, must be Muslim to be so. To each his own.

43

THE OTTOMAN EMPIRE: SELIM THE GRIM 1512–1520

THE JIHAD TOOK A BREATHER in Europe after the fall of Granada. In Hungary, where the fear of the Turks seemed temporarily to have vanished, it was the Christian aristocracy that lapsed into barbarism while the country went into a violent civil war under its new new king, Ladislas II, who had followed Mathias, Hunyadi's son, to the throne in 1490.

The peasants, hideously oppressed by the aristocracy, rebelled under the leadership of one George Dozsa, who was captured by the nobles on the charge of having attempted to become king and made to sit on a red hot iron throne, with a red hot iron crown on his head and a red hot iron scepter in his hand. Partly roasted, Dozsa was then handed over to a dozen of his followers who had not eaten for two weeks. The hideous consequences I leave to the imagination of the reader. The rebellious peasantry was then condemned in toto to eternal serfdom, to teach them to keep their place. It is no wonder that, compared to their own masters, the Turks seemed a lesser evil to many of the Hungarian peasantry. But fortunately for the savage Magyar rulers, the Turks were rather inactive in Europe at this time.

While Spain was throwing out the unfortunate Boabdil from Granada and throwing off its Muslim yoke, the dreary sultan Bayazid II did manage to impose his own version of Muslim rule on three Venetian trading posts on the Greek mainland, Modon, Koron, and the more famously named Lepanto, the site a few dozen years later of one of the greatest naval battles of all times. Turkey was in the process of becoming a naval power. In 1499 an Ottoman armada of some 238 ships under Daud Pasha and Kemal Reis defeated a Venetian fleet of some 170 vessels, which included a French squadron of twenty-two galleys, and took Lepanto, which was also being besieged at the time by a Janissary force which had marched in from overland. The Spaniards at this time made one of their early entries on the Ottoman scene: a mixed Venetian-Spanish contingent led by Gonzalo de Cordoba recaptured the Ionian island of Cephalonia from an occupying Turkish army.

Like all campaigns by the faithful against the infidels, the war against Venice formed part of the Jihad, with all the spiritual and mystic connotations and rewards which Holy War held in the Muslim mind. "Above all, religious enthusiasm roused the Muslim of every class to share in the Holy War against the misbelievers. The Koran . . . teaches also that, when there is a war between the true believers and the enemies of Islam, it is the duty of every Mussulman to devote to such a war his property, his person, and his life," says a nineteenth-century historian. And, mentioning the Turks in particular, he adds: "The general tone of the Mahometan Sacred Book [The Koran] is eminently warlike and must in the palmy days of Islam have stirred the bold blood of the Turks."

The next sultan, Selim I, the Grim as he was rightly known, came to the throne in 1512, when his do-nothing father, Bayazid II, abdicated. He reigned only eight years, but managed during that short period to almost double the size of the Ottoman empire. All his conquests were made in Asia and Africa, notably in Persia, Iraq, Syria, and Egypt, so he can find only limited space in this Europe-orientated book, which is unfortunate, because he was perhaps the most militarily successful of all the Turkish sultans. He was not only a sultan, but also the first of the Turkish caliphs, which also means Vicar of the Prophet of God (i.e., Muhammad) and Supreme Imam of Islam (at least of the Sunnis; the Shiites, mainly in Persia, had their own dignitaries).

He secured the religious title, the main one in the Muslim hierarchy, from the last Abbasid, whose ancestors had taken refuge in Cairo after the massacre of the Baghdad caliphs by the Mongols two hundred years before. From this time onward the Ottoman sultans benefited from the religious authority their caliph title gave them over Muslims all over the world, not only within the Turkish empire.

Selim is even more unlovable than Mahomet II. The sultans, at least most of them, seemed to have a strong streak of sadism in them. In Selim the Grim this characteristic seemed particularly well developed. He reveled in killing and his reign as one of ceaseless carnage. On his accession to power he had his five nephews between the ages of seven and twenty all strangled, although the youngest ones begged him for their lives. His two brothers, Ahmed and Korkon, were similarly strangled. Each of his viziers usually lasted only a few months before they were strangled. He was a Sunni of profound religious faith, hated the Shiites, whom he considered heretics, and had a census made of them within in his dominions. They numbered 70,000; 40,000 of whom were arrested and beheaded by teams of executioners sent all over the empire. The rest were imprisoned. He disliked the message brought to him by an envoy from the shah of Persia, and had the messenger torn to pieces. When, in a battle at the gates of Tabriz, he defeated the Persian army, all Muslims, he ordered all the prisoners executed on the spot. When one of his generals, Hemdar Pasha, pointed out the difficulties of a march through the desert, he had the general beheaded immediately. He ordered several hundred Mameluke prisoners in Egypt, who had surrendered on the promise their lives would be spared, to be executed on the spot. When he took Cairo and became caliph, he had 50,000 of the city's inhabitants put to death, not forgetting 153 treasury officials whom he ordered executed for incompetence (he relented, however, when the empire's brave mufti interceded on their behalf). Toward the end of his life he decided that all the Christians in his empire should be put to death and only the intercession, once again, of the mufti prevented the sentences from being carried out by bands of roving executioners. When he died in 1520 every man, woman, and child in the empire, Muslim, Christian, and Jew, heaved a sigh of relief. His son, Suleiman, became sultan and caliph. He is known in history as Suleiman the Magnificent. It was during his reign that the Ottoman empire reached its apogee and became the strongest military and economic power in Europe.

44

THE RED DANUBE: MOHACS 1526

U NLIKE HIS FATHER SELIM, WHOSE mind was turned to the east, Suleiman's mind was turned to the west. Not only his mind, but his policy always gave priority to Europe over Asia. During his forty-six years as sultan and caliph, he did make war three times against his main Muslim rival, Persia: in 1534, largely because the shah of Persia had become the ally of the Hapsburg Holy Roman Emperor Charles V, who ruled over Spain, Mexico, Austria, and the Netherlands; again in 1548, when his Janissaries occupied Tabriz; and again in 1553 when he ravaged Mesopotamia. The rest of the time Christian Europe was the enemy.

These campaigns against Persia were essentially wars of religion, since, although the Persians were Muslims, they adhered to the hated (by the Turks and other Sunnis) Shiite sect. In Asia, Suleiman also expanded his empire into the Arabian peninsula, taking the Hejaz, Yemen, and Aden. The birthplace of the Prophet thus became a Turkish possession and was to remain so for four centuries, until T. E. Lawrence and his Arab legion helped to free it from Ottoman rule during World War I.

Suleiman's conquests in Europe were much more impressive than these Asiatic enterprises, which covered less than six years in all. Europe was where his heart, his Janissaries, and his Jihad were. Within seven years of his ascension to the throne he recaptured Belgrade, which the Turks had lost to the Hungarians; he captured the island of Rhodes; and he laid siege to Vienna. But before Suleiman took off on this vast campaign of imperial expansion across Europe, he had first to repeat the old Jihad campaigns. In the first Ottoman military actions in Europe, Serbia had met its fate at Kosovo; Bulgaria had disappeared into the Islamic night after Nicopolis; Wallachia and Bosnia definitely joined, in whole or in part, the Dar-al-Islam after Varna; Christian Albania died with its hero Skanderbeg; and the Greek empire vanished in the din, massacre, and rape of Constantinople.

There remained just one Christian nation in the region fighting still, sometimes beaten but always unbowed, torn by its own dissensions, fearful never, frivolous sometimes, barbarous often, valorous always. Hungary was still present, ready to fight the Turks, ready to fight for its God, its pope, and its king. Thanks to Janos Hunyadi, the last victory had been hers, a long time ago, in 1456 at Belgrade, which was then a Hungarian frontier town. Hungary had gone her own chaotic way ever since. But Suleiman, still only a young man of twenty-six, was determined to bring Hungary to heel again. He sent an envoy to Buda to demand, in return for a long-lasting peace, a heavy annual tribute from the seventeen-year-old harum-scarum King of Hungary, Louis II, a youthful nitwit, already a remarkable playboy for one so young, who liked to surround himself with irresponsible scamps like himself. Treating the matter as a huge joke, the young monarch foolishly replied to the sultan's demand with the contempt which it perhaps deserved, but which it was tactless to show so openly. The Hungarians insulted the envoy and threw him in a cell before sending him back empty-handed to Istanbul. Some reports say they even cut his nose and ears off as a final insult to the sultan.

Suleiman was delighted at the excuse Louis II gave him for going to war. Determined to retake Belgrade, he marched out of Istanbul in February 1521 at the head of a huge army of undetermined numbers, but which must have been very great as it required, Antony Bridge tells us in his biography of Suleiman, no fewer than 33,000 camels and 10,000 carriages to carry its supplies and its one hundred pieces of artillery. The whole force was backed by a fleet of forty ships that sailed up the Danube in support. As the Muslim invaders came down the mountains onto the plains of Hungary, they captured in July the town of Sabac, defended by only five hundred men under the patriots Simon Logody and Andrew Torma. The entire garrison was killed to a man. "A hundred heads of the soldiers of the Sabac garrison who had been unable to escape across the river were brought to the camp," noted Suleiman laconically in his diary. The next day the heads were stuck on pikes to decorate the Ottoman camp. Sixty Hungarian defenders of Sabac who had refused to try to escape were still alive on the sixteenth day of the siege. They drew up in the main square, and in a disciplined line like the soldiers they were, stoically awaited the last Turkish assault and fought their attackers until not one Hungarian was left alive.

By the end of the month the Janissaries were outside the walls of Belgrade, defended by a garrison of fewer than seven thousand men who were expecting a relief force to come to their aid from Buda. But no one came. Louis II was on his honeymoon and could not be disturbed. Two powerful lords, Bathory and John Szapolyai, each commanded a large personal army not far from the besieged city, but each feared the other more than the Turks and would not engage his troops. The Janissaries took the town by assault in early August. The defenders, now reduced to a few hundred, took refuge in the citadel, where they held out until the end of the month. Among them was a Monsieur de Croissy, a French knight who had mysteriously and bravely strayed into this fight which had no clear connection with France. A mixed force of Serbian mercenaries and Hungarians, and perhaps Monsieur de Croissy, surrendered when only seventy-five of them were still alive, on a promise that their lives would be spared. But the Turks, as usual, reneged on their promise, and spared only the Serbs. The Hungarians were decapitated. History fails to tell us what happened to Monsieur de Croissy. Most of the local inhabitants were marched off to the slave markets of Istanbul.

The Hungarians wondered where and when the next Turkish blow would fall. They had to wait five years for it, and it fell at a place called Mohacs, which plays the same role in Hungarian history that Kosovo has in Serbian lore: the graveyard of their country.

Before heading for Hungary again, Suleiman attacked and took the island of Rhodes from the Knights of St. John of Jerusalem, one of the fighting orders of Christian warriors, who had been in possession of it for two centuries. The Turks feared and hated them as much as the Christians feared and hated the Turks. The Grand Master of the Order was the Frenchman Philippe Villiers de l'Isle d'Adam, who had recently taken over the command at the age of fifty-seven. A few months later the Turks attacked with a fleet of seven hundred vessels, mainly galleys, carrying some 20,000 troops and manned by 40,000 sailors while Suleiman marched south from Gallipoli with an army of

140,000 men. Hearing of the approach of these vast forces, the Knights Hospitaliers prepared for battle. They were five hundred in number, divided according to the language they spoke into Provencaux, Auvergnats, Frenchmen, Italians, Aragonese, Englishmen, Germans, Castilians, and Portuguese. The section from Provence was the most numerous. Frenchmen from the south and north, were always in the van of these fighting organizations of the Church. The Knights were backed by a hundred fighting chaplains, about a thousand mercenaries, and about another thousand Rhode islanders.

On September 4, 1522, the Turks attacked the island's capital, and the knights did not sign their formal surrender until December 21. Turkish losses in the fierce fighting had been enormous, probably over sixty thousand. Suleiman was still young enough to be generous. He gave the Knights the right to depart in safety and in peace, provided them with the shipping they required, and promised to respect the lives and homes of the islanders as well. He gave orders that the escutcheons and armorial arms of the Order and of its knights inscribed in the walls on the conquered island should remain as they were as a token of the heroism of the knights in the battle. Napoleon's Marshal Marmont, who served in Turkey during the Napoleonic wars, noted the heraldic marks were still there, 315 years later.

The Knights did not sail until January 1. One of the survivors of the siege was the young Provençal knight Jean Parisot de la Valette, who in later years was to become head of the knightly order. He took part in their search for a new home and helped them to establish it on the island of Malta, which itself underwent an even more brutal siege in later years. The capital of Malta, Valletta, is named after him.

The siege of Malta took place forty-three years after the siege of Rhodes, and Suleiman lived long enough to oversee it and deplore that he had ever allowed La Valette to live to fight another day. The siege of these two islands—Rhodes and Malta—are in themselves a microcosm of the entire Jihad. The perennial clash between Christianity and Islam over hundreds of years was concentrated on two small spots of the globe and fought out with all the fury and hatred of more than a thousand years converged into a few months. But the battlefield of the Jihad has always been a universal one, whether the foe was Christian, Jewish, Hindu, Sikh, Buddhist, Zoroastrian, or animist. To Islam, the outside non-Muslim world is officially the Land of War, the Dar-al-Harb.

A few years after Rhodes we can place the Jihad again in Hungary. This time the Turks have an ally: His Most Christian Majesty King

François I of France, who was eager to see the Austrian army of his enemy Charles V caught up in a war against the Turks as the best safeguard for France on the dangerous checkerboard of international diplomacy. François I had been captured in battle by the Austrian emperor and had pleaded to the sultan for his aid. Suleiman patronizingly assured the king of France that now "that he has laid his petition before the throne which is the refuge of the world, he no longer need fear the enemy who has threatened and ravaged his dominions and made him captive."

The first Turkish target was Catholic Hungary, ruled by Charles V's ally Louis II, the playboy king. "Suleiman the Magnificent set out from Istanbul with an army of 300,000 to conquer the world," wrote Zoltan Bodolai in a phrase as magnificent in its own way as Suleiman himself. Perhaps François I ordered a majestic Te Deum to be sung in Notre Dame when he heard that the great Turkish host had gotten under way to fight his enemy. Religion, alas, sometimes allows itself to be manipulated by princes and politicians.

In Hungary, torn apart by all sorts of internal dissensions, with the peasantry condemned to perpetual servitude and alienated from their own country, King Louis II set out with his guard of four thousand men to meet the enemy. John Zapolya, the richest lord of the kingdom, with a private army of forty thousand men, hovered on the sidelines of the coming events. King Louis managed to gather around him another twenty-two thousand men, and it is with this army that he met the army of Suleiman on the field of Mohacs, near the Danube, on August 29, 1526. Back in England, Henry VIII was too busy preparing to divorce Catherine of Aragon to have a thought for the distant Hungarians facing the Islamic foe. In France, François I was indecently praying for a Muslim victory, because the defeat of the Hungarians by the Muslim Turks would greatly weaken his enemy Charles V, the absent ally of the Hungarians. At Mohacs, King Louis's military advisers counseled patience. "We are greatly outnumbered," they said. "Let us wait for John Zapolya's army." But King Louis II was young, inexperienced, and foolhardy. "We shall not wait," he said.

Bishop Perenyi, one of the numerous Hungarian prelates who accompanied the king to the battlefield, looked at the masses of Turks lined up, swords drawn, waiting for the Hungarian charge, made the sign of the cross, recommended his soul to God, and said to another bishop, astride a horse next to him, "Today is the feast of St. John the Martyr. Let us rename this day the Feast of twenty thousand Magyar martyrs." Magyar is the name by which Hungarians call themselves. They originally came from Asia and invaded and occupied Hungary in the 800s, and have been Hungarians ever since. Now, at Mohacs, they were facing a new set of invaders who had, like them, originally come from Asia. They faced the Turks like the brave men they were: they charged. The best cavalrymen of Europe, predecessors of the hussars, shouting and singing, they broke through the first Turkish lines. But beyond there was no victory for them, only more and more Turks waiting, heavily armed and with guns they were keeping in reserve. The Hungarians charged on only to be mown down by the Turkish gunners. It took Suleiman only two hours to smash the Hungarian army. King Louis, wounded in the head, escorted by his bodyguard, managed to escape from the battlefield, but his horse slipped while crossing a muddy creek, fell back on him and, dragged down by his heavy armor, the king drowned. Seven bishops and archbishops, including Perenyi, were among the slain. Sixteen thousand Hungarians died in the battle, two thousand taken prisoner were all beheaded, and their heads, impaled on pikes, were scattered as decorative pieces around Suleiman's tent that night.

Mohacs settled the fate of Hungary for nearly two centuries. Its population was to fall from four million to two and a half million in a little more than one hundred fifty years. The English impact on Ireland is a model of decency compared to the Turkish record in Hungary. The Turks hunted the Hungarians in the countryside as if they were partridges. Probably three million Hungarians were enslaved and deported all over the Ottoman empire. A few months after Mohacs, Suleiman marched back to Istanbul with the first batch of 100,000 Hungarians, men, women, and children, to be sold in the slave markets, some in the capital, others in Anatolia, Egypt, Syria, and the Balkans. The ghazis, the soldiers of the Jihad, Janissaries, spahis, and all were richly compensated for their fighting skills. The usual one-fifth of the spoils was allotted to the sultan, now doubly entitled to his share as the caliph of Islam, but the bulk was shared among the soldiery. The Jihad was people's capitalism at its best. Everybody benefited from it. Later, when Janissaries were allowed to marry, their wives and children also profited from all the wheeling and dealing that became part of the Ottoman military tradition.

Suleiman's successful campaign not only depopulated Hungary; it left the country a broken nation, scattered into three parts: one ruled by the Turks, another ruled by Charles V's brother, Ferdinand of Hapsburg, and the third part ruled by the wily aristocrat John Zapolya who had, like scum, risen to the top of the situation he had, by his disregard of his king's call, helped to create. He now fashioned a kingdom for himself out of the bits and pieces that remained from the land of the Magyars and became the Turks' liegeman. Zapolya, when threatened by Ferdinand, appealed to Suleiman for help and received a promise of Ottoman support. "I will march in person to aid him," Suleiman promised Zapolya's envoy. "I swear it by our prophet Muhammad, the beloved of God, and by my saber." God, Islam, and the sword, to Suleiman, were one, the trinity of the Jihad.

To Ferdinand's anxious ambassador, whom the king of Austria sent hastily to Istanbul when he heard of his rival's mission to Suleiman, the sultan only had words of arrogance and dismissal. "What the sword has won, the sword must keep," he said crushingly. He would go and fight Ferdinand and take away his part of Hungary from the Hapsburg king. "I will look for him on the field of Mohacs or even in Budapest," Suleiman said. "If he fails to meet me there I shall fight him beneath the walls of Vienna itself."

45

THE UNTAKEN CAPITAL: VIENNA 1529

IENNA. HERE WAS THE CHALLENGE. Vienna was the ultimate, barely mentioned target, the capital of Charles V's Holy Roman Empire, the worthy objective of the Ottoman empire. It was toward Vienna that Suleiman's thoughts and ambitions were bound. The Hungarians were now a beaten foe, barely worth a glancing blow. The Danube, the river on whose banks Vienna lay, should soon be as much part of the Moslemah as the Nile, the Euphrates, the Tigris, and the Indus. The Danube would run red with Christian blood. Vienna would become the Baghdad of the West. Suleiman was taking the message of the Prophet to Charles V, whose title he refused to recognize. There was only one emperor in the world: Suleiman. But as Charles V was not available, "occupied with his own ambitions and schemes in Italy," Creasy tells us in his *History of the Ottoman Turks* (vol. 1, p. 269), his brother Ferdinand would suffice. Vienna was the next target of the Jihad.

On May 10, 1529, Suleiman set forth again on a new campaign of conquest in the West with an army of 250,000 soldiers backed by three hundred heavy cannon, and countless thousands of mules, horses, and camels. He was met at Mohacs—specially chosen for the meeting by the sultan so as to humiliate the Hungarians—by Zapolya, who kissed his hand in homage, recognizing thereby his vassalage to the sultan. With his Hungarian allies in tow, Suleiman journeyed on to Vienna,

taking a few towns on the way, massacring a few garrisons, and torturing, killing, and enslaving haphazardly the inhabitants of the villages through which his army passed once they entered Austria. The
vanguard of Suleiman's army arrived outside Vienna on September 23
and galloped around the walls of the city on their horses, shouting
insults at the defenders and promising them death. Each horseman held
his lance aloft, with the head of an Austrian speared at the end of it.
The bulk of Suleiman's army reached Vienna a couple of days later and
the city settled in for a long siege, in dread and anticipation of defeat,
knowing they were outnumbered at least ten to one. Vienna was
defended by only sixteen thousand men.

The siege lasted only three weeks. Suleiman had expected Vienna
to be defended by King Ferdinand, but the king had wisely, if not hero-
ically, made a point of being elsewhere for the Turks, and the defense
of his capital was left to the veteran German general Nicolas von Salm,
for Suleiman an inferior person unworthy of the king's attention. The
weather, moreover, was vile and prevented the Turks from bringing in
their heavy guns. The Viennese proved stubborn in their defense of
their city. Although they were gravely threatened by the huge mass of
Ottoman infantry and the use of mines and explosives, it soon became
clear to Suleiman, always a realist, that he had no hope of winning
quickly and that his prestige was bound to suffer from a protracted
siege against a city defended by an obscure general. The refusal of
Charles V and Ferdinand to meet him in battle was an admission of
defeat on their part, Suleiman claimed, and on October 16 the Turks
packed up their bags and started on the long journey back home to
Istanbul. Before leaving the Turks burned their camp and massacred all
their prisoners, thousands of them, mainly peasants and their families
kidnapped from neighboring villages. No one was fooled by Suleiman's accusations of cowardice against Charles and Ferdinand.
Everyone knew that Vienna had defeated the Ottoman empire, and the
Viennese exulted in their victory.

The failure of the Turks to take Vienna was hailed throughout
Europe as the first big victory of the Christians over the Muslims since
the appearance of the Turks on the continent. Forty thousand Turks and
twenty thousand Christians are reported to have died during the siege.
The retreating Janissaries committed the usual outrages associated
with a beaten sixteenth-century army. Even more so, in fact. "The
memory of their atrocities was to sink so deeply into the consciousness
of Europe and win them such an indelible reputation for barbarism that

three centuries later the British Prime Minister Mr. Gladstone could still refer to the 'unspeakable Turks,' " as Bridge reminds us in his biography of Suleiman

The memory lingers on, and the Turks of today unfairly pay the psychological price for the atrocities committed by their Ottoman ancestors. It is rather as if Mr. Blair's Englishmen were today held responsible for the massacre of the helpless and defenseless people of Limoges by the Black Prince during the Hundred Years' War, or if the French of today were held to account for the massacre of two thousand Ottoman soldiers who had surrendered to General Napoleon Bonaparte at Jaffa in 1799 during the Syrian campaign.

46

SAILORS, SLAVERS, AND RAIDERS: THE MEDITERRANEAN 1504-1546

T HE JIHAD ALSO HAD A NAUTICAL side to it. The naval war against the Christians really began after the Moors were expelled from Spain. When they went to North Africa, many of them settled in Algiers, where the fishermen of Granada turned into pirates and slavers. They began to raid the Spanish coast they knew so well as a means of earning their living. Christian slaves were the main commodity they were after. There was also undoubtedly an element of revenge in these expeditions. The Moors were getting their own back for what the Spaniards had caused them to suffer.

These profitable nautical jaunts were an essential ingredient in the life of Islam, for they were part of the Jihad, and so the local Muslims all considered it. No doubting was possible in the war against the infidels. Allah, through the Prophet, had instructed the the faithful to kill them. Sura ix. 5-6 of the Koran says quite clearly, "Kill those who join other gods with God wherever ye shall find them; and seize them, besiege them, and lay wait for them with every type of ambush." Those who "joined God with other gods" were the Christians whose Trinity, for the Muslims, was composed of three Gods. Killing and "seizing" them wherever they found them was an activity blessed by Allah and given religious cognizance by their religious leaders. The Moors regarded these raids as a combination of business, pleasure, and duty. A very comforting outlook for desperadoes seeking mayhem, money, and vengeance. Since for a good Muslim the duty of religious war was permanent, and was so laid down in the Koran, these raids were regarded as saintly acts.

The first Muslim raiders of the sea have not left much obvious trace of their activities. But many of these Moors and Arabs with fair hair and blue eyes whom we see today in Islamic lands must be the descendants of the men and women abducted by Muslim raiders from European shores. The pirates of the Barbary coast are the stuff of legend. "The shores of Tripoli" provide their share to the hymn of the United States Marines. But let's not forget that the Spaniards were fighting the Barbary Coast pirates three centuries before the Americans. A Spanish grandee, Don Pedro Navarro, was the first to raid the shores of North Africa. In the 1500s he led a Spanish expedition there to bring the piracy to an end, seized and occupied a fort overlooking the harbor of Algiers, and forced the pirates to bring their operations to an end.

But the respite only lasted a few years. From the island of Lesbos in the Aegean the Ottoman pirate Uruj sailed west to North Africa and persuaded the dey of Tunis to allow him the use of his port in return for a fifth of the proceeds he would bring in from his expeditions. From that moment Uruj ruled the western Mediterranean. He assembled a collection of tough sea captains around him, the chief of whom was his brother Khayr-ad-Din, more widely known in history by the name of Barbarossa, "Red Beard" in Italian, from the color and abundance of his whiskers. Barbarossa took over the Muslim corsair fleet after the death of his brother in battle in 1518. From then on the Mediterranean became a Muslim lake.

The underlying Islamic motive for the war Barbarossa waged against the Christians was obviously a fact of military and political life in his own day. His exploits were numberless. He was the greatest provider of laborers for the work force in Algeria and the greatest provider of concubines for the harems. He raided all over the Mediterranean. In Fondi he landed at night to kidnap the local beauty, Julia Gonzaga, known all over Italy for her looks, figure, and charm. He wanted to present her to the sultan as a worthy addition to his harem. Awakened suddenly, she managed to escape in her nightdress on horseback, protected and escorted by a young Italian knight. (The story adds that the gallant young Italian was executed afterward for having seen too much of the damsel he had saved.) Barbarossa landed in Minorca under false colors and carried off six thousand of the local inhabitants to Algiers. In the first town of Calabria to be raided, all who resisted were slain and all the pretty girls in the town raped, cowed, and abducted. He raided Apulia and carried off ten thousand inhabitants for sale in Istanbul. The number of victims of these raids always sounds grossly exaggerated, but there is no doubt that there were a great many of them, even if the official figures should perhaps sometimes be divided by ten.

Slavery was accepted as normal by Muslims. It was also tolerated by Christians, with this difference: slavery was considered by Christians to be a reprehensible institution, notably in the later days of Wilberforce and Harriet Beecher Stowe and even well before, when Bartolomeo de Las Casas preached in Peru in the sixteenth century. During the period that we are writing about, the Venetian slave traffic was strongly, frequently, but ineffectively attacked and condemned by the papacy. The pope time and time again threatened with damnation Venetian shipowners whose vessels used to load up with Russian and Georgian slaves in the Black Sea and sell them to the Turks and to Venetian sugar plantations in Crete and Cyprus. But, threats of excommunication notwithstanding, the greed of the Venetian merchants was stronger than their fear of hell. These Venetian businessmen could have claimed, of course, that their traffic was tolerated in the Bible. We are, for instance, told in Genesis that Joseph was sold by his brothers to a slave trader, in Exodus that slaves could be flogged to death, and even St. Paul persuaded the runaway slave Onesimus to go back to Philemon, his Christian master, as related in Paul's brief letter to him. For Muslims slavery was divinely ordained, since it has the sanction of the Koran and of the Hadith. For many Muslims there was and is nothing reprehensible about it. Even today it is still practiced in a number of Muslim lands. Muhammad himself by his example showed that he was in favor of slavery. He refused to set at liberty four of the six slaves who has been freed by his disciple Imran ibn al-Husain at his death (Mishkat book xiii, chapter xx) "and he spoke severely of the man who had set them free."

In his *Dictionary of Islam* Thomas Patrick Hughes rather forcefully insists that "Slavery is in complete harmony with the spirit of Islam, while it is abhorrent to that of Christianity." The Koran allows a master all the rights he wants over his slaves. It even allows him (in sura iv. 28) to commit adultery with a married woman if she is a slave, a toleration hardly in harmony with more strait-laced Christian doctrine, or with the frequent Islamic stoning to death for adultery. Since the Koran, unlike the Bible, is for the Muslim eternal and uncreated, and every word of it valid for all times, it makes slavery today, and certainly also in the sixteenth century, as admissible as it was in the days of the Prophet.

In the year 1625 there were some twenty thousand Christian slaves in Algiers. The Order of the Holy Trinity, founded in the twelfth century, ransomed a total of ninety thousand Christians from slavery during its centuries of work in North Africa. One of them was the writer of *Don Quixote,* Cervantes, for whose release the Trinitarians paid five hundred gold ducats.

At one time Barbarossa had thirty-six galleots, all his personal property, raiding hither and thither out of Algiers, of which he was virtually the king. Some seven thousand Christian slaves, most of them captured at sea or on raids in Spain, Provence, and Italy, labored on the defenses of the port. Barbarossa and the Genoese admiral Andrea Doria, his most feared foe, warily kept away from each other as much as possible during those years of warfare, for each, virtually unbeaten, feared the genius and naval skill of the other. But ships from their fleets often clashed.

Barbarossa yearned for wider authority than the headship of Algiers gave him. He had recognized the sultan in Istanbul as his sovereign and brought Algiers into the Ottoman empire. At Suleiman's request, Barbarossa left Algiers in 1533 for Istanbul with the bulk of his ships to reorganize and rebuild the Ottoman fleet which, unlike the army, was in a very rundown condition. As admiral of the Ottoman fleet the old pirate, although outnumbered and outgunned, was to hold off at Prevesa the Genoese fleet under Andrea Doria.

The war in Europe extended to North Africa. Tunis had, in the meantime, fallen to Charles V, who had put the local ruler, Hasan, back on the throne. This unprincipled scoundrel was now the ally of the Christian emperor, who ignored his vicious and criminal past in order to assure himself a sound base and a local ally in North Africa from where to fight the Ottomans. Hasan had originally ordered forty-four of his forty-five brothers strangled when he came to power (the forty-fifth happened to be out when the killers called on him). His hobby was sodomy and he kept two harems, one female and one male. The male harem was manned (that seems the most suitable word) by four hundred young boys while the official (female) harem was peopled by a large number of wives and concubines whom he neglected abominably in favor of his boy playmates.

Charles V landed in Tunis in 1535 to restore Hasan to his throne.

The plunder of Tunis by Charles V's troops ranks—along with the sack of Rome by imperial troops in 1527—among the vilest campaigns of the emperor. The Turks couldn't better it for sheer horror. There was, however, a difference between the two sets of massacrers, and it is an essential one. Jack Beeching, in his book on the battle of Lepanto, pins it right down. "All through their imperial history, the Ottoman Turks had used cruelty as an implement of dominion: there was nothing in their religion to forbid it," he wrote. Here we come to one of the basic divergences between Christian and Muslim war crimes. Both sides murdered and tortured equally well, but, says Beeching, the "bloody deeds done by nominal Christians went contrary to the utterances of the founder of their religion. . . . The Christians guilty of such deeds must have been aware at the backs of their minds that what they did was wrong." But the Muslims who carried out the same deeds, and worse, felt no guilt at all. On the contrary, they felt they were obeying the will of God. Surveying the Christian scene with an unblinking eye, Beeching adds, "From this friction between doctrine and practice might come a change for the better. Perhaps," he adduced, "this is the reason why the Christian West has never stagnated."

Meanwhile the Christian powers were fighting as bitterly against one another as the Turks fought against them. François I of France had lost Milan to Charles V a few years previously and wanted it back. The two sovereigns found themselves at war again. Charles V's troops invaded Provence but were beaten back outside Marseille. The French king, to the horror of the other European countries, aghast at this unnatural alliance between the believers and the unbelievers, allied himself to Suleiman on condition the sultan attack the Hungarians, thus forcing Charles V to fight on another front.

His Most Catholic Majesty François I was now the ally of a sovereign whose proclaimed purpose was to destroy Christianity. In practical terms, this mainly meant having a French liaison officer on Barbarossa's ship when the Ottoman fleet sailed out of the Dardanelles to attack Italy. Barbarossa raided Messina and Reggio in Calabria, where the salacious old admiral (he was in his mid-sixties at the time) captured the eighteen-year-old daughter of the local commander, forced her to become a Muslim, and ravished her. He sailed to Ostia, on the outskirts of Rome on the Tiber, and went on to spend a quiet winter on the French Riviera, in the port of Toulon, to the indignation of the local population, who could not understand why their king would be the friend of these infidels, particularly since some of the rowers on board the Muslim galleys, most of whom were Christian slaves, were French. But just the same, Barbarossa, with the support of some French vessels, raided nearby Nice, at that time not French but part of Charles V's imperial domain.

Outraged by the religious offense of this aberrant alliance between a Christian king and a Muslim sultan, the king of England, Henry VIII, promised Charles V his help. During a busy schedule over the next few years—marrying and divorcing his fourth wife, Anne of Cleves; sending his adviser Thomas Cromwell to the scaffold for arranging the marriage; marrying his fifth wife, Catherine Howard; having her and her two lovers beheaded for adultery and treason; and marrying his sixth wife Catherine Parr—the portly English king managed to find the time to send an expeditionary force to France to help the emperor by a diversionary attack on Paris. But instead of marching on the French capital to fight the French, the English troops stayed in Boulogne, enjoying its fine seafood and the local wine brought in from Bordeaux.

At the other end of Europe, meanwhile, Barbarossa had landed at Otranto, in the heel of Italy, at the head of twenty thousand Janissary infantrymen and spahi cavalrymen. The plan was to march on Rome, turning St. Peter's into a mosque and occupying all of Italy. The various garrisons around Otranto were the first attacked. All were slaughtered when they surrendered, although Barbarossa had promised to spare their lives. Finding his planned expedition too difficult to mount, Barbarossa returned to Istanbul with ten thousand young men and women for sale as slaves. The Turks were now also at war with Venice, so Suleiman sent Barbarossa on a tour of the Greek islands, most of which were owned by Venice. He picked them off and occupied them one by one and sailed back to Istanbul with a thousand girls and fifteen hundred boys worth a million pieces of gold. The Mediterranean, thanks to Barbarossa, became for a few years a Muslim sea. He turned it into the center of Turkish warfare against the Christians and, like Lord Nelson, he assembled around him a group of captains rather like Nelson's undefeatable band of brothers.

In this book we tend to use the word "Turkish" as a synonym for "Ottoman." It's the same as calling all the British English. Many of the Ottomans were not Turkish; in fact the majority came from elsewhere. Some, like Barbarossa, were Greek. Others were Bosnians, Serbs, Armenians, Moldavians, Moors, and Arabs. There were lots of others. They were often enrolled in Ottoman ranks as Christian young men, as Janissaries, or palace officials and servants. Subsequently they often converted to Islam. Many of the sailors, perhaps a majority, were Greeks. Dragut, who served at the siege of Malta and who specialized in raids on the Corsican coast, was a Greek born in Asia Minor. He was captured by Doria, who had him chained as an oarsman in one of his galleys until Barbarossa paid a big ransom to get him back. Uluch Ali, who led a squadron at Lepanto, was a Calabrian who lived in Algiers. Another much-feared Turkish naval leader, Piale, was a Croatian. But Barbarossa was the greatest. He remains one of the most illustrious names in the history of naval warfare. But he was more a sea robber and plunderer, slaver and massacrer, than a fighting sailor. Kidnapping helpless men, women, and children to sell them as slaves was his forte. Battle was not a profitable activity, and he avoided it. He cannot be compared to the illustrious fighting sailors of the West. There is nothing of Nelson about him. He was certainly a great seaman and a great leader, but he was by instinct and methods first and foremost a pirate.

47

IN ARMS ALWAYS
AND PREPARED FOR COMBAT:
MALTA 1565

W E SHALL BEGIN THIS CHAPTER on the Great Siege of Malta by recalling the name of a young man who was not there but who desperately wanted to be: Don John of Austria.

That year Don John had recently been acknowledged by King Phillip II of Spain, his half-brother who was twenty-two years older than he, as a kinsman of the imperial Hapsburg family that ruled over Spain, southern Germany, Austria, western Hungary, Burgundy, Holland, Flanders, southern Italy, and Sicily. Don John was therefore a member of the most exalted dynasty in Europe, and he was anxious to make his name in the world of chivalry, soldiering, and courage. Instead he was fretting away his young life in Madrid.

Don John was the illegitimate son of a young Bavarian entertainer with the improbable name, for the mother of a prince, of Barbara Blomberg, who had started her imperial romance with the Spaniard Charles V by singing to him one night at dinner. Her son, Don John, was conceived and born in 1545 in the Bavarian township of Regensburg, the most westward point reached in 1529 by the Turkish cavalry. There could have been no more suitable birthplace for a man destined one day to win, at Lepanto, the most resounding of all the battles of Christendom against the Turks. Lepanto brought to an end the Muslim advance across the Mediterranean which had threatened to overwhelm southern Europe. Regensburg has a minor place in world history, Lepanto a major one. Lepanto lives on. Don John of Austria links the two.

Now aged twenty, Don John of Austria hankered for glory and action. Malta, besieged by the Turks, was the place to be. Without telling his brother the king, the young man ran away from his palatial home in Madrid and made his way to Barcelona, from where he hoped to take ship to the mid-Mediterranean island where seven hundred Knights of St. John of Jerusalem and a few thousand Spanish infantrymen and Maltese islanders were holding at bay Suleiman's forty thousand Muslim invaders. Don John "resolved to win his maiden laurels under the banner of the cross," Prescott tells us. But the laurels eluded him for a few more years. The king, anxious for Don Juan's safety, ordered him to return to court immediately. You didn't disobey a king, even if you were his brother. So Don John of Austria returned to Madrid and the defense of Malta continued without him.

Malta under siege had become the Mediterranean key to western Europe. Christendom could not allow the island to fall into enemy hands. Malta was far more than a symbol. It was a key spot in the war between Christianity and Islam. Situated halfway between Christian Sicily to the north and Muslim Tunisia to the south, it controlled the passage between the western and the eastern Mediterranean. Its importance went beyond these tactical considerations. A quick glance at the map reveals immediately its immense strategic importance for an intended conqueror of western Europe.

The strategic consequences of the fall of Malta could be more disastrous for Christendom than the fall of Constantinople had been when it fell to the Turks in 1453 and became Istanbul. Constantinople was no longer of considerable military importance. It had been bypassed by the Turkish Muslim invaders a century before, and they had already spread far across the Balkans. Its symbolical and moral importance had remained high, for it was the capital of eastern Christianity and a former capital of the Roman empire. But located in a faraway corner at the eastern end of Europe it was a dead-end town, important for the Turks only as the link between the Asian and European parts of the Ottoman empire. Its capture, heartbreaking as it was to Christendom, and its subsequent possession by the Turks, presented no military risk to the West.

With Malta in hostile Turkish hands, however, the fate of southern Europe would be in doubt. Even the heretical Queen Elizabeth in distant foggy London saw the defense of Malta, in spite of its Catholicism which she loathed, as essential to the existence of a European, Christian Europe. "If the Turks should prevail against the isle of Malta," she wrote, "it is uncertain what further peril might follow to the rest of Christendom." Christendom, in her mind, was the prey. The peril was Islam, with its negation of European Christian values.

Malta taken and occupied would have meant an immense victory for the Jihad. Perhaps no collision between Islam and Christendom was so nakedly Holy War as the siege of Malta. Two forces, each of which called itself "holy," affronted each other: on one side the might of the Ottoman forces of the caliph of world Islam, on the other the small, battered forces of an order of militant Christian knights.

Finally—and the history of the last four hundred years is the witness—this was a clash not only of differing conceptions of God and religion, nor merely the clash of antagonistic eastern and western imperialisms. A successful attack on Malta by followers of Islam who refused to countenance any sort of change might have smashed the new enlightenment that was arising in the West during and after the period we call the Renaissance. Perhaps Queen Elizabeth, when she expressed her concern, was already aware, however dimly, that this was the most imminent peril.

Initially the impulse for the Jihad attack on Malta did not come from the sultan's highest religious advisers; it was prompted solely through the most down-to-earth, commercial interests and harem intrigues by one of the numerous women in Suleiman's life: his daughter. It concerned a shipment of merchandise seized by an adventurous French Knight of Malta, the Provençal Mathurin d'Aux de Lescaut Romegas, known more simply as Romegas. Romegas had recently intercepted and seized a Turkish merchant vessel in the Ionian islands, near Corfu, loaded with 80,000 ducats' worth of merchandise and luxury goods that belonged to the harem's chief eunuch, Kustir-Aga. Several of the sultan's wives and concubines had invested in the venture and they all stood to lose a great deal of money after Romegas took the ship to Malta where, spies reported, it was moored alongside Castle St. Angelo, the strongest fortress of the Knights of St. John of Jerusalem.

Suleiman's favorite daughter, Mihrmah, had invested heavily in Kustir-Aga's commercial venture, and she and the other harem speculators, who had been looking forward to a large profit from their investment, now faced ruin instead. They pleaded with the sultan to take Malta instead of Vienna, which he was at the time planning to attack again after his first unsuccessful campaign against the Austrian capital, four decades before. To add religious fervor to her pleadings, Mihrmah frequently reminded the sultan of the hundreds of faithful Muslims who had been captured by the knights and who now lingered as slaves in Malta, pulling on the oars of Christian galleys. Even the imam, who had perhaps invested in Kustir-Aga's shipping expedition also, urged Suleiman in the Friday prayers to attack Malta and "shatter the chains of these unfortunate people, whose cries are ascending to heaven, and afflicting the ears of the Prophet of Allah."

Suleiman listened attentively to the prayers and entreaties of the members of his family, particularly of his surviving children. He had become very aware of the impermanence of life in the past few years, particularly as, fearing quite wrongly that his eldest son, the strong and capable Mustafa, was plotting against him, he had had him strangled, and Mustafa's small son immediately afterward. Four years before, as a result of the intrigues of one of his viziers, the weaselly Lala Mustafa, Suleiman had also ordered his second son Bayazid to be strangled as well as Bayazid's five sons, including a three-year-old child.

Lala Mustafa, once tutor to Bayazid and his brother Selim when they were teen-agers, had early in their lives recognized that Bayazid was the nobler and more able of the two brothers. Selim was already a sot, easily manipulated. And Lala Mustapha wanted to be the man who might one day mastermind Ottoman policy. It would be easier through the wine-sodden Selim than through the obdurate Bayazid. So, behind the scenes, he slyly maneuvered events so that they forced Bayazid to rebel, be captured, and subsequently to be strangled by his father's eunuchs. All in all, Suleiman the Magnificent's record as a father and grandfather had been rather shoddy these past few years, and perhaps to soothe his conscience he now wished to be especially nice to his surviving children, notably his favorite daughter, and attack Malta to please her.

It is also part of Muslim thinking that any land where Islam had once reigned and that had been taken away by the infidels should, by right, revert to Islam. Malta had once been part of the Moslemah. So had nearby Sicily, Sardinia, Corsica, and Spain itself. By taking Malta and breaking the power of the knights, Suleiman could turn the island into a springboard for the reconquest of these lost territories. Spies had told him that Malta, whose fortifications were still incomplete, could be taken in a few days. Suleiman, now almost seventy years old, sought the advice of Barbarossa's old shipmate, Dragut. The retired pirate, now aged eighty, was all in favor of an attack on Malta, a nest of vipers that stood in the way of further Ottoman expansion. It must be destroyed. Perhaps it is this advice from a man whose opinion and fighting record he valued that decided Suleiman. The attack on the Austrian capital was put off to another year. Malta would be the target in 1565, not Vienna.

The Ottoman fleet sailed through the Dardanelles into the Mediterranean in early April. Suleiman came to the harbor to bid good-bye to the expedition, one hundred eighty-one ships in all, including thirty large galliots. Most of the rest were galleys rowed by criminals and Christian slaves, forty thousand fighting men, including more than six thousand elite Janissaries and four thousand laylars, a special corps of Jihad fighters renowned for their religious zeal. The expedition leader, Mustapha Pasha, in his seventies, was a direct descendant of Khalid, Muhammad's fightingest general, a happy omen for the expedition, everyone thought. The fleet was under the command of Piale, born of Christian parents near Belgrade and abandoned (or lost) by them during an earlier Turkish attack in Hungary. The governors of Alexandria and Algiers had also been ordered to join the Ottoman fleet with the vessels under their command. Dragut had promised he would join the expedition later as adviser.

Christian watchers in Malta sighted the fleet on May 18, fifteen miles off the island. One of them rushed to warn the Grand Master of the Knights of Malta, Jean Parisot de la Valette, who had fought in the defense of Rhodes forty-five years ago and was now seventy-one years old. La Valette was a Frenchman, as were nearly half of the seven hundred knights. Spaniards and the Italians provided most of the rest, probably close to a couple hundred men in each contingent—the units, called "langues" were divided on a language basis. The Spaniards served in the Aragonese and Castilian units, the French in the contingents of Auvergne, Provence, and France, the latter being mainly from the northern provinces of France: Normandy, Picardy, Artois, and Champagne. The smallest contingent was English, with one knight: the valorous Sir Oliver Stukeley, reputedly an illegitimate son of Henry VIII. England, torn by the Reformation, was no longer "the spearhead of militant Christendom," as one writer drily observed. There were about twenty Austrians and Germans among the knights of Malta, and a sprinkling from other European lands, all assembled in a unit commanded by Stukeley.

When he heard the news of the Muslim fleet's approach, La Valette sent out Romegas with four ships to keep an eye on the enemy vessels, but with strict orders to avoid any engagement with the enemy, a necessary instruction as the fire-eating Romegas was the greatest fighting sailor in the Mediterranean at the time. He had been warring against the Turks for several decades. He was what the French call "un homme de guerre," a "man of war." War was his trade. He feared nothing and no one. A few years previously he had sailed right into the Nile delta to capture several Muslim ships and in the recent capture of the Kustir-Aga merchantman he had had to fight two hundred Janissaries specially placed on board the Muslim ship to prevent its capture.

The Grand Master had earlier summoned all his knights to urge them to show "that contempt for death which alone can render us invincible." The upcoming battle would decide "whether the Gospels are to be superseded by the Koran." On the Muslim ships the imams were encouraging their troops and praying with them, reminding them that they must fight without fear. "Whosoever shall show his back to the enemy will earn the anger of God and his abode shall be in hell." Allah wanted only brave men in Paradise.

The next morning, after a feint approach to the north, the Muslim fleet entered the bay of Marsasirocco in the southeastern tip of the island and, unopposed, the Turks landed in the tens of thousands. Here we must pause to describe Malta in some detail, and in particular the W-shaped (with the W lying on its side, the top of the letter pointing east) Grand Harbor region in the southeast of the island, where most of the fighting took place during the four months the siege lasted. The Grand Harbor is a long narrow bay into which, from the southern side, three spits of land jutted towards the peninsula of Mount Scibberas (the center of the W). Malta is only eighteen miles long and nine miles across. Marsasirocco is located some four miles to the southeast of the Grand Harbor toward which the Turkish troops began to march, capturing two knights, a Frenchman and a Portuguese, who had been sent out on a reconnoitering mission, and torturing them to death.

The invaders headed toward the Grand Harbor, at the eastern tip of which stood the small fort of St. Elmo, commanded by a 71-year-old Italian knight, Luigi Broglia, seconded by the Spaniard Don Juan de Guaras. As the siege began, the defenders were joined by the French knight Pierre de Massuez Vercoyran, recently arrived from Sicily with two hundred Spanish soldiers, and sixty-four knights from St. Angelo who volunteered for the more exposed and dangerous posting at St. Elmo and who were all rowed over at night.

It was on this castle that the whole weight of the Muslim assault was to fall from May 24 until June 23. The fighting afterward took place around the peninsulas of Birgu and Senglea, spits of land jutting out into the Grand Harbor, with assaults by land and sea on the fort of St. Angelo, at the tip of the peninsula of Birgu, and against the castle of St. Michael, at the base of the peninsula of Senglea. On the other side of the larger Mount Sciberras peninsula lay the bay of Marsamuscetto, into which the bulk of the Muslim fleet was intended to anchor. Its location there presented just one problem: the Muslim fleet would come under the fire of the St. Elmo guns. The admiral, Piale, therefore requested Mustafa to protect his fleet by taking the fort of St. Elmo before undertaking any other action. The Muslims expected the small fort to fall in four days. That was the first, and most devastating, error of judgment made by the Turkish command. In the end it took them four weeks and the lives of eight thousand Muslim soldiers to take St. Elmo. That long resistance saved Malta.

The fighting for St. Elmo began on May 24, after the Turks had dragged their guns from their base camp at the Marsa up to the rocky Mount Sciberras, from where they began blasting the fort. The Turks, rich from their battlefield experience in the Balkans and Hungary, were at the time the best gunners in Europe. The biggest Turkish gun, the "basilik," fired a solid cannonball weighing 160 pounds. They also brought up two 60-pound culverins, and ten 80-pounders. But the Christians were not cowed. A few days later the Turks brought up 36 more guns, while several ships lying offshore joined in the assault. "On most days an average of six or seven thousand shots were fired against St. Elmo," noted an Italian knight in the diary which was found after his death.

Dragut, arriving a few days after the bombardment began, bitterly reproached Mustafa and Piale for starting the siege by an attack on a secondary target like St. Elmo. "You should have attacked St. Angelo right away," he shouted at Mustafa. Dragut had sound notions not only of tactics but of strategy, and he pointed out that the Ottomans by maintaining all their forces in the Grand Harbor region, and leaving the north of Malta unoccupied, had permitted the Christian defenders of Malta to keep their lines of communication open with the Spanish base in Sicily where the viceroy, Don Garcia of Toledo, was preparing to send a relief force. Having had his say, the tough old warrior went off to the trenches to join the gunners there. In spite of his eighty years, Dragut was a fighter, and so he remained until the day he died.

On St. Elmo's feast day, June 3, the Turks launched their first big infantry attack against the fort. The Christians fought back with every weapon at their disposal, including Greek fire, which they poured down from the parapets onto the storming Janissaries who, in their long flowing white robes, were often turned into living torches. Urged forward, rather in the glamorous style of some of the American southern evangelists, by screaming and whirling dervishes who called on "the Lions of Islam" to "separate the trunks of the infidels from their heads," the attackers captured one of the fort's outerworks, which gave them a clear view down into the fortress. From that moment the defenders became particularly vulnerable to sniper fire.

The next day, just before dawn, while it was still night, two knights arrived off St. Elmo in a small boat. They were Rafael Salvago and the Spanish hidalgo, Captain de Miranda. They had come from Sicily to inspect St. Elmo on behalf of the viceroy. In their report, prepared by Miranda, part of which Ernle Bradford quoted in his splendid book on the siege, the captain describes in the simple, unsensational words of a soldier the conditions in which the Christians, knights, Spanish infantrymen, and Maltese volunteers held St. Elmo. Miranda notes that the defenders of St. Elmo, since the ground is too rocky, could not bury their dead but deposited them "in in the parapets of the fort, the bowels and limbs of men all torn to pieces," and that the defenders of the fort were too few to "ever stir from their posts, but sleep there and eat and carry out all other human functions there, in arms always and prepared for combat."

"By day," Captain Miranda went on,

> they are exposed to the burning sun, and by night to the cold damp, and they suffer from privation of all kinds, from the blasts of gun-powder, smoke, dust, wildfire, iron and stones, volleys of musketry, explosions of enormous gun batteries, insufficient and unwholesome food. They are so disfigured, they hardly know each other any more. They are ashamed of retiring for wounds not obviously serious or nearly mortal. Their livid faces are bruised with frightful sores, or they are very lame and limp woefully. . . . They look like sceptres rather than living men.

Captain Miranda was rowed under fire to St. Angelo where he wrote his report, left it with La Valette for forwarding to Don Garcia in Sicily, and then asked the Grand Master for permission to return to St. Elmo and take his place among the defenders of the fort. Permission was granted. Captain Miranda returned to St. Elmo that same night and was killed there nineteen days later.

The battle for St. Elmo raged on. Every night, to replace the casualties, volunteer Maltese boatmen would ferry across the few hundred feet of harbor that separated St. Angelo from St. Elmo, knights, soldiers, and other volunteers to join their companions in the doomed fortress. St. Elmo looked "like a volcano in eruption, spouting fire and smoke," wrote a Spaniard who watched the daily battles from the still relatively safe haven of St. Michaels, on the other side of the harbor.

Panic is contagious, but so is heroism, perhaps more so, for men, deep in heir heart of hearts, aspire to do great deeds. Among the volunteers who rowed across to the beleaguered fort were two young Maltese Jewish lads, Ernle Bradford tells us in his remarkable history of the great siege. They had no cause to love the knights, or any Christians for that matter, but they felt their rightful place was among those doomed defenders of a faith that was not theirs. The Neapolitan knight Constantino Castriota, eager to get into the heart of the fray, presented to the Grand Master a list of six hundred volunteers, knights, Spanish soldiers and Maltese islanders, willing to accompany him into the hell of St. Elmo to replace the "sceptres" who, too sick and wounded, might wish to get back to Birgu and Senglea. From the embattled fortress came the message that no one in St. Elmo wished to be relieved. They wished to stay and, if necessary, to die in St. Elmo. So the company of the brave Neapolitan knights remained where they were. Their time for carnage and heroism was to come later. The defenders of St. Elmo fought on.

Thousands of Turkish corpses littered the approaches to St. Elmo, killed by the fire of the St. Elmo garrison or by the guns on Birgu and Senglea across the water which pounded the Turks in the hope of helping their besieged comrades in the devastated citadel. The stench of death and putrefaction hung heavy in the hot Mediterranean air. The island of Malta is made of almost solid rock; it is hard work fashioning graves out of rock. There was not enough manpower, not even among the slaves, to dispose of the mounds of corpses which lay massed around St. Elmo.

June 16 was the day of the strongest Turkish attack on the fort. It lasted all day, guns posted in the surrounding hills pouring shot without respite into the fort while a new breed of fighters, the fanatical layalars, wearing animals skins and high on hashish, swarmed across the landscape in wave after wave while their mullahs and their imams in a frenzy of devotion promised them the joys of Paradise if they had the good fortune to be killed. The Christians warriors, weary after these weeks of unceasing fighting, received this new assault with Greek fire and incendiary grenades. The bodies of the dead filled the ditches below the battlements. The Janissaries who followed the lay-alars were also slaughtered. None could break through the Christian wall of arquebus fire and boiling oil.

Among the Christians, Miranda, struck by a musket ball, collapsed, the Frenchman Pierre de Massuez was badly burned by a cauldron of Greek fire that fell back on him, and Juan de Guaras was so lacerated with sword cuts and had lost so much blood that the men around him wondered how he could still stand. The next day the old pirate Dragut, hit by a splinter of rock behind the ear and bleeding profusely, was rushed into his tent to await death in the comfort and with the consideration that his eighty years deserved. But his approaching death brought no respite to the Christians of St. Elmo. It was clear that the end could come at any time. Yet the fort still managed to hold out for four more days.

On the 19th, Miranda—he had volunteered to go to St. Elmo, it seemed such a long time ago, but it was less than three weeks—sent a message to La Valette that St. Elmo could fall at any moment. The next day Miranda sent another message to the Grand Master begging him to leave St. Elmo to its fate. "Every new reinforcement sent into the fort is lost; it is cruelty to send any more men to die here." But unafraid, the Provençal Romegas volunteered to try to reach the fort with a group of volunteers. They included fifteen knights, dozens of Maltese and Spanish soldiers, and the two young Jews. Ready to share the fate of their comrades about to die in St. Elmo, they filled five boats. But Romegas's little flotilla was spotted by the Turks, who intercepted the boats and forced them back to Birgu.

On the 23rd, St. Elmo fell. A messenger hurried to tell Dragut the news, whereupon the old pirate died. That same day Miranda and Guaras also died. Unable to stand because of his wounds, Miranda had been eased into a chair and, sword in hand, awaited the Turks in a breach in the fort wall. Not far from him Juan de Guaras, also too badly wounded to stand, sat near the breach with a lance in his hand, also waiting to die fighting. They were both overwhelmed in the final Muslim assault. The Turks decapitated their dead bodies and fixed their heads, as well as that of the Frenchman Pierre de Massuez, to the tip of three long pikes facing their comrades across the water. Then they crucified their headless corpses to three wooden planks nailed together in the form of a cross and sent them floating across the water of Grand Harbor toward St. Angelo. That day La Valette, always so reserved and unemotional, lost the self-control he had shown throughout the siege and ordered all the Turkish prisoners to be beheaded and their heads to be fired by cannon into the Turkish camp across the water. It was done, we are told, "to teach the Turks a lesson in humanity." In this war, holy as it may have been to both belligerents, God was often absent. He always is when men kill one another in his name.

The siege of Malta was to continue for two and a half months after the fall of St. Elmo. The forts of St. Angelo and St. Michael were now the main targets, as well as the fortifications and ramparts defending the entrance into Birgu and Senglea. With St. Elmo now in Turkish hands, the harbor of Marsamuscetto was safe for Piale's fleet, but the northern part of the island still remained in Christian hands. Nearly seven hundred soldiers, a force made up of forty-two knights; twenty-five volunteers, including two Englishmen, John Smith and Edward Stanley; and six hundred Spanish infantrymen arrived from Sicily and managed to make their way to Birgu during a foggy night to add their strength to the garrison already there. On July 15 the Muslims launched their first attack against Senglea. Fort St. Michael was attacked by the Algerian contingent, led by Dragut's son-in-law, Hassem, who was also dey of Algiers. The Algerian warriors were preceded by three boatloads of chanting imams calling for Allah's blessing on this Holy War against Christians and promising quick entry into Paradise for any who were killed.

While the Algerians were attacking the southern end of Senglea and Fort St. Michael, ten vessels full of Janissaries pushed off from Mount Sciberras to assault the tip of the Senglea point of land, but they came within range of a St. Angelo gun battery that smashed nine of the vessels and sent them all to the bottom. Despairing of victory, the Turks returned to their encampment after five hours of heavy fighting. Three thousand Muslims died that day. Christian losses amounted to 250. But those figures do not include the galley slaves, most of them Christian, who, fettered to their places at the oars, went down with the nine vessels.

Mustapha Pasha now took personal charge of the attack against St. Michael. Piale was ordered to take St. Angelo, and the naval operations were placed under the command of Hassem's deputy, Candelissa. Between assaults the Turks bombarded Birgu and Senglea without respite. On one hill alone, St. Salvatore, the Turks set up thirty-eight guns which pounded the Christian positions.

The bombardment went on day and night. Some 70,000 shots fell in two months, an average of more than a thousand a day, but every Turkish assault was repulsed. On the 18th the Turks broke into a fortification held by the Spanish knights on the defensive wall called "Castile," which lay across Birgu. The Turks raised their banner on the rampart and La Valette led in person the counterattack which threw the Turks out, but he was wounded in the leg by the explosion of a grenade. Maltese townfolk, Spanish soldiers, and his own knights rushed to his side and then ran forward to attack the Turks who, unable to face this raging riposte, began to fall back. Urged by those around him to withdraw and leave the fighting to younger men, the septuagenarian La Valette limped on toward the enemy, now in full flight. "I will not withdraw so long as those banners still wave in the wind," the old man replied tartly, pointing to the Muslim star and crescent flags on top of the battlement.

During the fighting the next day, La Valette's nephew and a young knight were killed together while trying to destroy a wooden siege tower the Turks had placed against "Castile." La Valette looked sadly at the two dead young men. "Those two young men have gone before the rest of us by only a few days," he said quietly. As August drew to an end, conditions in the two garrisons of Birgu and Senglea were resembling more and more those of St. Elmo in its last days. Many bodies lay where they had fallen in the streets, and there were many corpses of women and children among the unburied dead, for the civilians suffered as much as the warriors under the heavy bombardment of the Turks, and valorously fought side by side with the knights against the invaders. The Maltese, Christians for 1,500 years, since the visit of St. Paul to the island, and the victims for centuries of Saracen raiders, were above all faithful and loyal disciples of the Church. For them this was truly a Holy War, far holier than the Jihad was for the kill-and-loot campaigners from the Moslemah.

The Muslim leaders in Malta, Mustapha Pasha and Piale, were desperately anxious to end their Maltese campaign with some sort of success instead of the ghastly defeat they were facing. They were only too well aware that Sultan Suleiman did not like failure, and their costly defeat might mean the execution block for them on their return to Istanbul. Many men had been decapitated or strangled for considerably less weighty fiascos. Suleiman was unlikely to execute Piale, who was his daughter's husband, but Mustapha felt very vulnerable, and anyway Piale remembered uneasily that Suleiman had recently ordered his eldest son to be strangled. In the desperate hope of showing one victory, Mustapha decided to capture the old Maltese capital, Mdina, and dispatched a strong contingent of troops to take the town. But the governor of Mdina, the Portuguese knight Don Mesquita, ordered every man and woman in the town to get into uniform and man the battlements. Tricked into believing Mdina was heavily defended, the Turks, by now thoroughly demoralized, retreated back to their old positions around Birgu and Senglea without fighting.

In Sicily, meanwhile, events were at last stirring. The viceroy, Don Garcia, who had delayed sending reinforcements to Malta fearing the island was doomed anyway, was shamed at last into action. He dispatched a relief force supposedly of eight thousand men, but widely believed to be double that number, mainly Spaniards from the Sicily garrisons, and on September 6 they began their unopposed landing at Mellieha Bay, in the north of Malta. For the Turkish besiegers, the arrival of these fresh troops meant the end of all hope, even of the tiniest success. Mustapha decided to go home with his ships, his sailors, and his army. There was one last battle, near St. Paul's Bay, where the apostle had been shipwrecked 1520 years before. Where St. Paul had walked along the shore, hundreds of arriving Christians and departing Muslims were killed in fierce hand-to-hand combat with battle-axes, swords, scimitars, and maces. The water of the bay, sacred to the Maltese through its association with early Christianity, was red with the blood of Muslims and Christians. By the evening of the 8th the defeated Turks had all left for home. Europe was saved and Malta remained a Christian bastion. "For two or three days afterwards the water of the bay was so thick with enemy dead, more than three thousand, that no man went near the place because of the stench," an Italian crossbowman wrote in his memoirs afterward. The stench always remains after a battle, be it holy or unholy. A dead Muslim stinks as much as a dead Christian.

Thirty thousand Moors and Turks died in Malta during the siege, more than eight thousand of the nine thousand knights and Spanish soldiers who had served under La Valette were killed or wounded, and five thousand islanders were also dead, many of them killed in combat fighting for their island.

The West acclaimed the victory of Malta. Even in Queen Elizabeth's Protestant England—where the heads of three hundred decapitated Catholics would soon adorn London Bridge—the Archbishop of Canterbury announced that special prayers would be said three times a week for the next six weeks to thank God for the victory of the (Catholic) Knights of Malta. In Istanbul, Suleiman the Magnificent had lost much of his magnificence in this shattering defeat. "There can only be one Emperor on earth, me, and one God in Heaven, Allah," Suleiman shouted at the ashen-faced Mustapha Pasha and Piale, who stood with bowed heads before him. But at least he did not order them to be beheaded. "It is only in my own hand that my sword is invincible," he whined in peevish self-pity. In his adversity, he had become just a petulant old man. "I myself, Sultan Suleiman, will lead an expedition against that accursed island. I will not spare one single inhabitant. Not one."

But Suleiman never led another expedition against Malta. The next year, instead of attacking Malta he headed with a large army for Hungary, that old stomping ground of the Jihad, and for Vienna, which he felt he must take. There was not room on this earth for two emperors, the Ottoman and the Hapsburg. The Hapsburg had to go.

48

THE RHAPSODY OF DEATH: HUNGARY 1566

T HE LARGE OTTOMAN ARMY—200,000 men, 300 cannon—that marched out of Istanbul against Vienna in 1566 was advancing through territory that had been conquered decades and, in some cases, centuries before. Most of the Balkans, Greece, Bulgaria, Albania, Serbia, and Bosnia, had begun to come under Ottoman rule in the mid-fourteenth century; the same fate had befallen much of central and eastern Europe from the late fifteenth century. Hungary, restless and suffering, was split in three: a third was now Turkish, Suleiman had occupied Budapest in 1540; another third came under the Hapsburgs; and the province of Transylvania was the fief of the Zapolya dynasty.

At the time of Suleiman, and for the rest of the century, various bits and pieces of Hungary were in a state of rebellion against their foreign, notably Turkish, masters. Hungarians view the resistance of their ancestors against the Turks in very much the same way as the Spaniards regard their struggles against the Arabs and the Moors. Although they were fighting against different foreign occupiers, they were both in fact fighting the same ideological enemy. There was a heavy touch of imperialism about medieval Islam. The Jihad was its sword.

In mid-sixteenth century Hungary, a number of localities remained for decades centers of fighting resistance against the Turks. One was the small town of Erlau, some seventy or so miles to the northeast of Budapest, where the local governor, Stephen Dobo, with an army of nine gunners, nine guns and a few hundred peasants, repulsed after a 38-day siege a large professional army of Janissaries backed by 120 guns. The women of Erlau had fought on the ramparts side by side with the men, cutting down the attackers with the swords they took from the dead and pouring boiling oil on the Turks as they tried to climb over the top of the ramparts. Finally the Turks had withdrawn, leaving Erlau in the hands of the Hungarians. This was an affront Suleiman was determined to avenge, and Erlau figured high on his list of targets to be obliterated. Suleiman the Magnificent was a man who liked to nurse his grudges. But on reaching Hungary, he was diverted to another rebellious town, Sziget, where the troublesome Hungarians had failed to show proper respect and obedience to their Ottoman overlords.

One of Suleiman's favorite generals, Mohammed Pasha, had been killed trying to take the town which was held by one of the most infernal Hungarian nuisances of his time: the wealthy Count Nicholas Zriny, who owned many castles in the border country with Slovenia, financed his own armies, and for whom fighting the Turks had become a way of life. Suleiman, who considered that his right to rule Hungary had been allotted to him by Allah and that any challenge to his authority was not only an outrageous blasphemy against the Islamic religion but also an unforgivable crime of *lèse-majesté,* decided that the rebellious count must be instantly crushed. En route to Vienna, therefore, he paused at Sziget, intending to take and plunder the town, enslave its inhabitants, execute its defenders, and reduce the rebellious count by torture to a gibbering, quivering lump of pain-wracked flesh pleading for death. Suleiman and his vast army reached Sziget on July 31; the siege of the town, held by an army of 2,500 Magyars, began on August 7.

It took the Janissaries only five days to occupy the town, but Zriny and his men simply retired into the citadel, from which they continued to fight for more than five weeks. They were outnumbered by 80 to 1, considerably more in fact, as the Hungarian garrison was reduced by death to only six hundred men whom Zriny gathered about him on September 8 in the sole remaining strong point in the citadel after a huge mine had destroyed its outer defenses.

Zriny knew the end had come and he met it with style, in the best Magyar tradition of courage, elegance, and insolence. "He wore his most splendid apparel, and a diamond of high price glittered in the clasp of his crest of the heron's plumes. . . . Then from among the four richly ornamented sabers, he chose the oldest one. 'With this good sword gained I my first honors and with this will I pass forth to hear my doom before the judgment seat of God,'" he announced. With his standard bearer by his side, sword in hand, Count Zriny went forth to meet his doom. The Count, four and a half centuries after the siege of Sziget, is still one of the great heroes of Hungarian history. Whatever his failings, there was nothing weaselly about Count Zriny.

Of course the panache of yesterday rings strange in this modern age whose values are mainly centered on the pursuit of money. Style and honor seem perhaps ridiculous notions nowadays until one encounters them in one's own life, and then they can still stir the imagination. People still yearn for what is great and fine and good. Paradoxically, war, horrendous war, the foulest human activity, has also always been a cradle both of vileness and of nobility. But these contradictions are part of the human condition. They are part of ourselves and of our history. So it was on the day Count Zriny died. Death so near that it was only seconds away, in a voice of prayer and reverence, not in a voice of fear, Count Zriny three times uttered the words "Jesus, Jesus, Jesus."

The screaming Turks were attacking the citadel gate where a loaded mortar had been placed facing the entrance, ready to be fired. As soon as the Turks smashed the gate and poured through into the citadel, Count Zriny fired point blank into the frenzied horde, killing dozens of them. Then, his sword slashing around him, he rushed into the melee, and died with two musket balls in the body and an arrow through the face. The Turks, seeing him fall, shouted three times "Allah, Allah, Allah."

The day of slaughter was not over. A chamber under the citadel was full of gunpowder which, connected to a slow fuse, exploded a few minutes later and blew three thousand Muslim soldiers into the eternal revelry of their Paradise of houris and banquets.

Suleiman the Magnificent never learned that his troops had taken Sziget and that he had won. He had died from a heart attack the day before. The Turkish army did not continue its journey toward Vienna. The Turks campaigned for a few more weeks and then turned around and marched back to Istanbul. Suleiman's son Selim had already reached the capital, where he was enthroned as the new ruler of Islam and of the Ottoman empire. He was a tippler and even in his lifetime his subjects knew him as Selim the Sot. He loved the wine of Cyprus and, thanks to the Jihad conquest of the island a few years later, he would be assured of a plentiful supply to the end of his days. In Spain, too, the Jihad was stirring again in the Alpurrajas mountains of Granada where, seventy years after the Reconquista, the 100,000 Muslims still left in the peninsula dreamed of its return to the Moslemah.

49

THE ALPUJARRAS RISING:
SPAIN 1568–1570

Some seventy years after the fall of Granada to the Christians, there were approximately one hundred thousand Muslims still living in Spain, most of them in Andalusia, but with a sprinkling also in Murcia and Valencia. About forty thousand lived in and around the city of Granada itself. The Jihad and the days of triumph for them were over. They were the remnants of a former population trying to maintain a toehold in the country which their ancestors had conquered and from which the Christian Spaniards were trying, slowly, with the minimum of fuss, to evict them. A few minor revolts had occurred in recent decades, and the Spaniards had used them to denounce the terms of the peace treaty that had been drawn up between Castile and Granada. The Moors, Moriscos as they were known in Spain, were given the choice of becoming Christians and staying, or of remaining Muslims and going. Most of them had chosen to remain but, although on the surface they observed the Christian faith, were baptized, and went to Mass on Sundays, in fact they continued to secretly practice their former religion, and their first and only real loyalty was to Islam. Their second loyalty was to al-Andalus, Moorish Spain, the land that had once been theirs but was theirs no more, because it didn't exist any more. The comparison that comes to mind is pre-1994 Palestine.

Throughout all these years considerable hostility existed between the old Christian population of Granada and the Moriscos. The Mus-

312

lims were now the defeated ones. The Inquisition was particularly active against them as it considered that in the majority of the cases their conversion to Christianity was a sham and they continued, in fact, to be Muslim and to live according to the rules of the Koran rather than those of the Bible. If they were found guilty, the Inquisition had the right to confiscate their property. It is not difficult to imagine the abuses to which the system gave rise. Morisco-bashing was one of the favorite pastimes around Granada.

The Moriscos were well aware of the strength of their co-religionists in the Mediterranean, or rather, to be precise, their ex-co-religionists. The power of the Ottoman empire was a major fact of the political life of Europe. Moreover, Muslim corsairs from Algiers and other ports of North Africa regularly raided the coast. The Malta campaign had drawn away much of the Spanish fleet and the corsairs of Algiers and Morocco, well aware of the current Spanish naval weakness in its home waters, were raiding the Spanish Mediterranean coast more than ever and with almost complete impunity. Documents discovered in Granada revealed a plot to raise the standard of revolt in Granada if the Turks won at Malta. All in all, the Spaniards had every reason to fear the existence of a powerful fifth column in their southern provinces, people who were in a large measure supported by the foreign Muslim powers of North Africa and the Near East.

Shipments of arms were landed at secret spots on the coast and rushed for hiding to the caves of the wild and rugged Alpujarras mountains behind Granada, where many of the defeated Muslims had made their home after Boabdil's surrender in 1492. The Alpujarras had become the refuge for every Muslim malcontent of Granada. Within Granada itself the movement of revolt was led by a dyer called Farax, who promised that eight thousand Turks would be landing soon to back the rebellion. Inigo Lopez de Mendoza, marquis of Mondejar and captain-general of Granada, warned Madrid of approaching trouble with the Moriscos. His warnings were ignored. On Christmas day of 1568 nearly two hundred men wearing Turkish turbans penetrated surreptitiously into the old Moorish quarter of the town while everyone was at midnight Mass, killed a few guards sitting around a fire, and plundered a shop. Farax harangued the townsfolk, announced that the men (who were not Turks at all but villagers from the Alpujarras) were the vanguard of a force of eight thousand all set to invade Granada. But the locals were skeptical and Farax marched away at the head of his little army with only a few volunteers. Just the same, the word spread across the Alpujarras: "The Turks have landed," and the mountain people, believing that the days under Christian rule were over, went berserk. Priests all over the countryside were attacked, mutilated or murdered; some were burned alive; one was sown up inside a pig and barbecued; the pretty Christian girls were assiduously raped, some sent off to join the harems of Moroccan and Algerian potentates. The Jihad was obviously back in action. Farax, knowing that no Turks were on the way and sensing he might soon be in deep trouble, abdicated and handed power over to one Hernandez de Valor, a callow youth of twenty-two, who promptly changed his name to Mahomet ibn Umaiya, declared himself king of the Moors of Andalusia, and began to rule his little mountain kingdom with zest and enthusiasm, one of his first cares being to set up a harem suitable for a person of his station, youth, and virility. From Granada and the seaports of Andalusia the young Moriscos flocked to the mountains to join the war of liberation and fly the star-and-crescent banner.

The Jihad called, of course, for a counter-Jihad. From the west the Marques de Mondejar marched in with an army of nearly four thousand men, and from the east the Viceroy of Murcia, the Marques de Lopez, arrived with five thousand; but neither could dent more than superficially the considerably larger Morisco force scattered all over the mountains. Still, they did fight a Morisco force at Ohanez, killed a thousand, enslaved a few thousand more, and rescued thirty Christian girls destined for the harems of North Africa. Ibn Umaiya sent his brother Andalla to Algiers and Istanbul to try to raise a large force of volunteers, but in Turkey Sultan Selim the Sot was more interested in preparing an attack on Cyprus, whose wines he particularly appreciated and whose vineyards, he felt, should come within his imperial domain. As for the Algerians, they were disinclined to engage themselves too deeply in the Alpujarras adventure, which they felt might be short lived. This was not the feeling, however, in Spain, where Philip II officially informed the pope that the kingdom of Spain might collapse if the fighting went on much longer.

It is at this juncture that Don John of Austria—a Spaniard in spite of his title—appeared on the scene again. There is always a touch of Zorro about Don John, without the farce but with a lovely Spanish flourish of courage and flamboyance that places him among the great heroes of history. He manages to stride with panache and nobility across all this gore, blood, cruelty, treachery, and filth, sword in hand, in search of glory, ready to fight for his faith and his country; yet always compassionate and understanding, concerned for the men he led, concerned for the poor and helpless, concerned even for his enemies, loyal to his king and his friends. The word is always abused, I know, but Don John does emerge from the pages of these troubled years as a hero for all times, the Christian warrior knight as he should have been but, alas, was so rarely. Don John was young, good looking, loved by many pretty women, yet deep down he had the vocation of a monk. He was saint, sinner, and hero in one. How well G. K. Chesterton understood "Don John of Austria going to the war." Those whom the gods love die young. He was among those whom the gods loved.

Philip II asked but did not order Don John to take command of the Alpujarras campaign. When he arrived in Granada in April, the king, to be near the action, moved the court to Cordova. Don John passed his troops in review, and met and seduced the beautiful Margaret de Mendoza. In the Alpujarras, a few hundred Turks and Algerians arrived to help the rebels. The governor of Algiers, the corsair Ochiali, had told the Morisco envoy he could recruit four hundred Algerians—but only from the city jail! Four hundred criminals joined the Morisco forces and made themselves famous as rapists. In the mountains, revolt was brewing against Mahomet ibn Umaiya. One of his friends, ibn Abu, who had been castrated by the Christians for refusing to reveal the whereabouts of the self-styled king of the Moriscos, now turned against the leader for whom he had made that sacrifice. The Morisco king was strangled in the middle of his harem revels and the eunuch ibn Abu became king.

However, the new monarch must have been aware that his kingdom was doomed. In October Philip II ordered his half-brother to take to the Alpujarras "a war of fire and blood," and in January 1570 Don John of Austria was ordered to attack and take the town of Galera. It was his first campaign as a soldier and in the siege the Morisco women of Galera fought side by side with the men. Don John led the troops in person, ignored the king's orders that every person in the town should be killed, and spared the forty-two hundred women and children he found in the captured fortress. While Don John was leading his men in battle as usual, a musket ball hit his helmet but failed to penetrate it. Told that his brother was always in the van of the fighting, Philip II admonished him firmly. "You are not to risk your life, as you have hitherto been wont to do." Perhaps Don John was risking his life unnecessarily because he was shamed by the brutality of the campaign and of the men under his command. Perhaps he had expected them to be as noble as he was. "They cared for nothing but plunder and an easy life," he wrote. "There was not the least sense of honor among them." In May, Hernando al-Habaqui, the commander of the Morisco forces defending the town of Tijola, capitulated to Don John, who gave him back the scimitar he deposited at his victor's feet, and told him to use it in the future in the service of Spain.

Many of the more than one thousand men in the surrendered garrison of Tijola did not observe the terms of the capitulation, but joined Ibn Abu, who was determined to continue fighting and was still hoping for considerable help from Algeria and Turkey. In September Luis de Requesens, the king's vice-admiral, led the final campaign into the Alpujarras to settle once and for all the fate of the Moriscos. It is an ugly story. One hopes that Don John of Austria was somewhere else. This was the scorched-earth type of warfare. "Every house, fence, fruit tree, or vine that they passed was either cut down or burned to the ground," writes Jack Beeching. And he adds: "All Morisco women encountered were made slaves. Every man they caught was shot or hanged. Those who tried to hide in mountain caves were smoked out. . . . One thousand five hundred men were slaughtered in cold blood, three thousand women and children enslaved. Within six weeks the Alpujarras had been devastated from end to end." Twenty-one thousand Moriscos of Granada died during their two-year rebellion. Five months later Ibn Abu was murdered by a follower anxious to receive the bounty and pardon promised to anyone who would bring in the Morisco king's body or, at least, less cumbersomely, his head.

In November 1570 the decision was taken in council to deport the Moriscos from Granada and scatter them all over Spain. Don John of Austria, in the minority, opposed the decision. He left Granada a few days later but witnessed the first deportations of the Moriscos. He described it in a letter to a friend as "the saddest sight in the world . . . one cannot deny that the spectacle of the depopulation of a kingdom is the most pitiful one can imagine." After this tawdry war he would like, he wrote, to take part "in a war that concerned all Christendom." Lepanto was only a year away. But the Jihad can have innumerable facets. In the meantime, back in Istanbul, Selim the Sot wanted to assure himself a plentiful and constant supply of that lovely ruby-red wine from Cyprus of which he was so fond. And Lala Mustafa, his old tutor, was the man to get it for him.

50

THE FLAYING OF BRAGADINO: FAMAGUSTA 1571

INE, AT LEAST GOOD WINE, is the nectar of the gods, and a war fought over wine therefore deserves religious sanction. In any case, the attack on Cyprus, a colony of Venice, required the endorsement of Allah, because there was a treaty of peace between Turkey and Venice, sanctified by the Koran, as were all pacts with Muslim nations. So Selim II summoned the Mufti, an acquiescent prelate, and told him he required a sound Islamic reason for breaking the peace and invading Cyprus. The Mufti dutifully issued an edict, a fatwa, stating that, whatever treaties might be in existence, any land that had once been Muslim should return to Islam. The case of Cyprus fitted perfectly the finding. It had been Muslim as far back as 649. Cyprus, moreover, was only a few miles off the Turkish coast, and its vineyards therefore were within easy reach. The rightful place of Cyprus was in the Moslemah. In fact it had been the first European (at least, quasi-European) land to be invaded by the Muslims. Cyprus was coming back home to roost. Four hundred years later, Cyprus is still roosting, divided between antagonistic Greeks and Turks.

There was no time to be lost. Selim announced that in obedience to the holy will of Allah he would bring Cyprus back into the fold of the true believers. Cyprus was to be the first of many other conquests in the Mediterranean. Indeed, the Venetians had a little colonial empire at his doorstep. They owned Corfu and the Ionian islands, and several other

317

beauty spots in the Aegean and Adriatic seas. Every new sultan made it his duty to increase the size of the Ottoman empire. Selim wanted, like his father, to be a great expander of Muslim territory. So he raised an army of one hundred thousand men, gave the command to his old tutor, Lala Mustafa, and put the fleet in the hands of the young and very personable Admiral Ali Pasha, said to be a great favorite of the sultan's wives (he called his ship *Sultana*). Ali, unlike the great majority of Turkish naval commanders, had the reputation of treating his galley slaves, many of them Christian captives, with care and kindness.

The invading army landed at Limasol in July 1570. The campaign was expected to last only a few months, with no resistance anticipated from the Greek Cypriot population, most of whom worked as field hands in the sugar and vine plantations of the island. They were Orthodox by religion and disliked intensely their Venetian Catholic and capitalist bosses. But they were soon to discover that their new masters were worse. The Turks laid siege to Nicosia, which capitulated after a six-week siege on the condition that the lives of the Venetian garrison and of the townspeople were guaranteed. But Lala Mustafa disregarded his pledge, and nearly all the soldiers and civilians were immediately massacred, often after torture, which was a sort of a hobby of the Janissaries. Two thousand young boys and girls were spared and enslaved for the sexual titillation of the folks back home. One ship, with eight hundred young slaves on board, blew up before reaching the Anatolian coast when one of the young women captives threw a burning stick into the powder magazine. The name of this heroine, Amalda de Rocas, deserves to be remembered. She was eighteen years old.

Famagusta, ruled by a governor, Marcantonio Bragadino, had been expected to fall quickly. But, defended by several thousand soldiers—about eight thousand at its peak—under the military command of Astor Baglione, it refused all calls to surrender, to the fury of Lala Mustafa, who was anxious to get back to his scheming and weaseling in Istanbul. Selim II, in his capital, angrily told his military chiefs not to start on any other campaign until the Famagusta siege was over. He had plans to invade other islands and maybe Venice itself, but first he wanted Cyprus and Famagusta secured. Just as Count Zriny by his defense of Zsiget four years before had disrupted Suleiman the Great's eastern Europe invasion timetable, and thus saved Vienna, so the Venetians by their long defense of Famagusta were preventing Selim's offensive in southern Europe from ever getting under way.

Time and time again the Turks attacked the ramparts, each time losing many combatants, and were thrown back. After nearly a year of siege, in July 1571, Turkish sappers managed to blow up a large part of the main wall. By this time the defensive force was down to fewer than two thousand men. Munitions and food were also down to dangerous levels. Now was the time to yield honorably. Bragadino agreed to capitulate, and on August 1 the Venetians officially ceded Famagusta to the Turks. Now began one of the most horrendous scenes of individual savagery recorded in the history of the Jihad. Because the victim of this episode was just one man, toward whom all our pity can be directed, the reader cannot escape the singular horror of Bragadino's agony. It is not dispersed among many anonymous victims in a general massacre such as those that occurred time and time again when a town was captured, and its inhabitants were, we are told, "all put to the sword." It's a nicely balanced and pretty phrase, all the prettier that it does not convey the abominable and messy slaughter that "putting to the sword" must imply, particularly when hundreds, if not thousands, of people are cold-bloodedly slaughtered.

The pain and cruelty of Bragadino's death are made more real than so many of these mass murders which marked the progress of the Turkish armies, and of the Christian armies in their wars against each other. Their crimes were too many and too overwhelming, the victims too many and too impersonal for us to assimilate. They are part of the universal and unending saraband of death. But the torture and death of Bragadino, one man among thousands, became a personal injury and source of grief for every soldier and sailor who fought against Islam. Causes need one man, alive or dead, preferably dead, to represent what they are all about. Bragadino, dead, represented to the Christian warriors the Christian cause. It steeled in every Christian warrior in Europe the resolve to fight and conquer Islam.

On August 4, at the request of Lala Mustafa, Marcantonio Bragadino rode out of Famagusta on horseback to confer with the Turkish commander. By his side marched his military commander, Astor Baglione, and behind them were forty arquebusiers as bodyguards, and a young, handsome page, Antonio Quirini, whose father commanded a Venetian war galley. Was Lala Mustafa enraged because there was nothing cringing about the men of this defeated but unconquered army who stood straight before him, unafraid, and who gazed fearlessly around them, proud men who had done their duty and who had no reason to cower? Or was it the impeccable accoutrement of Baglione, upright, shoulders back and square, striding like a victorious knight instead of a beaten soldier? Venetians are a proud people, proud of their city and proud of themselves. They do not fawn, cringe, or crawl. Or was it the haughty attitude of Bragadino who, in the purple robes of a Venetian senator and who, with a parasol held over his head by his page, was as magnificent in defeat as he was when in power? Or was it the comeliness of the young page Antonio which made the pederast Lala lose his reason? Or was it all part of a calculated and secret ploy? We shall never know what suddenly turned Lala Mustafa from a man into a monster. All we know—for years later Antonio Quirini, a survivor, returned to Venice—is that Lala accused Bragadino of having killed some Turkish prisoners and ordered that Antonio should stay with him as a hostage, for reasons which were quite obvious to the worldly and realist Bragadino. He refused Lala Mustafa's new condition. The terms of the surrender had already been signed and there was no mention of hostages, he said. Lala Mustafa, furious, then gave a signal, Janissaries seized Bragadino and all who were with him. A couple of young boys were spared, but all the others except Bragadino were immediately sliced up and cut into little pieces. Turkish soldiers cut off his ears and nose and dragged him down into a cell. They arrested the Italian soldiers who were still in the surrendered city and massacred them all although they had agreed in the capitulation terms to let them return home. Lala Mustafa had special plans for Bragadino. He was not to reveal them until nearly two weeks later.

On August 17, Lala Mustafa ordered Bragadino to be taken out of his cell. The time had come for the big show for the people of Famagusta and for his troops. For the Muslim soldiers, it was like circus day, a moment of relaxation and laughter. For the Christian citizenry of Famagusta the objectives were different, more subtle, more satanic, a moment in the propaganda war, a moment in the war of terror. At the sight of their former Venetian governor, shriven and humiliated, the Cypriots would acquire new respect for their new Turkish masters who had conquered their old Italian masters. By so humiliating the man who had once been the ruler of their daily lives Lala Mustafa wanted to make clear to the citizens of Famagusta that the old order had truly changed. Bragadino was saddled up like a donkey and dragged and kicked around the town like an animal, with bags of dirt and soil tied on his back. Each time he passed before Lala Mustafa he had to lick the ground in front of him. He was then hauled up to the high spar of a galley mast exposed to the multitudes so that all could see what had become of the proud Venetian patrician, now noseless and earless, hauled down and tied to a post. Then Lala Mustafa told him what his fate was to be: to be flayed alive. He died during the torture. His torturers then filled his flayed skin with straw, placed it astride a cow and took this pathetic, tortured effigy, still streaked with blood, around the town under the shelter of a parasol. Then they hung the straw-filled skin, like a large, bloody, bloated balloon, from the yardarm of Lala Mustafa's galley. The distance isn't too great from the people who flayed Bragadino alive to those who, in the 1980s, blew airliners and their passengers out of the sky.

Yes, we should be shocked and horrified. But we must remember that Bragadino's hideous death was only one of the many acts of immense cruelty of that epoch.

> The massacre of St. Bartholomew (fifty thousand killed) took place in France not a year before the murder of Bragadino and scarcely another year had passed away when at the capture of the fortress of Wittenstein, in Finland, the garrison was cut to pieces by the Russians, and the commandant tied to a spear and roasted alive. (Creasy, *History of the Ottoman Turks,* vol. 1, p. 348)

The flaying of Bragadino, says Creasy, was in the spirit of that age.

51

A GOOD DAY TO DIE:
LEPANTO 1572

LUCKILY FOR ADMIRAL ALI PASHA, he did not have to be a witness to the sadistic death of Bragadino. With his fleet of two hundred twenty-two war galleys and sixty other vessels he was at anchor in the bay of Lepanto, that long, narrow gulf in southwestern Greece just above the peninsula of Morea, west of Athens, waiting for a Christian fleet that he knew would soon be looking for him. That naval force was the weapon of the Holy League, Christendom's newest answer to the Jihad, founded that year by Pope Pius V, who for years had been striving to unite Europe against the Muslim invaders.

The Holy League had formally come into being in May 1571. Its fleet flew a huge flag of Christ crucified, and consisted of 316 ships, including 208 galleys and six galleasses, a cross between a galley and a galleon, with between thirty and forty heavy guns instead of the usual four or five of a galley. The Venetian fleet was under the command of a 75-year-old firebrand, Sebastiano Veniero, with the redoubtable Agostino Barbarigo as his second-in-command. The bearer of a famous name, the Genoese Gianandrea Doria, commanded a squadron in the service of Spain. A shipowner in his native city, Doria had hired out more than twenty of his own galleys to the king of Spain. Anxious to keep his ships intact, he was the most cautious of all the Holy League's commanders. The quiet and competent Marcantonio Colonna, of an old Roman aristocratic family, was in charge of the papal squadron. Two Spanish admirals, Don Alavaro de Bazan and Don Juan de Cardona, with their squadrons were also among the pillars of the Christian force.

Don John of Austria was the Commander-in-Chief. Universally accepted, and appointed by Pope Pius V, Don John, aged twenty-five, was less than half as old of most of these seasoned sea fighters. Even so, there were no dissenting voices to his appointment. The young warrior had the respect of all. "If I had but a little better health I would ship myself as a soldier or sailor under Don John," Don Garcia of Toledo, who had waited so long to go to the relief of Malta, wrote to a friend. The son of the Spanish emperor and of a German singer, after fighting the local Alpujarras rebels in Granada, Don John was now fulfilling the destiny he had sought "in a war that concerned all Christendom." The fleet he was to lead into battle consisted not only of vessels commanded by the highest officers in the Holy League—Spain, Venice and the papacy—but also of men and sometimes ships contributed by many other Italian cities: Genoa, Florence, Turin, Parma, Lucca, Ferrara, and little Urbino. The Knights of St. John were there, of course, as always present in every affray against the infidels, some with their own flotilla and some scattered throughout the other ships of the fleet. There were also volunteers from the rest of Europe, including recalcitrant France and Protestant England. The Provençal Romegas, hero of the siege of Malta, commanded one of the papal galleys. Another famous Provençal, Crillon, one of France's most famous fighting men, from the French Riviera town of Murs, was also among those of the European provincial nobility who placed their sword in Christianity's cause. So were at least a dozen Englishmen. One of them was another hero from the Malta siege, Sir Thomas Stukeley, reputedly Henry VIII's bastard son, fighting the Turk once again with the same courage as he had shown at St. Angelo. But Spaniards and Italians were the mainstay of the international force that was to meet the Turks in battle. Seventy-two of the Christian galleys flew the Spanish banner, 140 were Venetian, eight belonged to the Knights of Malta, and the papacy had twelve.

The port selected as meeting point for all the Holy League ships was Messina, in Sicily, where Don John of Austria arrived on August 23, barely a week after the martyrdom of Bragadino, of which no one in Christendom yet knew anything about. But in Lepanto, Ali Pasha did hear of the gathering of the ships against him from Ochiali, the foremost Algerian corsair. He did not believe the Christians would sail until next spring, he told Ali Pasha. But he was wrong. Ali Pasha and Don John would soon meet, for the first and last time, in the Gulf of Lepanto, for the biggest naval battle of all times since Actium in 31 B.C.E., as every book on the Battle of Lepanto tells us, without ever explaining what the battle of Actium was all about.

Here's a reminder for the reader who may not know or who has forgotten. Actium was fought just north of Lepanto and, like Lepanto, it was a battle between West and East. One side was under the command of Octavian, the future emperor Augustus, with a fleet of four hundred galleys; the other side consisted of a Roman/Egyptian fleet of four hundred eighty ships led by Mark Anthony and Cleopatra. The two lovers lost the battle and committed suicide a few months later. Under Mark Anthony, the center of power in the Roman Empire had been gradually slipping east and might well have become established in Alexandria. Under Augustus it returned to Rome and remained there for several more centuries, until Constantine moved it east in the fourth century C.E.

So, more than 1,600 years later, the battle of Actium was certainly not on Don John's mind as the fleet he commanded gradually gathered around him. Galley warfare was a naval rendition of land warfare. Ramming and boarding were the essential tactics, and all the vessels carried a large number of troops with swords, pikes, muskets, arquebuses, and bows and arrows, whose main purpose was to board and capture the enemy vessels in usually savage hand-to-hand fighting. In his two hundred eight galleys Don John of Austria commanded thirty thousand soldiers and nearly thirteen thousand sailors. Two-thirds of the soldiers were on the Spanish payroll; one of those was Miguel de Cervantes who, surviving the battle, was to become Spain's most famous writer, author of *Don Quixote*. The Muslim force was about of equal strength. The 250 Ottoman galleys carried thirty-four thousand soldiers, and thirteen thousand sailors. But neither side knew the strength of the other. A battle of giants was in preparation, and neither had feet of clay.

Don John sent out a French knight of the Order of St. John with four galleys to discover where Ali Pasha's fleet was. The Frenchman reported back on September 28 that they had recently been in one of the Ionian islands, had now returned to Lepanto for the winter. "The time for counsel is past, the time to fight is now," Don John replied to the cautious Doria, who had suggested that the leaders of the Christian fleet meet in counsel to decide what action to take. In Lepanto Ali, who was wondering whether he should seek battle or avoid it, received firm orders from the sultan: If the Christian fleet comes anywhere near yours, fight it. The determination on both sides was unmistakable. Battle was the order of the day, for both Muslims and Christians.

On October 5, at Viscando, not far from Actium, a Venetian vessel brought the news to the anchored Holy League fleet that Famagusta had fallen and that Bragadino had been flayed alive. The news rapidly spread all around the ships, and a mood of rage and fury and hate and an overwhelming desire to avenge the martyred Bragadino seized every man in the fleet. Tough soldiers beat their heads with clenched fists in helpless rage and anguish, sobbing at the torment of the Venetian and the cruelty of the Turks. No enemy who fell into Christian hands could expect mercy.

On October 7 the Christian fleet entered the bay of Lepanto. Don John knew he would fight the Turkish fleet that day. The soldiers and sailors all went to Mass. Every galley had a chaplain, sometimes two, usually Jesuits, Dominicans, or Franciscans. This was a holy war for the Christians as much as for the Muslims. A banner of Christ crucified flew from the mast of Don John's flagship, the *Real*. A lookout shouted that he had spotted the first Turkish ships. Over the Muslim flagship, the Prophet's banner also flew high, bearing the name of Allah inscribed on it 28,900 times. On the *Sultana,* Ali Pasha knew that victory or defeat that day could depend on the tiniest of circumstances, the two fleets were so evenly matched. He had to secure the cooperation of his rowers, most of them Christian captives chained to their posts. He was a humane man and he had always treated them well. He walked down to the lower deck among the oarsmen. They all listened to him because they respected him, but in complete silence. "Amigos," he said to them in Spanish, "I expect you today to do your duty by me in return for what I have done for you. If I win the battle, I promise you your liberty; if the day is yours, Allah has given it to you."

Among the Christian vessels, Don John of Austria, holding aloft a crucifix in his hand, moved in a launch along the line of his ships: "My children, we are here to conquer or die. In death or in victory, you will win immortality," he shouted to them across the water. This was as much a religious occasion for them as a martial one. When he sailed in front of the Venetian ships, he called on them to avenge the death of Bragadino. The men cheered, or wept, some knelt and made the sign of the cross. Don John shouted a few respectful pleasantries across to old Sebastiano Veniero, who commanded the Venetian squadron and who was fifty years older than his commander. "This would be a good day to die," Veniero told one of his officers. He held in his hand a blunderbus, and a strong young sailor stood by him with another blunderbus already loaded them for him, as the old man no longer had the strength to load it himself and he wanted to personally fire, and keep on firing, at the Turks. He had known Bragadino and served with him in the old days.

The Holy League fleet was divided into four squadrons. The center was commanded by Don John in person from his flagship the *Real,* surrounded by Veniero, Colonna, and the small flotilla of the Knights of St. John, about sixty galleys altogether. The galleasses, floating batteries that were to cause havoc in the Muslim ships, kept their positions just ahead of the rest of the Christian fleet. The Christian right wing was commanded by Gianandrea Doria, some sixty ships also, and the left wing, numerically about the same, was under the command of Barbarigo. The reserve flotillas, under Don Alvaro de Bazan and Don Juan de Cardona, sailed a little behind, with orders to go wherever they were most needed during the fighting. Sailing toward them in the vague form of a crescent, the Muslim fleet was also split into four squadrons. The center led by Ali headed straight for Don John; the right wing, commanded by Mehmed Suluk, was lined up opposite Barbarigo's squadron. Uluch Ali, however, was heading straight south with the obvious intention of outflanking Gianandrea Doria's squadron and attacking the Christians from the rear. The Turkish reserve stood massed behind Ali's battle fleet, about ninety galleys in three lines. The center was obviously going to be the main point of contact as, at about eleven o'clock, the two fleets sailed toward each other, each armada presenting a battle line of about three miles across at the entrance to the narrow gulf of Lepanto. Don John ordered the captain of the *Real* to lay his galley right alongside the approaching *Sultana* when the time came. Don John of Austria and Admiral Ali Pasha headed straight for each other. The two young warriors were to meet at last.

As the two galleys ground into each other with the splintering, smashing sound of pulverized oars, Don John danced a little jig of joy on the *Sultana*'s gun platform. The three hundred Janissary arquebusiers and one hundred archers on the Muslim galley fired into the mass of Spanish soldiers, knights, and gentlemen volunteers who crammed the *Real*'s decks. Four hundred arquebusiers on the *Real* fired back. The Christian oarsmen on the Holy League ships had all been unchained and armed, and they fought against the Turks with as much fury as the soldiers and sailors on the Christian galleys. Very soon the whole battle zone turned into a floating battlefield with the galleys all crammed together and ramming into each other, so that the naval battle was soon a melee of infantrymen killing one another with fierce intensity and without mercy, most of the killed dying on each others' decks, but with some also slipping into the sea and drowning. The sea literally turned from blue to red. It was a ferocious brawl, Christians and Muslims all fighting with one purpose in mind: to kill each other.

Don John, his sword held straight before him, led the boarding party that clambered onto the *Sultana*. Colonna, coming up alongside the *Real,* crashed his vessel into the poop of the *Sultana.* By 2 o'clock in the afternoon the Muslim flagship was overwhelmed. Nearby, the septuagenarian Veniero clambered with the awkwardness of his age onto an Ottoman galley, was wounded by an arrow in the leg, left his crew to capture the enemy vessel, went back to his own galley, and attacked and sank two more ships. Barbario, on the left wing, was hit by an arrow that went through his eye and into his brain, but he died knowing the Christian fleet was victorious. In three hours of frantic and unceasing hand-to-hand fighting 32,500 soldiers and sailors, Christian and Muslim, were killed. In sheer numbers of casualties there has never been a more costly naval battle than Lepanto. Trafalgar, the most famous battle in history, cost the lives of some three thousand French, Spanish, and British sailors, not even one-tenth of the casualties at Lepanto.

The meeting between Don John and Ali Pasha was both macabre and grotesque. Ali Pasha, hit by an arquebus shot, fell wounded to the deck. A Spanish soldier, one of the boarding party fighting on the deck of the Turkish flagship, saw him fall, pounced upon him, pulled out his knife and cut Ali Pasha's head off. The Spaniard then rushed over to Don John to present him with the trophy and, hopefully, earn a big reward. But Don John, an aristocrat although conceived on the wrong side of the blanket, had a delicate nature. "What can I do with that head?" he asked with distaste. "Throw it into the sea," he ordered the soldier. Another soldier recovered the head, fixed it to the top of a lance, and the whole of the Turkish fleet soon knew that their admiral was dead. By 3 P.M. the battle was over. Only Uluch Ali made it back to Istanbul with most of his flotilla. The Turks had lost 210 ships, of which 130 had been captured and eighty sunk. Twenty-five thousand Muslims and some 7,500 Christians had been killed. Uncounted among the dead must have been at least eight to ten thousand Christian slaves chained to the oars of the Turkish galleys. However, fifteen thousand of them survived the battle and were freed from the captured Turkish vessels. The Christians lost twelve galleys, which on sinking must have taken close to 1,500 Muslim galley slaves to a watery grave. All in all, it was a great victory, but for the Ottomans it was less of a defeat than they might have feared.

Don John of Austria wanted to follow up his victory with an attack through the Dardanelles on the heartland of the Moslemah: Istanbul, but bad weather and jealousies and quarrels between Venetians and Spaniards stymied his efforts. Bragadino, too, was to remain unavenged with Cyprus remaining unattacked. Instead Don John led a dead-end expedition to Tunis, which the Turks had taken back in 1574. The Jihad and Don John then parted. He was never to fight against Islam again.

Right to the end of his life Don John's instinct for gallantry never left him. Sent to govern the Netherlands, he tried to defend the interests of the local peasants and, reported a local English spy by the name of Fenton, "he maketh deep impression in the heart of the people." Radcliffe, another English secret agent, sent by Walsingham, the English secretary of state, to kill Don John, was arrested in the prince's audience chamber. Instead of having his would-be killer hanged, Don John pardoned him and had him sent back to England. Walsingham, who met Don John a short time later reported that he had never seen before a gentleman "for personage, speech, wit and entertainment comparable" to the Spanish prince. But Walsingham, a shrewd judge of human nature, also noted a great conflict underway in Don John, a man always torn between "honor and necessity."

If this conflict did exist within Don John, it was not honor that lost. He died suddenly on October 1, 1578, of typhoid—some say of poison—in a pigeon cote in Namur, Belgium, to which he had been urgently rushed to shelter him from the rain. Selim the Sot had died four years earlier, after falling down in his bathroom and fracturing his skull. Appropriately enough, he was drunk, having just swigged down a whole bottle of that fine Cyprus wine which a few years previously had inspired him to launch a Jihad across the seas.

52

COLONIALISM MUSLIM STYLE: EASTERN EUROPE 1574–1681

ITH THE BATTLE OF LEPANTO we reach a plateau in Ottoman-European military affairs that was to last some 115 years and that almost lulled western Europe into a belief that the Muslim threat was past. But during this period of just over a century there was no lull for the Hungarians in the process of colonization which they endured. They continued to bear the oppression, humiliations, and sufferings of a ruthless occupation by an alien race of a different faith and way of life. During this long Muslim occupation, upward of some three million Hungarians were probably enslaved and shipped off to garnish the bagnios and seraglios of their their masters in Istanbul, all over the Balkans and the Ottoman empire, all the way to Egypt and the Euphrates.

Turkey can rightfully be said to have been the first major colonial power, well before Spain, long considered the inaugurator of the colonial race with its occupation of Hispaniola after the discovery of America by Columbus in 1492. But, unlike Spain and the other powers who followed, Turkey—geographically located at the eastern extremity of the Mediterranean, far from the open Atlantic seaboard—established its colonies in neighboring southeastern Europe instead of tropical America and Asia, and started doing it in the late 1300s, more than one hundred years before Spain.

The Christian victory at Lepanto should have smashed Ottoman power for at least the next couple of generations. It did nothing of the sort. In fact, through the inaction and quarrels of the Holy League members, and through the wiliness of the Turkish Grand Vizier, Sokolli, the Muslims snatched victory from defeat and, on the promise of a great expansion of trade, even persuaded Venice to forget the hideous death of Bragadino and abandon its claim to Cyprus. In return the Venetians received many commercial advantages.

After Selim II ended his reign with a cracked skull on his bathroom floor, his son Murad III came to the throne, had his five brothers executed in the usual way, and gave up the Jihad in favor of the harem. He fathered 103 children and was assiduously courted by Queen Elizabeth of England, not as a prospective consort, but as a prospective ally against Philip II of Spain, because Elizabeth was desperately worried about the great Armada with which Spain planned to invade England. Through her envoy in Istanbul, the English Queen urged Murad to send sixty to eighty galleys "against the idolator, the King of Spain, who relying on the help of the Pope, and all idolatrous princes, deigns to crush the Queen of England, and then to turn his whole power to the destruction of the Sultan and then make himself universal monarch." That's not all, Elizabeth added. If Murad came to the aid of England, "the proud Spaniard and the lying Pope with all their followers will be struck down" and God would protect his own and punish the idolators of the earth thanks to the combined might of England and Turkey.

Presumably aware that the sultan did not know English, the queen wrote her letter in Latin, which the sultan didn't know either. But Murad was uninterested in Elizabeth's letter anyway and returned to his harem. Besides, the letter came two years too late. Turkey and Spain had made their peace in 1585. Still, a battle between Spanish galleons and Muslim galleys off the Isle of Wight, however improbable, might have been interesting.

Not only did Murad fail to encourage the Jihad, but it was during his reign that the Janissaries' iron discipline, through inaction, began to break down, a process of disintegration that was to go on for the next two and a half centuries. During Murad's 21-year reign, revolts broke out in Transylvania, Moldavia, and Wallachia; and Turkey also engaged in a minor war with Austria. The campaigns in eastern Europe dragged on intermittently for several years. The most important operation was the siege of Canissa in 1600, held in turn by Austrian and then Turkish forces, in which a young English volunteer, John Smith, then aged twenty, got his first taste of fighting. When the Austrians abandoned the siege in November 1601, "it was so cold," John Smith wrote, "that three or four hundred froze to death and two or three thousand were lost in that miserable flight." John Smith went on later to take part in the colonization of Virginia where, in that warmer climate, he met and married the Indian princess Pocahontas, who had saved his life.

With the Jihad temporarily shelved, there was not much plunder to be obtained in any of these conflicts in the Balkans and, as a substitute, the Janissaries began to be more interested in trafficking, bribery, and corruption in Istanbul. They attacked the palace and clamored for the heads of a pasha and another official who had displeased them. They received both heads and then dispersed. But the precedent had been set. They revolted twice more during the next few years, demanded that their nominee (who was paying them for their support) be placed on the throne of Moldavia, engaged in a minor civil war against the Spahis in the streets of Istanbul, and scared the whole city except for Murad III, who continued his harem activities unabated ("he lay immersed in lust," the Venetian envoy reported) until he died, presumably of exhaustion, and his eldest son, Mahomet III, came to the throne.

Forty-seven of Murad's one hundred three children were still alive at the time of their father's death, of whom twenty were sons. Mahomet III, the new sultan, had them all strangled, and to make sure no others were on the way he had seven of his father's concubines, all pregnant, sewn up in sacks and thrown into the Bosporus. His reign was marked by a major victory at Cerestes in 1595 against an army made up largely of troops from Germany and Transylvania. One of the Ottoman heroes of the battle was the former Sicilian nobleman, Scipio Cicala, captured as a youth in North Africa, who subsequently threw in his lot with his Muslim captors and became one of their most illustrious warriors and, after the victory of Cerestes, Grand Vizier of the Ottoman empire.

Mahomet III died in 1603, after ordering one of his sons, whom he feared was planning to take his place, to be strangled. Ahmed I, at age fourteen the elder of his two remaining sons, took over the throne, sparing his younger brother Mustapha, reputedly an imbecile. When the Grand Vizier objected to leading an army into Hungary, he received a note from the youthful sultan, short and to the point: "If thou valuest thy head, thou will march at once." The Grand Vizier duly marched. Shiite Persia, not Europe (busy with its Thirty Years' War), was considered the major threat to the Ottoman empire, and the Jihad was as assiduously practiced against these heretics as against the Christians.

The mufti in Istanbul a few years ago had issued a fatwa calling for a Jihad against these Muslim dissenters and proclaiming that it was more holy to kill one Persian Shiite than seventy Christians.

On the death of Ahmed, Othman II came to the throne of this decaying empire in 1618. He spent a large part of his four-year reign trying to master the Janissaries, sending them off to fight the Poles in a hopeless Jihad which he hoped would kill off a lot of them. He also practiced his skill as an archer by using prisoners of war as targets or, if none were available on the spot, summoning one of his pages for the job. Unloved, and quite rightly so, by everybody, Othman II was arrested by the Janissaries, thrown into a cell and strangled while Ahmed I's imbecile brother Mustapha took over the empire for a brief spell in 1622, until his mental state became obvious to all. The Ottoman empire was in a state of physical and moral chaos. "In the general dissolution of all bonds of government, and in the absence of all protection to industry or property, the empire seemed to be sinking into the mere state of wilderness of beast of prey," says Creasy (*History of the Ottoman Turks*, vol. 1, pp. 391–92). The British diplomatic envoy in Istanbul, Sir Thomas Roe, in his report to King James in London, described Turkey as "an old body, crazed through many vices, which remains when the youth and strength is decayed," and mourned "the want of justice . . . and the violent oppression" which then reigned in the Ottoman empire. Turkey, he said, "was as a sick man about to die upon one's hands" thus coining the expression by which Turkey was to be known for the next three centuries: "the sick man of Europe."

The next sultan, Murad IV, came to power in 1623 at the age of eleven and restored order in the empire at the cost of a hundred thousand executions. He had to quell, in the course of his seventeen-year reign, mutinies by the Janissaries and Spahis, and to assent to the execution of his Grand Vizier, Hafiz, who rather than imperil the sultan voluntarily walked to his death among rebellious Janissaries who stabbed him seventeen times. Murad IV bided his time. He sent his own killers to roam Istanbul at night and one by one the ringleaders of the rebels were killed. Unfortunately Murad IV grew to enjoy killing, not only of his enemies, but of anyone who happened to cross him. A pedestrian who got in his way when he was riding through the city was immediately killed with an arrow. A group of girls dancing in a meadow irritated him; they were all seized and drowned. A passenger boat sailed too near his harem; it was immediately sunk by gunfire. A young Frenchman who tried to seduce a Turkish woman was impaled. A moody man, as he had every right to be with so many killings preying on his mind, he next took to drink and the local drunk, Mustapha Bekir, became his best friend. Mustapha, brandishing a bottle, taught the sultan that "this liquid gold outweighs all the treasures of the world." Inside the palace drinking became Murad IV's favorite pastime. But outside the palace drinking, whether alcohol or coffee, was treated as a capital offense. The penalty: immediate execution. So was smoking. The caliph once found a gardener and his wife having a quiet smoke behind a shed. He ordered his executioner to cut off their legs on the spot and left them bleeding to death among the tulips.

But occasionally Murad IV was guilty of a kind act. Perhaps it was in a moment of alcoholic euphoria that he put an end to the tribute in children to which the Christian villagers in the Balkans had to submit, thus obliging the Janissaries to find a new source of manpower. His moods, however, remained somber and unpredictable. After an expedition into Asia, irritated by the comments of the Mufti, Murad had him strangled, the only recorded execution in Ottoman history of this highest religious prelate by a sultan. In a Jihad campaign against Persia in 1638, he captured Baghdad, had the entire thirty-thousand man garrison executed, except for a lucky three hundred, and returned home with the intention of declaring war on Venice. Instead he fell ill and died of the gout, brought on by excessive drinking, at the age of twenty-eight. He last act, on his deathbed, was to order, two minutes before his death, the execution of his sole surviving brother, Ibrahim. But the brother hid and was called to the throne as Murad IV expired.

Ibrahim, in spite of his close escape from strangulation, was as savage as his recent predecessors in the sultanate. He resumed the much-interrupted Jihad in Europe in a campaign, aided by the Crimean Tatars, against the Cossacks—"a horde of malefactors" according to the Russian czar—who had occupied the city of Azov on the Black Sea. Next Sultan Ibrahim decided to attack the Knights of St. John in their island fortress, Malta. But his horrified advisers, well aware of the strength of the island which had so successfully withstood the great siege of 1565, persuaded him to break the signed truce with Venice and attack instead their island possession of Crete. The Muslims landed unopposed on the island in 1645 and laid siege to Candia. They were still besieging the town twenty years later. In the meantime the Venetians, furious at the Turks for breaking the truce, sent their galleys into the Dardanelles to blockade Istanbul. The local population, unhappy over their very short rations, began to mutter against the inanity of their sultan and his well-known bizarre practices, chiefly sexual. The sultan was able to enjoy in his harem all the facilities of a high-class brothel. One of Ibrahim's favorite pastimes, in a special room lined with mirrors, was "to strip all his women naked and pretend they were mares while he would run among them acting the part of a stallion as long as his strength lasted." Believing one of the 288 concubines in his harem had had an affair with an improperly castrated eunuch, he had all the concubines tied in sacks and thrown into the Bosporus. Only one, whose bag was not properly tied, managed to break out, swam to the surface and, calling for help, was picked up by a passing French ship that rescued her and took her to France, where she was last seen enjoying the sights of Paris. The weirdness and savagery of palace life in Istanbul is recounted with great verve by Noel Barber in *Lords of the Golden Horn.*

Ibrahim's opponents found willing listeners among the Janissaries; Hungry and angry, too, they revolted, arrested the sultan and, with the connivance of the Grand Vizier and of the mufti (whose daughter he had forced into his seraglio), strangled him. His son, aged ten, became Mahomet IV in 1648. It is during his reign that the Ottoman empire was restored, however temporarily, to its former greatness and was launched again into one of its great European Jihad adventures—which, however, thanks to the Italian soldier Montecuccoli, failed miserably.

Montecuccoli's name is one of the three that stand out during this period of the Jihad. The other two were Albanians, father and son, Mohammed and Ahmed Kiuprili, both Grand Viziers of the Ottoman empire. Mohammed Kiuprili was installed in his position in 1656 at the age of seventy. In spite of his advanced years, Kiuprili was a man of action. During his five-year tenure in office he put to death all the people he considered corrupt, thus ridding the Ottoman empire of no fewer than thirty-six thousand miscreants, an average of more than seven thousand a year. One of his executioners, by the name of Sulfikar, later confessed to personally executing four thousand people, an average of nearly three a day, and disposing of the corpses by throwing them into the sea. Mohammed Kiuprili was succeeded to the vizerate by his son, the equally able Ahmed Kiuprili. The third outstanding figure, Count Raimundo Montecuccoli of Modena, Italy, was the most brilliant of the Imperial generals—Imperial referring of course to the Holy Roman empire of the Austrian Leopold I.

Montecuccoli smashed the Ottoman army in 1664 at the Battle of St. Gothard, about a hundred miles south east of Budapest, and brought the Muslim campaign and Ahmed Kiuprili's first venture into the military arts to a sudden end. The Grand Vizier's objective had been to crush once and for all the power of Austria. The Turkish army had set out from Istanbul in June of the previous year under the command of Ahmed Kiuprili and of the sultan (who abandoned the enterprise at Edirne, preferring the joys of hunting to those of the Jihad). It was made up of 120,000 men, backed with 60,000 camels, 10,000 mules, and 135 guns, light and heavy.

Montecuccoli, a military genius with a long list of hard-fought battles to his name, had been fighting since the age of twenty-two for the Holy Roman Empire, mainly against the Swedes and the French, and his opponents had included the warrior king Gustavus Adolfus of Sweden and the Frenchmen Turenne and Condé. But at St. Gothard Montecuccoli had a French contingent fighting at his side, along with the usual steady and professional Austrian, German, and Hungarian infantry. They were greatly outnumbered by the Turks, but Montecuccoli was a more experienced soldier than Ahmed Kiuprili. The battle was fought along the bank of the river Raab. The Italian placed his German auxiliaries in the center of the line, the Austrians and Hungarians to the right, the French under Count de Coligny to the left. When the Turks crossed the river and attacked the Imperials in the center, Prince Charles of Lorraine charged at the head of an Austrian cavalry regiment. More Turks were coming across the river, and Montecuccoli now called on Coligny to attack. The French count sent in a thousand infantry and two squadrons of cavalry under the Duke de la Feuillade and Beauveze. Says Creasy: "When Kiuprili saw the French coming forward with their shaven chins and cheeks and powdered perruques, he asked scornfully, "Who are these young girls?" But the French cavalry, unimpressed by the formidable Turkish battle-cry of "Allah!" replied with their own battle-cry of "Allez, Allez"—just as the French rugby crowds shout today when their team is playing—and rushed upon the Turks, killing or scattering a large part of the Ottoman army. The Muslims, however, were not defeated yet. The Turks were coming across in larger numbers at points up and down the river and heading toward the fighting. General John Spork, Montecuccoli's cavalry commander, dismounted, knelt on the ground and prayed to the "mighty Generalissimo" in heaven. "If thou wilt not this day help thy children the Christians, at least do not help those dogs the Turks, and thou shall soon see something that will please thee." He then remounted his horse and, at the head of his men, charged, shouting insults at the enemy.

The Turks, finally destabilized by the vigor of the Imperial attack, bolted toward the river. That day, ten thousand Muslim warriors were killed and twenty thousand fled the battlefield. The survivors particularly remembered the Duke de la Feuillade and he became known among them as "Fuladi" which means "The Man of Steel."

The battle of St. Gothard broke a long list of land defeats to the Turks that went right back to Kosovo. The two sides signed a twenty-year-truce (which was not kept) and Ahmed Kiuprili went off Jihading to other parts. He landed in Crete to lead the siege of Candia, where the defenders, led by the Venetian firebrand Francisco Morosini, had recently been reinforced by the arrival of a contingent of French volunteers commanded by the irrepressible La Feuillade, anxious to get at the Turks again. Morosini is one of the great names of Venetian history, and his defense of Candia is one of the epics of the Mediterranean Jihad campaign. Louis XIV sent three unofficial French expeditions to Candia to help the Venetians defend the city.

The first, four years before the Battle of St. Gothard, was made up of four thousand men. It was in the second French expedition that La Feuillade appeared, again at the head of a coterie of French knights, three or four hundred in all, who insisted on attacking the Turks on arrival although they had been refused the permission to do so. La Feuillade led the charge with a whip instead of a sword in his hand, a sort of Murat before his time. He was much admired by his Turkish enemies, who respected valor and panache. Casualties were heavy. One hundred Frenchmen were killed or wounded. Most of the survivors died of the plague. A third expedition, six thousand men in all, arrived the following year under the command of the duke of Beaufort. Again, the French insisted on charging in particularly unpropitious circumstances; five hundred of them were killed in action or beheaded after capture. Possibly because of the ravages of the plague, the rest went home, and the fate of Candia was now sealed. The siege went on, under the command of Ahmed Kiuprili, for another few months. During its last three years, thirty thousand Turks and twelve thousand Venetians were killed. When Candia fell, there were none of the ghastly massacres and tortures that had so tainted the capitulations of Nicosia and Famagusta in Cyprus nearly a century earlier. The inevitable surrender, at the end of the twenty-year siege, and the change of sovereignty were carried out in dignity and honor. No flaying alive, no cutting off of ears and noses, no torturing. But, of course, Ahmed Kiuprili was no Lala Mustafa. Many of the local people, unwilling to live under Muslim law, migrated to Corsica, where they founded the town of Carese, where some of their descendants still live and where, three centuries later, some of the inhabitants still speak Greek.

Ahmed Kiuprili's final Jihad was fought in Poland in 1672. One wonders, with the passage of time, how much of the original spirit of the Jihad was retained and whether, by the seventeenth century, these campaigns were not essentially those of a European (though Muslim) imperialist power clashing in the pursuit of international politics with other European imperialist powers all striving for a dominant position on this side of the Bosporus. Undoubtedly the two elements, imperialism and religion, prevailed, particularly as Islam was both a religion and an ideology and the Jihad, therefore, can be at the same time both religious and imperialist. By this time the political side of Islam dominated the religious, while the religious provided support for the political. In fact, probably the religious was a front for plunder and the acquisition of power and wealth. The Jihad made the state of war permanent and natural between Islam and Christendom, even when they were not actually fighting. Whatever the reasons for its existence at any particular time, as long as the Jihad continued to be the policy of Islam, that enmity and distrust inevitably also continued. Nearly a century ago, the *Encyclopedia of Islam* (1913 edition) stated the problem quite unequivocally: "Islam must be completely made over before the doctrine of jihad can be eliminated." But the Jihad appeared to be immovable. It gave Islamic imperialism the holy tinge it sought for its colonial conquests. Rudolph Peters, in his treatise on the Jihad, has been at pains to stress the imperialist aspect of the Muslim Holy War. "Historically speaking there has often rather been question of purely political grounds, such as the wish for expansion of territory or the necessity to defend it against attacks from outside."

A Jihad founded upon "expansion of territory," as it has often been both on the part of the Arabs and of the Turks, can hardly be considered a Holy War. Yet for hundreds of years it was considered to be exactly that by both powers, not only in Europe but also in Africa, Asia, and the Near and Middle East. "Imperialism" and "colonialism" are better words for it.

The Jihad took over again after an obscure quarrel between Turkey, Poland, and Russia over the Don Cossacks in 1670. Both Poles and Russians were claiming sovereign rights over the Cossacks of the Don and of the Ukraine. A Polish army under John Sobieski, the ablest Polish general, was sent to the Ukraine to "coerce the Cossack malcontents," as Creasy puts it. The malcontents were willing to place themselves under the czar, but he was unable to accept them because of a treaty which then existed between Poland and Russia. So the Cossacks sent an envoy to Istanbul to ask the Turks for protection against the Poles. It was a very confusing situation. The Poles protested to the Sublime Porte over their interference, as did the Russians, who threatened to go to war against the Turks at the side of Poland. The Turks haughtily dismissed Russian protests. "Such is the strength of Islam that the union of Russians and Poles matters not to us. Our empire has increased in might since its origin; nor have all the Christian kings that have leagued against us been able to pluck a hair from our beard. With God's grace it shall ever be so and our empire shall endure to the day of judgement." There was a threat of war in the Ottoman message, but it was still essentially one inspired by religion: respect for one's own religion and contempt for the foes'. It was a warning of an approaching Jihad. With a bit of theology thrown in, this was naked imperialism.

The reply that Ahmed Kiuprili next made to the Poles was also a threat of war, but much more political and much less religious in nature. "The Cossacks, a free people, placed themselves under the Poles, but being unable to endure Polish oppression any longer, they have sought protection elsewhere, and they are now under the Turkish banner. If the inhabitants of an oppressed country, in order to obtain deliverance, implore the aid of a mighty emperor, is it prudent to pursue them in such an asylum?" Kiuprili finally also invoked Islam, wrapped up in a threat of military action. "If the solution of differences is referred to that keen and decisive judge called 'The Sword,' the issue of the strife must be pronounced by the God . . . by whose aid Islam has for a thousand years triumphed over its foes."

It's all there, the diplomatic and political presentation, the righteous indignation, and finally the warning of war, aided by a God who has always helped Islam to triumph: the threat of the Jihad. There is, of course, considerable hypocrisy in this reference to oppressed people seeking Ottoman aid. Turkey held many unwilling peoples in a state of servitude and was hardly in a position to lecture anyone on the evils of oppression. Turks and Christians practiced oppression equally when it suited them.

So the Ottoman empire went to war against Poland in 1672, defeating the Poles, who were made to cede Podolia and the Ukraine to the sultan and to pay him a heavy annual tribute. But John Sobieski, who had not been consulted over the treaty made by the "imbecile" (the quote is from Creasy) King Michael of Poland without consultation with the country's leaders, refused to accept it. The Ottoman army set out to fight both the Poles and the Russians. When Ahmed Kiuprili died, he was replaced as Grand Vizier by Mahomet IV's bisexual son-in-law Kara Mustapha, said to have been a close friend of his homosexual sultan father-in-law. Kara Mustapha was not particularly interested in fighting the Poles and the Russians. His main ambition in life was to fight and defeat Austria, and establish a new Muslim state west of Vienna, between the Danube and the Rhine, on the borders of France, with him as viceroy. Louis XIV's France would be the Ottoman empire's neighbor. The Dar-al-Islam would be dangerously near the Channel.

But for the moment the Cossack cause took up most of Kara Mustapha's time. Dissatisfied with the Sublime Porte, they revolted and Kara Mustapha was soundly beaten. By 1681 the Poles and the Russians were everywhere victorious. Within a few years, the Ukraine and Podolia would be back completely in the Slav domain. The shrinkage of the Ottoman empire was already under way, although Kara Mustapha failed completely to discern this fact. On the contrary, he planned to expand the empire. Vienna was on his mind, and beyond the Danube the rich Germanic lands all the way to the borders of France. On with the Jihad!

PART NINE

THE WANING OF HOLY WAR

53

NEVER WAS THERE
A VICTORY MORE COMPLETE:
VIENNA 1683

"IN 1682, KARA MUSTAPHA COMMENCED his fatal enterprise against Vienna," Creasy begins his account of the second attack against Vienna by the Turks—the first had been in 1529. "A revolt of the Hungarians under Count Tekeli, against Austria, which had been caused by the bigoted tyranny of the [Austrian] Emperor Leopold, now laid the heart of that empire open to attack; and a force was collected by the Grand Vizier, which, if ably handled might have given the House of Hapsburg its death-blow." (*History of the Ottoman Turks*, vol. 2, pp. 55–56)

Alas for the Muslims, and fortunately for the West, the force collected by Kara Mustapha was not ably handled at all. In fact, it was so mishandled that it wasn't the Hapsburg empire that received its death blow but the Ottoman empire that received the worst of the many heavy blows that were sending it reeling toward its own downfall, although that took another couple of centuries.

"It is probable that not less than half a million of men were set in motion in this last great aggressive effort of the Ottomans against Christendom," says Creasy, who obtained much of his information from Joseph Von Hammer's monumental *Histoire de l'Empire ottoman depuis son origine jusqu'à nos jours*, translated from the German and published in Paris between 1835 and 1848.* Along with its thousands

---

*Von Hammer's 10-volume opus remains the basic reference book on the Ottoman empire. It was Mr. von Hammer's lifetime mission, and is a work of staggering scholarship and thoroughness.

of camels, horses and mules, and even elephants, and guns, and muezzins to call the Janissaries and Spahis to prayer, and a harem to keep Kara Mustapha happy on the march, and scores of black eunuchs to keep the harem women in order, the last great Muslim assault on Christendom started from Edirne on March 31, 1683. Some quarter of a million fighting troops were once again sent off on a Holy War and promised all the sexual and gastronomic joys of Paradise if they died in battle. Picking up reinforcements in Wallachia, Moldavia, and Transylvania on the way, the great host arrived under the walls of Vienna three and a half months later, on July 14. A few miles from the city they massacred the four thousand inhabitants of the village of Perchtoldsdorf. It was a foretaste of what the Viennese could expect if their city fell to the attackers. From the top of the dilapidated battlements of the capital, the garrison watched the Turkish cavalrymen cantering around their city while a huge tent city sprang up where Kara Mustapha established his harem and his headquarters. Anxious not to damage Vienna, which he hoped would soon be his, Kara decided to starve out the inhabitants. That was his fatal mistake.

In the meantime, in soundly applying the popular dictum that discretion is the better part of valor, Emperor Leopold I had left the defense of his capital to the doughty Count Rudiger von Stahremberg and a garrison of eleven thousand men, while from the town of Passau, well away from the marauding Turks, Leopold I issued pathetic appeals for help to his fellow sovereigns all over Europe. Most of them didn't rush to reply. The pope sent his benediction, prayers, and best wishes; Louis XIV of France, whose kingdom to the west was constantly at war with the Hapsburg empire, magnanimously agreed not to attack it while Leopold was fighting the Turks to the east, thus at least sparing the Austrians from the peril of war on two fronts simultaneously. From Paris there also arrived in Passau a young aristocrat, Prince Eugene of Savoy-Carignon, determined to leave the service of the French king, who had ordered him to become a monk instead of a soldier. Prince Eugene joined his cousin, the margrave of Baden, and left for the Vienna region to fight in the army of Charles, Duke of Lorraine, against the Turks. In due course he became one of the greatest generals of his time, the victor a quarter century later, alongside Marlborough, of Bleinheim, Ramillies, Oudenarde, Malplaquet, and other great battles, not against the Turks, but against the French.

One king did reply, loud and clear, to Leopold's call for help. John Sobieski, now King John III of Poland, said he was on his way. The grateful Hapsburg, remembering that Sobieski had defeated the Turks in four battles in ten days in Poland nine years before, sent him an ecstatic message of thanks. "Your name alone, so terrible to the enemy, will ensure a victory," it read. John Sobieski had set out with three thousand cavalry to fight the Turkish army of 250,000 men to save Christendom. From across Germany eighteen thousand more soldiers joined the Polish hero, and from Poland another twenty-three thousand, all infantry, marched forth. By September 5 some sixty thousand Polish and German soldiers were assembling on Kahlenberg mountain to the northwest of Vienna, overlooking the city. The delivery of Vienna was at hand.

It came none too soon. The walls of the besieged city were crumbling under the continual pounding by the Turkish guns. Its few thousand defenders, by now maybe around ten thousand, were still ready to fight, but they were starving. Outside the city walls, Kara Mustapha waited for the city to surrender. "We'll wait," he told his military advisers who were urging him to attack, then disappeared behind the folds of his portable harem to enjoy the simple uxorious pleasures of a Muslim Grand Vizier, who was entitled to several dozen wives and concubines. He wanted to take an undamaged city, not one half destroyed by fighting. Patience was the only quality required, he said. Until the Poles actually arrived, Kara Mustapha did not believe that they were on their way. The siege of Vienna, with its city of tents and its exuberant social life, was pleasant and comfortable for the besieging army. One of the Poles who captured it described it as "an immense plain and all the islands of the Danube covered with pavilions, whose magnificence seemed rather calculated for an encampment of pleasures than the hardships of war."

Kara Mustapha's own tent was particularly luxurious. According to the German writer Paul Frischauer, it was full of "gardens with fountains, bathrooms with scented waters and soaps, sumptuous beds, shining lamps and chandeliers, carpets worked in silver and gold and all manners of other costly objects. . . . Besides richly chased weapons and embroidered clothing, Kara Mustapha's tent contained rabbits, dolphins, and every kind of bird. There was even an ostrich." The Jihad against Vienna was truly a sumptuous affair, for the Grand Vizier believed in the magnificence of Holy War.

From the top of Kahlenberg mountain, John Sobieski with his practiced military eye looked over the huge enemy camp. But he was was unimpressed, and wrote to his queen back in Poland that night,

"The general of an army who has neither thought of entrenching himself nor of concentrating his forces, but encamped as if we were a hundred miles from him, is predestined to be beaten." In spite of the huge superiority in numbers and weapons of the enemy, Sobieski felt certain of victory. "Kara Mustapha is badly encamped; he knows nothing of war; we shall certainly beat him," he said to the officers around him.

Von Starhremberg, advised by a secret messenger of the impending attack by his allies against the Turks in order to relieve the city which he had been staunchly defending for over two months, ordered all shingles to be taken off the roofs to avoid fires. The town had been unceasingly under attack from cannon fire and he also feared that being now aware of the arrival of the relieving force, the Turks might make a surprise attack under cover of darkness. Huge fires were lit throughout the city to turn the night into day and show up the enemy if they broke into the city.

But they never did. Instead the Poles and the Germans came down the mountain to assail the Turks. But first Sobieski addressed his troops. He knew how to go straight to the heart of the devout Poles. "It is not a city alone that we have to save, but the whole of Christianity, of which the city of Vienna is the bulwark. The war is a holy one," he cried out. The men from Warsaw crossed themselves, shouted hurrah, praised the Lord of hosts, and prepared to fight and die for God, for the Black Virgin of Czestochowa, for Poland, and maybe a bit for Vienna, too.

On the morning of September 12, the battle began with the long, four-hour descent by Sobieski's and Charles of Lorraine's troops down the mountainside. Kara Mustapha realized by this time that he was no longer the attacker but the attacked, and on two fronts; by the Poles and Germans coming down the Kahlenberg, and by the Vienna garrisons, who were preparing to make a sortie against their besiegers. He ordered the Janissaries to remain in their trenches facing Vienna, and then galloped off at the head of his Spahis to fight the Poles as they came down the mountainside. But the hearts of the Muslims were no longer in the fight. They were, above all, shaken by the presence of the dreaded Sobieski. "By Allah, the king is really among us," the khan of Crimea, Selim Ghirai, cried out in dismay when he recognized the Polish hero, and he turned his horse around and left the battlefield as fast as his horse could gallop.

By two o'clock in the afternoon, the Polish cavalry, seven thousand strong, were massed at the bottom of the mountain, armed with their long lances and pennants. So anxious were they to go into battle that some horsemen prepared to charge without orders, and were beaten back by their officers with the flat of their swords. "Wait until the king charges!" they shouted. Charles of Lorraine also stood nearby with his infantry, waiting to give the order to advance. In front, the Turks brought up the Muslim battle flag, a revered relic from Mecca. "By this sign," wrote a French soldier who was fighting among the Poles, "the Ottoman commander-in-chief reminded his troops that under this flag they must be victorious, or die in the attempt."

Sobieski, his sword drawn and pointing ahead, stood in his stirrups, turned around and shouted, "Charge!" Sitting upright on his saddle, he then rode straight for the Muslim banner. Shouting "Hurrah!" seven thousand Polish lancers and hussars galloped behind him, the pennants of their lances fluttering in the breeze. The Turks, usually so brave but now thoroughly demoralized, dropped the revered, holy banner from Mecca and fled, Kara Mustapha leading the flight. The young Prince Eugene entered Vienna with two regiments of Austrian dragoons; then with some of the garrison they charged the trenches where the Janissaries were posted facing the city, but on reaching the Turkish trenches, the Austrians found them empty. The Janissaries, the elite of the Turkish military, had fled, too.

It was no longer just a defeat, but a rout. The entire Turkish army had disappeared, Grand Vizier, Janissaries, harem and all. They were in such a hurry to leave that they didn't even have time to massacre the thirty thousand prisoners; men, women, and children, they had gathered from the surrounding countryside. But they did manage to decapitate the ostrich, and they deposited in a corner of the harem the headless corpse of Pearl of Loveliness, one of Kara Mustapha's concubines who apparently had refused to accompany her lord back to Istanbul. As the defeated, panic-stricken Turks fled back east, there were more beheadings as Kara Mustapha, in rage at his defeat, ordered the executions of the officers who had disagreed with him over the course of the campaign. One of them was the Pasha of Buda. That was another fatal mistake by Kara Mustapha, because the favorite wife of the executed Pasha was the beloved sister of Sultan Mahomet.

Back around Vienna, the jubilant Sobieski that night slept in Kara Mustapha's huge tent, after ordering the removal of the luckless and headless Pearl of Loveliness. The tent, he wrote to his wife, was as large as Warsaw. As for Prince Eugene, he hoped to be promoted to the rank of colonel for his role in the Austrian victory, but promotion was not yet forthcoming for the young Savoyard prince who was now committed to service for the Austrian emperor. The victors went around the abandoned camp gathering the spoils: 20,000 buffalo, 20,000 bulls and cows, 20,000 camels, 20,000 mules, 10,000 sheep and goats, 25,000 tents, 100,000 bags of corn, and thousands of bags of coffee, which the Viennese took home and brewed in their own way. And so the famous Vienna coffee was born.

The Jihad had turned sour for Kara Mustapha. It was to turn even more sour a few months later. On Christmas eve, back in Poland, John Sobieski solemnly entered the old capital of Cracow and went to midnight Mass in the cathedral, already three hundred years old. In Istanbul the next day, Christmas Day, Kara Mustapha was ordered to surrender the seals of office of Grand Vizier. He knew what that could mean. "Am I to die?" he asked, trying to sound nonchalant. The executioner nodded. "As Allah pleases," Kara Mustapha said. Like a true Muslim, he was a fatalist. He placed the silken cord around his neck and was duly and ritually strangled. The executioner then cut off Kara's head, stuffed it with straw, and nailed it to one of the city gates to remind passersby how fleeting life is and that it doesn't pay to be a loser.

54

THE JIHAD TOTTERS: GREECE AND HUNGARY 1685–1699

HE JIHAD WAS NOW WELL set on a downward course. The next blow against Islam came from the Venetians two years after the siege of Vienna. Francisco Morosini, the hero of the siege of Candia, reoccupied much of the Morea (the Peloponnese) in 1685. But alas, his successful campaign resulted in one of the greatest artistic disasters of all times. While bombarding the Turkish positions on the Acropolis in Athens, Morosini blew apart a large part of the Parthenon when one of his shells hit gunpowder stored in the building, which the Turks were using as an ammunition depot. So the temple of Athena, the most perfect expression of Doric art, built by the genius Phidias in the fifth century B.C.E., was indirectly a victim of the Jihad brouhaha. But it's the enemies of the Jihad who blew it up, or at least a great part of it; bits of it littered the Acropolis for more than a century. The Turks, who did not have an eye for great artistry, melted down some of the fragments into mortar.*

---

*About a century later a British diplomatic mission, headed by Lord Elgin, Ambassador to the Porte, a man seeped in art and good taste, arrived on the scene, and Lord Elgin immediately perceived the immense artistic value of all this broken masonry scattered on the ground. He collected the debris, to the delight of the Turks, who were very pleased to get rid of all this rubbish, shipped it in dozens of crates to England, usually in British warships—even Lord Nelson carried some home—where, known as the Elgin marbles, they have become one of the glories of the British Museum.

Meanwhile, another enemy, the Russians, besieged Azov in 1687; the next year the Austrians took Budapest, using bayonets for the first time in battle. In these wars, although the call to Holy War was inevitably invoked, the spirit was gone. The Jihad was becoming a loser. Another defeat awaited the Muslims in 1691 at Salankeman, on the Danube, not far from Belgrade. Under their Grand Vizier, Kiuprili the Virtuous, the Ottomans prepared to charge the Imperial army fighting to free Hungary from the Turks. "Courage," cried the Muslim general to his massed troops, eager to fight the Christians, "the houris are waiting for you." The Ottoman cavalry, six thousand horsemen, mainly Kurds and Turcomans, shouted "Allah is great" and charged. Thousands were killed, but they died happy, in the expectation of Paradise. The Austrians captured 150 of the Turkish guns, marched on, and liberated a large chunk of Hungary.

Throughout these centuries, the Jihad had been a masquerade, but at least it had been a winner. The Jihad was still a masquerade, but now it was a loser. Fighting for the Jihad, the Janissaries had become the best professional soldiers in the world, as well as the most efficient looters and rapists. But they were no longer the elite troops of yore. In fact, by now they had become an unruly, mutinous, and murderous assemblage of soldiers. When Sultan Mahomet IV died and was replaced by his brother Suleiman II, the Janissaries objected to the nomination as Grand Vizier of one Siavuch Pasha. They attacked his palace, killed him while he was trying to defend his harem, cut off his head, raped his wives and concubines, and dragged his sister and one of his wives naked through the streets.

The Ottoman empire was not only collapsing at home; it was collapsing even more spectacularly abroad. After the victories of yesteryear, defeats and trouncings were now the order of the day. In 1685 Charles of Lorraine, Prince Eugene's commander at the relief of Vienna, defeated the Turks at Gran, took Buda, and in 1687 attacked and defeated them at Mohacs, a name of sinister memory for the Christians of the Balkans and central Europe. The Austrians took Croatia, which had been a Muslim colony for 145 years. Transylvania soon afterward slipped off the Ottoman leash and put on the Hapsburg one. In 1688, Budapest, after having been temporarily lost to the Turks, was taken again by Prince Max Emmanuel of Bavaria. Turkey was no longer the terror of Europe. The time had come, Emperor Leopold said, to throw the Turks out of Europe, back into Anatolia. But the Turks had other ideas. A mixed Tatar/Ottoman force occupied Kosovo in 1690, the Austrians abandoned Belgrade, and, so it is claimed, thousands of Serbs (estimates vary from 30,000 to 40,000), many of them from Kosovo, in an operation known as The Great Migration, fled to Hungary for refuge.

Fortunately for the Turks they had a powerful, if unofficial, ally in western Europe. Louis XIV of France was increasingly concerned over the growing power of Austria. He visualized the Austrian Hapsburgs as the main rivals to the French Bourbons in the power struggle underway in continental Europe. Turkey was obviously making its way out of the European big league. For the Sun King, as Louis XIV was known to his contemporaries, the Hapsburgs represented far more of a threat than the Turks did. He was not unduly perturbed over the Jihad. He was probably right. By now the Jihad was a spent force. The Turks were becoming more and more absurd and less and less terrifying. To create a diversion, Louis attacked the Rhineland, on the outer fringes of the Austrian empire, and Charles of Lorraine marched west to fight the French instead of marching east to fight the Turks. Austria was not alone on the anti-French front. In the west, Sweden, Spain, Bavaria, Saxony, and England were all also busily fighting the armies of the French king in an obscure, nine-year conflict known as the War of the League of Augsburg. In the east, Islam was the enemy and Austria was the sole champion of Christendom.

As the century was drawing to its close Prince Eugene, only thirty years old but now a field-marshal, took command of the armies of the Hapsburgs and went out to challenge the Turks to battle. Christians and Muslims clashed for two hours before sundown on September 11, 1697, at Zenta, some eighty miles northwest of Belgrade on the Tisza River. Prince Eugene caught the Turkish army with one half on one side of the river, the other half on the other side. By nightfall, twenty thousand Turks were lying dead on the battlefield, and the drowned corpses of ten thousand others, who had tried to flee by swimming across, were floating in the river. Prince Eugene's soldiers were busy counting the booty for days. It was enormous. Oxen, camels, and horses became some of the cheapest commodities on the market. It was too late in the season to take the well-defended town of Belgrade; Eugene moved across to raid Bosnia and took Sarajevo.

Two years after the battle of Zenta, the Turks sued for peace. It was signed at Karlowitz in 1699, and by the general opinion of historians it marks the beginning of the end of the Ottoman empire as a great power. It certainly marks the first obvious collapse of the triumphant

Muslim Holy War. For the first time in the history of the Ottoman empire, the Turkish delegation traveled abroad to negotiate with its foe. Before that, any king, emperor, or nation wishing to treat with the Turk had to send its delegations to Istanbul to humble itself before the sultan. The journey from Istanbul to Karlowitz must have been a very chastening one for the Turks.

"The elementary tidal force of Turkish conquest had ebbed and subsided. . . . The Treaty of Karlowitz marked a final, decisive turning point in the military balance between Europe and the Islamic world. . . . After Karlowitz, the Turkish empire found itself perpetually on the defensive, seldom able to equal the armed strength of any European power," is how Professor Paul Coles described the Turks' first moment of decline. "The Treaty of Karlowitz marks a turning point in Ottoman history," comments the *Cambridge History of Islam*. The Jihad had become a toothless tiger. "The Ottoman Empire, which had terrified Christendom for over three hundred years, ceased to be an aggressive power. From now on, it mainly fought rearguard actions against the overwhelming might of Christian Europe." In *Kosovo* (p. 139), Noel Malcolm described the story of the Ottoman empire from this point forward as one "of historical contraction and loss."

Creasy saw Karlowitz as the moment when "all serious dread of Turkey ceased in Europe." And, quoting Schlosser's *History of the 18th Century*, he added: "Turkey's importance has become diplomatic. Other nations have from time to time sought to use her as a political machine against Austria, or the growing power of Russia" as the British later did in the Napoleonic wars, and the French and British in the Crimean War. From being a superpower, the standard-bearer of the Jihad, the fighter for the cause of Islam, Turkey after Karlowitz gradually slipped among the ranks of the plain, ordinary, second-rate powers, to be slightly courted for the help it could give in any conflict, major or minor, in which it would never again be the major participant. After Karlowitz, Turkey no longer bestrode this narrow world like a colossus; it had joined the ranks of the has-beens.

The architect of victory had been Prince Eugene, the affable aristocrat from Savoy, man of the world, of indefinite identity, a Parisian who fought against France alongside Marlborough in his greatest battles, and usually won. Prince Eugene, perhaps more than any other single man, set the Ottoman empire on the way to its final destruction. Thanks to his victory at Zenta he won freedom for Hungary, which had been under Muslim rule for nearly a century and a half. One should say "a sort of freedom," because Hungary only exchanged Turkish domination—in which as "rayahs" they were literally considered the equivalent of "cattle" by their Turkish masters—for domination by the Hapsburgs, who turned their imperial realm into the Austro-Hungarian empire. Transylvania, Croatia, and much of Dalmatia were also allocated to the Hapsburgs by the Treaty of Karlowitz. Venice received the Morea, Poland acquired Podolia, and Russia took over the region of Azov. The Ottoman empire, after Karlowitz, was tottering. But, miraculously, it went on tottering for another 220 years, and with it the Jihad also tottered on.

55

THE GRAVEDIGGERS:
CENTRAL AND SOUTHEASTERN
EUROPE 1716–1770

W E ARE NOW IN AN Ottoman empire awaiting burial. The chief gravedigger is Prince Eugene. The successful repulse of the Turkish assault on Vienna in 1689, followed by Prince Eugene's victory at Zenta in 1697, to be crowned by the Treaty of Karlowitz two years later, were the main stages in a final series of reverses that led to a lasting disappearance of the Jihad as a major ingredient in European land and sea warfare. It also disappeared for nearly three centuries, until these last two or three decades, as an element in international politics. The self-styled Jihad of today, however, has no connection with Turkey—a country greatly admired by all for the past eighty years—although it does have an important one with some other countries. But that is a mainly extra-European matter, not ours, and within Europe we must remain.

These Ottoman wars against the Venetian doges, the Austrian emperors, and the Russian czars (and, we could add, the Persian shahs) formed part of a long seesawing series of military campaigns, part holy war, part imperialist, but all expansionist, in which huge numbers of people were killed, tremendous acreages of land were lost and won and lost again, while the Ottoman empire gradually slipped into the strange combination of coma and chaos which turned Turkey for a couple of hundred years into "the sick man of Europe" (Creasy, *A History of the Ottoman Turks,* vol. 1, p. 392).

"Of Europe," let it be emphasized. From the nineteenth century, no one doubted the Europeanness of Turkey. Turkish delight is as European as English toffee. But the Europeanness of Turkey, although resented sometimes for historical or religious reasons, was never queried and it should not be now. Its state of political health was another matter. Yet remember, Turkey and Britain, so very different, are both part of Europe just as India and Japan, equally different from each other, are both part of Asia. I am inclined to think that Turkey is as least as European in its sentiments as England is. Perhaps more.

The sick man of Europe was moribund, but taking a long time dying through defeat after defeat and the massacres it either inflicted on its subject peoples, notably the Greeks, or suffered from them. Massacres were mutual and equally ferocious. Generally speaking, the Muslims were more efficient at it than the Christians. They had, after all, more experience, and the Koran, unlike the New Testament, does not discourage its readers from slaughter. Pacifism is a Christian virtue, not a Muslim one; Muhammad never told his followers to turn the other cheek.

The Turks, through their appalling military debacles, had become more and more the subject of international derision and less and less the object of universal fear. The wars they were fighting by the eighteenth century were even less related to religion than before and were more concerned with European power politics than with spreading the Koranic message. The Jihad had become excess baggage of the Muslim armies rather than their motivating force. The ardor had gone, inevitably after so many hundreds of years of continual ideological usage, and Islam is even more an ideology than a religion. Turkey, unlike so many other Muslim countries, has had the courage to look into itself. Islam was throttling it.

The Dardanelles, because of their strategic position, always played a major part in the military operations of the Ottoman empire. In 1715, precisely 200 years before our Gallipoli campaign of World War I, a flotilla of Turkish warships passed through the straits on their way to the Adriatic and a Turkish army from Bursa crossed them on its way to new European battlefields. It was clear to the fearful European powers that Turkey was preparing to fight another war in Europe. When the Austrians asked for an explanation, the Turks assured them that Venice was their target. Perhaps they assured the Venetians that Austria was the target. Prince Eugene now reappears in our narrative He felt sure that Austria was the Turkish objective, and his instinct was right. Now only fifty-two years old, Prince Eugene was back in Vienna after his great victories a few years earlier with Marlborough against the French at Blenheim, Ramillies, and other battlefields.

Eugene did not appreciate the Turks. When he wrote to the Grand Vizier advising him that Austria might have to defend itself by taking the offensive, he received a vituperative reply, not at all in the refined style of European diplomacy, warning him that an Austrian attack against Turkey "would cause his ignominious downfall and everything unholy would overtake his children and grandchildren." As Eugene had no children or grandchildren—his nearest relative was a nephew— the Turkish threats passed over his head and, in 1716, he installed his headquarters near the town of Peterwardein, not far from Belgrade. A force of at least 100,000 Turks crossed the Save River and marched to meet him. With an army half as big, Prince Eugene marched out of Peterwardein and the two armies clashed in battle on August 5. The victory went to the Savoyard prince once again. Austrian casualties came to five thousand; the Turks lost twenty thousand killed and wounded. The pope sent Prince Eugene a hat and a sword set in diamonds, with a message thanking him for "his services for the cause of Christendom and the Catholic Church." On the Christian side the battle had a touch of the Holy War about it, too.

From Peterwardein Eugene swept on, sent one of his armies into Rumania and the next year captured Belgrade and the last shreds of Hungarian territory, Temeavar, and the county of Temes, which had been under Turkish rule for 165 years. All of Hungary was now free; the Magyars had at last come into their own. But for Prince Eugene the victory was only partial. He wanted to march on to Istanbul, retake the old capital of the Byzantine empire, and drive the Turks into Asia Minor. His old adversary, the French duke of Villars, marshal of France, whom he and Marlborough had fought six years ago at Malplaquet, wrote to him a warm letter of congratulations after his victory at Peterwardein. "This is a great day for the emperor and his famous general. I renew my prophecy and set the Black Sea as the goal of your victories." Istanbul is only a dozen miles from the Black Sea; the inference was quite obvious. No great army now stood between Prince Eugene and Istanbul. But the Hapsburgs hankered for a rest and the Turks were happy to end the war, so peace was signed the next year at Passarowitz and Prince Eugene's fighting days were over. The capture of Belgrade had been his last big battle.

Listed by Napoleon as one of the seven greatest military commanders of all times, Prince Eugene lived for another eighteen years as an elder statesman and army reformer. More than any other man of his time, he gutted the Jihad and turned it into one of the redundant forces of history. He died in 1736 at the age of seventy-three. The year of his death the Ottoman empire again went to war, this time against the combined forces of Austria and Russia. History judges this conflict as merely one more passage of endemic warfare in the convoluted annals of European power politics. It is difficult to consider this war as a Jihad, although the Janissaries and the spahis who fought in it undoubtedly viewed it as such. After all, if they were killed, their entrance into the Muslim Paradise depended on its official status as a Holy War. No Holy War, no Paradise (at least, not in the immediate future), no houris, no lovely meals on gold plates. For a Muslim warrior, this was an important matter which would make a big difference both to his life and to his afterlife.

During the last years of his long reign (1703–1730), Sultan Achmed II had waged a Jihad against the Persian Shiites over territory in the Caucasus mountains; during the final year of the sultan's reign the Persians drove the Turks out of the region, at least for a few decades. Sultan Mahmoud I, who followed Achmed to the throne, had to cope with a revolt in Istanbul led by a Janissary rebel named Patrona, who obliged Mahmoud to appoint to a high post Patrona's friend, the Greek butcher Yanaki. The loyal Janissaries mutinied against Yanaki and the upstart Petrona, who were both executed along with seven thousand of their followers. The Grand Vizier, the "skilful, sage and valiant" (says Creasy) Topal Osman, led the Ottoman army against the Persians, who were laying siege to Baghdad and managed to save the city, but the Ottoman troubles were not over. Turkey's next source of war was Russia, the foe whom the Turks feared most of all. A Russian victory was judged inevitable. "The decay in [Ottoman] military force was considered to be irretrievable," observed a nineteenth-century historian. But the French military writer Chevalier de Folard considered there were no better fighters anywhere than the Turks. He attributed Turkish inferiority on the battlefield to their neglect of the bayonet as a weapon. "The Turks are defeated only because of the deficiencies of their weapons," he wrote. "They do not know what is a bayonet at the tip of their guns. For, since this weapon was invented, they have never been able to beat the Christians." The demise of "the sick man of Europe" was seen everywhere as inevitable in the immediate future, and the European chancelleries were already discreetly carving the empire up among themselves, a pastime that went on for a couple of hundred years.

One highly respected observer of the European political scene who gauged the future of the Ottoman empire accurately was the Frenchman Charles, Baron de Montesquieu, whose philosophy of government, contained in his famous 31-volume *The Spirit of the Laws* (which went through twenty-two editions in two years, but who reads it nowadays?), was to help frame the American Constitution a half century later. With the clarity of mind that marked all his studies of the human political genius, Montesquieu bluntly stated in his lesser known *On the Causes of the Greatness of the Romans and of their Decadence*: "The Ottoman Empire will survive a long time." His statement was in complete contradiction to what all the political and diplomatic experts were saying at the time. But he considered, and events proved him right, that Turkey's great weakness was, in fact, her great strength, for "if any ruler placed this empire in danger by extending his conquests, the trading nations of Europe know their business too well not to go to its defense immediately."

This is precisely what happened. Britain and France at various times gave their full diplomatic, and sometimes military, support to Turkey in its wars against the Russian and Austrian empires. The Austrians and the Russians were extending their conquests too far and by becoming too powerful at the expense of the Turks were also thus becoming a threat to their rivals in western Europe. The Jihad didn't enter into their considerations. It was tough, nose-to-the-grindstone, balance-of-power international politics. Holy War was developing into public relations usage, a propaganda weapon of war, a technique which, used with guile and cunning, can be very effective against a gullible enemy.

A connection that suddenly reappears between Turkey and Poland seems both unreal and remote. Yet, for some reason which, to us today has a touch of delirium about it, the Turks attacked Russia for aggression against Poland. Russia retaliated by accusing Turkey of conniving at Tatar attacks against the Cossacks in the Ukraine, and the two countries went to war. The Russians took Azov, raided Crimea, and ordered the Muslim Tatar khan to sever all his country's links with Istanbul. The khan refused. The Muscovites and the Cossacks under field marshal Burkhard von Munnich, a German in Russian service, invaded Crimea in 1736 and, in a campaign of incredible ferocity, laid the country waste, slaughtered thousands of innocent villagers, burned hundreds of villages, and finally had to return to Russia leaving behind 30,000 dead from hunger and disease. In a retaliatory campaign the Tatars invaded the Ukraine, defeated the Russians, and took 30,000 Ukrainian and Russian captives back to Crimea for a lifetime of slavery. Further east, Russian troops who invaded the Kuban, in Asia, forced the Muslim inhabitants to change their alliance from the sultan to the czar, or rather the czarina, for Russia was then ruled by a woman, Anne, one of Russia's lesser imperial lights, best remembered today for having an English husband and a German lover.

The Russians, joined by the Austrians, met the Turks at Nimiroff in 1737 to hammer out a peace agreement which hammered out nothing but expressed many pious thoughts. However imperialist the three countries may have been, there was always a dash of Holy War within their pronouncements, even if it was quite plain that everyone was fighting for land and power rather than for Jesus or Muhammad. The Turks were on the defensive, with the Austrians claiming more lands in Serbia and Bosnia and Wallachia, and the Russians, anxious to establish themselves on the Black Sea, demanding Crimea and the Kuban, free passage to and from the Black Sea and the Mediterranean through the Bosporus and the Dardanelles, and, like the Austrians, a slice of Bosnia and Wallachia.

The Turks quoted from the Koran copiously and also, curiously, from the New Testament. The Christians repeatedly reminded the Turks of the belligerent passages in the Koran calling for the deaths of the Christians. No one agreed about anything, but they did agree to say they disagreed, both sides prayed together, then everyone went back to fighting. The sword, finally, was the argument everyone understood best.

The Russians under General Lascy invaded Crimea, field marshal von Munnich marched into Moldavia, part of which was under Turkish rule, and Russians and Turks met in battle at Khotin, where an army of 68,000 solid, stolid Russians defeated an army of 90,000 mercurial Turks. An estimated seventeen thousand Turkish soldiers who had surrendered after the fall of the city of Ocsakow were massacred by the Russians.

It was a bloody victory for the Russians, but a dead-end one. That year the Austrians, aghast at the successes of their Russian allies, began to fear for their own future, that the Russians might next triumph against them. So they made peace with the Turks—at the whispered instigation of the French.

France, well versed in the delicate and devious techniques of bal-

ance-of-power politics, wanted a strong Turkey to counterbalance Austrian and Russian muscle. If a country grows too strong, take his
enemy's side: Montesquieu's commonsense prophecy was already
coming true. At the Treaty of Belgrade (1739), Russia agreed to dis-
mantle her fortresses at Azov, and Austria evacuated northern Serbia.
Turkey recovered a small part of the empire it had recently lost. Islam
was still strongly embedded on European soil, but the threats against it
were growing. Under Catherine the Great, who came to the throne of
Russia in 1762 and reigned for thirty-four years, the gutting of the
Ottoman empire continued in earnest.

An overall geographic view of the zones of the Russo-Turkish
wars is in order, for the "front" was a widespread one. There were four
major zones of operations. We could call one of these zones the
Danube front, which included southern Poland and the Balkans. The
second front was the central and eastern Black Sea shores, with Crimea
the vital center, and the Russians' Muslim enemies included the
Crimean Tatars as well as the Turks. Third, there was what we could
call the Mediterranean campaign, largely naval, fought mainly in the
Aegean Sea and in Greece itself. The Caucasus, on the outer fringes of
Europe, where it slips into Asia, with its Christian lands of Armenia
and Georgia, was the fourth front. Meanwhile, the Turks were also
fighting the Austrians in the Danube region.

The wars between Russia and Turkey that broke out again in 1768
were to be continuously repeated over the next century and a half.
Moreover, the male chauvinist Turks to their puzzlement were now
facing two mighty female opponents: Catherine the Great in Russia,
and Maria Theresa of Austria. The ostensible reason for the war
between the Turks and the Austrian was, again, Poland. Although
Turkey's record toward its own subjects was appalling ("You can see
from the road naked and still living men caught on long spikes where
they will have to remain until death delivers them," wrote the Italian
traveler Bocaretto visiting Turkey in the 1760s), the Ottoman empire
preened itself as an international defender of human rights. The Turks
were determined to protect the Poles from the Russians, Prussians, and
Austrians. Polish rebels fighting for their country habitually found
refuge in the nearby Ottoman territories of Moldavia and Wallachia to
the south. The Tatars, descendants of the Mongols of the Golden
Horde, and Muslims for four hundred years, were always actively anti-
Russian. There was also intense diplomatic and sometimes military
activity by the western European countries who, hoping for tidbits,

swirled hungrily around a diminishing Turkish empire, widely considered to be in its death throes.

Everyone was lining up for his slice of the Ottoman imperial domain. At the same time, the western European governments viewed Russian interventions in Europe with grave disquiet. The Austrians wondered how the demise of Turkey would strengthen the position of Russia in the Danube region; the British, for their part, were worried that Russia's determination to find herself a warm water port in the Mediterranean region would inevitably lead to a clash with the Royal Navy, always suspicious of any budding foreign naval enterprise. But Turkey was now an active participant in eastern and central European politics, in which the Jihad factor, although not dominant, was always present.

Catholic Poland now turned snarlingly against its Muslim friend Turkey. Pressed by the Russians, the Polish government declared war against the Ottoman empire. The furious sultan, Mustapha III, profoundly vexed at ungrateful Poland's turnabout policy, transformed this new conflict into a full-blown Jihad and ordered his mufti to declare the war sacred. The mufti, Pirizadi Osman Effendi, who knew the virtue of obedience to the sultan-caliph, and who was, as well, a fanatic who believed that all Christians should be massacred, pronounced a public fatwa against Poland. For good measure, he then issued a second fatwa calling for the massacre of Moldavians and Wallachians who, in a recent conflict, had cooperated with the Russians. When the two principalities immediately went over to the Russian side, the angry mufti then tried to persuade the sultan to have all the Christians throughout the Ottoman empire executed. The proposal went before the ruling Divan, who voted against it, and all of Istanbul heaved a sigh of relief when this zealous cleric unexpectedly died that year.

56

THE ORLOFF-SUVAROV DUET: THE MEDITERRANEAN AND CRIMEA 1770–1792

THE WAR BETWEEN RUSSIA AND Turkey also had a picturesque naval side. In 1770 an imposing Russian fleet, made up of twelve ships-of-the-line, twelve frigates, and several troop transports sailed from the Baltic port of Kronstadt for the Mediterranean to help the Greeks, who were in revolt against their Turkish masters. The squadron was commanded by the brother of the Empress' lover, Count Alexis Orloff, but at least one admiral, John Elphinston, several of the captains, and many of the officers were British, on leave from the Royal Navy. The Turks, whose notions of geography were often erratic, did not believe it possible for ships to sail from the Baltic to the Mediterranean, and when the Russian ships reached the Greek coast, the Porte sent a bitter note of protest to the Venetian Republic for allowing the Russian ships to sail down the Adriatic to Greece.

The fleet landed its troops on the Greek mainland where the local population, encouraged by their appearance, at once rose in revolt and massacred thousands of perfectly peaceful Turks, men, women, and children. One of the favorite Greek pastimes was to climb up to the top of the minarets and drop Turkish children to the ground, preferably in front of their parents, whom they would also slaughter afterward. "They practiced the most revolting cruelties upon all the Turks whom they could overpower in the open country or less defensible towns," says Creasy. Misitra in particular was the scene of fearful carnage,

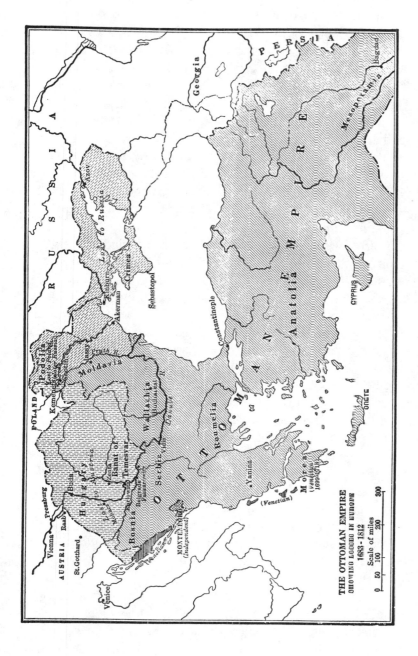

Source: William Stearns Davis, *A Short History of the Near East* (New York: Macmillan, 1922).

afterward still more fearfully avenged. Four hundred Turks were slaughtered there in cold blood.

Admiral Orloff called on all Greeks to rise in defense of their religion against their Turkish masters, "as their fellow Christians had done in Moldavia and Wallachia, to the number of 600,000," he claimed. He then sailed away with his troops, leaving the locals in Morea to cope. They didn't. The Turks reestablished their authority with appalling reprisals. The Greeks who survived hunched their heads into their shoulders, sat tight and waited for their day to come around again. It did, fifty years later, and the poet Lord Byron that time made their struggle famous.

As for Orloff, he went on waging a successful naval war against the Turks in the Aegean Sea, defeated a squadron off the island of Chios and pursued its defeated ships into the narrow harbor waters of Chesme. A handful of volunteer British officers in Orloff's squadron, led by Admiral Elphinston, sailed fireships right into the Turkish fleet, burned nearly every one of the vessels at anchor, including a 100-gun battleship, another of 96 guns, four of 84 guns, a 74, and 70, and six 60-guns ships. Only one ship of the line survived the firestorm to be boarded and captured. After the battle, fought on July 6, 1770, Elphinston impetuously proposed that the Russian fleet head for the Dardanelles and Istanbul, but Orloff dithered. The Turks took advantage of the delay and of the visit of a French artillery expert, the Baron du Tott, to strengthen their defenses in the Dardanelles, through which the Russians would have to sail to attack the capital. So the opportunity was lost. Orloff made a half-hearted attempt to sail into the strait, turned back, landed his sailors and soldiers on Lemnos, and laid siege to a castle on the island. The siege lasted sixty days and ended suddenly and brutally when a force of four thousand Turkish volunteers, recruited from among the criminal riffraff of Istanbul's jails, landed on the island shouting "Allah is great," and, led by an Algerian corsair named Hassan, chased the Russians back to their ships.

For the rest of the war Orloff crisscrossed haphazardly the eastern Mediterranean, captured an island or two and a few Ottoman merchantmen, and allied himself with an Egyptian bey in rebellion against the Turks. But the whole enterprise ended in ashes when four hundred of the Russians who had been ordered to join the Egyptian rebels were nearly all killed, some in battle, some by decapitation. Only four lucky survivors managed to make their way back to Mother Russia.

Crimea, home of the Muslim Tatars, associates and tributaries of the Turks, was a favorite Russian target. It was perhaps particularly attractive to Catherine the Great and her advisers, facing the long, cold winters of St. Petersburg, because of its balmy, sunny climate. One of Catherine's great claims to historical fame—in addition to her numerous lovers—is that she won the Crimea for Russia. "It had been reserved for Catherine II to strike down the last stem of the Tatar stock by subjugating the Khanate of the Crimea," grandly comments Creasy.

When Crimea was invaded by several Russian armies, the khan of Crimea fled and the Russians captured all the main towns of the peninsula. The Russians seemed irresistible and the Tatars, faced with their overwhelming numbers and strength, and the inability of the Turks to come to their rescue, took an oath of allegiance to Catherine of Russia, much as it must have irked them, as Muslims, to do so to a woman who was, moreover, a Christian. In the meantime the Russians also occupied the come-and-go principalities of Besserabia, Wallachia, and Moldavia in the Danube region. Russia was, in fact, becoming so powerful that Frederick the Great of Prussia, to deflect the fears and channel the strength of Russia's neighbors, particularly Austria, came up with the suggestion that the weakest among them, Poland, should be partitioned among his country, Austria, and Russia, which was duly carried out in 1772.

Two years later, in the small Danubian village of Kainarji, the first war between Catherine the Great and the Turks came to an end with a treaty which made Crimea independent of the Turks, returned Moldavia and Wallachia to the Turks on condition that they rule the two principalities more leniently in the future, and gave the Russians the right of supervision. In fact, Turkey had been turned into a semi-tributary of Russia. In what turned out to be the most important clause in the treaty, Turkey, the land of the Jihad, agreed to protect the Christian churches in its empire, and to give Russian representatives in Istanbul the right to intervene on their behalf. Poland, the country over which Turkey had gone to war against Russia, was not even mentioned. It didn't exist any more, anyway.

Turkey's Jihad role was now so diminished that it was unrecognizable. Turkey, once an unquenchable fighter in the cause of Islam, had now become officially the protector of Christianity and of Christians throughout its imperial domains. But Turkey had been placed in a very favorable political position. No country wanted Turkey, no longer just the sick man but the joke of Europe, to fall to any other country. Every European power labored to keep the Ottoman empire, once so feared, alive and independent to prevent its alliance with a foe. And so the empire miraculously lingered on until the 1920s. Muted and subdued, the Jihad also lingered on.

As the eighteenth century wound down to its close, the situation did not stagnate. Catherine the Great, who disputed the Europeanness of the Turks, as Prince Eugene had a few decades earlier, was anxious to drive them out of Europe. But she wanted foreign help. With the assistance of Prince Potemkin, her adviser and lover, she offered the British a deal: "I'll help you to fight to keep the American colonists if you help me to get the Turks out of Europe." Nothing came of the proposal, which simply lapsed into oblivion. Britain fought without Russian aid against the Americans and lost, and Russia fought without British aid against the Turks and lost too in her grand anti-Turkish design. The Turks stayed in Europe and became, by geography, history, and vocation, more and more European.

In 1783, without seeking approval, Russia incorporated Crimea into the Russian empire, to the impotent fury of the Turks. Four years later Sultan Abdul Hamid "unfurled the Sacred Standard of the Prophet, proclaimed a holy war, and summoned the True Believers to assemble round the banner of their faith." The Jihad sounded as if it was back in its old fighting form, but it was merely an old and tired version of the holy war that had once been. Catherine the Great, an expansionist, now had Georgia on her mind and Austria as an ally. She gave the command of her armies in the southern Ukraine to field marshal Count Alexander Suvorov. The old campaigner was coarse, brutal, and fearless. The bayonet was his dream weapon. "Push hard with the bayonet," he urged his soldiers, whom he always addressed as "Brother," and who worshiped him. He was perhaps an unattractive man, but he was a brilliant soldier. He had fought against the Prussians in the 1750s, against the Poles in the 1760s, and against the Turks in the 1770s. In the next couple of decades, he was to fight against the armies of the French Revolution in Italy.

The new Ottoman war against Russia went on for five years, until 1792, and was fought largely to the northwest of the Crimea, in what is today southern Ukraine, between Odessa and the mouth of the Danube, where Suvorov defeated the Turks at Kilburn and, later, further east at Ismail, on the northern bank of the Danube, about forty miles from the Black Sea. The Scots-born American sailor hero John Paul Jones suddenly and unexpectedly appeared in the middle of this little-known conflict in command of the the Russian Black Sea fleet and sank fifteen Turkish ships with the loss of only one frigate.

Some 33,000 Turks were killed during the battles of the southern Ukraine siege and battle, and 10,000 taken prisoner. Thousands more men, women, and children were butchered by the Russians, and the record of this massacre stains the memory of Suvorov to this day. The Austrians fought a desultory war in Wallachia and Moldavia, and against the Bosnian Muslims. Britain and the other European powers were more concerned over Russia's new and manifest imperialism than over Turkey's dying Muslim Holy War. The British prime minister, William Pitt, expressed the concern of his country in the House of Commons debate in which he made it clear that "the principle by which the foreign policy of this country should be directed is the fundamental principle of preserving the balance of power in Europe." And, Pitt added, "the true doctrine of the balance of power requires that the Russian Empire should not, if possible, be allowed to increase, nor that of Turkey to diminish." It was now no longer the scaring eagle of bygone days but a pigeon with a broken wing.

Mr. Pitt quite obviously no longer considered the Jihad a threat. Perhaps he was not even aware of the existence of the Jihad as such. Of one thing he felt certain: Muslim Turkey was less of a threat to international peace than Christian Russia. In the context of the times, Mr. Pitt was right. The Jihad barely existed at the time except in the sermons of powerless mullahs, and perhaps as a slogan to be repeated at the mosque on Fridays. The Jihad was a relic; it seemed a thing of the past.

The Treaty of Jassy ended the war in 1792. Russia's new border was fixed much further south, along the Dnieper River. Moldavia and Bessarabia were given back again to the Turks. And the Christian Caucasus principality of Georgia, so close to Catherine's heart, where no fighting had taken place at all, was recognized to be under the protection of Russia.

A new lineup of power was underway in Europe, under Russian aegis in the east; and under French aegis in the west, where France had proclaimed itself a Republic, beheaded its king, and launched a new international ideological crusade based on republicanism and the Rights of Man. The revolution was as intense and virulent and idealistic as the old Jihad, and with just as much taste for plunder, terror, and conquest as its Muslim counterpart. But God, this time, was not involved. Not even Robespierre claimed to be his prophet. Only the Supreme Being was concerned, and no one knew exactly who he was. The French Republican experience was indeed bloody in its violent birth pangs during its first couple of years, but no bloodier than the Islamic one after 1200 years of settled existence.

PART TEN

WARRIORS OF A WILLING DOOM

57

TO THE SHORES OF TRIPOLI: NORTH AFRICA 1798–1830

MANY OF EUROPE'S MOST ILLUSTRIOUS Christian warriors have, down the ages, fought the Jihad. This book has mentioned quite a few, Don John of Austria, Charles Martel, Leo the Isaurian, Prince Eugene, Montecuccoli, Andrea Doria, El Cid, Sobieski, Charlemagne, Suvorov, Boucicaut, Hunyadi, Fernando III of Castile, Alfonso I of Aragon, Guiscard, and Harold Hardrada. There have been many others and now, as we reach the late eighteenth century, we can add Napoleon Bonaparte to the list.

It was unthinkable that Napoleon, the greatest soldier of them all, and the Jihad should not run into each other at some time. They did, in Egypt, notably at the famed Battle of the Pyramids in 1798, in Syria the following year at the siege of Acre and at the battle of Mount Tabor, and that same year again back in Egypt at the Battle of Aboukir.

As one of the world's greatest practitioners of *realpolitik* the future emperor of the French tried, most blatantly during his two years in Egypt, to recruit Muhammad and Allah into the French camp. In Cairo he would from time to time prance around dressed up in some sort of Muslim costume, in which he looked absurd, masquerading as a Muslim scholar. He would spout verses from the Koran to his bewildered listeners or learnedly chat about Allah to imams and mullahs who pretended to be impressed but were not. One of his senior commanders, General Menou, tried to win the confidence of the locals by

371

converting to Islam and changing his first name from Jacques to Abdallah. He also married some local bint (Arab word for a young girl) and prayed several times a day, bowing ostentatiously in the direction of Mecca.

None of these posturings was of any avail. The local Muslims judged these performances for what they were: humbug. And the Muslims were always ready to revolt against their French occupants. The dominant presence in Cairo of the French was foreign and Christian, and therefore intolerable, and when a revolt broke out messengers ran through the street, shouting, "Let those who believe there is but one God take themselves to the Mosque El Azhar! For today we fight the infidel!" It was the Jihad, in its pure, basic form. Shedding his Islamic pretensions, Bonaparte on this occasion ordered his artillery to start shelling the mosque. "Exterminate everybody in the mosque!" he shouted to one of his generals. The mob, led by their religious leaders, went on a rampage that lasted until the evening of the next day. They massacred thirty-three French hospital patients caught in a convoy of ambulances and gave the body of a murdered French general to the dogs to eat. Two thousand Muslim warriors attacked the river boat *Italia,* beached just below Karnak and carrying down the Nile some three hundred blind and wounded French soldiers, two hundred sailors and marines, and a military band. They forced ashore those who survived their onslaught, then obliged the band to play while, in the name of Allah, they methodically sodomized, tortured, and killed all the survivors, including the sick, blind, and wounded. They then slaughtered the members of the band. The Jihad, holy war though it may be, is never gentle. It wasn't in Egypt. Neither was the French occupation. Because of the prevalence of syphilis, one of the French generals ordered that all prostitutes caught in the soldiers' barracks should be arrested and executed, which was duly carried out by the Janissaries, who, being disciplined soldiers, were now working for the French. They rounded up and beheaded four hundred women, placed their headless bodies in sacks, and threw them into the Nile.

When Bonaparte invaded Syria and laid siege to Acre, the local governor, Djezzar Pasha, a Bosnian from Sarajevo, ordered that all French prisoners have their heads cut off. But the massacring was two-sided; Bonaparte had ordered some two thousand Muslim prisoners captured at Jaffa to be bayoneted to death.

Of course, it was Napoleon Bonaparte who was the aggressor in Egypt. He had never regarded the Jihad as his enemy, but the Jihad marked him down as an enemy of Islam from the day he landed near Alexandria and attacked the city. The famous battle of the Pyramids, near Cairo, was simply another incident for the Muslims in their Jihad against the Franks. They considered Bonaparte the descendant of the first crusaders who had tried to conquer the Holy Land seven centuries earlier. So for three years they endured the infidel French occupants of their country. The French also invaded Palestine and Lebanon in the Syrian campaign, were beaten at Acre, won nearly everywhere else, and marched up the Nile Valley to fight the Mamelukes, the local equivalent of the Turkish Janissaries. For the Egyptians, the French were a plague who one day would vanish. And they did. Bonaparte, in the end, failed in Egypt and, after the departure of the French invaders, Allah came back into his own in the mosques of Cairo where the French cavalrymen, callous and mocking, had ridden their horses over the mosaic tiles and among the marble colonnades. When Allah came back, hundreds of Cairo women—including Bonaparte's former 16-year-old Egyptian mistress Zeinab—were beheaded for having shared their charms with the enemy.

For Bonaparte and the French, there was nothing holy about their war in Egypt. Egypt was, in any case, a surrogate for Britain: Bonaparte went east because he could not go west. He occupied Egypt because it was impossible, thanks to the Royal Navy, to cross the Channel and invade England. He had hoped to weaken Britain, to launch from Egypt an invasion of India by sea from Suez or overland across the Middle East to the Indus River. Foiled at Acre by the Turko-British resistance, instead of attacking India, he returned to France to become emperor a few years later. In Egypt, he had endured the Jihad and felt its insanity; so seemed the self-destructive fervor of Muslim Holy War to him and to the men he led to battle in the desert. And, in an act of pure Jihad fanaticism, General Kleber, who later replaced Bonaparte as commander-in-chief in Egypt, was stabbed to death by a young Syrian clerk called Soleiman who was not particularly interested in ridding his country of a foreign occupant, but who, as a devout Muslim, wished to do a great deed "for the glory of God." Killing this important infidel soldier seemed the best way to do it, and by his execution to become a martyr and obtain immediate entry into Paradise.

In later years the Muslims were to become Napoleon's allies against the British when, in 1807, he sent a military mission under General Sebastiani to Istanbul, then being threatened by the British; and a force of three hundred French army gunners to man the Turkish coastal guns in the Dardanelles and train the Turks in modern gunnery methods. The Turks went into action against an attacking force of eight British warships under Admiral Sir John Duckworth, who was lucky to get his squadron back to the Mediterranean after losing one hundred sixty-seven men in the attack during which several of his ships were severely damaged.

Thwarted in Istanbul, the British decided to recoup their losses and prestige the same year in Egypt. An army of six thousand men landed in Alexandria under the command of General Alexander Fraser, who was defeated by the Ottoman army outside Rosetta, where a thousand British soldiers were killed by the warriors of the Jihad, and several hundred were captured. Fraser capitulated, recovered the British prisoners, and returned home. The only apparent result of the expedition were a few hundred spiked British heads left rotting in the sun outside Rosetta.

A few years earlier the Americans had undergone their first experience of Jihad warfare, along the Barbary coast, on "the shores of Tripoli," as we are told in the battle hymn of the United States Marines. For centuries, under the suzerainty of various deys, beys, and pashas, these piffling local potentates had been of immense power in their little fiefdoms in Algiers, Tunis, Tripoli, and other places along the coast. For generations the pirates of the Barbary Coast had been preying on the shipping of the Mediterranean, kidnapping passengers and crews, enslaving them and only releasing their captives on payment of ransom money. Those who could not pay, or the pretty young women whom the sultan coveted for his harem, faced a lifetime of servitude. The kingdoms of Europe, even the most powerful, found protection by paying tribute. One of the pirates' victims had been the lovely Aimée Dubucq de Rivery, a French cousin of the future empress Josephine of France, on her way to Martinique, whose ship was captured at sea. She was sent to grace the sultan's harem in Istanbul, spent the rest of her life in the Palace seraglio, and gave birth to a son who became Sultan Mahmoud II.

The ships of a new nation, the recently founded United States of America, had recently come sailing into the blue waters of the Mediterranean and, to assure its freedom of the seas, the United States built a squadron of frigates to protect its ships. Before the vessels were even launched, the dey of Algiers had assured the Americans their ships would sail unharmed against payment of an annual tribute. The frigates were therefore totally unnecessary, the dey forcefully said. So the Americans, like everybody else, paid, but built their frigates anyway.

If the Americans pay tribute to the dey of Algiers, why not to me, wondered Yusouf, the pasha of Tripoli. The President of the United States offered friendship to the pasha instead of money. The pasha of Tripoli was not interested in friendship; he wanted money. "We would ask that your flattering words be followed by deeds," he warned the president. Unless tribute was paid without delay, Tripoli would declare war on the United States within six months. Yusouf's word was his bond. The necessary tribute not being forthcoming, war was. On May 14 ,1800, Yusouf sent his henchmen into the grounds of the United States consulate and chopped down the flagstaff.

"Millions for defense but not one cent for tribute," retorted the Americans. The first American ship on the scene, two years later, was the USS *Philadelphia,* a 36-gun frigate commanded by Captain Bainbridge, who promptly captured the corsair *Meshboa,* out of Tangiers, which itself had just attacked and seized the American brig *Celia.*

Commodore Edward Preble, in command of the American squadron, sailed to Tangiers to demand reparations and explanations. The local ruler assured him it was a mistake and pledged eternal friendship for America. Preble then sent USS *Philadelphia* on patrol off Tripoli. At the end of October the *Philadelphia* went to intercept a Barbary Coast pirate ship trying to nose her way through the American blockade. Bainbridge tried to cut it too fine, sailed too close to the shore and found himself held fast on a reef. Surrounded by a swarm of small, armed vessels, Bainbridge tried to scuttle his ship. half did so in the shallow water, and then surrendered. The Americans were taken to the local fortress while the pasha of Tripoli worked out how much ransom money he could expect. From the barred windows of their cells, the crew of the *Philadelphia* witnessed with anguish their ship being refloated and rearmed by its Muslim captors.

Commodore Preble, when he heard that the *Philadelphia* was in the hands of the pirates, prepared an immediate rescue operation. The command was given to Lieutenant Stephen Decatur, one of the future great names of the budding U.S. navy, known all over the world as the man who once said, "My country, right or wrong." Aged twenty-four, Decatur was captain of USS *Enterprise.* He exchanged her for the ketch USS *Intrepid* and a do-or-die crew of seventy,with orders to burn the captured USS *Philadelphia.* The seizure of an American warship by a pirate vessel was an unacceptable humiliation. Decatur received his orders, sailed on February 3, 1804, in company with the brig USS *Siren* under Lieutenant Charles Stewart, and six days later they were off Tripoli battling high winds. They did not enter the harbor until February 19.

Decatur sighted the *Philadelphia* moored near a fort, under the protection of the castle guns, surrounded by three large warships and several twenty-gun boats. Disregarding them, the American sailed his ketch straight for *Philadelphia*. The unsuspecting Tripolitanians tied the *Intrepid* to the ship Decatur was preparing to attack. "Board!" the young lieutenant shouted. "Americanos," shouted the bewildered Tripolitanians. Within seconds the seventy Americans were swarming all over the captured *Philadelphia*, setting her aflame. Withing minutes the American frigate was a burning and smoking wreck, and the *Intrepid* crew was back on their ship, sailing out of Tripoli's history and into the heart of American pride, history, and legend.

On July 25 another American warship arrived off Tripoli. Commodore Preble, his flag aboard USS *Constitution* (affectionately known as *Old Ironsides* in the U.S. navy) and backed by three brigs, three schooners, six gunboats and two bomb vessels, attacked the town. Another attack was later made overland on the neighboring town of Derna by a joint naval and marine force commanded by Lieutenant O'Bannon of the United States Marines. In 1805 the Americans and the Tripoli pasha signed a treaty under which Tripoli agreed to release all the captured Americans. After their release, the United States would pay sixty thousand dollars to the Pasha of Tripoli. It looked to everybody very much like tribute. The Americans insisted it wasn't; it was only an exchange of money for a few hundred sailors. Not tribute, just a deal maybe. Nothing very holy about it, anyway. But the final chapter of this first American Mediterranean saga remained to be written—ten years later, and not in Tripoli but in Algiers.

In 1815 the Americans sent a naval squadron to escort an American diplomat, William Sharer, to Algiers to sign a treaty with the dey. He was assisted by two well-qualified assessors for the negotiations that were about to take place, both well acquainted with the Mediterranean: Bainbridge and Decatur. The two countries came to an agreement in two days. Algerians and Americans signed a treaty abolishing all tribute, freeing all captives, and restoring to their owners all captured ships.

But before he left, Stephen Decatur fired the final shots of this nautical Jihad. Meeting at sea a suspicious-looking frigate flying the British ensign, he ran up the British ensign, too. The two ships cautiously approached each other, then suddenly both false flags came down and their true flags went up: Algerian and American. Decatur had to put the recent War of 1812 well behind him: instead of the British, he was fighting against the Jihad. At almost point-blank range the two ships poured shot into each other. The Americans were more successful. "The Algerian captain, Reis Hamidou, was cut in two by a solid cannon shot," we are told in J. B. Wolf's *The Barbary Coast* (W. W. Norton, 1979, p. 150), and the Algerian privateer surrendered. For years Hamidou had been the most successful fighting sailor of Algeria. The son of a tailor, he had finally become admiral of the Algerian navy.

The Americans went home, and the following year a famous British sailor, the former frigate captain Edward Pellew, hero of the Napoleonic wars, now Admiral Lord Exmouth, went to both Tunis and Tripoli and demanded that the two North African states end, once and for all, the practice of Christian slavery. After a considerable amount of hemming and hawing he obtained satisfaction. He then visited Algiers for the same purpose, but had to back down when an Algerian mob, outraged at this impudent demand, pulled two of his officers from their horses and dragged them through the streets, their hands tied behind their backs. Lord Exmouth decided to temporize and sailed back to England where, on arrival, he was informed that dozens of Italians who were living in Oran and Bore under British protection had been put to death during the visit of a Royal Navy squadron in the region. The British reply this time was a no-nonsense one. A joint British-Dutch naval force of twenty-four battleships, led by Lord Exmouth aboard HMS *Queen Charlotte,* a 108-gun ship-of-the-line, sailed into Algiers harbor and bombarded the town. Christian gunboat diplomacy was replacing the Muslim Jihad. "The battle was fairly at issue between a handful of Britons in the noble cause of Christianity, and hordes of fanatics, assembled round their city, and enclosed within its fortifications, to obey the dictates of their despot. The cause of God and humanity prevailed," wrote Lord Exmouth unctuously in his report. The British fleet fired 118 tons of powder, 50,000 shot and nearly 1,000 shells that day. The British suffered 128 killed and 600 wounded. One of the minor casualties was Admiral Lord Exmouth himself, wounded in three places, a telescope smashed in his hand, and his coat torn to strips. All the Algerian navy ships but two were destroyed

The next day, the dey agreed to free all the foreign slaves in Algiers, who numbered 1,642, most of them Italians. But he remained truculent, overbearing to any Christian who came his way. In 1827 he struck the French consul across the face with his fly whisk over a dispute concerning a French debt on a shipment of Algerian wheat to France. This undiplomatic gesture caused a diplomatic uproar in France. The dey, who was his vassal, reported to the sultan in Istanbul that the French consul had insulted Islam and the honor of the sultan, "the protector of the world." He told the French envoy to go home and fired on the ship that was taking the diplomat back to France. The time for insults passed imperceptibly into the time for war, and the greatest showdown in North Africa came in June 1830, when a French fleet commanded by Admiral Duperré, who twenty years previously had fought and defeated the British in the inshore waters of Mauritius at the Battle of Grand Port, sailed into the harbor waters of Algiers at the head of a convoy which included thirty-seven thousand soldiers crammed into his warships and troopships. Three weeks later the victorious French packed the dey, his harem, his children, and his eunuchs aboard a French frigate, and deposited them in Naples to start a new life amid the tangerine groves of southern Italy, while the French army conquered Algeria and began an occupation that lasted 132 years.

"There is no more humiliating record in the annals of annexation than this miserable conquest of Algiers," wrote Stanley Lane-Poole in his history of the Barbary corsairs, although he acknowledged that in its early stages "the conquest was marked by a moderation and humanity which did infinite honor to the French arms." But moderation and humanity were certainly absent when, during the conquest of Algeria, General Pélissier trapped five hundred Berber and Arab men, women, and children in a cave, closed it, and smoked them all to death.

For the Muslims, the hero of the war was the rebel Abd el-Kadir who returned to Algeria from Egypt at the age of twenty-four and became the leader of the Muslim insurgents fighting French rule. The war, in which tens of thousands of French troops were involved, did not end until 1847 when Abd el-Kadir surrendered on condition he could retire to a Muslim country. Instead, he was jailed in a French prison for five years, then finally allowed to settle in Damascus where, as an old man, he saved many of the local Christians from massacre by the Muslims during the insurrections of 1860. After Algeria, Tunisia was taken by the French in the 1880s.

For the Muslim Arabs, these wars against the Christian French and Americans in Egypt, Syria, Libya, Algeria, and Tunisia were an integral part of the Holy War against Christendom. It was, in Muslim minds, particularly Arab minds, part of the natural order of life that the Muslim should reign and the Christian should serve. The Muslims could not fail to be aware, however, that the old order was now changing and, in the new order, the Christian was master and the Muslim the servant. Moreover, in Christian minds, particularly Western European minds, this state of affairs was part of the natural order of life. The Jihad was turned upside down and for many of the faithful, whose history and lives had flourished in perpetual victories, the experience was an emotionally shattering one that many Muslim minds were not able to accept. Defeat and humiliation were not the stuff of which Islam was made. It had always triumphed in the past, and it awaited triumph in the future. Today, with decolonization and with the backing of its immense oil riches, the hour of Islam has perhaps come around again.

The Jihad, begun by Muhammad in the seventh century, is required to persist until the whole world belongs to Islam. It is doubtful if any of the Americans and Europeans engaged in battle against Algiers and Tripoli felt, at the time, that they were in any way engaged in a religious war, holding off an intended Muslim conquest of the world. Empire building was, anyway, Britain's and France's own pastime in the 1800s. So it was too for the United States, which called it its "manifest destiny."

Soon after the French conquest of Algeria, the British also became active in Arab lands. In 1839 they took the fishing village of Aden, on the Red Sea, and from there began, for Britons, a colonial journey into the Arabian lands that was to culminate for them about seventy-five years later with Lawrence of Arabia, and to end piteously with the Suez expedition in 1956. The winds of change had at last arrived.

58

THE SURROGATES OF PERICLES: GREECE 1821–1827

I N ANOTHER PART OF THE Mediterranean, on the European continent, well to the north of Tripoli, another war, religious as well as national, had pitted the rayah Christian Greeks against their Muslim Turkish masters. The Greek War of Independence, as history has called it, broke out in 1821 and ended six years later. It was a war of unspeakable atrocities by both sides. In this Holy War (at least, so the Turks saw it), famous for the presence of the poet Byron in Greek ranks, Turks and Greeks wallowed in an immensity of massacre, mass inhumanity, and mass torture which the mind, even today, more than 180 years later, still cannot quite grasp. But with the example of our own time in mind, let us remain horrified but not too surprised at all the hideous things human beings can do to one another.

One surprising facet of the Greek-Turkish war was the idealized version of the struggle given to the conflict. To the cultured Europeans of the early 1800s, the downtrodden Greeks of their epoch, however downtrodden and depreciated, were still the distant kin and descendants of the splendid Greeks of the fifth century B.C.E., when the great figures of antiquity, not only Pericles but also Euripides, Aeschylus, Aristophanes, Thucydides, Herodotus, Phidias, Sophocles, Socrates, the Sophists, and so many others graced the history of Attica, and the Parthenon was rising above the city of Athens.

Fair Greece! sad relic of departed worth!
Immortal, though no more; though fallen, great!
Who now shall lead thy scatter'd children forth
And long accustom'd bondage uncreate?

wrote Lord Byron, clinging romantically and lovingly in his cantos to the memories of the golden age of Greece when white-robed poets, playwrights, and philosophers sat in shady groves, nibbling idly on grapes they had just picked, reciting iambic verse, comparing the prowess of Olympic athletes, and discussing the harmony of the Pindaric odes.

The lovers of Greece—Philhellenes they were called, and nearly a thousand of them from all over western Europe, including Byron, went to fight for Greece between 1821 and 1827—conceived of the Greek War of Independence in ancient classic terms, and saw the Turks as latter-day Persian barbarians whom the Spartan Leonidas had fought at Thermopylae in 480 B.C.E. They saw the whole war in an antique Grecian setting. But their vision meant nothing to the vast majority of contemporary Greeks, who were peasants and fishermen, simple Christian people who lived under an oppressive alien rule. There was, however, a minority of rich and educated Greeks, living often abroad, mainly in France and Russia, who were well aware of the classical Greece. The ruined monuments of Greece were their heritage. But most of the people, unmindful of Greece's past, regarded the great ancient monuments, the ruins of many still standing in their midst, as the work of pagans who had distantly preceded them on Greek soil.

But the uncultured majority knew who the Turks were. The Turks were alien, were Muslims, and were their masters; and the Greeks wanted them dead or out of the country, preferably dead, because that way there would be no risk of their return. That is what the Greek War of Independence was all about, Byron notwithstanding. The Greeks were not fighting for civilization and as surrogates of their antique and artistic ancestors. They were fighting strictly for themselves.

By a strange sort of paradox, the catalyst for the Greek War of Independence was a revolt in February 1821, in Wallachia, against the Greek officials who ruled their province on behalf of the Turks. The Ottoman rulers often used talented Greeks to govern and administer their more distant Christian possessions in the Balkans, and these Greek appointees were often corrupt and oppressive. The Wallachian revolt precipitated another revolt two months later in neighboring Moldavia by a Greek officer serving in the Russian army, Prince Alexander Ypsilantis, who deserted his post to fight the Turks. The czar refused to help him and Ypsilantis, defeated by the Ottomans in battle in June, took refuge in Austria.

The rebellion was now anchored in the soil of Greece. Yet its first inspiration had come from abroad. The Greek Society of Friends, the Philike Hetaeria, centered in the Black Sea port of Odessa in the Ukraine, had furnished the original historical and intellectual stimulus. A Corfu Greek, John Capodistrias, also in the service of the czar, was the original choice of the rebels for leader, but he declined. Prince Ypsilantis's brother Demetrios, a young man in his twenties, also a serving officer in the Russian army, was then appointed by the Society of Friends to the leadership of the rebellion. But he was unpopular with the local Greek guerrilla leaders, ran out of money, and was in due course replaced by Alexander Mavrocordato, a fat and short-sighted aristocrat of Istanbul who became nominal head of the Greek government.

The Greeks in the Peloponnese, or Morea as the most southern portion of the Greek mainland is also called, had in the meantime gone around the countryside killing all the Turks they could find. More than twenty thousand were slaughtered, nearly all quietly and savagely exterminated in a few weeks, perhaps in a few days. Suddenly there were no longer any Turks in Morea, only Greeks. The Turks had simply vanished. One more holocaust to be added to a list which reached its peak in the Ottoman empire in the Turkish holocaust of the the Armenians during World War I.

"All over the Peloponnese roamed mobs of Greeks armed with clubs, scythes, and a few firearms, killing, plundering, and burning. They were often led by Christian priests, who exhorted their parishioners to greater efforts in their holy work," recounts St. Clair. The religious—with its murderous practices, we cannot decently call it "holy"—character of the civil war was obvious from the beginning. But it was no longer the traditional, offensive, Koranic Jihad, bidding the infidel to convert to Islam, or die, or pay tribute. It was a Jihad in reverse. For, in this moment of history, when Islam was on the decline, in the words of Albert Hourani, the Jihad "tended to be seen in terms of defense rather than expansion." The Jihad was no longer a war of conquest. It had become a battle for survival. Islam was on the run. Right from the beginning the Turks had considered their empire to be above all a Muslim empire, multi-racial, certainly, but above all in the service of Islam. Ottoman nationality and the Islamic religion had been the two parts of their identity. Now both were disintegrating. In Greece, both were in fact disappearing.

The revolt in the Peloponnese spread to several of the Aegean islands and further north to Rumelia, Epirus, and Thessaly. Furious at the slaughter of their co-religionists in the Peloponnese, the Turks retaliated by hanging the Christian patriarch in Istanbul, Gregorios. His body remained publicly dangling at the end of a rope for three days and was then dragged through the streets and thrown into the sea. Twelve other Greeks, including three bishops, were also executed the same day. In nearby Edirne a former patriarch, nine priests, and twenty merchants were hanged outside the church. On June 15, five archbishops and three bishops were hanged or beheaded in Istanbul. Another seventy Greeks were hanged in the capital in July. A few more hundred Greeks were massacred by unruly Muslim mobs in the capital. Rotting corpses lay around the streets for weeks. In Smyrna, the Muslim judges who refused to sign a document ordering the extermination of the Greek inhabitants were themselves massacred. Some three thousand armed Turks marched into the Greek quarter of the town and killed every Greek they met. A few hundred Greeks were massacred in the island of Coz, a few thousand in Rhodes, in Cyprus the archbishops, five bishops and thirty-six priests were dealt with either by hanging or by beheading. A few thousand more Greeks were slaughtered at Kydonies, on the nearby Asian mainland. Those who were not executed were sold as slaves. In the north, the Turks recaptured Thessaly, killing thousands and enslaving thousands more.

The massacre on the island of Chios (population over 100,000) remains unforgotten by history to this day. Famous for its mastic, a sort of chewing gum widely favored by the bored ladies of Turkish harems, the Christian island of Chios (which was trying to stay neutral in the civil war) was occupied briefly by a Christian raiding party from another island, Samos, who sailed away a few days later after killing all their Turkish prisoners. The Turkish troops from the nearby mainland, backed by thousands of freelance local Muslim warriors led by imams preaching Holy War, invaded Chios, killed thousands, and enslaved thousands more who were taken over to Istanbul and Anatolia. Each Muslim volunteer tried to take back a slave or two for his own use, plus a few more to be sold on the local slave markets. The number of casualties remains unknown to this day. Official customs figures give the total as forty-one thousand shipped out as slaves, most of them women, boys, and girls. The Sciote community in Istanbul was hunted down, tortured, and massacred.

"For them" writes St. Clair, "simple death was not considered sufficient. They were taken to the torture house within the seraglio and subjected to the highly refined punishments of the East." These included the breaking of their limbs and joints by screws and being burned to death slowly in huge ovens. Sacks full of Sciote heads, ears, and noses were scattered around Istanbul, rotting in the sunlight. "They lay where they fell," St. Clair gruesomely adds, "sticking to the feet of pedestrians."

The Greeks were also on the rampage. When the Turks in Navarino surrendered, the Greeks, in spite of their assurance of a safe passage for the entire Turkish population, killed between two and three thousand Muslims. Not even babies were spared; they were taken from their mothers and smashed against the rocks. When Tripolitsa, the main Turkish town in Morea was captured, the Greeks killed every Turk they could lay their hands on. Let St. Clair tell the story:

> Upward of 10,000 Turks were put to death. . . . Prisoners who were suspected of having concealed their money were tortured. Their arms and legs were cut off and they were slowly roasted over fires. Pregnant women were cut open, their heads cut off and dogs' heads stuck between their legs. . . . For weeks afterward starving Turkish children running helpless about the ruins were being cut down and shot at by the exultant Greeks. . . . Three Turkish children [were] slowly burned to death over a bonfire while their father and mother were forced to watch.

If the reader has had enough reading of these atrocities—I could add more—so have I, writing about them. But it is right, however unpleasant, that we should be aware that cruelty is a commodity savored by all men, Christians as well as Muslims. There is no effective taboo anywhere, in any time or any place, against it. The last words of Mme. Rolland, on her way to the guillotine during the French Revolution, reproached Liberty for the crimes committed in its name. One can equally reproach God for the crimes committed in His name. But the crimes disgrace neither Liberty nor God, they disgrace only these murderers and torturers who quote God or Liberty to justify their abominable deeds.

Many of these atrocities were witnessed by Philhellenic European officers fighting to bring to Greece a civilized nineteenth-century version of the Age of Pericles. Many former soldiers of Napoleon's

Grande Armée made their way to Greece from Marseille to fight for Greek independence. Many, sickened by what they saw, returned home. But most stayed, some to die of disease, others to perish in battle, a few to commit suicide from despair, some to be tortured and massacred by the Turks. The Germans furnished the largest contingent of volunteers for Greece, although it was a Frenchman, a former soldier of Napoleon, Baleste, who was given command of the first Greek regiment. Seventy of a battalion of about a hundred Philhellenes were killed in battle against the Turks at Peta, in Epirus, in 1822. The Turks cut off the heads of the dead and the wounded and forced twenty survivors, including two of the officers, Colonel Tarella, a Piedmontese who had been a battalion commander in the army of Napoleon I, and the Genoese cavalryman Dania, who had also fought as a captain in the French army, to march under escort to the nearby Turkish base at Arta carrying the heads of their decapitated comrades. There, the twenty men were all immediately condemned to death by the Turks and impaled on the spot. Thus, atrociously, on a windspent Grecian plain, died a handful of the former soldiers of Napoleon, in the cause of Greek freedom, seven years after Waterloo.

New Philhellenic arrivals took the place of the slain. The most prestigious was, of course, Byron. But there were other famous names among the volunteers. Sir Richard Church was one of them. He had fought against the French in Egypt in 1800, against the French in the Ionian Islands in 1810, and for the Bourbon King of the Two Sicilies in 1817. Sir Charles Napier, conqueror of much of India for the British empire (his statue is in Trafalgar Square), offered his services, but they were not taken up. Count General Normann, a German, survived the Russian campaign only to die in Greece of a broken heart after the battle of Peta, the disaster for which he felt responsible. The maverick Admiral Thomas Cochrane, former hero of the British, Chilean, and Brazilian navies, fought in Greece where, however, he failed to relieve the Greeks besieged by the Turks on the Acropolis.

One of the men defending the Acropolis was the French artillery officer Colonel Charles Fabvier, "a soldier of heroic proportions" St. Clair describes him, "who seems to come straight from one of those huge canvases of Napoleonic battles so beloved by the French." Fabvier had served with a French military mission in Persia in 1807, and had survived Napoleon's disastrous Russian campaign. After Waterloo he had refused to accept the return of the Bourbon kings in France, and had participated in a plot to abduct Napoleon from St. Helena and return him to the throne. Bonapartist to the core of his being, he had gone to Spain to try to raise an army of exiled Frenchmen with the hope of one day liberating France from what he considered its royal interlopers. While awaiting that day, he volunteered to help the Greeks liberate themselves from the Turks, and was given the task of training a Greek army in European methods of warfare. Many of his old comrades from his fighting days in France joined him in Greece. In all, about two hundred Frenchmen, most of them old Bonapartists, fought for Greek independence. The only larger contingent (342) was from Germany. Some 137 Italians came to Greece, and 99 British. Even the distant United States sent a contingent of sixteen volunteers.

The liberation of Greece was perhaps facilitated by the immolation by the sultan of his whole corps of Janissaries who, in 1826, vanished from history. They were no longer, of course, the redoubtable Janissaries of the early days of the Ottoman empire, but an unruly mob of mutinous, whiney creatures who had refused to modernize their weapons, their training, or their tactics. They were primarily interested in influencing the sultan to give them as many advantages as they could force from him by threats and blackmail, promising mayhem if their demands were not met. Sultan Mahmoud II raised a new corps of gunners, "unfurled the Sacred Standard of the Prophet, and called on all True Believers to rally around their Sultan and Caliph." It was a sort of a new Jihad, within the context of the still-prevailing Jihad, against the Greek rebels. The new was more successful than the old. While the Janissaries were marching against the imperial palace, demanding that the sultan's chief ministers all be beheaded, Mahmoud's gunners fired into their ranks. The Janissaries rapidly retired to their barracks, which was for them a fatal move. The artillerymen surrounded the buildings with their guns and fired point blank into them until not one single Janissary was left alive. Between five and ten thousand were killed. Those in the provinces of the empire were then rounded up one by one and executed. So vanished the Janissaries from Islamic history, themselves the victims of a Jihad which they had done so much to create against themselves. The Janissary standards were all destroyed. A new force of forty thousand men was raised, to be trained according to European methods. Known officially as "The Victorious Mohammedan Armies," their mission in life was to fight for "the cause of religion."

Two years previously, in April 1824, Byron had died in the malaria-ridden town of Missalonghi, a few miles west of Lepanto, not far from where Don John of Austria has so decisively beaten the Turks

250 years before. Byron died "not on the field of glory but on the bed of disease," as he had always dreaded. His lungs were given to the local people to be buried there as a relic of his sojourn in Greece, and the rest of his body shipped out to nearby British-ruled Corfu. His military role in the Greek War for Independence may have been secondary but, by his very presence in the conflict, he had given it an idealistic panache which has survived to this day.

Unable to defeat the rebellion with his Turkish troops, the sultan called on his Egyptian vassal, Mohammed Ali, who was promised Morea and Crete as a reward if he won. He did, for a while. Missalonghi was captured in 1826, two years almost to the day after Byron's death. The Acropolis surrendered to the Muslims the next year under the supervision of a neutral French naval force that escorted to safety its defenders through the lines of the besiegers. The Bonapartist rebel Fabvier had been saved by the ruling French royalists whom he despised and whom he had sworn to overthrow. On his return to France, Fabvier, a Frenchman above all, placed his sword again at his country's disposal.

Perhaps the Turks might have recovered Greece and continued their misrule over that land a few more years had the fighting between Turks and Greeks not, by this time, acquired an international diplomatic dimension. By the Treaty of London, signed on July 6, 1827, France, Britain, and Russia warned Turkey that if it refused to sign a cease-fire with the Greeks, as the Greeks were prepared to do with the Turks, the three countries would use their ships in support of the Greek cause. Three months later they did at the Battle of Navarino when, faced by the refusal of the Muslim fleet to cease fighting the Greeks, a combined British/French/Russian fleet under British Vice-Admiral Sir Edward Codrington, a veteran of Trafalgar, sailed into the Bay of Navarino. Codrington's orders were strict: no ship was to fire unless fired upon. With only twenty-four ships—ten ships of the line, ten frigates, four brigs—under his command, he was heavily outnumbered. The Turks and the Egyptians had 89 ships between them. Hit by a shot from one of the Egyptian vessels, the French frigate *Sirène* fired back. And so began the last battle in history between wooden sailing ships. It lasted four hours. For the Muslim sailors the naval battle was simply a maritime aspect of the Jihad. It also was what one could rightly call a crushing defeat for them. When it was over, sixty of the Muslim ships had been sunk. Twenty-nine were still floating, though many of them were so badly damaged they were no longer fit for service. Between four and eight thousand Turkish and Egyptian sailors (the numbers vary according to the book you read) died that afternoon. Codrington lost no ships, but between 172 and 450 (the numbers, again, vary according to the book you read) British, French, and Russian sailors were killed.

The British government, politically correct and anxious to maintain good relations with Egypt and Turkey, referred mildly and officially to the victory of Navarino as "an untoward event." The Greeks, of course, were jubilant. Without a fleet to bring in troops and land them in Greece and all its islands, the Turks could not win. Greece was now free and Jihad was now becoming a synonym for Turkish defeat in all the Balkans.

59

WAR GALORE: THE BALKANS 1828–1878

HESE WERE LONG YEARS OF wars of liberation for the Christian countries of the Balkans. With Greece leading the way, the others followed. For the Muslims, as we wrote in the previous chapter, the Jihad no longer meant conquest; it meant the hope of survival. Survival in these campaigns meant a fighting retreat. That was now the Ottoman fate. Defeat, however, was still nearly a century away. The Ottoman empire may have been finished, but Turkey wasn't. And elsewhere a so-called Jihad was to assume new forms, and to acquire a new lease of very violent life, the results of which we are still experiencing now.

More than a hundred years after Hungary, thanks to Prince Eugene's victories, was totally liberated in 1716, Greece became the next country in Europe to win freedom from the Turks. The others followed in an untidy avalanche of five major wars which engulfed the Ottoman empire: the Russo-Turkish War of 1828–29; the Crimean War of 1853–56; the Russo-Turkish War of 1877–78; the Balkan wars of 1912–13; and the 1914–18 war, World War I.

After the Eastern Roman empire, after Serbia, after Hungary, after Venice, after Austria, czarist Russia was now Ottoman Turkey's main enemy, and the Christian countries of the Balkans largely rode to victory as Russian protégés. But, for one war, the Crimean, Turkey found new allies against Russia: Britain and France. In fact, the two Western countries did most of the fighting against the Russians. The British and French involvement was based on their fear of Russia's growing power. They knew that Russia aspired to take over the Dardanelles and link up with the Mediterranean. For Britain, a Russian Istanbul (which, of course, would have been renamed Constantinople) would have meant Russia almost astride the road to India, a threat to the lifeline linking London and Delhi. For France, a Russia established in Istanbul meant a danger to her own dominant position in the Mediterranean. The two countries preferred to deal with a weak Turkey than with a strong Russia. For the Europeans, these wars were now almost solely to do with empire, power, and imperialism. For the Turks, the inspiration was still largely religious. The Jihad was a sort of a call to patriotism. The call to battle was still, "Allah is Great and Muhammad is his Prophet." And, in addition to the usual military medals and decorations, houris were still the reward that awaited a dead Muslim warrior.

One tends to forget the Holy War quality that these wars maintained for the Ottomans. It also appeared sometimes in Turkish wars against other Muslim countries—quite illegally according to Islamic law—notably against Persia, and even against their vassals Egypt, Syria, and Arabia. But the Jihad was particularly invoked in conflicts against Christian powers. In December 1827, sensing the Russians would soon declare war against him in the wake of the Navarino naval battle, Sultan Mahmoud II, in a speech to his imperial pashas, called on all Muslims to show the valor which they had always displayed when they established Islam as the true religion in the world, and to annihilate the enemies who wished to destroy Islam. The Persians too were in the van of the Jihad. The previous year the ayatollahs had forced the shah, Fath Ali, to open hostilities against Russia. But Moscow had won, secured a large part of Armenia, turned the Caspian into a largely Russian lake, and caviar into a Russian delicacy exported all over the world.

The sultan's appeal to his Muslim subjects' religious fervor was perhaps made because so many of them had been outraged by the massacre of the Janissaries, particularly European Muslims. Because of his reforms many criticized him as "the Christian sultan." The fact that the sultan's mother, Aimée Dubucq de Rivery, was a French woman made many suspicious of his intentions and loyalties. When he raised his new "Victorious Mohammedan Armies," which replaced the old and turbulent Janissaries, many people commented on their unsoldierly appearance, including a famous professional soldier from Europe.

"The splendid appearance, the beautiful arms, the reckless bravery of the old Muslim horde had disappeared," wrote the future Prussian field marshal Helmuth Carl von Moltke, who in his youth took service in the Ottoman army for a few years, "but this new army had one quality which placed it above the numerous hosts which in former times the Porte could summon to the field: it obeyed."

Dissatisfied with its new sultan, Bosnia, "a remarkably warlike and strongly Muslim province" according to Creasy, refused to send any troops at all to fight the Russians when they declared war against the Turks in April 1828. The Russian army crossed the Danube in June, took Varna in October, laid up for the winter decimated by disease, then continued its advance south across the Balkan mountains under the command of the Prussian veteran of Austerlitz, General Hans Diebitsch. The Russians took Edirne, only about fifty miles from Istanbul, in August and then stopped. With the plague raging in the army, there were no longer enough soldiers to attack Istanbul. But the Turks, unaware of their enemy's weakness, were willing to make peace. By the Treaty of Adrianople, signed on September 14 at Edirne, they agreed that the Russians would occupy the Danubian principalities of Wallachia and Moldavia (Rumania) pending the payment of an indemnity of 15 million ducats in ten years.

The Turks also agreed—and this is interesting as it shows the depth of ill feeling that local Christians had toward Islam—that no Muslim would ever be allowed again to reside in Wallachia and Moldavia. They also recognized Russia's right to Georgia in the Caucasus. By this time Russia had become the spokesman and defender of the Christian Balkan countries (notably those inhabited by southern Slavs, like the Serbs), as well as those of Greece.

The next year, while the French were taking Algiers, several of the Muslim provinces of the Ottoman empire revolted against the sultan, perhaps because they sensed the empire's coming demise. Bosnia, Albania, and also Egypt, on the other side of the Mediterranean, were all in a state of revolt. The sultan's Egyptian vassal, Mehemet Ali, whose domain, with a French-trained and equipped army, was stronger and better organized than that of his patron, wanted in fact to break away and establish his own dominion in Syria, Palestine, and Arabia as well as Egypt.

As a further goad to the Porte, Mehemet Ali, with the strong backing of his son, Admiral Ibrahim Ali, removed the Turkish soldiers who guarded the tomb of Muhammad, replaced them with Arabs, and then refused to pay tribute to his Turkish overlord. Turkish army and

Source: William Stearns Davis, *A Short History of the Near East* (New York: Macmillan, 1922).

navy units sent to bring the recalcitrant Egyptians into line all deserted to the enemy. In the middle of all these convoluted proceedings, Mahmoud died and his son, the new sultan Abdul Medjid, called in the French and the British to help him restore order.

We are now in the year 1839 and fully involved in the exercise of power politics, with the Jihad now almost redundant. Britain was delighted to help, for London was determined to keep the Ottoman empire strong enough to confront the growing and worrisome power of Russia. A British naval squadron bombarded the Egyptian occupants in Beirut in August 1840 and landed a regiment of Turkish troops to take over the Egyptian-held town. The Egyptians also withdrew from Candia, in Crete, which they had occupied, and from Acre in Palestine. Under negotiations carried on through the good offices of France and Britain, the sultan gave Egypt to Mehemet Ali and his descendants in perpetuity.

The Jihad had become, indeed, a very wobbly factor in Middle Eastern politics, and many devout mullahs and imams must have been very concerned over the strange political paths their religion was taking.

For a dozen years peace reigned intermittently in the Muslim desmene until the Turks declared war on Russia in October 1853. A few months later Britain and France in their turn declared war on Russia in order to protect Turkey. One can refer to the ensuing Crimean War as part of the Jihad only with great difficulty, but for the Muslim Turks, obliged to fight infidels, even alongside other infidels, the conflict was undoubtedly a Holy War since in any case they were fighting non-Muslims. The Charge of the Light Brigade by the British cavalry and the taking of the Malakov redoubt by the French infantry were among the outstanding military feats of the Crimean War. The Turks, who played only a very secondary role in the fighting, must have been very puzzled by the presence of Florence Nightingale and her squad of nurses, all unveiled, among those rough Christian fighting men and, it is said, were absolutely bewildered by the Scotsmen in kilts who showed their knees.

Just the same, the Muslim empire was at last coming to grips with some of the realities of the outside world. In February 1856, the sultan issued an important reform edict, the Hatt-i Humayun, prepared by the French, British, and Austrian ambassadors in Istanbul. It guaranteed full liberty of conscience to all Ottoman subjects and opened all offices to them, whatever their religion. Christians could now even join the army, which inevitably would mean the end of the Jihad. But they could also buy themselves out if called up for military service. Torture was abolished and prisons reformed. The Treaty of Paris, signed the following month as the last act of the Crimean War, recognized Turkey's identity as a European nation; the future of the Danubian nations was left to be settled later. Russia, the loser, gave up to Turkey the mouth of the Danube and a bit of Bessarabia, peopled by Turkish Muslim migrants. Interestingly, when the Indian Mutiny broke out at about this time (1857), the British were convinced the revolt was inspired by the Jihad, and one of the first actions carried out by the large Muslim contingent in the rebellion was to restore the old Muslim Mogul empire to power. After defeating the mutineers, as Rudolph Peters reminds us, the British began to give more and more government jobs to the Hindu and Sikh population of India, while the Muslims were more and more shunted aside.

A new crisis was hovering in eastern Europe. In 1875, an insurrection broke out in the provinces of Muslim Bosnia and Herzegovina, followed by another rebellion in the Christian town of Batak, in Bulgaria, which was put down with so much savagery that, as Noel Barber describes it in *Lords of the Golden Horn,* "repercussions of horror rippled across the world." The awful atrocities were revealed to the world by an American journalist, J. A. MacGahan, of the *London Daily News,* who happened to arrive in Istanbul three months later and who traveled to Batak to find out what had happened. Barber reproduces part of MacGahan's article in his book. Because of its very awfulness it is, once again, necessary reading. Massacres deserve more than a sentence like "more than three thousand people were killed." We must, to remember, read what massacring three thousand people can mean.

> I counted from the saddle a hundred skulls, picked and licked clean: all of women and children. We entered the town. On every side were skulls and skeletons charred among the ruins, or lying entire where they fell in their clothing. They were skeletons of girls and women with long brown hair hanging to their skulls. We approached the church. There these remains were more frequent, until the ground was literally covered with skeletons, skulls and putrefying bodies in clothing. Between the church and the school there were heaps. The stench was fearful. We entered the churchyard. The sight was more dreadful. The whole churchyard for three feet deep was festering with dead bodies partly covered—hands, legs, arms and heads projected in ghastly confusion. I saw many little hands, heads and feet covered with beautiful hair. The church was still worse. The floor was covered with rotting bodies quite uncovered. I never imagined anything so fearful. There were three thousand bodies in the churchyard and church. . . . In the school, a fine building, two hundred women and children had been burned alive. All over the town there were the same scenes. . . . The man who did all this, Achmed Aga, has been promoted and is still Governor of the district. No crime invented by Turkish ferocity was left uncommitted.

Quite a few Englishmen must have retched over their eggs and bacon when they read MacGahan's dispatch in the *Daily News* on the morning of August 7, 1876. Perhaps some present-day readers will retch, too. Whatever the squeamish may think, it is not in bad taste to reprint such hideous extracts. Human beings need to be reminded all the time of the savagery of which we are capable. The men who massacred the townfolk of Batak believed they were doing the work of God. Maybe not. Some of the massacrers were Bulgarian.

At the Berlin Congress in 1878, chaired by Bismarck and also attended by Russia, Austria, Britain, France, Italy, and Turkey, Bulgaria's request for independence from the Turks was immediately recognized by the participants. Rumania and Serbia were also given their freedom from Turkish rule. Montenegro, which along with Serbia had also fought against Turkey the previous year and which had been independent since 1389, had its boundaries extended two years later. For centuries it had been a refuge for all in the Balkans who had refused to accept Muslim rule. Bosnia and Herzegovina left the Ottoman empire and joined the Austrian one. The Ottoman empire was dwindling fast in size. A bit of it even went to distant Britain, who cunningly managed to snatch Cyprus out of the mess.

By this time Britain, with her numerous Muslim subjects in India, had acquired a certain expertise in Islamic affairs. The *Quarterly Review,* in its January 1877 issue—twenty years after the Indian Mutiny —had commented at length on a recent meeting of Muslim lawyers in Hindustan on the question of the allegiance of their co-religionists to Queen Victoria. The issue was "nothing less than the question whether Hindustan was a Dar-al-Harb or enemy country, that is whether the Jihad was in active or potential existence there, and consequently whether or not Muslims could, consistently with their faith, preserve their allegiance to their Christian rulers." In other words, whether a Jihad against Britain was called for.

"The decision was given almost unanimously in favor of peace and submission to the existing rulers," the *Quarterly Review* reported, concluding hopefully:

> The chief argument adduced in support of this view was a convincing proof of the truth of the theory that not only is the spirit of Islam favorable to peace and progress but that such spirit really actuates its professors now. The practice of Muhammad himself was adduced, namely, that when he laid siege to a town, or declared war against a tribe or people, he invariably delayed his operations till sunset, that he might ascertain whether the "izan" or call to prayers was heard amongst them. If it were, he refrained from the attack, maintaining that when the practice of religion was allowed by the rulers of the place he had no grievance against them. This one argument, and the fact that the name of our most gracious sovereign is now inserted in the "Khotbah" or Friday "bidding-prayer" in all mosques throughout India, is sufficient proof that Islam is not antagonistic either to religious or political toleration, and that the doctrine of Jihad, or holy war, is not as dangerous or barbarous as is generally imagined.

PART ELEVEN

THE JIHAD RETURNS

60

THE GREAT UNHOLY WARS:
DAR-AL-HARB 1912–1945

RITAIN ITSELF, THANKS TO ITS geographical position, had always
been safe from the Jihad. Moreover, the self-liberation of
Britain's Indian Muslim subjects did not lapse into a blood-drenched
upheaval—at least not until seventy years later when, after World War
II, Pakistan tore itself out of the Indian political fabric and became an
independent Muslim state. But in the Balkans, the terminating divisions between Muslims and Christians had been, as we have seen, and
still are, occasions for ferocious massacres and, afterward, for more
wars among the liberated Christian states.

The Jihad process of cleansing itself of its victims has often been
as bloody as the Jihad itself, as new nations have emerged out of the
mess. The experience of history largely fashioned each of these nations' futures, each in its own way. But they all resembled one another
by their common experience as Christian subjects of Muslim masters.

There was no tolerance, at least at first, among the people of these
new Balkan states being carved out of the multi-hued racial non-
melting pot of the region. As they had fought and killed their Muslim
occupants (who had often been the first to start the massacring process)
in past decades, they now fought and killed one another with all the
gusto expected of mustachioed brigands of the mountains and the
plains. The new Balkan countries were often not only inexperienced in
self-rule, they also had no example to follow except the Ottoman one,

in the most recent centuries, of intolerance and corruption. Many of the worst aspects of Ottoman government and bureaucracy were taken over by these new states as the norm. Backwardness, moreover, was part of the Ottoman way of life. It became part of of the Ottoman legacy to its former dependencies.

Until the death of Suleiman the Magnificent in 1566, the Ottoman empire had been, in terms of economic progress, the equivalent of western Europe. But afterward it had stagnated for three centuries while the rest of Europe had drawn well ahead. The East European and Balkan frontiers, moreover, were not always drawn with any sense of balance, justice, language, or ethnology. Some populations sometimes found themselves in one country when most of the people wished to be in another. Transylvania—sometimes Rumanian, sometimes Hungarian—is a classic example of these confused boundary shifts. Finally, the Ottoman heritage, and the divisions that came with it, proved a political disaster for these new countries trying to emerge into a new political spectrum. It still is.

Their differences culminated in the First Balkan War between Bulgaria, Serbia, and Greece, against Turkey, in 1912, which ended in confusion and the next year in the Second Balkan War when Bulgaria attacked the Serbs and the Greeks, and then was attacked in turn by these two countries, which were joined by Rumania and Turkey in their assault. Next, Albania raided Serbia and Serbia invaded Albania, the Austrians demanded that the Serbs evacuate Albania and that Greece leave Albania alone. Every country in the Balkans seemed to be making territorial demands on the countries around it. Albania became independent in 1913; Serbia expanded the same year by annexing a slice of Macedonia. Bulgaria added Rumelia and expanded south to the Aegean Sea. Greece expanded east and acquired Salonika; Crete also became Greek. The whole region was a cauldron of political and ethnic turbulence.

The archduke of Austria, Francis Ferdinand, decided that he should help to unravel the situation in his own empire where its Bosnian province, which was ruled from Vienna, was claimed by the Serbs. On June 18, 1914, the archduke and his wife visited Sarajevo, the capital of Bosnia, where they were promptly murdered, with Serbian connivance, by a young revolutionary, Gavrilo Princip. Princip was acting for the Serbian terrorist organization the Black Hand, which was demanding that Bosnia be detached from Austria and be made over to Serbia. Austria, dissatisfied by Serbian explanations, declared war against Serbia on July 28. An avalanche of declarations of war followed as alliances between countries came into force one after another: on August 1 Germany declared war on Russia, on August 3 Germany declared war on France; on August 4 Germany declared war on Belgium, and Britain declared war on Germany. On August 5, tiny Montenegro, loyal to her alliances, declared war against the Austrian Empire; on August 6 Austria declared war on Russia, and Serbia declared war on Germany; on August 8 Montenegro declared war on Germany; on August 12 both France and Britain declared war on Austria; and on August 28 Austria declared war on Belgium. The Jihad still had no apparent place in this war, not even a very small one. But its time was approaching. John Buchan wrote his novel *Greenmantle* around the submerged conflict that raged between Britain and Germany's ally, Turkey, in Asia. The Turks called it a Jihad. The British called it "The Great Game," with the Turks as adversaries now instead of the Russians.

On August 3, the day before war was declared, Winston Churchill, then First Lord of the Admiralty, had announced that two warships being built in British shipyards for the Turkish Navy, the *Sultan Osman* and the *Reshadiye,* because of the coming war with Germany, would not be delivered to the Turks, but would be requisitioned for the British Navy instead. The Turks were outraged. The next day, by chance, two German cruisers, the *Goeben* and the *Breslau,* after evading a pursuing British squadron, appeared at the entrance to the Dardanelles asking for permission to enter. Events, manipulated by a clever German diplomat, the German ambassador to Turkey, Prince von Wangenheim, now moved very fast. The ambassador, alerted of the German cruisers' arrival, immediately proposed to the Turkish war minister, Pasha Enver Bey, that Turkey buy the German ships to replace the undelivered British vessels, payment to be arranged as some indeterminate future date. The German crews would remain on board and sign on for service in the Turkish navy. The Germans were delighted to have saved their ships. The Turks were delighted to have acquired at virtually no cost these two fine vessels.

Turkey quietly and carefully prepared to enter the war on the side of Germany. On October 29, without any declaration of war, several Turkish warships, including the two Germano-Turkish cruisers, attacked the Russian Black Sea ports of Odessa, Theodosia, and Sebastopol, sinking a number of ships in their harbors. Four days later, on November 2, Russia declared war on Turkey, and on November 5 both France and Britain followed suit. Nine days after that, on November 14, the sultan, in his capacity as caliph, head of the world-wide Muslim community, proclaimed a Jihad against all countries and all people making war against Turkey—and her Christian allies, Germany and Austria.

The inspiration for this Muslim Jihad had, in fact, come from a Christian monarch, Kaiser Wilhelm II of Germany. As Peter Hopkirk reminds us in his *On Secret Service East of Constantinople,* the German emperor, who longed to destroy Britain and its empire, ordered his agents "to inflame the entire Muslim world against Britain, this hateful, lying, and unscrupulous nation." The main target was British-ruled India, with nearly sixty million followers of Allah, the most populous Muslim nation in the world. Earlier, in the first years of the twentieth century, the kaiser had begun to cultivate assiduously the Islamic world, also spreading the rumor that he had secretly converted to Islam and, incognito, had made the pilgrimage to Mecca. He now called himself "The Protector of Islam."

The call to war was aimed also at the Muslim North African troops serving in the French army, at the Muslims in the Indian Army, and at the czarist soldiers from the Muslim provinces of Russia. It was a smooth operation that Turks and Germans cunningly hoped would cause chaos in allied ranks. It caused a big scare, but that was virtually all. The only troops on which it had the slightest effect were some Indian Muslim troops defending the Suez Canal. Some of the Indian troops, mainly Muslim Baluchis from the Iranian-Indian-Afghan border region, refused to fight their fellow Muslim Turks and deserted to the Turks. A number of Indian troops in faraway Singapore mutinied. Several dozens, not all of them Muslims, were shot. But Muslims in the Allied armies, Jihad notwithstanding, in fact generally fought as bravely against the Muslim Turks in the Dardanelles and Mesopotamian campaigns, as they did against the Germans on the western front.

The Jihad against the Russian army was more violent, but equally unsuccessful. We can consider the Turkish offensive against the Russians in the Caucasus as the fist phase of this new Jihad, led by Enver Pasha, one of the leaders of the ruling Young Turks political movement. Part of the Turkish Third Army, renamed for the occasion "The Army of Islam," attacked the Russians through the freezing mountain passes in midwinter snow and blizzards. Their target was the small town of Sarikamish. Many of the attacking troops were tough and devout Arab tribesmen from the desert in their thin uniforms, picturesque headdresses, and sandals. Fifteen thousand Muslim soldiers froze to death in the mountains of Armenia. Fighting bravely but repulsed everywhere, only some fifteen thousand of the ninety-five thousand men of the Turkish Third Army survived the campaign. Blaming the Christian Armenians for their defeat, the Turks began in April the wholesale deportation of the Armenians in which about one million died during their death march to the south. Some young women survived by converting to Islam and agreeing to marry their Muslim abductors. In eastern Turkey, the Russians also attacked and took the fortress city of Erzerum in February 1915. On the eve of the fall of the city Russian soldiers claimed they had seen a huge cross appear in the sky, a special omen for them in the war between the Cross and the Crescent.

Meanwhile there was also fighting in the Dardanelles where an Anglo-French fleet attacked the straits in January and March 1915, before the army landings a few weeks later by British and French troops and those of the Australian and New Zealand Army Corps (ANZAC). The attack had turned into another manifestation of Muslim piety by the devout Turkish defenders who, under the direction of their imams, sang appropriate verses of the Koran as they fired their heavy shells at the allied dreadnoughts, turning the battle into an unscheduled Jihad. Former private W. Carrol of the 21st AIF (Australian Imperial Force) Battalion remembers the Turks as particularly "ferocious soldiers" as, he said, "they were not only fighting in defense of their homeland, they were also fighting a Jihad, a holy war against the infidel. They were filled with holy zeal, Allah, Allah, Allah, they shouted as they plunged forward to attack." Then the Turks suddenly found themselves the target of a Jihad called by their Arab subjects in the Hejaz—the Prophet's own birthplace—against their Ottoman rulers.

Negotiations had been underway since October 1914 between the British and the Hashemite, Hussein ibn Ali, Grand Sharif of Mecca, thirty-seventh straight linear descendant of the Prophet. The British war minister, field marshal Lord Kitchener, had offered Hussein independence for the Hejaz (which it was not his to give) if it came over to the Allied side. The Arabs had been in a seething rage of revolt against the Turkish overlords for a considerable time and in June 1916, from the very birthplace of the Prophet Muhammad, the sharif of Mecca called all the Arabs to a Holy War against the Turks, proclaimed the independence of Hejaz with himself as king, and attacked the Turkish garrison at Medina, which surrendered two days later. The Jihad was now primarily a war of Muslim against Muslim.

Aided and advised by a capable young British officer, Colonel T. E. Lawrence, the Arabs attacked the Turkish strong points all over the Hejaz and blew up the railway line linking the province to Damascus and the outside world, thus preventing any Turkish counterattack. Under Lawrence and Hussein's son, the emir Feisal, the Arabs from the Hejaz fought their way into Palestine and Syria. A local internecine Jihad continued in the Hejaz well after World War I had ended with the Allied victory over Germany, Austria, Bulgaria, and Turkey in November 1918. Britain, France, and Russia had then recognized Hussein as king of Hejaz and head of the Arab people. But in eastern Arabia, along the Persian Gulf, there existed another Arab kingdom, Nedj, ruled by Ibn Saud, the leader of the Wahabis, a Muslim puritanical sect, who led his people to war (a Jihad, too, since Wahabis once considered all other Muslims heretics, deserving only of death) against King Hussein in May 1919, and defeated him. In 1924 Ibn Saud captured Mecca and Hussein was forced to abdicate. With British assistance Hussein replaced his lost kingdom by Iraq and Jordan, Transjordan as it was then called, while Ibn Saud in 1926 was proclaimed king of the Hejaz and Nedj, which six years later was renamed Saudi Arabia.

In the strangely convoluted and twisted ambiance of Middle Eastern politics, in which calls for a Jihad were and can still be murderously symbolic or simply be impulsive orders carried out on a whim, we must recall, if only because decency requires they not be forgotten, the massacres of perhaps one million Armenians in 1915. They died mainly while being deported from Turkey to what is now Syria and Iraq on the orders of Enver Pasha, then the Turkish war minister. There was another holocaust in which an estimated one hundred thousand Greeks in Smyrna died in 1922, all of them victims of particularly addled forms of Holy War. Many Turks would insist that these holocausts were only the inevitable consequence of flouted Turkish patriotism. Let it be noted, however, that the victims were all Christians, which does seem to give the massacre of Greeks and Armenians a Jihad-like quality.

Enver Pasha appointed to the post of governor of the eastern region of Van, where many of the Armenians lived, his brother-in-law, Jevet Bey, known locally as "The Blacksmith," since his favorite torture was to nail horse shoes to the feet of his victims. The official Pryce Report, presented to Parliament in London in October 1916, estimated that approximately one-third of the two million Armenians who lived in Turkey were killed or died from ill treatment; one-third escaped to Russia; and one-third, those living in the large cities, were unharmed.

But cold statistics don't tell the whole story. This extract from a U.S. State Department report, quoted by Noel Barber, at least gives an idea of how their deportations were carried out. It concerns a convoy of three thousand Armenians sent to Aleppo.

> On the first of June 1915 a convoy of 3,000 Armenians (who were later joined by 12,000 more), mostly women, girls and children, left Harpoot. All the way to Ras-ul-Ain, the first station on the Baghdad line, the existence of these wretched travelers was one prolonged horror. The gendarmes went ahead, informing the half-savage tribes of the mountains that several thousand Armenian women and girls were approaching. The Arabs and Kurds began to carry off the girls, the mountaineers fell upon them repeatedly, killing and violating the women, and the gendarmes joined in the orgy. One by one the few men that accompanied the convoy were killed. . . . When the diminishing band reached the Euphrates, they had been so repeatedly robbed that they had practically nothing left except a few ragged clothes, and even these the Kurds now took, the consequence being that the whole convoy marched for five days completely naked under the scorching sun. For another five days they did not have a morsel of bread or a drop of water. Hundreds fell dead on the way, their tongues were turned to charcoal, and when, at the end of five days, they reached a fountain, the whole convoy naturally rushed toward it. But here the policemen barred their way and forbade them to take a single drop of water . . . .

The journey took seventy days. Out of the 18,000 deported Armenians, only 150 women and children reached Aleppo alive.

The last days of Greek Smyrna (today's Izmir) does not make for pleasant reading either. But it is necessary reading, in the same way that we are urged to remember the murder of six million Jews by the Christian Germans in the gas chambers of Auschwitz and the other Nazi concentration camps during World War II. Lest we forget. The expression is made to measure. I quote Barber again:

> The Turkish commander Nurredin, a man with a reputation for sadism, sent for the Greek patriarch, Monsignor Chrysostomos. As the Patriarch entered the room, Nurredin spat at him, pointed to a dossier and told him that he had been sentenced to death by a tribunal

in Ankara. "There is nothing left but for the people to give their judgment," he shouted. "Now get out of my sight."

The old man was walking down the steps when the Turkish general appeared on the balcony above and yelled to the mob, "Treat
him as he deserves."

A patrol of twenty French marines had accompanied the patriarch to the general's headquarters, but as a gesture, and under the
strictest orders not to interfere. Now they watched horrified and
helpless as the crowd tore the old man to pieces, gouging out his
eyes, cutting off his ears, nose and hands. . . . The murder of the
Patriarch was soon accepted as a license to murder and loot. The wife
of an American missionary, who escaped at the last moment,
watched terrified as Turkish troops stormed into their home and
stripped it. In her words, the Turks started the most horrible looting,
raping, and killing. . . . The American teachers in our American
Girls' School watched the soldiers kill civilians in the street in front
of the school, enter homes and kill families, and throw them out into
the street. Within a few hours, twenty women who had taken refuge
in a British house were taken out and violated. An American's grave
was opened, the body exhumed and torn to pieces. Every Greek and
Armenian made, as though by instinct, for the quayside. . . . Thousands lined the edge of the harbor. Hundreds jumped into the water
and swam—but not to safety; for under the policy of strict neutrality
the warships could not take them aboard.

There were twenty-one foreign warships in Smyrna harbor that day:
three American destroyers; two British battleships, three cruisers, and six
destroyers; an Italian cruiser and destroyer; and three French cruisers;
and two destroyers. Their orders were to observe strict neutrality as the
Turks took over the city from the departing Greeks. They carried out
their orders with aloof and superb inhumanity. Thousands of tightly
packed Greek and Armenian refugees, men, women, and children, stood
all night, shoulder to shoulder on the wharf, screaming for help. The
band on the deck of a British battleship played a light musical selection
to show that whatever might be happening around them, stiff upper-
lipped Britons knew how to remain cool in the direst circumstances.

"We were in the harbor and they were all on the pier and at midnight they started screaming," wrote Ernest Hemingway, then corre-
spondent for the *Toronto Star,* recalling the plight of the refugees.
Some fell into the water and drowned. Some were crushed to death.
The captains of the Allied ships looked on. Noninterference was the

order of the day. The wretched Greeks and Armenians screamed all night for help in the name of God and humanity. But God and humanity were elsewhere that night. In the morning the Allies relented and sent their boats to pick up some of the women and children who had spent the night screaming on the waterfront.

That night the European, Greek, and Armenian quarters of the town went up in flames. Kemal Mustafa Ataturk, soldier hero and future president of Turkey, watched the fire from his mansion, high on a hill overlooking the inferno. "It is a sign that Turkey is purged of the traitors, the Christians and the foreigners, and that Turkey is for the Turks," he said. Holy War, racism, ultranationalism, hatred of the foreigner, they're all there. It is not one of Kemal Ataturk's proudest declarations. But the ghazi, as he was known to his compatriots, knew what he wanted for Turkey: the abolition of the Ottoman empire and of the caliphate. He considered these institutions foreign to those of Turkey. He also wished to jettison the influence of Muhammad, the Prophet himself. The French historian J. Benoist-Méchin recounts Kemal Ataturk's comments, which he often repeated in his moments of anger: "Cruel and criminal laws in Turkey have been fixed for more than five hundred years on the rules and theories of an old Arab sheik, and through the abusive interpretation of ignorant and filthy priests. . . . Islam, this absurd theology of an immoral Bedouin, is a rotting corpse which poisons our lives" (*Le loup et le léopard,* p. 323). But there were no fatwas against Kemal Ataturk for these withering views which he expressed about Muhammad and the Muslim religious establishment.

Admiral Mark Bristol, American high commissioner in Istanbul, who commanded the American naval forces in the area, blamed the Greeks, "about the worst race in the Near East," for the fire. He considered it "a calamity to let the Greeks have anything in this part of the world." Edward Hale Bierstadt, executive secretary of the United States Emergency Committee, blamed the Turks for the fire. "They wished to hide forever all traces of sack, massacre, and rapine that had been going on for four days. And more, they had determined that Christianity should be obliterated from the Christian capital of Asia Minor, that it should be utterly wiped out by fire and sword. So it was done." Perhaps Smyrna was the last belated Jihad overlap from World War I. The Jihad also inspired the defeated leader of the Young Turks, Enver Pasha, who in the closing months of the war created the ambitiously named but short-lived Army of Islam, with which he planned to invade the disintegrating Russian empire and liberate the Muslim republics from their Slav masters.

Mustafa Kemal, who assumed the added name Ataturk in 1934, led Turkey into the modern world when he became president of his country in 1923. He gloried in his quality as a Turk and felt no loyalty to the multicultural Ottoman empire of the past with its Greek, Arab, Moorish, Copt, Macedonian, Bulgarian, Albanian, Bosnian, Moldavian, and other minorities. He also jettisoned the official status of Islam along the way, and with it disappeared the sultanate and, above all, the caliphate. Since 1924, Islam has survived without a caliph, although efforts have been made by international Muslim congresses to bring the caliphate back into existence.

The caliphate vanished. So did the Jihad. Even the word became unknown to most Westerners. But eclipse of the Jihad was only temporary. The Jihad has since returned.

It first reappeared during World War II in Europe, in Yugoslavia, incognito and not really itself, unrecognized by all except maybe some Muslims. It was part of the murderous confusion in the inextricable disorder of an occupied country already divided by centuries of ethnic, political, social, national, and religious rivalries. If that sentence is so convoluted that it is unclear, that is the way it should be, because it reflects the darker, twisted side of much of the political reality of the Balkans since World War II. And for centuries before.

Yugoslavia, and particularly Bosnia, is where three religions meet: Muslim, Orthodox, and Catholic. Adherents of the three groups were active, usually on both the Allied and the Nazi sides during World War II, but in a mainly Yugoslav context. Noel Malcolm recalls in his history of Bosnia that at least one million Yugoslavs were killed during the four years of Axis occupation, from 1941 to 1945, most of them probably by other Yugoslavs. The Muslims of Bosnia played their part, as did the Catholic Croats and the Orthodox Serbs, in the orgy of killings that distinguished that unhappy and divided country during the four years of German and Italian occupation.

The Ustachis of Croatia massacred Serbs, Bosnians, and Tito's Partisans. The Cetniks of Serbia massacred Croats, Bosnians, and sometimes Tito's Partisans. The Partisans massacred Cetniks, Croatians, Bosnians, Ustachis, and Germans. Everyone was killing everyone else. Presumably the Herzegovinians were also doing their share of killing, but one doesn't hear about them so much. Malcolm mentions, however, that in 1941 Serb peasants of Herzegovina destroyed a Croat Ustachi group, following it up a few months later with a massacre of local Croat and Muslim villagers, including six hundred Muslims from the Bileca district, and some time later with another group of five hundred in the Visegrad district. In those circumstances, Noel Malcolm reflects, "the most natural and popular course for Muslims to follow was to form their own local defense units and try to protect themselves against all comers."

So the Muslims were involved, sometimes spectacularly, for and against all factions in the World War II Yugoslav imbroglio, at first largely on the German side, but after 1943 largely against the Germans. In 1941 the Bosnians even raised a Waffen S.S. Division, the "Handzar" Division, of 21,000 men, so named after the fearsome Turkish scimitar of former wars. Sent to northern and eastern Bosnia for "peacekeeping" operations in March 1943, the Handzar division distinguished itself by the large-scale massacre of the local Serb population. The precise number of their victims is not known. It may have run into the thousands. Serbs were recently massacring Bosnian Muslims. The infernal cycle of massacre and revenge, stamped out by Tito, has started again.

The Grand Mufti of Jerusalem, al-Haj Mohamed Amin al-Hussein, president of the Supreme Muslim Council, chased out of Palestine by the British for his alleged Nazi sympathies, made an unexpected appearance in Yugoslavia to preach holy war against the Jews and their British allies. He was received by Hitler and discussed with him the future of Palestine and of the Arab nation after the war. His arm raised in the Nazi salute, the mufti reviewed the "Handzar" S.S. division in their barracks and urged the soldiers to fight against Tito, "a friend of the Jews and a foe of the Prophet." In 1944, in an address to the S.S. troopers, some 2,000 of whom had gone over to Tito during the past year, he put Islam and Nazism on the same lofty level, claiming "there are considerable similarities between Idslamic principles and National Socialism." In a March 1, 1944, radio address from Berlin to the Arab countries, the mufti called on his listeners to "kill the Jews wherever you find them," for, he said, "this pleases God, history, and religion."

However much Hitler himself may have sympathized with the mufti's views, the Handzar division was not a military success story. Faced with mass desertions and the disintegration of the Muslim division, the Germans disbanded it at the end of 1944. Noel Campbell estimates the number of Muslims killed during the war at 75,000, just over 8 percent of the total population of Yugoslavia. "Muslims had fought on all sides—Ustasa, German, Cetnik, Partisan—and been killed by all sides," he sadly concludes.

61

TERRORISM:
THE WEST 1980S–1990S

S O, HALF A CENTURY LATER, we come to our modern Jihad. This Jihad, however, is no longer history or an expression of religious intolerance or persecution. It is mainly an expression of political terrorism. In fact, of terrorism pure and simple. It is not merely a forlorn and hopeless enterprise in the Balkans—it is that as well—but it is a well-directed, world-wide movement, with Europe as one of its main targets.

With the Hezbollahs, the Islamic Jihad movement, Muslim extremism of every type, the ayatollah Khomeini, writers threatened with death as apostates, airliners hijacked or blown out of the sky, the kidnapping of hostages, bombs in Paris department stores and New York skyscrapers, killers on the loose and murder, murder everywhere, Jihad has become an everyday word in our language. Let us not fail to note, however, that the Jihad of terrorism is repudiated by large numbers of Muslims who do not identify themselves with it.

The Jihad also has come back in its traditional military guise, but in a confused, untidy way in which Muslim countries go to Holy War against one another. For Islam, more than ever, is at war against itself. During the eight-year-long first Gulf War between Iran and Iraq in the 1980s, both sides invoked the Jihad against each other. During the second Gulf War, between Iraq and the United Nations coalition, which included several Muslim nations—Kuwait, Saudi Arabia,

410

Egypt, the United Arab Emirates, Pakistan—both sides were on a Jihad again. In the name of Allah, Muslim fought against Muslim as well as Christian. Most worryingly, both Islam and the West see each other as potential enemies of tomorrow. The future is a source of concern, not of optimism.

It need not be so, the massacre and pillage of yesteryear notwithstanding. This book recounts only one side of the reality of Muslim-Christian confrontation over more than a thousand years. But the truth has two facets, and my book presents only one of them. We must accept what our ancestors, Christian or Muslim, did. It was done and nothing can change that now. We must know our past and accept it. It is all part of the immense mosaic of mankind, whose history is a complex picture of good and bad. Let us keep it in the past where it belongs.

Now we have arrived at the brink of the twenty-first century. What the future holds for the relationship between Islam and the rest of the world, notably the West, is still a matter of conjecture. The present is not encouraging. Whither the Jihad?

It needs to be said: Islam considers itself doctrinally a religion whose destiny it is to dominate and to rule the world. In the spiritual sphere it believes that it has taken over from the older Jewish and Christian religions. It considers them outdated and itself therefore entitled to the recognition of its true and superior status, and to their deference. Politically others see Islam and it sees itself as the would-be successors of the Russians and now, strangely enough, of the Americans. Let us never forget the ideological dimension of Islam.

In Muslim countries which are far from the West and its protective mantle—Pakistan, the Sudan, Saudi Arabia, and Iran, among others—Islam requires religious submission from its own people. Prison or death can be the penalty for those who do not acquiesce.

After the past 150 years or so of political eclipse, Muslim countries are no longer under colonial tutelage, and thanks to their oil deposits, they are now rich and powerful. They intend to make full use of these advantages and, in fact, are already doing that. Hopefully, some will draw their inspiration from tenth-century Cordova, where a gracious and highly cultured mixed civilization of Muslims, Jews, and Christians flourished. But I fear that an anti-Christian miscalculation may take over, inspired by the overconfidence that the presence of a few million Muslims in Europe may give. A Muslim friend in Paris told me a couple of years ago, "Our great strength is that people are afraid of us." That type of thinking is also likely to lead to a major miscalculation in the way Islam approaches the West. Similarly, a British publisher who rejected this book, because it feared reprisals, told me, "We have to play the game according to Muslim rules." Obviously I have failed to do so.

They were both wrong.

Let us end with an epilogue that should serve as a model for the future, or at least as a guide.

EPILOGUE

AN ACTION IN ALL ITS LUSTER

T HE FRIENDSHIP BETWEEN THE EIGHTEENTH-CENTURY Turkish Grand
Vizier Topal Osman and the French harbor master Vincent
Arnaud shows us what the relationship between men of good faith can
be, however wide apart their religious, or for that matter, their political
beliefs may be. I end with a passage from Creasy's *History of the
Ottoman Turks*:

"The conduct of the war in Persia against the Turks was resumed
in 1733, by Nadir Kouli Khan (during whose absence the Ottomans
had obtained considerable advantages), and that chieftain gave the
sultan's forces several defeats, and laid siege to the city of Baghdad.
But that important bulwark of the Ottoman empire was rescued from
him by the Grand Vizier, Topal Osman.

"This is a name justly celebrated by Christian as well as Moslem
writers; and it is gratifying to turn from the scenes of selfish intrigue,
violence, and oppression which the careers of Grand Viziers generally
exhibit, and to pause on the character of a Turk . . . who was not only
skilful, sage, and valiant, but who gave proofs of a noble spirit of generosity and gratitude such as does honor to human nature. . . .

"Osman was born in the Morea: he was educated in the Serail, at
Constantinople, where native Turks were now frequently brought up,
since the practice of levying Christian children for the sultan's service
had been discontinued. At the age of twenty-six he had attained the

rank of Beylerbey, and was sent on a mission from the Porte to the governor of Egypt. On the voyage his ship encountered a Spanish corsair and was captured after a brave defense, in the course of which Osman received a wound which lamed him for life, from which he obtained the name Topal, or Lame, Osman.

"The Spanish pirates carried their prize to Malta, where a Frenchman of Marseilles named Vincent Arnaud was then harbor master. Arnaud came on board the prize and was scrutinizing the prisoners when Osman addressed him and said, 'Can you do a generous and gallant action? Ransom me, and take my word that you shall lose nothing by it.' Struck by Osman's appearance and manner the Frenchman turned to the captain of the vessel and asked the amount of the ransom. The answer was a thousand sequins, a sum nearly equal to five hundred British pounds. Arnaud then said to the Turk, 'I know nothing of you, and you would have me risk a thousand sequins on your bare word!' Osman replied that Arnaud could not be blamed for not trusting the word of a stranger, 'but,' he added, 'I have nothing at present but my word of honor to give you, nor do I pretend to assign any reason why you should trust it. However, I tell you that if you *do* trust it, you shall have no occasion to repent.'

"The Oriental proverb says that 'there are paths which lead straight from heart to heart.' Arnaud was so wrought upon by Osman's frank and manly manner that he prevailed on the Spaniards to set him at liberty for six hundred sequins, which sum the generous Frenchman immediately paid. He provided Osman with a home and medical assistance until his wounds were healed; and then gave him the means of proceeding on his voyage to Egypt. As soon as Osman reached Cairo, he sent back a thousand sequins as payment to Arnaud, with a present of five hundred crowns, and of rich furs, which are considered the most honorable of all gifts in the East.

"A few years afterward, Osman signalized himself greatly in the Turkish reconquest of the Morea, and in 1722 he was appointed Seraskier, and commanded all the Turkish troops in that country. He immediately invited Arnaud's son to visit him in the Morea, and conferred mercantile privileges on the young man, and placed opportunities for lucrative commerce within his reach, which enabled him to accumulate large wealth, with which he returned to his father.

"In 1728 Osman was governor of Rumelia, and he then invited his French benefactor and his son to visit him at Nissa, his seat of government, where he treated them with distinction and honor such as no

Ottoman Turk had ever before been seen to accord to a Christian. On taking leave of him at Nissa, Arnaud said, as a compliment, that he trusted to live to visit Osman as Grand Vizier at Constantinople. When Topal Osman attained that rank in 1731, he again invited Arnaud and his son to become his guests, and, receiving them in his palace, in the presence of the highest dignitaries of the state, Osman pointed out the elder Arnaud and said, 'Behold this Frenchman: I was once a slave loaded with chains, streaming with blood, and covered with wounds; this is the man who redeemed and saved me; this is by master and benefactor; to him I am indebted for life, liberty, fortune, and everything I enjoy. Without knowing me, he paid for me a large ransom, sent me away upon my bare word, and gave me a ship to carry me where I pleased. Where is there even a Moslem capable of such generosity?' He then took both the Arnauds by the hand and questioned them earnestly and kindly concerning their fortune and prospects, ending with an Asiatic sentence, 'God's goodness is without bounds.' He afterward gave them many receptions in private, when they met without ceremony as friends, and he sent them back to their country loaded with the richest presents.

"Hanway well remarks on this exhibition of gratitude by the vizier . . . that 'this conduct appears the more generous, when it is considered what contempt and aversion the prejudices of education often create in a Turk against the Christian. . . .' "

If history has a lesson for us all, Christians and Muslims, it is here.

BIBLIOGRAPHY

Ahmed, Akbar S. *Discovering Islam*. London, 1988.

Al-Banna, Hasan. *Peace in Islam*. London, 1996.

———. *Jihad*. London, 1996.

Ameer Ali Moulvi, Sayed. *A Critical Examination of the Life and Teachings of Mohammed*. Edinburgh, 1873.

Armstrong, Karen. *Holy War*. London, 1988.

Aziz, Ahmad. *A History of Islamic Sicily*. Edinburgh, 1975.

Aziz, Philippe. *Les sectes secrètes de l'Islam*. Paris, 1983.

Aziza, Mahomed. *Le retour de l'Islam*. Paris, 1978.

Barber, Noel. *Lords of the Golden Horn*. London, 1973.

Barker, Thomas M. *Double Eagle and Crescent*. New York, 1967.

Barraclough, Geoffrey, ed. *The Times Atlas of World History*. London, 1984.

Barreau, Jean-Claude. *De l'Islam en général et du monde moderne en particulier*. Paris, 1991.

Bat Yéor. *The Decline of Eastern Christianity under Islam, from Jihad to Dhimmitude: Seventh–Twentieth Century*. London, 1996.

———. *The Dhimmi: Jews and Christians under Islam*. London, 1985.

———. *Juifs et Chrétiens sous L'Islam*. Paris, 1994.

Bazancourt, Baron de. *Histoire de la Sicile sous la domination des Normans*. Paris, 1846.

Beeching, Jack. *The Galleys at Lepanto*. London, 1982.

417

Bendiner, Elmer. *The Rise and Fall of Paradise.* New York, 1983.

Bennassar, Bartolome. *Histoire des Espagnols.* Paris, 1985.

Benoist-Méchin, Jacques. *Le loup et le léopard: Mustapha Kémal.* Paris, 1954.

Béraud-Villars, J. *Les Touaregs au pays du Cid.* Paris, 1946.

Bertrand, Louis. *The History of Spain.* London, 1952.

Bertuel, Joseph. *L'Islam—ses véritables origines.* Paris, 1981.

Biancamaria, J. T. *La Corse dans sa gloire et ses souffrances.* Paris, 1963.

Blachère, Régis. *Le Coran.* Paris, 1988.

Bodolai, Zoltan. *The Timeless Nation.* Sydney, 1977.

Boorstin, Daniel J. *The Discoverers.* New York, 1988.

Bradford, Ernle. *The Great Siege—Malta 1565.* London, 1961

Braudel, Fernand. *A History of Civilization.* London, 1993.

————. *The Mediterranean and the Mediterranean World in the Age of Phillip II.* London, 1973.

Bridge, Antony. *Suleiman the Magnificent.* London, 1983.

Brière, Claire, and Olivier Carré. *Islam, Guerre à l'Occident.* Paris, 1983.

Bruce, George. *Collins Dictionary of War.* London, 1995.

Bucaille, Maurice. *La Bible, le Coran et la science.* Paris, 1976.

Buchan, John. *Greenmantle.* London, 1949.

Burlot, Joseph. *La civilisation islamique.* Paris, 1990.

Buckhardt, Titus. *Moorish Culture in Spain.* London, 1972.

Cambridge History of Islam. Cambridge, 1950.

Cash, W. W. *Expansion of Islam.* London, 1928.

Chafiq Chahla. *La femme et le retour de l'Islam.* Paris, 1991.

Chevallier, Dominique, Guellouz Azzedine, and André Miquel. *Les Arabes, l'Islam et l'Europe.* Paris, 1991.

Clissold, Stephen. *Spain.* London, 1969.

————. *In Search of the Cid.* London, 1965.

Clogg, Richard. *A Short History of Modern Greece.* Cambridge, 1986.

Coles, Paul. *The Ottoman Impact on Europe.* London, 1968.

Collins, Roger. *The Arab Conquest of Spain 710–747.* London, 1989.

Condé, J. A. *History of the Dominion of the Arabs in Spain.* London, 1854.

Coppée, Henry. *History of the Conquest of Spain by the Arab-Moors.* Boston, 1881.

Crankshaw, Edward. *Maria Theresa.* London, 1969.

Crawford, Francis Marion. *Rulers of the South.* London, 1900.

Creasy, E. S. *History of the Ottoman Turks.* London, 1854.

Currey, Cdr. E. Hamilton. *Sea Wolves of the Mediterranean.* London, 1910.

Curtis, Lionel. *Civitas Dei.* London, 1934.

Davies, Norman. *Europe: A History.* London, 1996.

Davison, Roderic H. *Turkey, A Short History.* Huntingdon, 1988.

Dawson, Christopher. *The Making of Europe.* London, 1953.

Delcambre, Anne-Marie. *La parole d'Allah.* Paris, 1991.

Derry, T. K. *A Short History of Norway.* London, 1957.

Desmond, Stewart. *Early Islam.* New York, 1970.

Donia, Robert J., and John V. A. Fine Jr. *Bosnia-Herzegovina.* London, 1994.

Dozy, Reinhart. *Spanish Islam.* London, 1913.

Duby, George, ed. *Atlas historique.* Paris, 1987.

Dupuy, R. Ernest and Trevor N. *The Collins Encyclopedia of Military History.* London, 1993.

Durant, Will and Ariel. *The Story of Civilization.* New York, 1935–1975.

Edwards, William. *Notes on European History.* London, 1964.

Eggenberger. *A Dictionary of Battles.* London, 1967.

El-Bokhari. *Les traditions islamiques.* Paris, 1903–1914.

Eliot, C. ("Odysseus"). *Turkey in Europe.* London, 1900.

Elpeleg, Zui. *The Grand Mufti Haj Amin al-Hussain.* London, 1993.

Enciclopedia universal illustrada. Madrid, 1958.

Encyclopedia of Islam, The. Leyden, 1913, and London, 1960.

Epstein, Steven A. *Genoa and the Genoese.* Chapel Hill, N.C.,1996.

Esposito, John L. *The Islamic Threat, Myth or Reality.* New York, 1995.

Etienne, Bruno. *L'Islamisme radical.* Paris, 1987.

Famin, César. *Histoire des invasions des Sarrazins en Italie.* Paris, 1843.

Fernandez-Armesto, Felipe. *Fernando and Isabella.* London, 1975.

Finley, M. I. *Ancient Sicily.* London, 1979.

Fletcher, R. A. *The Quest for El Cid.* London, 1984.

Fletcher, Richard. *Moorish Spain.* Phoenix, Ariz., 1994.

Freely, John. *Istanbul.* London, 1996.

Freeman, Edward A. *The Ottoman Power in Europe.* London, 1877.

———. *The History and Conquests of the Saracens.* London, 1876.

Freese, J. H. *A Short Popular History of Crete.* London, 1897.

Fregosi, Paul. *Dreams of Empire.* London. 1989.

Frischauer, Paul. *Prince Eugene.* London, 1934.

Fuller, J. C. *The Decisive Battles of the Western World 480 B.C.—1757 A.D.* London, 1988.

Gabrieli, Francesco. *Mahomet et les grandes conquêtes arabes.* Paris, 1967.

Garaudy, Roger. *Promesses de l'Islam.* Paris, 1981 .

Gibbon, Edward. *The Decline and Fall of the Roman Empire.* London, 1897.

Gilman, Arthur. *The Saracens.* London, 1891.

Glubb, John. *The Lost Centuries.* London, 1967.

———. *The Empire of the Arabs.* London, 1963.

Grunebaum, G. von. *Medieval Islam: A Study in Cultural Orientation.* Chicago, 1947.

Guerdan, Rene. *Byzantium—Its Triumphs and Its Tragedy.* London, 1956.

Guillaume, Alfred. *Islam.* London, 1990.

Gumley, Frances, and Brian Redhead. *The Pillars of Islam.* London, 1990.

Haikal, Mohamed. *The Illusion of Triumph.* London, 1993.

Hakem, Ibn Abdel. *Conquête de l'Afrique du Nord et de l'Espagne.* Paris, 1947.

Hallak, Elizabeth, ed. *Chronicles of the Crusades.* London, 1989.

Halliday, Fred. *Islam and the Myth of Confrontation.* London, 1996.

Halperin, Charles J. *Russia and the Golden Horde.* London, 1985.

Hannay, David. *Spain.* London, 1987.

Hawkesworth, C. E. M. *The Last Century in Europe.* London, 1912.

Hibbert, Christopher. *Venice.* London, 1980.

Hitti, Philip K. *The Arabs—A Short History.* London, 1948.

Hole, Edwyn. *Andalus—Spain under the Muslims.* London, 1958.

Holmes, George, ed. *The Oxford Illustrated History of Medieval Europe.* Oxford, 1980.

Hopkirk, Peter. *The Great Game.* London, 1991.

———. *On Secret Service East of Constantinople.* London, 1994 .

Hourani, Albert. *A History of the Arab People.* London, 1991.

Housley, Norman. *The Later Crusades.* Oxford, 1992.

Howarth, David. *The Greek Adventure.* London, 1976.

Hughes, Thomas Patrick. *Dictionary of Islam.* Delhi, 1875.

Huntingdon, Samuel. *The Clash of Civilisations (Foreign Affairs).* Washington, 1993.

Hussey, J. M. *The Byzantine World.* London, 1967.

Inalcik, Halil. *The Ottoman Empire—The Classical Age 1300–1600.* London, 1973.

Irving, Washington. *Life of Mahomet.* London, 1856.

Jacobi, J. M. *Histoire générale de la Corse*. Paris, 1835.

James, Lawrence. *The Rise and Fall of the British Empire*. London, 1994.

Jelavich, Barbara. *History of the Balkans*. Cambridge, 1993.

Jelavich, Charles and Barbara. *The Balkans*. Edgewood Cliffs, N.J., 1965.

Jonquière, Vicomte de. *Histoire de l'empire ottoman*. Paris, 1914.

Kamen, Henry. *A Concise History of Spain*. London, 1973.

Keegan, John. *A History of Warfare*. London, 1994.

Keegan, John, and Andrew Wheatcroft. *Who's Who in Military History: From 1453 to the Present Day*. London, 1991.

Keesing's Record of World Events. London, 1987.

Kelsay, John, and James Turner Johnson, eds. *Just War and Jihad*. New York, 1991.

Kemp, Peter, ed. *The Oxford Companion to Ships and the Sea*. Oxford, 1988.

Kennedy, Paul. *The Rise and Fall of the Great Powers*. London, 1989.

Khomeini, S. *Principes politiques, philosophiques, sociaux et religieux*. In *Juifs et Chrétiens sous l'Islam*. Paris, 1979 .

Kinder, Hermann, and Werner Hilgemann. *The Penguin Atlas of World History*. London, 1978.

Kinross, Lord. *Ataturk, The Rebirth of a Nation*. London, 1964.

Kitsikis, Dimitri. *L'Empire ottoman*. Paris, 1991.

Koran, The. Oxford, 1982.

Landrau, Rom. *Islam and the Arabs*. London, 1958.

Lane-Poole, Stanley. *The Barbary Corsairs*. London, 1890.

———. *The Mediterranean Dynasties*. New York, 1965.

———. *The Moors in Spain*. London, 1887.

———. *Turkey*. London, 1887.

Langer, William L. *An Encyclopedia of World History*. London, 1987.

Lawrence, James. *The Rise and Fall of the British Empire*. London, 1984.

Lebeau. *Histoire du Bas Empire*. Paris, 1830.

Lemerle, Paul. *Histoire de Byzance*. Paris, 1990.

Lesure, Michel. *Lépante*. Paris, 1972

Lévi-Provencal, E. *Histoire de l'Espagne mussulmane*. Paris, 1950.

Lewis, Bernard. *The Arabs in History*. London, 1986.

———. *Islam and the West*. Oxford, 1993.

———. *The Muslim Discovery of Europe*. London, 1984.

———. *Le retour de l'Islam*. Paris, 1985.

Livermore, Harold. *A History of Spain.* London, 1966.

Livermore, H. V. *A New History of Portugal.* Cambridge, 1976.

Lomax, Derek W. *The Reconquest of Spain.* New York, 1978.

Luke, Harry. *The Old Turkey and the New.* London, 1955.

Macdonald, Lyn. *1915: The Death of Innocence.* London, 1993.

MacKay, A. *Spain in the Middle Ages.* London, 1991.

Makkari, Ahmed ibn Mohammed Ali. *The History of the Moham-medan Dynasties in Spain.* London, 1843.

Malcolm, Noel. *Bosnia: A Short History.* London, 1994.

―――. *Kosovo: A Short History.* New York, 1998.

Malleson, G. B. *Studies from Genoese History.* London, 1875.

Malouf, Amir. *Les Croisades vues par les Arabes.* Paris, 1983.

Mansfield, Peter. *The Arabs.* London, 1985.

Mantran, Robert. *Histoire de la Turquie.* Paris, 1988.

Mariejol, Jean Hyppolite. *The Spain of Ferdinand and Isabelle.* New Brunswick, N.J., 1961.

Marles, de, M. *Histoire de la domination des Arabes et des Maures en Espagne et au Portugal.* Paris, 1825.

Mascarenhas, Joao. *Esclave à Alger.* Paris, 1994.

McEvedy, Colin. *The Penguin Atlas of Medieval History.* London, 1961.

―――. *The Penguin Atlas of Modern History.* London, 1972.

―――. *The Penguin Atlas of Recent History.* London, 1982.

Mercier M., and A. Seguin. *Charles Martel à la bataille de Poitiers.* Paris, 1944.

Muir, William. *The Life of Mohammad.* Edinburgh, 1925.

―――. *The Caliphate, Its Rise, Decline and Fall.* Edinburgh, 1925.

Naipaul, V. S. *Among the Believers.* New York, 1981.

New English Bible, The. Oxford & Cambridge, 1982.

Nicole, David, Ian Heath, and Terence Wise. *Osprey "Men-at-Arms"* series. London, various dates.

―――. *The Age of Charlemagne.*

―――. *Armies of the Crusades.*

―――. *Armies of Islam, 7th to 11th Centuries.*

―――. *Armies of the Ottoman Turks, 1300–1774.*

―――. *Byzantine Armies, 886–1100.*

―――. *El Cid and the Reconquista, 1050–1492.*

―――. *Hungary & the Fall of eastern Europe, 1000–1568.*

―――. *The Knights of Christ.*

―――. *The Russo-Turkish War, 1877.*

———. *Saladin and the Saracens.*

———. *Saxon, Viking and Norman.*

———. *The Venetian Empire, 1200–1670.*

Nicosian, Solomon. *Islam—The Way of Submission.* London, 1987.

Noja, Sergio. *Maometto Profeta dell'Islam.* Cuneo, 1974.

Norwich, John Julian. *Byzantium, The Early Centuries.* London, 1988.

———. *Venice, The Greatness and the Fall.* London, 1981.

———. *The Normans in the South.* London, 1967.

Nutting, Anthony. *The Arabs.* London, 1964.

Ockley, Simon. *History of the Saracens.* London, 1757.

Oman, C. W. C. *The Byzantine Empire.* London, 1892.

Oman, Charles. *The Art of War in the 16th Century.* London, 1991.

———. *The Art of War in the Middle Ages.* London, 1991.

———. *The Sixteenth Century.* London, 1936.

Palm, Rolf. *Les étendards du Prophète.* Paris, 1981.

Palmer, Alan. *The Decline and Fall of the Ottoman Empire.* London, 1992.

Panteli, Stavros. *A New History of Cyprus.* London, 1954.

Partner, Peter. *God of Battles.* London, 1997.

Patai, Raphael. *The Arab Mind.* New York, 1976.

Peters, Rudolph. *Jihad, Medieval and Modern.* Leiden, 1977.

———. *Islam and Colonialism.* The Hague, 1979.

Pidal, Ramon Menendez. *The Cid and His Spain.* London, 1934.

Poli, X. *La Corse à l'expulsion des Sarazzins.* Paris, 1907.

Power, George. *History of the Musulmans in Spain.* London, 1815.

Prescott, W. H. *History of the Reign of Ferdinand and Isabella.* London, 1850.

Purcell, H. D. *Cyprus.* London, 1969.

Rabbath, Edmond. *Mahomet, prophète arabe et fondateur d'états.* Beirut, 1981.

Rahman, H. V. *A Chronology of Islam, 570–1000 C.E.* London, 1995.

Reinaud, M. *Invasion des Sarrazins en France.* Paris, 1836.

Riche, Pierre, and Philippe Lemaitre. *Les invasions barbares.* Paris, 1991.

Riley-Smith, Jonathan, ed. *The Atlas of the Crusades.* London, 1990.

Roberts, J. M. *The Triumph of the West.* London, 1985.

Rodinson, Maxime. *Mohammed.* London, 1971.

Roldan, J. M. *A Short History of Spain.* Madrid, 1987.

Ross, Cecil. *Rhodes under the Byzantines.* Cambridge, 1886.

Rothenberg, Gunther Erich. *The Austrian Military Border in Croatia 1522–1747.* Urbana, Ill.

Rushdie, Salman. *The Satanic Verses.* London, 1988.

Ruthven, Malise. *Islam in the World.* London, 1984.

———. *A Satanic Affair: Salman Rushdie and the Rage of Islam.* London, 1990.

Said, Edouard. *L'Orientalisme—l'Orient crée par l'Occident.* Paris, 1980.

St. Clair, William. *That Greece Might Still Be Free.* London, 1972.

Sardar, Ziauddin. *The Future of Muslim Civilization.* New York, 1987.

Schacht, Joseph, with C. L. Bosworth. *The Legacy of Islam.* Oxford, 1979.

Schevill, Ferdinand. *A History of the Balkans.* New York, 1991.

Sédillot, L. A. *Histoire des Arabes.* Paris, 1854.

Shaw, Stanford. *Histoire de l'Empire ottoman et de la Turquie.* Roanne, 1983.

Sinor, Denis. *History of Hungary.* New York, 1959.

Sourdel, Dominique. *Histoire des Arabes.* Paris, 1991.

———. *L'Islam.* Paris, 1990.

Stenhouse, Paul. *The Algeriazation of Europe in the Third Millennium.* Frankfurt, 1998.

Tharaud, Jerome, and Jean. *Les cavaliers d'Allah.* Paris, 1935.

Thomson, Ammad. *Blood on the Cross.* London, 1996.

Thubron, Colin. *The Venetians.* Amsterdam, 1980.

Tuchman, Barbara. *A Distant Mirror.* London, 1979.

Tucoo-Chala, Pierre. *Quand l'Islam était aux Portes des Pyrénées.* Biarritz, 1994.

Vambery, Arminius. *Hungary in Ancient, Medieval and Modern Times.* London, 1887.

Vilar, Pierre. *Histoire de l'Espagne.* Paris, 1991.

Vincens, Emile. *Histoire de la République de Gènes.* Paris, 1862.

Vives, Jaime Vicens. *Approaches to the History of Spain.* Berkeley, Calif., 1967.

Wallace-Hadrill, J. M. *The Barbarian West 400–1000.* London, 1985.

Walsh, William Thomas. *Isabella of Spain.* London, 1931.

Warraq, Ibn. *Why I Am Not a Muslim.* Amherst, N.Y., 1995.

Watt, W. Montgomery, and Pierre Cachia. *A History of Islamic Spain.* Edinburgh, 1977.

Wells, H. G. *A Short History of the World.* London, 1853.

Wheatcroft, Andrew. *The Ottomans: Dissolving Images.* London, 1995.

Whishaw, Bernhard, and Ellen. *Arabic Spain.* London, 1912.

Windrow, Martin, and Francis Mason. *A Concise Biography of Military History*. London, 1975.

Wolf, John B. *The Barbary Coast*. New York, 1979.

Wollaston, Arthur N. *The Sword of Islam*. London, 1905.

Woodhouse, C. M. *The Philhellenes*. London, 1969.

Wright, Robin. *Sacred Rage: The Crusade of Modern Islam*. London, 1986.

Zakaria, Rafiq. *The Struggle within Islam*. London, 1988.

Zebiri, Kate. *Muslims and Christians Face to Face*. Oxford, 1997.

INDEX

297.7209 Fregosi, Paul.
F
        Jihad in the West.

6-07